To the enduring memories of my late mother, Parvin Seyyedi Oskoui, who supported my scholarship with love, and my late hoca, *Halil Inalcik, who instilled in me the passion for Ottoman history.*

CONTENTS

Living Gender after Communism

Living Gender after Communism

Edited by
Janet Elise Johnson and Jean C. Robinson

INDIANA UNIVERSITY PRESS
BLOOMINGTON AND INDIANAPOLIS

Indiana University Press
601 North Morton Street
Bloomington, IN 47404-3797 USA

http://iupress.indiana.edu

Telephone orders   800-842-6796
Fax orders   812-855-7931
Orders by e-mail iuporder@indiana.edu

The paper used in this publication meets the minimum require-
ments of American National Standard for Information Sciences—
Permanence of Paper for Printed Library Materials, ANSI
Z39.48-1984.

MANUFACTURED IN THE UNITED STATES OF AMERICA

Library of Congress Cataloging-in-Publication Data

Living gender after communism / edited by Janet Elise Johnson and
Jean C. Robinson.
    p. cm.
Includes bibliographical references and index.
ISBN-13: 978-0-253-34812-8 (cloth : alk. paper)
ISBN-10: 0-253-34812-9 (cloth : alk. paper)
    1. Women—Europe—History—20th century. 2. Feminism—Europe—History—20th century.
3. Women—Europe—Social conditions—20th century. 4. Post-communism—Europe—History—
20th century. I. Johnson, Janet Elise. II. Robinson, Jean C.
HQ1587.L58 2007
305.40947'09049—dc22
                                                                    2006015170

1 2 3 4 5   12 11 10 09 08 07

Contents

FOREWORD: STUDYING GENDER AND POSTCOMMUNISM

More than a dozen years have passed since the collapse of communism and its attendant dislocations, crises, and opportunities. A whole generation of young people has come of political age without ever having experienced communism for themselves. For them, it is only a set of stories told by their parents and grandparents, yet it provides the context and the starting point from which their own lives will proceed. Studying these countries as postcommunist despite their obvious and increasing dissimilarities is thus important: the realities of present-day existence may differ greatly between postcommunist states, but without an appreciation of the commonalities of structure and history that were features of their shared past, it is very difficult to appreciate the extent of the differences between them or the reasons for these growing gaps.

So too when approaching the issue of the status of women and gender after communism. The postcommunist transition has impacted men and women differently. Across Central and Eastern Europe, there have been more benefits for men than for women from the transition: men are richer, more men head new companies, more men own privatized firms, and, as Iulia Shevchenko addresses in this volume, many more men hold political power. Women have suffered more from the loss of social services, women dominate professions that remain in the resource-starved state sector, and women and women's issues have not been a central part of the postcommunist political landscape. And yet, the impact of gender ideologies for many remain hidden. Anne-Marie Kramer shows that even when issues impacting women and gender become salient—such as abortion in Poland—the relevance for women's lives is neutralized. As Ewa Grigar argues for women artists in the region, an explicit critique of gender or use of feminism remains radical.

The transition has encouraged the gendering of nations and bodies in ways that are not positive for women. For example, the age-old gendering of recumbent nations in the Balkans as female to be protected by the resurgent and mobilized male states put feminists, such as Slavenka Drakulić, in the position of being accused of "raping Croatia" (or Bosnia, or Serbia) when they refused to give up their trans-Balkan campaign for women's rights in the face of impending war. In this climate, the rapes of individual Balkan women—and women's varied resistance to these rapes—are, as Azra Hromadzic argues in this volume, hidden under metaphors about the nation, ignoring the woman.

Anna Brzozowska shows that the gendering of the nation easily reinforces the identification of the feminine with weakness and passivity, with consequences for the autonomy of the state as well as for female citizens.

Hromadzic makes the case for recognizing women's agency, even in situations where the only outcomes are violent. The notion of agency and the enhanced space to negotiate gender in postcommunism have not necessarily made life "better" or easier for women, but postcommunism has meant spaces for women to manipulate their environment. Tania Rands Lyon shows the ways in which Russian women and men move back and forth between articulating traditional gender views and living more nontraditional lives. In Romania, Shannon Woodcock shows that women may manipulate ethnocentrism to "safely" raise the issue of such interpersonal violence in public by blaming the Other, such as the Roma, but leaving invisible the domestic violence many women face in private. In charting the new recognition of domestic violence, Janet Elise Johnson unveils the ways in which the assertion of agency and activism can begin to transform discourse as well as policy and people's lives.

Some of this activism of course is in response to the ways in which the opening of the communist world enabled the West's hyper-sexualization of women's bodies in advertising to become part of the postcommunist public space, as billboards and commercials replaced propaganda posters. Images in the market were not the only sign of this hyper-sexualization; as Svitlana Taraban describes, the Internet also became an avenue for virtual and actual gendering, as Western male and Eastern female found each other in hyper-space and stimulated the exodus of brides and prostitutes. The increase in trafficking in women and the new availability of Internet brides are matched by the rise of neotraditionalist conceptions of gender for both men and women and of an emphasis on women's bodies as their only valuable commodity. Many of the chapters included here address the fallout from the resurgence of rigid gender roles.

Considerations of the sites and spaces in and through which postcommunism has emerged as a gendered geography of transactions, institutions, and relationships are the subject of this book. These essays came out of a conference on "Placing Gender in Postcommunism" held in October of 2002 at the Havighurst Center for Russian and Post-Soviet Studies at Miami University. The goal of the center is to foster interdisciplinary study and research on the challenges facing the countries of this area by students and scholars from around the world. The conference was one of the center's annual series of international and interdisciplinary conferences for young scholars.

In this volume are contributions from the disciplines of political science, art history, sociology, anthropology, and history, and from scholars from Russia, the United States, Great Britain, Poland, Ukraine, Belarus, Bosnia, and Australia. It is a tribute to the editors, Janet Johnson and Jean C. Robinson, as well as to the discussants and the contributors themselves, that the articles are so well integrated and so provocative. Younger scholars, including those from the region, bring a fresh voice to the discussion of gender in postcommunism. In particular, their fieldwork is outstanding, and many of their case studies are little known in Western literature. In this sense, the volume makes a contribution to the recent work done in the study of gender and postcommunism, particularly the excellent volumes by Susan Gal and Gail Kligman on gender and postcommunism (*The Politics of Gender after Socialism* [Princeton, N.J.: Princeton University Press, 2000] and *Reproducing Gender: Politics, Publics, and Everyday Life after Socialism* [Princeton, N.J.: Princeton University Press, 2000]). They also follow recent journal issues on the topic, *Feminist Review* 76, no. 1 (2004), and *Signs* 29, no. 3 (2004).

The Soviet system was one that both preached a solution to the "women's question" and promised equality in the workplace. Despite the obvious failure to deliver on these and many other issues, Soviet-style regimes did at least place these items on the social agenda. In postcommunist countries, the social agenda is dictated less by ideology than by the market. The language and practice of capitalism make everyone "equal" before the market but also equally vulnerable. In this new climate, it is up to women to maneuver themselves so as to take advantage of capitalism's opportunities, while at the same time recognizing that power and opportunity structures are being constructed that disadvantage them. The chapters by Johnson and Lyon show that some Russian women have successfully organized against gendered violence while others draw upon more egalitarian gender roles in their intimate relations (even if they espouse traditional views about women's and men's place in their rhetoric). Thus, this volume highlights not just the constraints women face, but some moves to exert agency within these constraints, and in so doing makes a valuable contribution to analyzing women's conditions both in postcommunism and beyond.

KAREN DAWISHA
Director, Havighurst Center for Russian and
Post-Soviet Studies, Miami University

ACKNOWLEDGMENTS

This project emerged from our now decade-long conversation about gender after communism, during which we have been informed and assisted by many individuals whom we regret that we cannot thank individually. We appreciate the academic institutions that have facilitated this conversation, including Indiana University (Bloomington), especially the Russian and East European Institute and the Political Science department, where we began our relationship, and Miami (Ohio) University's Havighurst Center for Russian and Post-Soviet Studies, which gave us the impetus and support to publish our thoughts.

Individuals whom we would like to thank, in particular for their comments, include Susan Crate, Sheila Croucher, Karen Dawisha, Sara Friedman, Roz Galtz, Venelin Ganev, Kristen Ghodsee, Jeff Isaac, Sally Lloyd, and Mihaela Miroiu. We also are grateful to the participants and audience of the Post-Communist Cultural Studies Interest Group (SOYUZ) who shared their thoughts on our chapter at the 2005 symposium. In addition to those represented in this volume, we would like to express gratitude to the following scholars who were associated with this project at an earlier stage: Helena Goscilo, Karen Kapusta-Pofahl, Elaine Weiner, and Ecaterina Zatuşevski. We thank John Mark Summers for copyediting assistance and Janet Rabinowitch of Indiana University Press for her editorial support.

Janet Elise Johnson also wishes to thank her colleagues living and studying gender after communism, especially those in Russia, the Czech Republic, and Armenia, who were willing to share through long conversations their observations and theories. She is grateful to have found a forum for this discussion in her new home with the "Gender in Transition: Women in Europe" workshop sponsored by New York University's Center for European Studies and the Network of East-West Women, notably with the organizers Nanette Funk, Sonia Jaffe Robbins, and Ann Snitow. She appreciates the tough questions and additional empirical evidence from many students in her courses, in particular those in her seminars on gender, citizenship, and postcommunism at Miami and Charles (Prague) Universities. Financial support for the field research that informed this project came from the PSC-CUNY Research Foundation, Brooklyn College's Tow Faculty Travel Fellowship, the International Research and Exchange Board, the National Security Education Program, and the Russian and East European Institute at Indiana University. Finally, but not least, she thanks Jean Robinson for her warm support through-out her career (as well as for jumping right in when Janet suggested the crazy idea of putting this book together) and John Mark Summers for being her biggest fan.

Jean C. Robinson expresses her gratitude and appreciation to many schol-ars, especially those in East Europe who have helped her see and think through the problems of gender in communism and after. Her deep thanks to Mihaela Miroiu, Renata Siemienska, Kasia Staszynska, Jack Bielasiak, and Cynthia Dominik. She also thanks (current and former) graduate students who always push her to see gender in new ways: Amy Caiazza, Janet Johnson, Lynn Kamenitsa, Candice Ortbals, Kristen Parris, Sandra Reineke, and Rafia Zaka-ria. Some of her research travels have been funded by the Fulbright Scholars Program, the Russian and East European Institute, and International Programs at Indiana University. Additional support for publication was provided by the Office of the Vice-President for Research and the Mellon Endowment faculty grant of the Russian and East European Institute, both at Indiana University.

Living Gender after Communism

Living Gender

Janet Elise Johnson and Jean C. Robinson

The chapters presented in this volume—most by young scholars from postcommunist states—suggest that moving away from communism in Europe and Eurasia has provided an opportunity for gender to multiply.[1] As the communist party-state has retired, other institutions and processes—such as the market, political parties, ethnic identities, non-governmental organizations (NGOs), and the church/mosque—have emerged or reemerged as domestic sources of power. Simultaneously, the more porous boundaries of the new states have facilitated an increased influence from international sources of power—such as the World Bank, the global market, and transnational social movements—within postcommunist societies. The undermining of the communist party-state's monopoly, including its monopoly over gender, has enabled the development of more and more various forms of gender. This development, in turn, has enabled some women in the region to construct their own gendered identities for their own political, economic, or social purposes, although this has not necessarily made life better for all women. Nor have these new resources meant women have substantive power to change gender relations, but they have enabled many women to develop a toolkit of strategies and tactics that allow them to eke out some autonomy in a still limited range of choices.

1

By gender, we refer to the recognition that many characteristics and behaviors, often assumed to be a result of biological sex, are political, social, and cultural creations. We use gender as more than just a personal identity: females acting out "the feminine" and males acting out "the masculine." We build on a legacy of Western social construction–feminist scholars, such as Gayle Rubin, Candace West, Don H. Zimmerman, and R. W. Connell, who theorize gender as a society-wide institution that regulates people's lives, "a powerful ideological device which produces, reproduces, and legitimates the choices and limits."[2] We hold that sex/gender systems exist simultaneously at multiple levels of politics and culture, creating an overlapping and often contradictory web of gender constructions. These can sometimes be a source of stability for people living in societies facing extreme and unpredictable change, as, for example, in the ways that traditional myths of womanhood and manhood are often evoked in nationalist ideology. But most often they are powerful political, economic, social, religious, and cultural constraints.

But the turmoil of the social, economic, and political changes of the past fifteen years in the former Soviet Union and in Eastern Europe and Eurasia revealed just how much gender shifts. In the words of Nanette Funk from one of the first books to examine gender after communism, *Gender Politics and Post-Communism*, communism's collapse introduced "yet another difference, the difference of political system."[3] Social construction feminism, while recognizing the construction and contestation of gender, was founded on a trajectory of experiencing relatively stable and incremental social and political change. Similarly, gender under communism seemed relatively straightforward: living gender in public was constrained by the communist party-state ideology, by state socialist economics, and by authoritarian state power. While there were alternative gender constructions being produced, most importantly in the family, the village, and the workplace, private lives were often narrowly circumscribed, and privacy was a rare luxury in crowded and collectivized living.[4] We do not ignore the diversity that existed, nor do we deny that there was (at some times, and in some places, for some women) some personal agency in the process of constructing individual identities in opposition to the state. Women and men did act in ways that pushed the boundaries of what was acceptable gendered behavior. And yet, the powerful state dictates dominated: there were few alternatives to the ones presented by ideology.[5]

After 1990, many more gender ideologies seemed to flower—what we call gender multiplication. We observed increasing complexity and what appeared to be a wider range of gender ideologies available for women and men. By this we do not mean that there are necessarily better opportunities or lives for women or men after communism. What gender multiplication points to is that the market, globalization, a larger civil society, and the like enable a diverse array of strategies and tactics that women and men may use to construct the version of gender that they believe will help them survive, if not thrive. This signifies not so much a change for the better in terms of women's opportunities and life choices, but rather the impact of the shift from a public gender controlled by the socialist state to a more privatized gender shaped in large part by the impact of the market.[6] The changes after communism reveal that the static definitions of gender and the dichotomous representations of gendered behavior so often used during the period of communist rule are not only imperfect attempts to represent a changing reality now, but in fact they were imperfect heuristics (at their best) even in the communist period. Gender (and sex) must be understood to be multiple, fluid, and variable, albeit still (perhaps always?) shaping and constraining the choices women and men make about how to live their lives.

If this gender multiplication is accompanied by an increase in individual and collective agency, then the collapse of communism might also increase the opportunity for individuals or groups to negotiate gender in ways that sometimes can give them more options and choices in their lives. More individual freedom enhances the ability to resist being categorized as one particular gender construction. However, if the market and its domination merely replace the domination of the central coercive state, then there may be more choices, but not a substantive change in the gendered order. Thus, gender sometimes can be employed by groups or states to constrain women and men, but its various forms are employed by individuals, civil groups, and social movements to survive or thrive. Sometimes, new forms of gender are used to constrain women's and men's options in their lives. At other times, these new ways of living gender offer new, albeit often limited, opportunities.

This expands the understanding of gender used in this book. Sex/gender systems can also function as cultural "toolkits"[7] from which individuals and groups may sometimes be able to pick and choose among various frames of gender. These tools may sometimes, borrowing from postmodern feminisms, help subvert or "transvalue" the sex/gender system.[8] Indeed, negotiating around gender can be an effective weapon of resistance against normalizing gender constructs. Women of color have already shown it to be an effective tool. As Chela Sandoval points out, U.S. women of color and Third World women act as modern-day women warriors, recognizing, adapting to, and battling the power deployed by a specific power apparatus at a specific moment in time because they confront a multiplicity of oppressions. As driving with a manual transmission, they "shift" between oppositional consciousness based on culture, sex, and class, moving "between and among" ideological positions.[9] The experiences of U.S. Third World women bring into relief that each of us has multiple identities to draw from and that people can negotiate within and among those identities. Their experiences also illustrate that gender can be both a tactic of resistance and a strategy of constraint.

Sandoval argues that this negotiating between approaches (which she names "shifting")—for example, using one identity in one context and a second in another—can most effectively challenge oppression by eroding its organizing principle: blurring binaries, in this case, of male and female. In

Sandoval's words, "[t]he idea here, [is] that the citizen-subject can learn to identify, develop, and control the means of ideology, that is, marshal the knowledge necessary to 'break with ideology' while at the same time *also* speaking in, and from within, ideology."[10]

Employing this gender lens uncovers a provocative and untold story about living gender after communism. Young women in Russia or Poland have been using sex and sexuality to facilitate getting an (in)decent-paying job. Wives in Post-Soviet Russia have engaged in nontraditional behaviors such as expecting that husbands will share domestic responsibilities even as they subscribe to traditional ideologies about marriage. In their work, Polish women artists have presented stances that alternatively promote gender neutrality, essentialist femininity, or liberatory feminism. Ukrainian women, strategically seeking a route out of their homeland, have played to Western male fantasies about the beautiful but compliant Slavic woman while recognizing that such self-representation operates as an exit visa to a place where masculine domination is likely to still be mighty powerful. Even so, for these women, as for others, in addition to the myriad of problems created by communism's collapse, perhaps new opportunities for gender negotiation were also created.

Women's Lives and Gender after Communism

We recognize the huge costs to women and men of communism's collapse and of the particular way that these states in Europe and Eurasia transformed their regimes and economies. Many of the issues that plagued society and shaped the discussion about gender just after the fall of communism remain today.[11] If people expected that the advent of the market, the move to a competitive labor structure, and the institutionalization of competitive party structures, parliamentary games, and new roles for religious and other traditional institutions would be "good" for women, then they either were naïve or had been blind to the ways in which liberal democratic, market-oriented economies in the West perpetuated inequality and disparity in almost all aspects of economic, social, and political life.

Economic life continues to be a site of inequality, although that inequality has increased rather than diminished with the advent of the market and the retreat of the state. In Romania, Russia, and other parts of Eastern Europe and Eurasia (as elsewhere) women and men engage in sexually segregated occupations, where female-dominant occupations are typically lower paid—as an occupation employs more women, wages/salary levels go down. Even more significantly, though, both men and women have been deeply affected by the social and economic transformations in their own countries as well as by the increasingly powerful pull of globalization.

In all the societies of Eastern Europe and Eurasia there has been a destruction of the social safety net, with the sacrifices borne by those with least access to other resources. The extent of the destruction varies across nations, but it is no mere correlation that as state-sponsored social services have disappeared, the level of poverty has increased, inequality has risen, and women, in particular, seem to bear a heavier burden. Alongside the economic burdens have appeared increasing ideological support for female roles in domesticity and motherhood, and concomitant reduced participation in political representation and governmental agencies. All of the nations have seen an increased salience of religious and nationalist frames in politics, culture, and society. Finally there has been a reversal (in both directions) of reproductive policies from the communist period—some becoming more repressive and narrow, as in Poland, others becoming, at least on paper, more open, as in Romania. This leads to an impression that the window of opportunity to restructure political and economic institutions has reinvigorated that which had been suppressed under communist rule.

Thus, living gender after communism holds dangers for women. Many of the new power sources "sponsor" variations of neotraditional gender ideology, calling for re-feminization and re-masculinization. These neotraditional gender ideologies, in turn, legitimate dismantling the social safety net, excluding women from power, and ignoring many new (or newly recognized) problems for women. These problems range from women being unemployed because they are seen as mothers to being employed as sex workers because they are seen as whores; being glorified as the symbol of the nation to experiencing rape in ethnic conflicts because they are symbolic of the nation; living in societies where access to both birth control and abortion is problematic; needing state social services because they are entrusted with the responsibility to raise children while wanting secure and loving families but facing unrecognized violence in those families. After communism—as elsewhere—a woman cannot escape the gendering of bodies and selves; no matter whether she is on the street, in domestic spaces, imagined globally, or touched bodily, she is framed as gendered woman.

These problems serve as the backdrop to our edited volume, and many authors included here discuss them. We also refer readers to the many good books that already explore these questions, from Funk's and Mueller's (1993) *Gender Politics and Post-Communism* to Barbara Einhorn's (1993) *Cinderella Goes to Market: Citizenship, Gender and Women's Movements in East Central Europe*, Susan Gal and Gail Kligman's (2000) *Reproducing Gender: Politics, Publics, and Everyday Life after Socialism* and *The Politics of Gender after Socialism*, and Kathleen Kuenhast and Carol Nechemias's (2004) *Post-Soviet Women Encountering Transition: Nation-Building, Economic Survival, and Civic Activism*.

But our question here is different. We are not answering the question whether women's lives are better or worse since the fall of state socialism and the transition to more market economies and less authoritarian politics. Rather this volume seeks to uncover whether and how gender as an institution has changed, an intervening variable in the question of how postcommunism impacts women's (and men's) lives. What are the multiple ways in which gender is presented and performed after communism? What is the role of the state and the market in establishing preferential gender constructions and performances and behavior as well as in enabling new opportunities for gender identities, performances, and behavior? How has this changed from the communist period, and can one argue that gender in the postcommunist period is less stable, more dynamic, and more open to negotiation by individuals? What takes the place of the authoritarian state in establishing constraints, if any? How has the transition from an authoritarian state power to a weaker central state affected gender ideologies?

The work in this volume—whether delving into the relationship between the construction of gender and the Other in Romania, the creation of a narrative about rapes in Bosnia, the use of gender stereotypes to market oneself more effectively as a potential Internet bride, or the search for gender neutrality in Polish art—demonstrates that sometimes gender can be tactically deployed in ways that can be somewhat liberating for some women, although often at the expense of others. The volume shows that in certain circumstances, such as in the framing of domestic violence in Russia, negotiating gender may create new opportunities and freedoms for women. What we see happening here is indeed quite momentous, for it signifies the possibility that we can imagine different possibilities for gender. Coming after decades during which the public presentation of gender appeared to be fixed and regularized, this recapturing of gender by individuals themselves, and its transformation into a mutable, usable process that can shape social movements, is significant.

Socialism and Gender

What was the character of gender before the collapse of communism? Under state socialism as elsewhere, gender constructions were multiple, varying over time and place. Images of the ideal Polish woman, built within a mixed iconography of Catholicism and communism, differed from the ideal Romanian woman as a mother reproducing the Romanian nation, who differed from the clearly atheistic ideal Czech woman. Gender constructions of the Soviet woman worker differed from the Soviet heroic mother and the Russian peasant. There was also change over time. The 1930s gender fantasies of the elimination of most sexual inequalities shifted to the glorification of gender differences by dissidents and even by late socialist regimes.

Under socialism, as in other contexts, women (and men) also negotiated around gender. Sometimes women would choose to play up their similarities to men in order to get better jobs. Other times, they would play upon their idealization as mothers in order to get more time to do whatever needed to be done for their children, their husbands, their families. People's negotiation of gender under socialism became even more evident as coercion waned. In the late 1980s and early 1990s in Russia, for example, women and men strategically employed tales of women's "heroic shopping" and men's mischief-making as their resistance to Soviet rule.[12]

Yet while gender was regularly negotiated in these common ways, the context of communism was distinct from noncommunist states in two significant ways. First, the communist party-state held an almost complete monopoly over the politics of gender construction both because of the authoritarian institutions and practices of state socialism and because of the way that gender was veiled by the "woman question." Communist leaders "defined women's interests and introduced women's policy."[13] The Soviets by the 1930s believed that there were essential and innate differences between women and men. They framed the "woman question" not about how to restructure social values and society to make it less patriarchal or sexist, but rather as how to accommodate women's innate differences to the ideal of the New Soviet Man. To the extent that sex differences could be ignored, women were to participate like men in labor. To the extent that they could not, women were seen as fundamentally different creatures, determined by biology to be the "natural" caretakers—of infants, children, and men. In other words, the gender politics prevalent under communism never challenged the validity of *gender* difference because it was assumed that all differences flowed "naturally" from the sexual and physical differences between women and men. Unsurprisingly in this context, the terminology for gender—in the sense we are using it now—did not emerge.

This communist leap from body to practice blurred the gendered process that makes sexed functions a boundary of human meaning. One of the processes of gendering almost everywhere turned the consequences of birthing into a lifelong occupation and location. Another process of gendering found throughout the socialist world of East Central Europe and the Soviet Union presumed that women were (almost) men—when located on the factory floor or in the tractor seat. If women were men when at work, then the communist regimes were absolved, for the most part, from considering the full impact of productive work on women qua caretakers. The doublethink about women (women were men at work, but women at home, but gender was thought to be "natural") meant that communist regimes did not understand gender as distinct from sex.

During communism, although all critiques questioning "natural" gender were suppressed, everyday life remained highly gendered. Certain behaviors, occupations, practices, and styles were widely understood as feminine or masculine. It was the rare male who was employed in crèches; it was the rare female who worked underground in mines. And the roles of women (and men) were sometimes hotly contested. As Gal and Kligman argue, "While officially supporting equality between men and women, the regimes countenanced and even produced heated mass media debates about issues such as women's ideal and proper roles, the deleterious effects of divorce, the effects of labor-force segregation—such as the feminization of school-teaching and agriculture—and the fundamental importance of 'natural difference.'"[14] In contrast to the raising of the question of the social construction of gender, these debates revolved around what were the "natural" roles for women.

Communist leaders took control of the politics of gendering and, like regimes both before them and after, turned them to their own purpose. To do this is not unusual. But what Soviet and communist ideology about women's and men's roles in society, family, and reproduction also did was to (periodically) veil gender and its manipulation by the party-state. In an apparent and thoroughgoing erasure, Soviet-style communism ignored the ways in which difference permeated male and female lives. In so doing, communist party-states shrouded differences so as to simultaneously exploit them and, through disregarding them, make them disappear from public sight. At home, women were women, subject to the vagaries and whims of the men in their lives, tied to childcare, to household care, to laundry, and to lines—gender indeed thrived. In public, even as more and more women worked in female-dominated occupations at lower wages, women were treated as male workers except when pregnancy, childbirth, childcare, and leadership intervened. Here gender was veiled behind a claim to equality.[15]

We need to be attuned to the variation in the treatment of gender under communism. Communist states did not all work the same way, and there were varying emphases on women's equality. For instance in China, in an effort to promote their version of sexual equality, the Communist Party led by Mao experimented with a widespread process of gender erasure that has had significant impact on how women understood and negotiated gender in the post-Mao period and how they now imagine politics around gender issues. During the Cultural Revolution, gender erasure was taken to extremes: physical markers of femininity such as cosmetics, long hair, and skirts were attacked as counterrevolutionary, and a unisex gender ideology, based on peasant masculinity, prevailed.[16] In Poland, in contrast, little attention was paid to efforts to promote equality except in a ritualized form on International Women's Day. But in both locations, the party-state created a kind of gender erasure through the existence of ideological claims about socialism and equality coupled with the ostensible neutralizing of gender difference in the public sphere.

In other words, gender was always, under communism, "there but not there." It was simultaneously promoted in the rhetoric on motherhood and denied in the rhetoric on the "woman question" and women's equality. It was discarded in the rejection of feminism as a "bourgeois political movement in capitalist countries with the purpose of achieving formal equal rights for women"[17] and practiced, extolled, and contested in the household division of labor.

The second characteristic that Communist Party–led states shared as distinct from nonsocialist states was the limited personal agency for citizens to negotiate gender. There was some space within the home and close personal relationships, this space functioning as what Nanette Funk labels "an ersatz public sphere."[18] Although the amount of freedom varied enormously among the communist countries, this private qua public sphere was always constrained and controlled by the monopoly of the state over public discourse, including the social imaginings of gender. This limitation had an unintended consequence: the mobilization of (traditional) gender as "cultural resource for both survival and resistance."[19] Although women could negotiate the dominant gender ideologies—of women as mothers (essentially different from men) and workers (essentially the same)—their repertoire was limited. In comparison to less authoritarian contexts, the gender toolkit was small, and there was limited opportunity to expand it.

The party-state's treatment of gender is eerily similar to the way the nationality question was both mobilized and veiled under communism. When nationality was useful, it was embraced and wrapped in colorful costumes and folkloric dance, and when it was problematic and divisive, the authorities hid it, at times repressing it. After communism, nationalities were given an opportunity to explore who/what they are, much as women have been given an opportunity to explore what being female might mean. The intersection of nationality and gender ideologies is therefore a site of intense contestation of the two aspects of identity that were highly manipulated by the communist states. This intersection of nationality and gender also unveils the ways in which gender instability is shaped by both identity and ideology.

Therefore, while it has become fashionable to argue that gender has reemerged in the postcommunist states—or that there has been a re-feminization and -masculinization of these societies—we would argue that this claim misses the significant change that has taken place. It is correct that postcommunist states and societies have enabled more overt presentations of the hyper-feminized woman and, to a lesser extent, the hyper-masculinized man, partially because the states care less about appearing to support sexual equality and thus neglect equality issues in favor of searching for economic security and partially because the market has commodified certain forms of appearance and behavior. But it is not correct that with the fall of the Soviet Kremlin and the Berlin Wall, gender suddenly reemerged. Gender has always existed in Russia and in the countries of East and East Central Europe. What has changed is that there is now more variation and more opportunity to negotiate among different gender constructions. With a small feminist movement now using the word "gender" and a virtual explosion of studies on gender in the region, gender is coming out into the open.[20]

Transitions and Gender Multiplication

This way of thinking about gender and power suggests that, in addition to the myriad of problems that differentially impact women, the collapse of socialism may also create new gender opportunities. In most cases—with the notable exception of Belarus—the state dominates politics and ideology much less, and many other locations of power have emerged. In Poland, the Czech

	Communism	the transition	Postcommunism
Power	state monopoly over gender framed as the "woman question"	→ gender multiplication	more, and more diverse, locations of power that sponsor various gender ideologies
Resistance	limited agency to redefine gender (only in the limited private sphere and in reaction to the state gender ideology)	→ negotiating gender	more individual and collective agency to redefine and negotiate gender

Living gender after communism

Republic, Hungary, Slovenia, the Baltic Republics, Bulgaria, and Croatia, the process of democratization has been so substantial that Freedom House considers them consolidated democracies.[21] The demise of authoritarianism is also evident in that the Baltic states, Poland, the Czech and Slovak republics, Hungary, and Slovenia met the political standards for inclusion into the European Union in 2004; Romania and Bulgaria are hoping for inclusion in 2007. Although citizens in the region remain much less likely to join voluntary organizations than anywhere else,[22] multiparty systems have emerged, augmented by meaningful political participation, small civil societies, and relatively independent media. In most states, ethnicity and/or nationality has been mobilized in new ways, most dramatically and fatally in the former Yugoslavia.

Though these new institutions, identities, and processes can have, and have had, perilous consequences for women, especially the remobilization of nationalism and call for the abrogation of the states' social responsibilities, each sponsors its own gender ideology through the construction of ideal women and men. Instead of one highly problematic gender ideology, there are a variety of gender ideologies much more free from state control.

Within the diversity of new gender ideologies, one central tendency— often limiting for women—is what we call neotraditional gender—the idea that men and women have distinct roles: women the beautiful loving caretakers, men the strong providers—but this is not a simple traditionalizing of gender with throwbacks to Russian Orthodoxy, Polish Catholicism, or the preindustrial, pre-urban world. Rather, it is a traditionalizing of gender ideology that embraces the many variants of gender as practiced both before and under communism, including those incipient in national religions, in ethnic values, and in historical claims about who "the people" are. It is a traditionalizing of gender ideology that exists within a gendered global context where fantasies of 1950s American traditional gender roles can travel abroad.[23]

The neotraditional gender ideology is resonant with those that we more typically describe as traditional (that is, pre–communist regime) because it embraces privatizing and domesticating women's lives. But it is *neo*traditional because it responds to the impact of communism—a communism that was problematic for women and for gender. Communism was problematic because its ideological claims about equality were never realized, and women continued to be constrained by a gender ideology that framed women as feminine/female in private and in public, but also male in public (where male wasn't gender).

Neotraditional gender ideology exists in new times and sites; the contexts, correctly described as traditional gender organizations, such as the family or the Church, operate in new ways. Most significantly, women (and men) live in a different world than nineteenth-century Warsaw or early twentieth-century Soviet Union. They live in a more interconnected global context with a multiplicity of gender ideologies. These new locations mean that women and men can make new arguments to facilitate meeting their interests, even within the confines and boundaries of neotraditional gender ideologies.

The flip side to neotraditionalism is the sexualization of women, the whore to the Madonna. While less often articulated as an ideology, this version is implicit in the pornography that exploded following the end of communism. The use of the image of a sexed nude woman to sell journals, products, and even politicians has been assimilated into mainstream culture throughout the region. In contrast to a liberatory ideology that embraces women's sexual empowerment, the cult of beauty and sexiness has become key to the new market economy. Of course this is not new to the market, and for that matter, using women's bodies to market tractors wasn't unheard of in socialist Europe either. What links these gender ideologies together is that, whether seen as angel or as whore, women are not seen as merely people, who could have the same drives and aptitudes as men.[24]

But other gender ideologies may be more promising. Complementary but opposed to neotraditionalism is an ideology shaped by feminisms—a feminism born of Marxism, a feminism born out of the rejection of rigid determinism, and a feminism problematically bolstered by Western dollars and Western proselytizing.[25] This other gender ideology speaks to ways in which women can make a place for themselves in public, act collectively to extend and protect their interests, and act individually by negotiating the meaning of femininity, masculinity, and nationality. In Central Europe and Eurasia, this new gender ideology is advocated by a new cast of professional feminists at NGOs and new gender studies programs. They tend to speak the language of global feminism, with concepts that are strongly influenced, though, by Western feminisms, so that tensions remain between feminists and others in their own location as well as between feminists from the East and West.[26]

Transitions and Gender Negotiation

The collapse of socialism and the proliferation of gender ideologies in the region also enabled gender to be negotiated more explicitly and more collectively. Now that there is a [real] public sphere, gender negotiations can also be displayed there. New negotiations about gender identity and ideology are manifest in both public and private as postcommunism progresses. There are multiple sites for the expression of gender ideology—or rather for the expression of multiple forms of gender ideology. As Watson argues, "The transition from state socialism to liberal democracy involves a shift from frozen to fluid modernity."[27]

The chapters in this volume speak to the ways in which different women have embraced different ways of gendering—from neotraditional to feminist—depending on their particular context of the postcommunist experience. Sometimes the strategies are pulled by a search for gender neutrality, sometimes they use a feminist narrative to create new norms, and sometimes they negotiate neotraditional gender ideologies of hyper-femininity or hyper-sexuality. In all cases, gender is mobilized and negotiated. In many cases, the tactical use of gender enables them to resist and survive; in a few cases, to thrive.

We are not arguing that gender negotiation and multiplication are necessarily good for women, or that women are somehow advantaged just because communism has collapsed. Indeed, we are not sanguine about the opportunities for women to flourish independently under the neoliberalism of the new "democracies." The argument that the transition has been bad for women has been overdetermined; and the opposing rhetoric that postcommunist life is better for women and men misses the much more complex reality. Using the lens of gender, we highlight a different perspective. The collapse of communism created a little more room to maneuver, especially for individuals. This room to maneuver can create openings for women to constitute new forms of behavior and resistance. This is *not* to say that all women take advantage of resistance, nor that all women are actively engaged in playing with gender to establish autonomy or individuality. But choices have been expanded, and with these have come opportunities to try out new ways of being female (and male). In what ways this will work over the long haul remains to be seen.

As with other observers who place gender at the forefront of their analysis, this book illuminates the ways in which gender has been essential to the transitions. This remains in stark contrast to the ways that most participants and observers, within and outside the academy, understood marketization and democratization "as ungendered processes."[28] Thus, postcommunist countries have legislative and policy discussions about abortion, fertility rates, women's unemployment, and maternity leave as if these issues had nothing to do with women's bodies or with the cross-institutional practices of gender.[29] In the academy, most transition theorists have explored the establishment of democratic institutions and processes with no reference to gender. The chapters in this volume attest to the opposite: these studies affirm that gender is a constantly negotiated process that becomes relevant in a multitude of sites. Locating gender in women's bodies is insufficient and incomplete. Locating gender in society is necessary for understanding both the individual experiences of gender and its social processes.

Researching Gender after Communism

The research presented in this book is based on field research in the countries themselves. In some cases, the author is a native of the country; in others the author is from a neighboring formerly socialist country; in still others, authors are westerners who have spent years learning the languages, cultures, histories, and people. This diversity of nationalities and personal histories is matched by diversity in research methods and approaches.

The editors' aim here was not to present a monotonic image of gender research. Nor did we insist that the authors stick to a (Western) feminist approach. What we did ask of all the authors was that they contextualize their research and address the fundamental gender multiplication and negotiation questions that are at the heart of this collection. All of us thank the women and men who shared their lives, their insights, and their struggles with us as we sought to understand the ways in which gender works. Obviously this is not a positivist objective study—as in much of the work done in the past thirty years on gender, sexuality, and women, we seek to be honest and respectful researchers who admit from the outset that we hope and work for a world that has real opportunities and choices for both women and men.

It will be clear that a wide array of disciplinary approaches and language are used in the following pages. Whether art historian, anthropologist, political scientist, or philosopher, however, we are all concerned with how genders operate, and the ways in which women and men negotiate genders strategically.

There are many ways that gender works and shapes experiences, both in the lived experiences and in the after-analysis by scholars and researchers. The way gender is used in each of the chapters, whether in describing artists' works or the experiences of "Internet brides" or a woman who was raped in Bosnia, will vary. Doing research and writing about gender is a challenge—we are not outside of the gender negotiations since we too are gendered and ethnicized and sexualized just as are the people whose lives we are trying to analyze. And since gender is neither a stable nor a universal category, the research presented here seeks to embody the dynamics of being gendered while doing research on gender. Finally, a reminder that although the central subject of this book is gender, that often means we are talking about women, because women are not the stable defining gender in any society of which we are aware. But we recognize, and the research here at times addresses, the reality that men are also gendered, and also negotiate gender. At times a gender approach is about women's experiences, at other times, or at the same time, it is about the ways masculinity needs the Other, and so on.

Positioning the Chapters

This volume, which came out of a conference on Placing Gender in Postcommunism, sponsored by the Havighurst Center for Russian and Post-Soviet Studies at Miami University, presents multiple stories about gender that we believe add more fullness to the analysis of the way gender is lived in Europe and Eurasia. The research documents the destabilization and negotiation of gender and gender ideology in the postcommunist era. The chapters also highlight the multiple locations of gender contestation and the ways in which gender ideologies are negotiated and mobilized.

We present the chapters grouped into four sections that highlight different gendered processes and strategies employed by women in the region, based on the internal logic of oppositional gender consciousness.[30] Keeping in mind Sandoval's emphasis that none of us are just one gender, and that we can use and refuse gender identities in different locations and for different purposes, the editors sought to impose a logic on the presentation of the research by categorizing each of the chapters in terms of how gender ideologies and constructs were used to address needs and interests. In some cases, women explicitly negotiate gender. In other cases, gender—more accurately, the denial of gender—is used to mute and diminish the significance of gender. In still other cases, traditional gender ideologies are invoked. Taken together, the chapters illustrate the numerous ways in which gender is multiplied and negotiated in the period after communism.

In the first section, "Negotiating Gender," we see specific cases in which individual women and groups of women play with gender by varying gender strategies. Tania Rands Lyon's chapter, "Housewife Fantasies, Family Realities in the New Russia," illustrates how families who profess housewife fantasies end up with relatively egalitarian family relationships, fostered by the heritage of Soviet-style egalitarianism. Drawing upon fieldwork in Saratov, a fairly typical Russian city, Lyon contrasts individuals' questionnaire responses with their work-family life histories. She finds that despite articulating support for neo-traditional stereotypes, many couples enact far more egalitarian gender strategies in their own marriages and families. In other words, in addition to the neotraditionalist ideology to which they subscribe, many couples also employ Soviet egalitarian arguments about sexual equality and women as workers, arguments based on the Marxist, gender-neutral understanding of women as workers. This suggests that women have much more gender flexibility than legitimated under traditional gender discourses and that perhaps the Soviet egalitarian rhetoric had a lasting impact on gender.

To examine the opportunities for gender transformation after communism, Janet Elise Johnson's "Contesting Violence, Contesting Gender: Crisis Centers Encountering Local Governments in Barnaul, Russia," explores the frames of domestic violence employed by three crisis centers in one Siberian city. A series of encounters between these crisis centers and the state elucidate the differences between the sides' frames of violence against women and between their gender ideologies. Johnson finds that by 2001 the politics and discourses of violence against women had brought about a significant change: an agreement among several key players that domestic violence is a problem worthy of state response and that women are not to blame for it. The key to this transformation was the ability of the radical feminist crisis centers to compromise on the frame of domestic violence in one context while deploying a variety of other frames in other contexts.

The second section, what we call "Denying Gender," emphasizes the ways that women detour gender systems and ideologies by trying to avoid reference to genderedness, instead focusing on other identities. The desire to establish a space for gender neutrality can be born out of a political commitment to assert that femaleness is irrelevant, or by a social construction that seeks to make gender irrelevant, at least in most contexts. Other times, gender denial is a survival strategy used with little self-consciousness or political commitment. This kind of argument that exterior physical differences are irrelevant has formed the basis of many equal rights and human rights campaigns. Even the Soviet Marxists, when working to incorporate women into the workforce, were using a form of gender neutrality, arguing that women were physically similar enough to engage in the male-dominated workforce, and that gender was thus irrelevant in certain contexts.

In Anne-Marie Kramer's "Abortion Debate in Poland: Opinion Polls, Ideological Politics, Citizenship, and the Erasure of Gender as a Category of Analysis," we see the erasure of gender in the analysis of the abortion debate in Poland during the particularly contentious period between 1996 and 1997. Kramer argues that opinion polling has made gender invisible by simultaneously recognizing gender in the questions—for example, asking whether maternal health or rape are justifiable reasons for abortion—while denying gender in the findings by hiding women's distinct lived experiences with abortion and abortion activism. This gender-neutral framing has larger implications because dimensions of the debate are presented as emblematic of the (ostensibly gender-neutral) cleavage in Polish society between those with a "neutral world outlook" and those "respecting Christian values."

The next chapter, Ewa Grigar's "The Gendered Body as Raw Material for Women Artists of Central Eastern Europe after Communism," explores the postcommunist perspective of women artists from Poland, the Czech Republic, and Slovakia toward the concept of individuality, especially the gendered body of woman. Grigar contends that, following the communist silencing of the expression of individuality and discussion of gender, some Central Eastern European women artists claim a stance of "gender neutrality." Others, especially younger artists, specifically explore gender, fascinated with the tensions of gender within the new social and cultural environment of consumerism and family values.

The third section, "Traditionalizing Gender," highlights the power and limits of employing an essentialist view of women as fundamentally, biologically, and thus socially, different from men.[31] Gender neotraditionalism can be mobilized as a strategy to negotiate the dominant gender ideology by claiming that the ascribed gender differences legitimately give (certain) women a particular advantage in a certain situation. Gender neotraditionalism can illustrate a practitioner's astute observation of the dominant sex/gender system and choice to work within this system for change. On the other hand, the neotraditional sex/gender ideology can be used to foreclose this strategy by stressing that because of gender, women do not belong in spheres where power is wielded. Women and men may adopt neotraditional strategies because they see that is the most likely effective path to some goal, or because they recognize that the costs of not following that path are too heavy to bear.

Svitlana Taraban's chapter, "Birthday Girls, Russian Dolls, and Others: Internet Bride as the Emerging Global Identity of Post-Soviet Women," illustrates the opportunities created by negotiating neotraditionalism for women seeking to emigrate from Ukraine via the Internet bride market. She finds that though these women "are required to follow the established parameters of the sexual economy," they also strategically create identities within these parameters. Their verbal descriptions deploy "adjectives that are traditionally associated with femininity and motherhood" to construct fantasies of "true love" and "the perfect wife," while their photo images represent themselves as seductive and available. These neotraditional gender representations contrast with survey findings that expose Ukrainian women's increasing tolerance of nontraditional relationships and their motivations to leave their domesticity to live abroad.

Iulia Shevchenko, in her study, "Does the Gender of MPs Matter in Postcommunist Politics? The Case of the Russian Duma, 1995–2001," investigates the possibility of gender essentialism as a strategy for female parliamentary deputies seeking to protect women's rights. She analyzes the impact of parliament-related factors upon female legislators' capacity to vote together across party lines to support policies beneficial to women. Women's votes are analyzed on three key policy domains: public welfare issues, traditional women's concerns, and noneconomic issues of life quality. The study concludes that postcommunism has created unfavorable conditions for women's political representation. Claims to represent women as women, emphasizing the traditional roles of females in family, society, and church, have backfired so that women deputies have lost their legitimacy in the broader public. They are not effective as representatives of women's interests, nor are they considered effective as politicians and rulers simply because they are women. Neotraditional views on women's issues characteristic of the Russian society have reduced the salience of gender claims as a basis for voting for women deputies. At the same time, the study shows that such factors as legislative context and issue profile can modify the negative effects of postcommunism.

The fourth section, "Negotiating Genders within Nationalisms," focuses on the ways that gender is formed and negotiated through other social processes and identities. Especially the complex intersections of gender with race, ethnicity, and nationality emphasize the myriad ways in which gender negotiation and multiplication is shaped by cultural, ideological, and societal forces. Negotiating gender by playing into displacement and the social construction of the "Other" can be a strategy of resisting one form of ideological domination, such as gender, while conceding or even embracing another.

Shannon Woodcock's study of "Romanian Women's Discourses of Sexual Violence: Othered Ethnicities, Gendering Spaces" illustrates the power and limits for Romanian women of articulating that the threat of gendered violence occurs only in public spaces and is only perpetrated by "Țigani"—the derogatory slang for Roma—men. The discourse allows some Romanian women to claim protection from Romanian men and promote themselves as the site of the reproduction of the Romanian nation. At the same time, their warnings of the threat of sexual violence from "Țigani" displace Romanian male violence and create an alternative national fantasy. Almost all of Woodcock's interlocutors acknowledged experiences of domestic violence at the hands of their Romanian partners or family members and none had experienced rape by Roma men, and yet the problem is defined as that of the Other. Also made invisible is the violence experienced by Roma women at the hands of either Romanian or Roma men. In this case nationality claims trump gendered experiences.

Sometimes, recognizing the national dimension of gender or gendered violence can hide the experiences and agency of individual women. Azra Hromadzic's "Challenging the Discourse of Bosnian War Rapes" finds agency and individuality in women's personal testimonies of war rapes in contrast to the dominant ways of reducing these rapes to collective experiences. She categorizes the existing analysis on the Bosnian war rapes into three approaches: (1) ethnicity and gender, (2) (post)colonial, and (3) medical. Even though these approaches employ different methods to the analysis of war rapes, she finds that they all collectivize and homogenize the experience of the raped women.

In other cases, the gendering of national discourse can simultaneously weaken the nation and coincidentally reinforce traditional gender stereotypes. Anna Brzozowska, in "Deficient Belarus? Insidious Gender Binaries and Hyper-feminized Nationality," demonstrates that negative connotations of gender have trumped attempts at the construction of Belarusian national identity. The chapter examines the ways that Belarusians imagine the Belarusian national identity, especially the way that this identity is gendered. Brzozowska finds that, in contrast to most nation-states, where the nation-state is at least somewhat framed as masculine, Belarusians tend to frame the nation-state as weak and feminine. This suggests that many observers' description of Belarus

Janet Elise Johnson and Jean C. Robinson

as lacking a national identity fails to account for the particular, gendered form of national identity constructed by Belarusians. This particularly hyper-feminized construction of the Belarus nation-state not only might weaken Belarus vis-à-vis the international state system, but also might reinforce the equation of weakness with femaleness within Belarusian society.

Theorizing Gender through East–West Dialogue

For us, the conversation about gender after communism began with Funk and Mueller's *Gender Politics and Post-Communism*. In 1993, these editors initiated a dialogue between women from the East and West about gender and feminism. They too collected essays from women from formerly communist countries, revealing and examining the tensions already emerging. We continue this conversation by including the next generation of scholars; those from the West who have extensive fieldwork and those from the East who are graduates of postcommunist and/or Western institutions of higher education. In the afterword of this book, "Fifteen Years of East-West Dialogue," Nanette Funk reflects and expands on this conversation. Beginning with a reflection on what she has learned from Central and Eastern European women who immigrated to the West, she maps the various circumstances in which these dialogues have emerged and their various forms. In the end, she advocates for self-reflection not just to improve relations between East-West feminists, but for transnational feminism more broadly.

We see this conversation as teaching us as feminist theorists about the myriad ways in which gender is performed and understood contextually. Neither women nor men can escape gender. In postcommunist societies, women (and men) are learning both new and old ways of living gender. As gender options are multiplied, the relationships among and between men and women, private and public, and freedom and control are constantly renegotiated. Living gender after communism means living simultaneously with opportunity and constraint.

NOTES

1. The cases highlighted in the empirical chapters include Belarus, Bosnia, the Czech Republic, Poland, Romania, Russia, and Ukraine. We also seek to speak, in general, to experiences across postcommunist East and Central Europe—such as Hungary, Slovenia, the Baltic republics, Bulgaria, Moldova—but not to the Central Eurasian republics—such as Uzbekistan, Turkmenistan, Kazakhstan, and Kyrgyzstan.

2. Candace West and Don H. Zimmerman, "Doing Gender," *Gender & Society* 1, no. 2 (1987): 147. See also R. W. Connell, *Gender and Power* (Stanford, Calif.: Stanford University Press, 1987), and Linda Nicholson, *Gender and History: The Limits of Social Theory in the Age of the Family* (New York: Columbia University Press, 1986), 69–104.

3. Nanette Funk and Magda Mueller, eds., *Gender Politics and Post-Communism: Reflections from Eastern Europe and the Former Soviet Union* (New York: Routledge,

1993), 3. Note we use the term "postcommunism" following Funk and Mueller: "'Post-communism' does not refer to a fixed social form, but an ongoing process, in part political, that includes the writing of new constitutions and law, and the forging of new economic policies" (12).

4. The gender expectations for rural women, for instance, were quite different than for urban women, and similarly for single versus married women, women of different ages, with different levels of education, and so on (Kristen Ghodsee, personal communication, June 21, 2005).

5. See the now classic study by Lynne Attwood, *The New Soviet Man and Woman: Sex Role Socialization in the USSR* (Bloomington: Indiana University Press, 1990).

6. See, for instance, Elzbieta Matynia, "Women after Communism: A Bitter Freedom," *Social Research* 61, no. 2 (1994): 351–78, and Jeffrey C. Goldfarb, "Why Is There No Feminism after Communism?" *Social Research* 64, no. 2 (1997), 235–58.

7. Ann Swidler, "Cultural Power and Social Movements," in *Social Movements and Culture*, ed. Bert Klandermans and Hank Johnston (Minneapolis: University of Minnesota Press, 1995).

8. Jane Flax, "Postmodernism and Gender Relations in Feminist Theory," in *Feminist Theory in Practice and Process*, ed. Micheline R. Malson et al. (Chicago: University of Chicago Press, 1986), 51–74.

9. Chela Sandoval, *Methodology of the Oppressed* (Minneapolis: University of Minnesota Press, 2000), 58.

10. Sandoval, *Methodology of the Oppressed*, 44.

11. We thank the many scholars who are documenting these gendered problems, in both scholarly work and international NGO reports. A number of works that have been especially important to us include the following: Barbara Einhorn, *Cinderella Goes to Market: Citizenship, Gender and Women's Movements in East Central Europe* (New York: Verso, 1993); Susan Gal and Gail Kligman, *Reproducing Gender: Politics, Publics, and Everyday Life after Socialism* (Princeton, N.J.: Princeton University Press, 2000); Susan Gal and Gail Kligman, *The Politics of Gender after Socialism* (Princeton, N.J.: Princeton University Press, 2000); Rosalind Marsh, ed., *Women in Russia and Ukraine* (New York: Cambridge University Press, 1996); Sue Bridger, ed., *Women and Political Chance: Perspectives from East-Central Europe* (New York: St. Martin's Press, 1999); Peggy Watson, "Eastern Europe's Silent Revolution: Gender," *Sociology* 27, no. 3 (1993): 471–87; Funk and Mueller, *Gender Politics and Post-Communism*.

12. Nancy Ries, *Russian Talk: Culture and Conversation during Perestroika* (Ithaca, N.Y.: Cornell University Press, 1997).

13. Nanette Funk, "Feminism Meets Post-communism: The Case of the United Germany," in *Feminist Nightmares: Women at Odds: Feminism and the Problems of Sisterhood*, ed. Susan Ostrov Weisser and Jennifer Fleischner (New York: New York University Press, 1994), 312.

14. Gal and Kligman, *The Politics of Gender after Socialism.*

15. Why wouldn't the communist leaderships see gender? Did it threaten their claim that women's equality with men was merely a matter of bringing women into the paid labor force? Gender, it was often asserted, had no meaning in Soviet Russia, except for its heuristic use in linguistics, i.e., the gender of a noun. The Soviet assertion that gender had no place in the Soviet social, political, cultural, or economic environment beyond grammar arose from a refusal to see that class was not the sole source of

oppression and exploitation in modern societies. The "woman question" was not about the feminization of certain roles and behaviors and the masculinization of others. Rather it focused attention on the ways in which oppression was practiced in the privacy of the bourgeois domestic family. Communist ideology, as employed in both the Soviet Union and its neighbor states to the west, blithely regarded the equalization of women with men in the workplace as women's emancipation. Men were the public proletariat; Soviet, Polish, Romanian, Czech, and East German women could become public workers too, and thus become men. In public, it seemed, gender appeared to disappear.

16. Thank you to Sara Friedman for pointing out the similarities to gender erasure in China. See Mayfair Yang, *Spaces of Their Own: Women's Public Sphere in Transnational China* (Minneapolis: University of Minnesota Press, 1999).

17. Definition of feminism in a 1996 Russian dictionary.

18. Funk 1993, *Gender Politics and Post-Communism*, 323. See also Havelkova and Lissyutikina in that volume.

19. Watson, "Eastern Europe's Silent Revolution," 472.

20. From 2000 to 2005, there were over a thousand articles referencing the word "gender" (or its adjectival form) in Russian social science and humanities journals. See East-View database of Social Science and Humanities journals, http://online.eastview .com/login_russia/index.jsp (access restricted).

21. Adrian Karatnycky, Alexander Motyl, and Amanda Schnetzer, *Nations in Transit 2001: Civil Society, Democracy, and Market in East Central Europe and the Newly Independent States* (New York: Freedom House, 2002), http://www.freedom house.org/research/nitransit/2001/index.htm (accessed Oct. 2003; URL no longer active). Freedom House classifies all of the other cases specifically considered in this volume, except Belarus, as transitional governments.

22. Marc Morje Howard, *The Weakness of Civil Society in Post-communist Europe* (Cambridge: Cambridge University Press, 2003).

23. Alina Zvinkliene, "Neo-Conservatism in Family Ideology in Lithuania: Between the West and the Former USSR," in *Women and Political Change: Perspectives from East-Central Europe*, ed. Sue Bridger (New York: St. Martin's Press, 1999).

24. Olga Lipovskaya, "The Mythology of Womanhood in Contemporary 'Soviet' Culture," in *Women in Russia: A New Era in Russian Feminism*, ed. Anastasia Posadskaya (New York: Verso, 1994). A different view however is presented by Janine Wedel in her study *Collision and Collusion: The Strange Case of Aid to Eastern Europe* (New York: Palgrave, 2001). Also see Kristen Ghodsee, "Feminism-by-Design: Emerging Capitalisms, Cultural Feminism, and Women's Nongovernmental Organizations in Postsocialist Eastern Europe," *Signs: Journal of Women in Culture and Society* 29, no. 3 (2004): 727–53.

25. Sarah L. Henderson, *Building Democracy in Contemporary Russia: Western Support for Grassroots Organizations* (Ithaca, N.Y.: Cornell University Press, 2003).

26. Slavenka Drakulić, "A Letter from the United States: The Critical Theory Approach," in *How We Survived Communism and Even Laughed* (London: Vantage, 1993).

27. Watson, "Eastern Europe's Silent Revolution," 479.

28. Gal and Kligman, *Reproducing Gender*, 3.

29. For example Joanna Goven, "New Parliament, Old Discourse? The Parental Leave Debate in Hungary," in *Reproducing Gender*.

30. These categories are derived from Sandoval's categories of oppositional consciousness.

31. For some advocates of this kind of gender strategy, the assumption is not that women are naturally different from men, but that social conditioning has led to the difference. The determining factor of what constitutes this kind of gender consciousness is the manipulation of differences into a kind of supremacism. See Sandoval, *Methodology of the Oppressed*, 56–57.

PART I.
NEGOTIATING GENDER

Housewife Fantasies, Family Realities in the New Russia

Tania Rands Lyon

Since the early 1990s, the Western press has published a regular flow of articles about the changing gender climate in the former Soviet Union. These articles describe Russian women finding a high-earning husband and becoming the bored, beauty salon–hopping housewives of the new rich, or signing up in droves for international matchmaking services.[1] Popular media and survey data reveal that an overwhelming majority of both men and women believe in the supremacy of what Westerners would consider "traditional" gender roles: man as breadwinner, woman as homemaker. Russians generally presume these kinds of masculinity and femininity to be natural and rarely appear to question them.[2]

A wave of academic literature from Western and Eastern feminists also emerged in the early to mid-1990s critiquing the apparent resurgence of patriarchy in Eastern Europe. Most of these scholars agree that the proliferation of "traditional" gender norms in the late 1980s and 1990s was part of a backlash against Soviet models of androgynous worker-women and the blurring of sex roles. Many see this as evidence that Soviet policies spread only a thin veneer of "equality" over the entrenched patriarchy of pre-Revolutionary Russia,[3] leaving a patriarchal culture to reemerge virtually unscathed after 1991.

Unquestionably, women suffered setbacks during the transition period of the 1990s, and views about the natural supremacy of men have become more overtly pervasive in Russia's media.[4] I argue, however, that the impact of Soviet *egalitarian* policies and rhetoric has not dissolved with the collapse of the Communist Party and its ideology. Using survey data and in-depth interviews with both husbands and wives in Saratov, a fairly typical midsize Russian city, I find that in lengthy conversations and in the decisions they make for their lives, Russians do not consistently adhere to the opinions they express in more abstract written survey questions. This study of gender roles and work-family choices of men and women in the context of parenthood suggests that a Post-Soviet backlash has not crowded the Soviet icons of sexual equality or of the woman-worker completely off the shelves of available gender role models. Few women are interested in giving up work altogether, and Russian men rarely exercise the kind of patriarchal authority in the home that they claim in survey responses to uphold. I argue that the Post-Soviet gender culture is characterized by a multiplicity of competing gender role models, including both "traditional" and "Soviet," and is influenced by a freer flowing traffic in ideas and images from around the globe. I find empirical evidence of women negotiating gender —shifting in and out of different gender "gears"—within this neotraditionalist gender culture. Russia's "patriarchal renaissance"[5] is not as monolithic as some initially feared and described, and within certain limits, women are actively experimenting with the combination of gender models that suits them best. Moreover, their experimentation is itself hinged on the more rigid role of men as providers, a role that has been emphasized as part of that "renaissance." For both men and women, regardless of their support for neotraditional values, they negotiate their roles, make sacrifices, and experiment with new modes of work, in order to address both personal and family needs. This study examines the interconnectedness of male and female gender roles, going beyond the literature's previous emphasis on women's experiences.

In the chapter, I first clarify my terms, "traditional gender roles" and "Soviet gender roles," and describe in more detail the Soviet gender legacy. Second, I summarize the impact of the transition on women and men, highlighting neotraditional gender expectations' role strain on men . Then, I detail my data and methods and explore how these role strains are played out in the families I interviewed, demonstrating the disconnect between dominant gender beliefs and common gender strategies as men and women negotiate their family roles in a time of transition. I show that while on the surface there is much support for gender traditionalism, probing deeper reveals less traditional views and behaviors. I conclude with a discussion of how these trends may impact Russia's evolving gender culture.

Russian and Soviet Gender Roles

To Westerners, the phrase "traditional gender roles"[6] is understood to mean men as public actors and heads of families and women as primary caretakers for homes and families. I use the term "traditional" in the Russian context to evoke similar images: it legitimately refers back to the dominant discourse on proper gender roles in pre-Revolutionary Russia, which projected "a domestic and maternalist ideal of womanhood" in both religious and secular writings.[7] There are deep parallels between the nineteenth-century cult of domesticity developed in the West and its adoption into the upper classes of Russian society, where it settled as the discursive ideal for Russian women in general.[8] At the same time, as Johnson and Robinson outline in the introduction to this volume, the pervasive neotraditional approach to appropriate roles for men and women is also informed and shaped by the experiences of Soviet socialism.

By "Soviet gender roles," I do not refer to the lived reality of gendered life in the Soviet Union, which was saturated with essentialist assumptions about male and female nature and often exhausting role conflict for women. I mean it rather to evoke the Soviet rhetoric emphasizing equality between the sexes (at work and in marriage), the deep link forged between identity and work for both men and women, and in particular the idealized dual worker-mother role of women.

This Soviet gender rhetoric was situated within a complex approach to gender. Given the extensive documentation and analysis already in print of dominant gender norms during the Soviet period, I refer here only briefly to this Soviet gender legacy.[9] In short, although official emphasis on women's roles as workers in the productive labor force often expanded and contracted under pressure from the state's economic and demographic needs, women's dominant role in the domestic sphere was left unquestioned. As women were constantly working to balance between the productive and reproductive worlds, men's prescribed roles as breadwinners and heads of household remained relatively static. At the same time, women grew less dependent on men's income because of wage leveling, their own working status, and the growing state supports offered to women and children. Thus, men's roles were undermined in both material and symbolic terms by the dominant role of the state in both public and private spheres, while women consistently retained a measure of influence, power, and legitimacy in their homes. The range of acceptable roles for women to adopt was broader than that for men in Soviet times.

Beginning gradually with perestroika in the 1980s and accelerating rapidly through the 1990s, the state has relinquished its monopoly over economic and social life. Given its powerful influence in gender relations during the Soviet period, the receding state has, as Johnson and Robinson argue, now left new space for gender role negotiation. The transition to a market economy is also changing the perceived relative value of family and work spheres, with paid work gaining greater prestige over domestic work.[10] This revaluing has different impacts on men and on women.

Men and Women in Transition

International non-governmental organizations (NGOs) and feminist observers are practically unanimous in their assessment that the transitions following the collapse of the Soviet Union have been especially unfavorable to women as a group.[11] The most obvious erosion of women's status in Russia can be seen in women's relative disappearance from political life, their disproportionate numbers among the newly unemployed and the poor, and the eroding value and availability of social supports for women and children. Because these negative impacts on women have been well documented, the following section will focus more on how *men* have fared in transition. I then explore implications of these outcomes on strategizing gender roles within families.

Although they have been less likely than women to lose their jobs (especially in the early 1990s), men too have certainly suffered from high unemployment rates and severe wage arrears in the state sector. But they have faced other, more gender-specific pressures. The heavy-handed paternalistic Soviet state emasculated men as public actors by discouraging individual initiative and as heads of households by eroding their roles as primary providers in their families.[12] Now, with the retreat of the state and a greater emphasis on a more traditional division of labor, men are suddenly expected to provide single-handedly for their families in an economic climate that has favored only a small minority and in which a single earner for the family is rarely sufficient to maintain the standard of living, much less to advance it. How can a Russian man attain the ideal of patriarchal head if he cannot support his family? Most Russian men have no experience with unemployment or with the difficult burden of finding new work in a choked economy. This is not the world they were educated or trained for. The toll of the transition on men can be read in the well-documented higher levels of alcoholism and higher crime and suicide rates. It is also reflected in the alarming drop in life expectancy for men relative to women since 1990.[13] (It may also be documented in increasingly high levels of domestic abuse by husbands of wives, as the patriarchal power of the husband/father has been newly accentuated. See Johnson in chapter 2 for more on this.)

While men are primarily expected to fill the financial resource gap left by crumbling Soviet supports, women who "fail" in the workplace can blame the economic crisis and still derive a sense of identity and purpose from their role in the home. In some ways women have more options in this new context than do men. The wife of a busy surgeon, who curtailed her own medical career to handle the housework and child care, asserted:

> Work is always more important for a man's sense of self. A woman can prepare a good meal and make a family and that can be her self-affirmation. But for a man, self-esteem is his work, so of course he'll spend more time there. (Radiologist, mother of one)

Even though women have been the more expendable and malleable labor force, subject to mobilization according to state needs, their very mobility has also bequeathed them a broader gender-role base from which to derive their sense of identity. Women may face greater structural constraints in the new economy—most notably, options for pursuing meaningful careers—but they also have a wider range of gender models to choose from (as well as greater complexity and more options for gratification within each model) as they strategize gendered choices. Men have a more confined range of role models and less culturally accepted flexibility in choosing a gender strategy. Their more singular role of provider is relatively rigid and clearly defined, as well as being more dependent on external factors such as the economy. This leaves men more vulnerable to falling short of gender ideals and expectations than are women.

Data and Methods

To support and elaborate this argument, I draw on field research conducted in Saratov, Russia, in 1998 and 2000. I chose Saratov—a midsize city (population approximately one million) located on the Volga River about 250 miles south of Moscow—in an effort to capture the "typical" Russian urban experience. While Moscow and St. Petersburg have cultural and economic histories that make them unique in many ways, Saratov, in size, economy, and industrial makeup, is much more similar to the average Russian city.

The heart of the data consists of in-depth oral interviews and written questionnaire responses garnered from a core sample of twenty married couples with children. The extensive time I spent with each family provided a richness of data impossible to attain in survey data or in one-time sampling. I interviewed each spouse privately and then both as a couple. I spent hours in each household, often stopping by for unexpected visits (many households lacked telephones). In many cases, the lengthy interview process evolved into participant observation, and I spent weekends with families at their *dachas*, attended cultural events or church services with them, toured their workplaces, and visited socially in their homes. Interacting consistently with these families over the course of many months, including follow-up visits two years after the initial interviews, allowed me to observe fluctuations in their employment, living conditions, spousal relations, and family arrangements.

I chose to limit my sample to married couples with at least one child who was about 9–10 years old: these parents would have raised their children through the rapid social change of the 1990s. It was also important to me to include only opposite-sex, dual-parent homes in order to explore the issue of gender role negotiation in families considered the ideal. I located a few of the couples through networks of acquaintances. Most of my sample, however, I recruited directly by attending parents' meetings for third-grade classes in four different schools. I selected schools in different neighborhoods and with differing levels of competitiveness and cost in order to access parents from a range of socioeconomic backgrounds. This stratified sampling method yielded an interview pool that reflected about 50 percent struggling low-income families, 25 percent more stable, surviving families, and 25 percent wealthier and more upwardly mobile families.

Because my sample could not be random, I allow for sampling biases. Since I was dependent on participants' willingness to donate many hours of their time for long interviews, I may have selected for parents with an interest in talking about their lives, which could have biased my sample toward more stable and happy marriages than the average. In two cases, however, couples were separated or divorced when I followed up two years later. Secondly, because I was a foreigner asking to come into their homes, I may have selected for Russians with greater trust, openness, curiosity, income, and education than average. On the other hand, my data may have benefited from the "stranger on the train" syndrome. Train travel in compartments of four to six people is extremely common in Russia, and Russians often joke that they might tell a stranger on the train more than they ever would tell someone close to them. As an outsider passing through their lives only temporarily, to many I represented a safe ear to hear otherwise private information.

My data for this paper therefore consists of published material gathered in Moscow, Saratov, and the United States, field notes from participant observation, and transcripts of the tape recordings of every interview with my core sample of forty parents. I hired native Russian speakers to transcribe these interviews in order to minimize errors and misunderstandings, after which I translated the bulk of the texts into English and coded them by theme. In order to preserve confidentiality, I have changed the names of the participants.

My use of qualitative methods to provide a close-up view of a handful of couples in a single city comes with the usual strengths and weaknesses of that approach. Although my sample size is too small to generalize broadly to all of Russia, my in-depth data suggest important realities within families that are not easily captured in large-scale surveys. My findings are designed to reveal crucial questions and sensitize future research on the postcommunist gender climate.

Gender Beliefs versus Gender Strategies

My survey of twenty couples reflected the traditional and essentialist discourse on gender that many observers have argued characterizes postcommunism. The support of traditional gender roles—men as the rightful primary

Table 1.1. It is better for all family members if the husband provides for the basic material needs of the family and the wife cares for the home and the children.

	Husbands	Wives
Strongly Agree:	14	12
Somewhat Agree:	6	3
Neither Agree Nor Disagree:	0	3
Somewhat Disagree:	0	0
Strongly Disagree	0	2

actors in the public sphere and women as the primary caretakers of the hearth and home—was evident when I asked respondents to what extent they agreed with the following statement: "It is better for all family members if the husband provides for the basic material needs of the family and the wife cares for the home and the children" (see table 1.1). Overwhelmingly, both husbands and wives agreed, and only two respondents, both women, disagreed with this statement.

The in-depth interviews, however, demonstrated that the story is more complex. Although 100 percent of the men and 75 percent of the women in my sample agreed that a traditional arrangement of spousal roles is best for everyone, only one-quarter of the households could actually boast such an arrangement. Also, several of the women who indicated strongly traditional views in survey questions told me at some point in interviews that they would personally be unhappy as a full-time housewife and couldn't imagine staying home all day. There seems to be a difference in many minds between what is better for "everyone" and what is better for individual women.

In fact, all four full-time housewives in my sample claimed that they wanted to work—mostly for personal fulfillment. Some of their comments include:

> A woman should have work that she loves, something she enjoys doing—not for money. (Housewife 1, mother of two)

> A woman should be a woman and should have a choice: to tell someone to stay put and cook and clean isn't right. Everyone has his or her own leanings. Some women have very masculine tendencies to think logically and some men are wishy-washy and can't earn decent money. (Housewife 2, mother of two)

Many of the women who worked full-time expressed a desire for fewer hours and more control over their schedule to help manage housework and mothering duties, but were not interested in giving up work altogether, even if their income were to become unnecessary to household survival.

Larger-scale research has also indicated women's strong interest in work

Table 1.2. The husband should be the head of the family and should have the final say in family decisions.

	Husbands	Wives
Strongly Agree:	6	4
Somewhat Agree:	4	3
Neither Agree Nor Disagree:	7	5
Somewhat Disagree:	1	3
Strongly Disagree	2	5

outside the home. Numerous surveys from the late 1980s and early 1990s show that a majority of Russian women would prefer to keep their jobs even if their husbands earned enough to support their families. A 1995 survey conducted by the Russian Center for Public Opinion Research (VTsIOM) showed that women have commitments to work similar to men's.[14] Work is an important component of women's identities, they rely on their work collectives for companionship and support, and they value making a contribution to social production.[15] A more recent study with 240 respondents found that 80 percent of women would continue working even if their incomes became unnecessary, while only 72 percent of men would continue working.[16] In contrast to the portrayal of Russian women as rushing to become housewives—if only they could—these findings suggest the opposite. The survey suggests that Russian men are more likely to work purely for the income, while women are more likely to have other reasons, more personal and social, to pursue work.

My sample also suggested that, although most men said they would prefer their wives to be at home full-time, none of them felt they had a right to insist on such an arrangement. Most recognized that their wives' incomes were helpful to their families, but they also respected their wives' desire—and right—to work.[17]

Moreover, support for traditional family roles did not always equate with strong patriarchal views on who should have authority within families. My survey question about who should have the last word in a family decision is much more evenly distributed across the spectrum of opinions (see table 1.2). As might be expected, more men than women favored a patriarchal arrangement, and one-third of the entire sample agreed with it; thus, preference for a patriarchal model seems, for a solid minority, to have survived Soviet social engineering quite well. Overall, however, whereas only a few women opposed a traditional division of labor (see table 1.1), far more supported egalitarian decision making (see table 1.2), which seems to indicate a separate-but-equal ethos in marriages.[18]

And although half the men indicated in the survey question a preference for husbands to be heads of household (see table 1.2), most of their more detailed answers in interviews revealed a high level of self-consciousness about just what this patriarchal role entailed. Almost every man in my sample who claimed to be the head of the household (and believed that this was appropriate) qualified that role in some way:

> It depends. I don't think I should be the master and that's it. If a decision has to do with children's needs, then my wife takes care of it and the final word is hers. If the question has to do with the car, garage, and furniture . . . then the decision is mine. (Mechanical engineer, father of two)

> I try never to come to that point [where one person has the final word]. I try to work it out . . . we both have veto power in the family. (Electrical engineer, father of one)

> Basically yes [I consider myself to be head of the family], but I try . . . you know . . . it's not like without me there's nothing. I try not to degrade her with that. I don't act like I'm higher than her. (Engineer, father of two)

One husband, even though he noted in the survey that he agrees the man should be the head of household, described his actual family arrangement in very different terms:

> Sometimes I have the last word, sometimes [my wife does], depending on the question. We never have anyone proclaiming "I have said it, period!" We have a well-developed democracy. (Mechanical engineer, father of two)

It would seem that if patriarchy is alive and well in Post-Soviet Russia, it is often—at least in the intimate sphere of the urban family—a kinder, gentler patriarchy. Men seem to respect their wives and, in wielding the authority that most men and women seem to think men should hold, remain mindful of their wives' preferences. The fact that these men felt it important to qualify and soften their authority roles in these interviews reflects the influence of egalitarian values from Soviet ideology.

This comparison of survey data with interview data also clearly illustrates how abstract beliefs or preferences about gender roles (gender fantasies) are not always played out in actual gender role negotiation or in behavior (gender strategies). Thus the conservative social trends touted in popular and academic surveys do not tell the whole story.

Gender and Work-Family Choices

In contrast to claims about the popularity of traditional, patriarchal family arrangements, ambivalence toward traditional gender roles was also evident in how the couples in my study negotiated gender strategies as they made work-family choices. In my interviews, I traced the work histories of the twenty couples in my sample through the entire decade of the 1990s. I found that couples held a variety of work-family preferences and experienced, of course, a range of economic constraints.

Some couples would have preferred a traditional arrangement, but the wife had to work for the family to survive. In other cases, the couple would have preferred a more egalitarian arrangement with the wife earning more, but she couldn't find a professional job in a severely contracted and sexist labor market. These are examples of gender role negotiation being dominated by economic structural constraints.

In many households, I found that gender role negotiation and economics had an interactive effect—dual-earning parents had choices about how much to work, and selected options in keeping with their gender preferences. I was often likely to find men making significant personal sacrifices to increase their earning power, even as their wives scaled back on their jobs without quitting altogether.

It would appear that a dominant pattern has yet to emerge in Post-Soviet Russia. The stories I collected certainly do not show an overwhelming return to a patriarchal model of the home and family. Couples often experiment in à la carte fashion with different gender-role combinations. The following two stories represent a certain pattern.

Marina and Igor: Igor started the 1990s working for a factory in a technical engineering job he found both challenging and personally satisfying. When the factory's wages failed to keep up with inflation and then went into arrears, he reluctantly gave it up in favor of the cash-in-hand income he could earn from doing private remodeling jobs in other people's homes. Once Igor had built up his one-man contracting business to a point that it was supporting his family, Marina, his wife, took a cut in hours and pay and opted for a demotion from college administrator to college instructor. She felt it was important for her to be with their son when he came home from school and so opted for a less prestigious job with more control over her schedule. Igor and Marina were both satisfied with this arrangement. She liked the social and intellectual stimulation of her teaching and didn't want to give it up completely. She also had plenty of time for managing the household and devoting more attention to their son (who struggled with grades and health problems), including spending whole summers with him at the family *dacha* on the Volga River while Igor stayed in the city to work. Igor sorely missed the intellectual stimulation of the work for which he had been trained, but never doubted that he had made the right decision as a husband and father.

Lidia and Andrei: Both husband and wife in this couple were medical doctors and both had busy hospital jobs in the mid-1990s, but were still surviving only by pooling resources with Lidia's parents, who lived next door. When Lidia was downsized from her hospital department, she looked for a less lucrative alternative that would relieve her workload, in spite of their financial need. She joined a radiology department where she would have fewer hours, fewer demands, and no night shifts, allowing her to devote more time to managing their home and being with their ten-year-old daughter. Andrei was passionate about his work in emergency anesthesiology and spent long hours at the hospital. After the 1998 ruble crash, when it became clear that even his three separate positions at the hospital and extra shifts were not going to be enough to support his family, he quit the work he loved to become a businessman in a friend's pharmaceutical company. Andrei felt that his new work was "soul-less" and it pained him to take what he felt was a materialist path, but he also never questioned his duty to be the primary earner in the family.

Both of these men were married to capable, professional wives who enjoyed their work and cared about their professional identities. Nevertheless, it was the husbands who made personal sacrifices to maintain their gender role as providers rather than expecting or arranging for their wives to share more fully in that role. The women in these families contributed to the family income, but they also strove to keep a balance between family and work. For women, work is seen as a source of personal satisfaction and sanity rather than merely as a source of earnings. For men, earnings trump personal satisfaction. It seems universally more acceptable for women to experiment with where to put their energies than for men to do so. Take, for example, the case of Oksana.

Oksana and Viktor lived with their two children in a one-room apartment. He worked for the state utility company "Gazprom," which in 1998 was about six months behind in paying wages. She was an elementary schoolteacher earning about thirty to fifty dollars a month.[19] In spite of their very modest existence, however, Oksana decided in 1998 that she would take a year off work. Her salary was meager for the hours she put in, and she was already handling the lion's share of the housework. She wanted a rest. Both she and her husband had traditional views about household roles, and Viktor supported her decision. Oksana described it as an experiment to see if the family could get by.

Two years later, I asked how the experiment had fared. Oksana had stayed home full-time for a year and a half and had enjoyed the rest. She had read more fiction (her personal hobby) and spent more time comparison-shopping to save family money on purchases. Viktor had enjoyed having a cleaner apartment and ready meals when he came home from work. But Oksana confessed that she had soon felt restless and missed the teaching, which she loved. She told me, "I wasn't brought up to sit around at home. I need to feel like I am doing something useful for society." By January 2000, she was back in the classroom at a school nearer her home. To his chagrin, Viktor once again found the kitchen table covered with papers to grade rather than a hot supper when he arrived home in the evenings. He told me he much preferred to have Oksana home full-time for his own personal comfort, but would never insist on it. He honored her personal preferences and her right to work—even her right to experiment with the work-family role that suited her best.

Discussion

Russia is a profoundly sexist society—especially in the higher echelons of political and economic power. The Soviet ideals of sexual equality and the importance of paid work to personal identity have suffered from a strong backlash, and currently compete with widely appealing rhetorics of women as protectors of the hearth, spiritual centers of the family, and deservers of economic support from their husbands.

This is precisely my point: ideals of sexual equality and the importance of work to women's identity remain very much a part of the Post-Soviet cultural landscape as available models from which women can choose to legitimize their choices. Thus an unqualified portrait of contemporary Russia's entrenched patriarchy and essentialist gender beliefs is misleading. One of the scholars to write about this continuity is Rebecca Kay:

> Data indicate that attempts to convince women of a single ideal to which they must aspire have not been altogether successful. Ironically, the areas where women seem most acquiescent are those relating to inner qualities and personal relations, whilst the wider reaching stereotypes and constraints on women's lifestyles . . . meet with greater resistance. Whilst women may . . . seek a man's "strength and protection" [and] may be pleased to imagine themselves ruling over an exquisite and perfectly ordered home, they are not prepared to see themselves limited to the private sphere only, reduced to brainless bimbos with nothing to offer but their physical attractiveness, or condemned to a life of self-sacrifice and material hardship as over-worked, unappreciated mothers.[20]

These "unsettled times" of transition in Russia are forcing conversations and flexibility about gender roles that weren't possible a generation ago. As Johnson and Robinson write in their introduction to this volume, postcommunism has allowed for gender roles to multiply and for individuals to negotiate gender roles more freely. My evidence suggests that the gendered realities of family roles rarely match the patriarchal fantasies of the dominant gender discourse.

This lack of cultural consensus on appropriate gender roles is reflected in my finding that both men and women respondents contradict themselves within interviews and that their responses to survey questions are often inconsistent with other conversations and with their actual behaviors and choices. The widely accepted patriarchal role of men as heads of households is highly tempered by expressed beliefs in democratic decision-making processes on the part of both men and women. And many women are actively experimenting with their preferences for what balance to strike between work and family, with at least the tacit support of their husbands, no matter how traditional their stated beliefs.

It is simply too early to declare an overwhelming victory for patriarchy and women's oppression. The Russian economic crisis is taking its toll in different ways on both men and women. Women may actually be better off psychologically during this transition, given their legacy of multiple, malleable roles with which to identify, while men suffer from the pressures of a tightly circumscribed role made especially difficult to live up to in economic depression.

My argument is not intended to establish who is suffering more in transition. It is a step toward understanding the complexities of a shifting gender culture manipulated by active agents, especially women. Significantly, women's ability to experiment with different role combinations is inherently dependent on the men in their lives assuming the more inflexible role of primary breadwinner. In the face of retreating state supports for women and children, women without a male earner in the family are faced with the same lack of choice as men in traditional households in providing for themselves and their families. Although the intense pressure on men to support their families during an economic crisis is likely to ease as the Russian economy stabilizes and improves, the basic gender order seems unlikely to change. Women may continue to enjoy greater role flexibility, but as long as the acceptable range of male gender roles remains confined to the productive workforce instead of expanding into the domestic sphere, Russia will face the same stalled gender revolution as the West.

NOTES

I thank the twenty Russian families who gave generously of their time and opened their lives to me in Saratov. I also wish to thank Princeton University, and Sara Curran in particular, for supporting my field research and subsequent writing. Finally, thank you, Jean Robinson and Janet Johnson, for pulling together a remarkable conference at the Havighurst Center of Miami University and for shepherding the work of so many varied scholars into a single volume.

1. For example, see media articles: Alessandra Stanley, "Video Valentines to Russia, Seeking Patient Brides," New York Times, February 14, 1997; Alessandra Stanley, "Democracy in Russia: Women's Lib Is Just Cosmetic," New York Times, May 11, 1997; and Mike Trickey, "Russia: Women marrying western men to escape hard times at home," The Ottawa Citizen, July 3, 1995, C12. See also an academic analysis: Rebecca Kay, "Images of an Ideal Woman: Perceptions of Russian Womanhood through the Media, Education and Women's Own Eyes," in Post-Soviet Women: From the Baltic to Central Asia, ed. Mary Buckley (Cambridge: Cambridge University Press, 1997), 25.

2. See, for example, Dana Vannoy et al., Marriages in Russia: Couples during the Economic Transition (Westport, Conn.: Praeger, 1999), 61; Valerie Sperling, Organizing Women in Contemporary Russia: Engendering Transition (Cambridge: Cambridge University Press, 1999), 74; Kay, "Images of an Ideal Woman," 80; Barbara Einhorn, "Ironies of History: Citizenship Issues in the New Market Economies of East Central Europe," in Women and Market Societies: Crisis and Opportunity, ed. Barbara Einhorn and Eileen Janes Yeo (Aldershot, UK: Edward Elgar, 1995), 225; and Helena Goscilo, "Domostroika or Perestroika? The Construction of Womanhood in Soviet Culture under Glasnost," in Late Soviet Culture: From Perestroika to Novostroika, ed. Thomas Lahusen with Gene Kuperman (Durham, N.C.: Duke University Press, 1993), 237.

3. Einhorn, "Ironies of History," 227.

4. Irina Tartakovskaya, "The Changing Representation of Gender Roles in the Soviet and Post-Soviet Press," in Gender, State and Society in Soviet and Post-Soviet Russia, ed. Sarah Ashwin (New York: Routledge, 2000).

5. This phrase is used by Anastasia Posadskaia as quoted in Rosalind Marsh, ed., *Women in Russia and Ukraine* (Cambridge: Cambridge University Press, 1996), 302.

6. Codified by sociologists such as Arlie Hochschild in *The Second Shift* (New York: Avon Books, 1989).

7. William G. Wagner, "'Orthodox Domesticity:' Creating a Social Role for Women in Late Imperial Russia," paper presented to the conference on "Sacred Stories: Religion and Spirituality in Modern Russian Culture," University of Illinois at Urbana-Champaign, February 21–23, 2002. See also Catriona Kelly, *Refining Russia: Advice Literature, Polite Culture, and Gender from Catherine to Yeltsin* (Oxford: Oxford University Press, 2001).

8. Diana Greene, "Mid-nineteenth Century Domestic Ideology in Russia," in *Women and Russian Culture: Projections and Self-Perceptions*, edited by Rosalind Marsh (New York: Berghahn Books, 1998).

9. For excellent reviews of the history of gender norms and the constant push and pull on women as workers and mothers during the Soviet period see Ashwin, "Gender, State and Society in Soviet and Post-Soviet Russia"; Rebecca Kay, *Russian Women and their Organizations* (New York: St. Martin's Press, 2000); Metta Spencer, "Post-Socialist Patriarchy," in *Women in Post-Communism: Research on Russia and Eastern Europe*, vol. 2, ed. Barbara Wejnert and Metta Spencer with Slobodan Drakulic (Greenwich, Conn.: Jai Press, 1996); Beth Holmgren, "Bug Inspectors and Beauty Queens: The Problems of Translating Feminism into Russian," in *Postcommunism and the Body Politic*, ed. Ellen E. Berry (New York: New York University Press, 1995); Larissa Lissyutkina, "Soviet Women at the Crossroads of Perestroika," in *Gender Politics and Post-Communism: Reflections from Eastern Europe and the Former Soviet Union*, ed. Nanette Funk and Magda Mueller (New York: Routledge, 1993); Olga Voronina, "Soviet Patriarchy: Past and Present," *Hypatia* 8, no. 4 (1993): 99–111; Lynne Attwood, *The New Soviet Man and Woman: Sex Role Socialization in the USSR* (Bloomington: Indiana University Press, 1990); Gail Warshofsky Lapidus, *Women in Soviet Society: Equality, Development and Social Change* (Berkeley: University of California Press, 1978).

10. Elizabeth C. Rudd, "Reconceptualizing Gender in Postsocialist Transformation," *Gender and Society* 14, no. 4 (2000): 518.

11. *Women in Transition*, Economies in Transition Studies: Regional Monitoring Report, no. 6 (Florence, Italy: UNICEF, 1999); Miguel Angel Centeno and Tania Rands, "The World They Have Lost: An Assessment of Change in Eastern Europe," *Social Research* 63, no. 2 (1996): 369–402; Barbara Einhorn, *Cinderella Goes to Market: Citizenship, Gender and Women's Movements in East Central Europe* (New York: Verso, 1993); Lissyutkina, "Soviet Women at the Crossroads of Perestroika"; Lynne Attwood, "The Post-Soviet Woman in the Move to the Market: a Return to Domesticity and Dependence?" in *Women in Russia and Ukraine*, ed. Rosalind Marsh (Cambridge: Cambridge University Press, 1996).

12. For work on the prevalent theme of the superfluous man and heroic woman in Russian literature see Goscilo and Marsh. See also Marina Kiblitskaya, "'Once We Were Kings:' Male Experiences of Loss of Status" in *Gender, State and Society in Soviet and Post-Soviet Russia*; Sergei Kukhterin, "Fathers and Patriarchs in Communist and Post-communist Russia," in *Gender, State and Society in Soviet and Post-Soviet Russia*; Lissyutkina, "Soviet Women at the Crossroads of Perestroika"; and Voronina, "Soviet Patriarchy," for discussions of men's status and roles in the Soviet period.

13. The risk of premature death for men rose 70% from 1987 to 1994, and has begun to decline only in the last half of the decade (Goskomstat, 1999). Men's life expectancy is lower than the average for Latin America, the Middle East, and North Africa. The gap between men and women in Russia remains one of the largest in the world (World Health Organization, 2000). See also Kiblitskaya, "'Once We Were Kings,'" 95, for more discussion of the physical impact on men's health and life expectancy.

14. Given a list of statements about work, 14.0% of men and 14.7% of women opted for "Work is important and interesting to me irrespective of pay." The other end of the spectrum also showed similar views between men and women: 3.9% of men and 5.3% of women opted for "Work is an unpleasant occupation. If I could I wouldn't work at all" (cited in Sarah Ashwin and Elain Bowers, "Do Russian Women Want to Work?" in *Post-Soviet Women: From the Baltic to Central Asia*, 25.)

15. Ashwin and Bowers, "Do Russian Women Want to Work?" 25; V. Perevedentsev, "Women, the Family, and Reproduction," in *Women in Contemporary Russia*, ed. Vitalina Koval (Providence, R.I.: Berghahn Books, 1995), 123.

16. These figures increased to 90% of women and 80% of men in the younger age groups. See Sarah Ashwin, "'A Woman is Everything': The Reproduction of Soviet Ideals of Womanhood in Post-Communist Russia" in *Work, Employment and Transition: Restructuring Livelihoods in Post-Communism*, ed. Al Rainnie, Adrian Smith, and Adam Swain (New York: Routledge, 2002), 121.

17. Sociologist Elizabeth Rudd ("Reconceptualizing Gender in Postsocialist Transformation," 532) found a similar pattern in postcommunist East Germany.

18. This is very similar to the findings of gender attitude research in Italy, where young parents are choosing traditional divisions of labor as long as they are based on nonhierarchical family models with an emphasis on the arrangement being a voluntary choice subject to change: Ulla Björnberg, ed., *European Parents in the 1990s: Contradictions and Comparisons* (New Brunswick, N.J.: Transaction, 1992).

19. Before the September 1998 ruble crash, her salary was valued at about $50. After the crash it dropped to $30.

20. Kay, "Images of an Ideal Woman," 94.

Contesting Violence, Contesting Gender

Crisis Centers Encountering Local Government in Barnaul, Russia

Janet Elise Johnson

At the beginning of the twenty-first century, there was a momentous opportunity for the transformation in the Russian response to domestic violence. For the first time, most Russians—87 percent of men and 93 percent of women in a 2001–2002 survey—agreed that violence against women in the family is a problem.[1] From a Moscow suburb and the northern city of Arkhangelsk to the ethnic Republic of Tatarstan and the Siberian capital of Barnaul, politicians began to discuss the once taboo problem of violence in the family and to initiate moderate plans of reform, such as supporting crisis centers or small shelters and forming multidisciplinary working groups. Even the criminal justice system had begun, in some localities, to see the mutual advantages of collaborating with local activists. According to Natalia Sereda, the director of a women's crisis center in Barnaul, by 2000, discussions with policy makers and law enforcement about domestic violence and violence in the family had become almost "normal," illustrating that there was a new level of recognition of the prevalence and impact of the problem.

In the early years following the end of the Soviet Union, the concept of "domestic violence" had aroused blank looks, and the criminal justice system had mostly ignored domestic violence or blamed the victim for "provoking" the violence.[2] Throughout society, women were held responsible for mediating family conflicts, often making their suffering invisible. From the perspective of leaders of the Russian crisis center movement, increased recognition that domestic violence is a problem—even just discussing the problem in the media or with policy makers—reflected the possibility for significant changes in the dominant thinking about domestic violence and gender.[3] For feminist political scientists, increased problem recognition represents a de facto enhancement of women's status.[4] In the language of the introduction to this volume, new thinking about domestic violence represents a shift in gender ideology, especially the distribution of responsibilities between women and men.

To provide a richer account of this postcommunist opportunity, this chapter maps the encounters between various non-governmental organizations (NGOs) and state institutions as they struggle over different "frames" of domestic violence. By frame, I refer to "collective action frames," the "meaning work—the struggle over the production of mobilizing and counter-mobilizing ideas and meanings."[5] Frames diagnose injustices, identifying the source of the problem and its victims, and propose responses to alleviate the problems. The politics of framing within a movement includes generating and elaborating a frame and attempting to diffuse the frame to others in society, so they will accept its orientations. The contextual constraints on the framing process include the degree of political opportunity and the cultural "toolkit" that can be drawn upon in framing or can limit the resonance of frames.[6] Encounters between different sponsors provide a particular opportunity to highlight the differences between collective actions frames and their corresponding gender ideology.

Despite the almost universally gloomy analysis of women's status after communism, including my own,[7] I argue that the collapse of communism in Russia has also meant a new opportunity for feminist gender ideologies, not just in a small and marginalized women's movement, but also in ways that allow feminist orientations to be considered and adopted by those in power. The women's crisis center movement emerged and began to renegotiate the dominant understandings of domestic violence and gender. This debate was less at the level of formal politics, as Susan Gal and Gail Kligman found with another gender-specific policy issue (reproduction) across East and Central Europe.[8] Instead, the debate was mostly at the level of agenda setting—whether violence against women even gets on the agenda of issues that will be debated—the kind of politics where the most power is often wielded.[9] The crisis center movement's achievement, often overlooked by observers of the region as they aptly criticize Russian president Vladimir Putin's "managed democracy"[10] and downplayed by activists because there is so much more that needs to be done, is an illustration of the possibility inherent in postcommunism.

To bring this process of gender transformation into the most detail, I highlight one geographical location of these encounters between the society and state, the southwestern Siberian city Barnaul, capital of the Altai *krai*,[11] far from places most often analyzed in studies of Russian society. Barnaul is a medium-sized city of approximately six hundred thousand people, located on the Ob' river, a few hundred miles from Kazakhstan, China, and Mongolia. Though Barnaul represents fairly typical Post-Soviet Russian urban life,[12] it provides a glimpse into an exceptional case of robust non-governmental activity around the issue of violence against women.

The field data come primarily from my research trip to Barnaul in 2002.[13] I employed the method of "participant observation," observing and participating in the everyday activities of the organizations. In addition, I conducted interviews as well as analyzed literature from the organizations and regional news media. The research for this chapter is part of an ongoing project on the crisis centers and violence against women in Russia first begun in the early 1990s, and continued for over a decade, during which I have lived and researched across Russia.

As Azra Hromadzic discusses and illustrates in her chapter on Bosnian war rapes in this volume, for Western feminists such as myself, critiquing non-Western societies is rife with analytical risks of universalizing Western experience and objectifying Other women as victims. "Like Alice [in Wonderland], Westerners are likely to slip easily from the view that things in Central and Eastern Europe 'go the other way' to the view that they 'go the wrong way.' "[14] As my colleagues who study the Russian women's movement have observed, we may gloss over problems that Russians themselves see as important as well as use the critique of other societies to make us feel good about ourselves.[15] Yet, there is also the opposite risk, as Russian activists and scholars contend, that culture is used as an excuse for domestic violence.[16]

I claim, as does Uma Narayan, that even as we must be concerned about our Western "preoccupations," there is a place for moral criticism, especially when the West is held to the same standards.[17] In this chapter, I negotiate between the Western "provocateur" imposing beliefs and a more culturally relativist stance.[18] While I employ a schema based on Western experiences to understand various ways of thinking about domestic violence—making distinctions between radical, sociological, and psychological perspectives[19]—I provide a detailed case study of Russian views of domestic violence and gender. Though I critically analyze foreign intervention in other current projects because I believe this kind of analysis is important, the chapter assesses these views from my feminist perspective that all societies, including my own, need to take domestic violence seriously, holding men, not women, responsible for the violence men inflict on women. My goal is to honor what the crisis centers have achieved from a feminist perspective that, as I show, many of them have adopted.

Soviet Skepticism and the Women's Crisis Center Movement

The Soviet leadership understood violence against women in a limited way. Although the 1917 Bolshevik Revolution brought new consideration of women's problems, including a new criminal statute that criminalized quid pro quo sexual harassment,[20] by the 1930s there was little space for considering violence against women as a challenge to "women's emancipation." Instead, Soviet scholars tended to blame women and women's emancipation for "provoking" violence, for example, arguing that domestic violence was caused by women's failure to perform their domestic duties "selflessly" and by their declining moral values.[21] When violence against women was regulated at all, it was regulated only as part of the overall control of society, for example in campaigns against gang rape or "hooliganism."[22]

None of these ways of thinking about domestic violence involved the consideration that domestic violence might be a mechanism of gendered power. Biology was destiny, and the inability of Soviet leaders to see that gender was socially constructed left untouched the gendered beliefs that women are to be held responsible for family relations, even the violence inflicted against them. And for the most part, the state's "skeptical frame" of domestic violence was widely circulated and unchallenged in society.[23]

As Soviet power waned, whatever commitment there had been to "woman's emancipation" also waned.[24] Similarly, less state coercion meant that the criminal-legal system lost its justification for intervening in private life, regardless of whether individual women sought such intervention. Human Rights Watch found that police, prosecutors, and judges, when faced with victims of violence against women, consistently failed to comprehend the violence, considering it minor even when arguably severe and blaming the woman even when she was the one assaulted.[25] The skeptical view of domestic violence meant that it was "privatized."[26]

Yet, simultaneously, the liberalization of the Soviet Union also created the possibility for the emergence of feminist gender ideologies that foreground gender.[27] The global feminist movement was bringing violence against women to the forefront of their advocacy in alliance with several major donors, including the Ford Foundation and the U.S. Agency for International Development (USAID).[28] As independent non-governmental groups began to emerge in Russia, women's groups gathered, notably in Dubna in 1991 for what is now called the First Independent Women's Forum. This gathering, widely considered a watershed in the development of a Russian women's movement, and the follow-up meeting the next year, generated a sister movement, a women's crisis center movement.[29] More than many other issues, the critique of domestic violence resonated with many Russian women activists.[30]

The hallmarks of this smaller movement are crisis centers for women victims of violence. The first crisis centers were founded in Moscow and St. Petersburg in 1993.[31] By the mid-1990s, additional crisis centers were founded in these two cities, and the movement spread eastward. By 1998, researchers in Moscow found 24 organizations that worked in the sphere of "prevention and elimination of violence against women" within the Russian Federation, from Murmansk to Irkutsk.[32] By 2001, there were between 60 and 80 organizations.

In the summer of 2002, the director of the Russian Association of Crisis Centers for Women, an umbrella organization of 40 members, estimated that there were some 120 organizations involved in opposing violence against women in Russia.[33]

The primary—and defining—activity of these women's crisis centers is a hotline for victims of sexual and domestic violence. A hotline is an inexpensive way to reach out to women to provide emotional support, empowerment, and medical and legal referrals. Many centers also provide in-person assistance. Some centers also have more political goals, seeking to educate the public about the problem of violence against women and to change the behavior of the police, prosecutors, medical examiners, judges, social workers, and psychologists.

These more political activities require challenging the dominant gender ideology both locally and nationally. Responding to the global feminist movement, and in particular to American movement activists who were providing the early financial resources, the leadership of the Russian women's crisis center movement decided it was crucial to create new terms (from "violence against women," to "domestic violence," to "violence in the family") to make the problems more visible. These crisis centers also worked to disseminate these terms so that they had social meaning. For example, more than a dozen women's crisis centers worked with USAID on a national campaign from 1998 to 1999, introducing "domestic violence" onto talk shows at TV stations across Russia.

The Women's Alliance in Barnaul

The Women's Alliance in Barnaul is one of the second-generation crisis centers that emerged in the late 1990s. Natalia Sereda, the director, had founded a women's NGO in 1993 as a result of wanting to help the women that she was observing in her work as a psychologist at a women's hospital. In 1995, she took note of the role that domestic violence was playing in the lives of her women patients. In 1996, at a USAID-sponsored conference in Novosibirsk, members of one of the first generation of crisis centers in Nizhnii Tagil described their work and thus provided a model of what an organization might do to address violence against women. In 1998, Sereda refocused her organization toward the problem of violence against women, opening a hotline for women victims of violence. The Women's Alliance, in the summer 2002, consisted of a crisis center, a parenting training program, and a women's resource center. The resource center itself maintained a library and ran programs to advocate for women's rights and aid other women's NGOs.[34] Like many crisis centers, the Women's Alliance employed a handful of paid staff, with perhaps up to a dozen volunteers connected to the center.

The crisis center at the Women's Alliance included a variety of programs to help prevent domestic and sexual violence as well as sex trafficking. As described by the executive director, Elena Shitova,

Specialists of the Center provide victims of violence with support such as a hot line, free legal consultations, free psychological counseling, support groups, and escorting victims to court and the police. Center specialists conduct informational and educational campaigns against violence in our society through publications in mass media, as well as training and seminars for government employees such as law enforcement officials, social workers, doctors, teachers, and elected officials.[35]

As with the other political crisis centers, the Women's Alliance combines practical services for victims of violence with broader advocacy work targeted toward transforming both societal understandings and state responses. According to a staff member, the center had helped "6,500 victims—most of them female victims of violence" from 1998 to 2002.[36] Broader, transformative work has included public information campaigns, roundtables, seminars, and conferences. For example, the Women's Alliance distributed a variety of stickers, bulletins, and pamphlets, as well as photos and articles for the news media, designed to bring attention to the issue. The Alliance also sees itself as part of the larger women's movement. Shitova, for example, was involved in a 2001 project to support and link women's organizations in Altai *krai* by launching a "women's parliament" Web site. In 2002, Sereda was elected vice president of the Russian Association of Crisis Centers for Women.

Radical Feminism versus Post-Soviet Skepticism

The frame of domestic violence sponsored by the Women's Alliance became clearly evident through an encounter with the state at a July 1999 workshop on violence against women organized with the American Bar Association Central and East European Legal Initiative (ABA-CEELI). Dianne Post, who was then the Russian ABA-CEELI gender expert, made trips to the regions to raise awareness of the issues of violence and discrimination against women, working with indigenous women's organizations and inviting psychologists, local administrators, social workers, and police officials.[37] In similar trips to Kaluga and Orel in March of 1999, in which I participated and observed, Post brought tools from the American domestic violence movement, such as using post-traumatic stress disorder (PTSD), to demystify the ways that battered women tend to act.[38] She also brought members of first-generation crisis centers to share their work and invited local activists and social workers to speak. According to Post's journal from this trip, the workshop was organized with Natalia Sereda and the Women's Alliance and attended by members of the regional administration involved in education and healthcare and by the police.[39]

For both Post and Sereda, there was a chasm between their understanding of violence against women and that of members of the criminal justice system. Sereda remembered that the police claimed that domestic violence was the woman's fault, and that violence in the family was due to women's "provocation." Post noted that that the head of the regional education committee claimed that "Russian women love to be martyrs, they love to be beaten." She also noted that a local forensic doctor made multiple excuses for not conducting the medical exams almost always required for the prosecution of rapes. This doctor, according to Post, feared that an exam would allow any woman to blackmail any man. This doctor's and Sereda's understandings of the responsiveness of the criminal justice system were hugely different: the doctor estimated that 100 percent of rape cases are investigated and prosecuted, while Sereda's estimate was 1 percent. These differences in understanding violence against women meant that the police saw no benefit in working with the Women's Alliance.

This conflict between the Women's Alliance and the criminal justice system also illustrates just how limited was the criminal justice system's understanding of violence against women. Instead of bringing visibility to the problems of sexual and domestic violence, the Altai criminal justice system denied the existence of many incidences and types of violence against women. Their understandings dismissed the problems as idiosyncratic or as the fault of the victim. In this case, the Altai criminal justice system held contradictory understandings of violence against women, both of which concealed the violence. Mirroring the Russian criminal justice system of the 1990s, the Altai criminal justice system construed violence against women as either caused by the women-victims (i.e., it is real, but not worthy of state response because the victims are to blame) or so serious a crime that women often use false accusations to manipulate men (i.e., the violence so rarely occurs that an individual case is probably not real).

Sereda, though, saw herself as having been transformed by working with Post. She had come to the problem of domestic violence via her practice in psychology, but her observations of women's suffering contrasted with that of Soviet "experts." With Post, Sereda trained to become a "social advocate," and when I met with her in 2002, she was planning to attend law school in order to advocate more effectively for women who have been victimized by violence.

Through her positive encounter with Post and her negative encounter with the Russian criminal justice system, Sereda adopted a frame of domestic violence that resembled the radical feminist frame developed in the United States and Great Britain. As defined by American scholar Evan Stark, a proponent of this frame, battery is "the pattern of violent acts *and* their political framework, the pattern of social, institutional, and interpersonal controls that usurp a woman's capacity to determine her own destiny."[40] The feminist frame holds that men-perpetrators need some punishment and/or penalties for battering, and then perhaps batterer treatment. Women-victims, on the other hand, do not need to be treated by [patriarchal] psychologists or social workers, but rather to be empowered through naming their problem as a violation of their rights and through receiving social services that allow them to escape dependence on their batterers.

Sereda's version of the radical feminist frame was implicit in her dreams for the future. For example, she and her husband Sergei, who is the deputy of the Alliance and director of the parenting program, expressed a desire to find more effective ways to collaborate with men: they understand that it is important to persuade men of the problem of domestic violence. Further, because she understood that child abuse is also rooted in the gender-related problem of domestic violence and was therefore worried that victims of domestic violence might turn violent with their own children, Sereda told me that she would like to do a program on women's aggression. Finally, she saw her assignment as teaching the police that it is their job to respond to domestic violence, assuming that police response will illustrate to people (including children) that there is a punishment for domestic violence.

As this frame stems from radical feminism, it evokes a gender ideology resistant to the domination of men over women. As an explicitly feminist frame, it highlights the need for women to work together. These ideas about gender challenge not only the state's failure to see violence against women as a problem, but also the dominant, neotraditional gender ideology, which call for women's return to domesticity, discussed in this volume's introductory chapter and in Tania Rands Lyon's chapter.

Response (*Otklik*)

The Women's Alliance is not the only women's organization in Barnaul, nor is it the only sponsor of a new frame of domestic violence or new gender ideology. A directory of women's organizations in the Altai *krai* published in 2002 details the emergence of these organizations.[41] Between 1991 and 1994, there were seven women's organizations registered in the *krai*, and as is common in postcommunist Russia, four of these quickly collapsed.[42] Between 1995 and 1998, eight were registered; nineteen between 1999 and 2000. Nineteen of the thirty-four organizations described their major focus to be the defense of women's rights, while others focused on children, human rights, or the environment.

In response to a 2001 survey, approximately half of the Altai women's organizations reported that their focus was on the family or motherhood, but only two organizations besides the Women's Alliance identified themselves as involved in organizing against violence against women.[43] One, *Dobryi svet* (Good World), described the purpose of their organization as the "liquidation of discrimination against women, the social strengthening of women, the prevention of violence in the family."[44] This organization, located in the village of Pospelicha, targets rural women, and falls outside the scope of this study.

The second organization, *Otklik*, or "Response" in their English translation, was the organization that coordinated the publication of the directory. Otklik was founded and registered in 1997. In 1999, their original purpose was described as the defense of the rights of citizens, especially women. By 2002, the organization redefined its mission, drawing upon the language of national legislation, as the "equal rights and equal opportunities . . . to achieve gender equality."[45] At least since 1999, one of Otklik's many educational, legal, and social service projects has concerned the problem of violence against women. In 2001–2002, one of their two main projects was on "innovative forms of help to survivors of violence" against women. Otklik's resemblance to the women's crisis centers was confirmed by their inclusion in a fundraising workshop in June of 2002. The workshop was the second of ten seminar-trainings for organizations working on issues of violence against women, sponsored by ANNA, the founding organization of the Russian Association of Crisis Centers for Women. Further, Otklik has received funds from international organizations that tend to support women's crisis centers.

A Sociological Frame of Domestic Violence

Otklik articulated their frame of domestic violence in their gender dictionary. In the dictionary, "domestic violence (violence in the family)" is defined as

> any deliberate action of one member of the family against another, if that action restrains the constitutional rights and freedoms of a member of the family as a citizen, causes him physical pain and brings harm or issues threats of harm to the physical or individual development of the minor members (children) of the family. International rights regimes distinguish between the following forms of violence in the family: physical violence, psychological violence, sexual violence, and economic violence. The object of domestic violence can be any member of the family.[46]

Compiling a gender dictionary and including this definition of domestic violence indicates that Otklik takes gender and domestic violence seriously, just as the Women's Alliance does. I found further evidence of this in my encounter with them at the fundraising workshop run by ANNA.

Nonetheless, Otklik's frame is different from the radical feminist frame in that it is gender-neutral. While radical feminists accent the gender-specificity of domestic violence—claiming that violence is most often perpetrated by men, experienced by women, and indicative of the subordination of women— Otklik's above definition twice clarifies that anyone can be a victim of domestic violence. Otklik's frame is sociological, which is unsurprising given that the center is staffed by students and faculty from the Sociology Department at Altai State University. While sociologists can, of course, be radical feminists, there is relatively little of this radical feminist critique in Russian sociology departments. This sociological frame suggests that violence in the family is a result of the larger structures of society or the dynamics of the family. The sociological frame suggests that there might be as much violence committed by wives as by husbands, in contrast to the feminist frame, which highlights that severe violence is much more likely to be used by men against women.

From the perspective of a radical feminist, Otklik's sociological frame, while it uses some of the language of the Beijing platform from the 1995 United Nations Conference on women, has the potential to normalize domestic violence. This approach—which makes little distinction between individual instances where violence is used (such as slapping) and overwhelming physical and psychological control—has led some Russian survey researchers to underestimate and misconstrue the rates of violence.[47]

The emergence of another women's organization in Barnaul demonstrates that the frames of domestic violence have truly multiplied, not just doubled, in postcommunist Russia. Otklik's sociological frame, while distinct from the radical feminist frame of the Women's Alliance, countered the dominant reluctance to even discuss domestic violence. Similarly, Otklik's activity suggests an alternative gender ideology. Their domestic violence frame calls for increased responsibilities of men—albeit within the context of all individuals taking responsibility for inflicting violence. It is also articulated by a women's organization and within a context of academic gender studies, evoking an ideal of women working together to understand and address a problem facing them.

Altai Krai Crisis Center for Men

In addition to these two women's organizations, there was also a crisis center for men, the Altai Krai Crisis Center for Men (KCCM), which was founded in 1996, the most robust men's crisis center in Russia.[48] According to their 2002 brochure, the mission of the organization is "the prevention and rehabilitation of the physical, psychological, and social health of working-age men in the region."[49] Originally, most of the calls came from men concerned about their physical health. Social workers, psychologists, psychiatrists, several medical doctors, an attorney, and a "social pedagogue" staff the center. The center ran various groups for men and youth facing a variety of different life situations. The center provided psychological consultations twenty-four hours a day on a hotline. In addition to this concrete social, psychological, and legal work, the center conducted "gender research."

As with the Women's Alliance and Otklik, one of the main issues that the KCCM hopes to address is domestic violence. According to the brochure, the center provides "psychological help in the situation of domestic violence for men-offenders." Group projects aim to counsel those who employ violent behavior and to develop among youths nonviolent ways of relating. In addition, the director of the program since 1998, Maksim Kostenko, has an obvious intellectual interest in domestic violence and the broader women's crisis center movement in Russia.[50] Like the handful of other self-identified pro-feminist men in the women's crisis center movement, Maksim Kostenko is conversant in American feminist theories of masculinity and is familiar with Western (American and Swedish) batterer treatment programs.

A Psychological Frame of Domestic Violence

The KCCM's attention to domestic violence is significant because, unlike the Women's Alliance, it is primarily a state-sponsored institution.[51] It was founded under the committee of the administration of the *krai* on the social protection of the population and continues to receive funding from the government. Such state support for the provision of social services is not unusual in Altai, where the continuity of communist elites, the lack of independent economy, and subsidies from the federal government mean that the state is the primary source of funding for almost all activities in the region. Yet the KCCM's responsiveness to domestic violence represents a significant difference from the denial of the problem that was illustrated by the criminal justice system at the 1999 ABA-CEELI conference. Kostenko, who wrote a dissertation that discusses domestic violence and who was involved in the writing of Otklik's gender dictionary, has brought a keen awareness of the seriousness of domestic violence to a welfare-oriented state institution.

KCCM's attention to domestic violence is also significant because it is a men's organization, approximately half staffed by men and focused on men clients. Women's crisis centers such as the Women's Alliance work to challenge prevailing notions about women and to shift societal gender ideologies about men with their consciousness-raising campaigns. A men's crisis center can hold men-batterers directly accountable for their actions through their hotline and their group and individual counseling. That this accountability is accomplished under the direction of a man provides an example of men taking responsibility for domestic violence. The KCCM's work has potential for challenging a masculinity that does not hold men accountable for their violence. For the director, "when working with batterers the most important and at the same time the most difficult thing is to teach them responsibility for their behavior."[52]

Nonetheless, although the KCCM sponsors a third frame challenging the dominant understandings of domestic violence and gender in postcommunist Russia, there are limitations to its challenge. Similar to problems faced by batterer treatment programs in the West, the context of the KCCM's intervention, as part of the ministry of social protection and through its emphasis on consultations, shapes its frame of domestic violence into a psychological one. A psychological frame understands domestic violence as a specific pathology of an individual's personality, as a psychological disorder that primarily requires psychotherapy to overcome. This frame pathologizes the violence, often providing psychological excuses for the perpetrator. In Russia, particular emphasis is placed on the environmental and cultural stresses placed on men by the transition and by unyielding ideals of masculinity, what the director calls "male gender role stress."[53]

At the KCCM, there is a tendency to excuse, or at least diminish, violence. As explained by Natalia Kostenko of KCCM, most other "specialists [the women involved in women's crisis centers] see the solution of the problem of domestic violence in divorce; we seek to provide psychological counseling to the man so that the spouses can reconcile."[54] Reconciliation is a goal probably sought by many victims of violence, but there is little evidence that counseling, in the absence of any punishments or penalties for the violent offenders, is effective at stopping the violence. Research in the United States shows that programs work better when there are at least some consequences for violent behavior.[55] Moreover, without any punishments or penalties for domestic violence, there is less challenge to violent masculinity.

From my perspective, more problematic is the way that psychological frames of domestic violence tend to slip from the batterer to the woman, blaming the (woman) victim instead of the (man) perpetrator. In the United States, this is done by raising the question "Why didn't she leave?" In Russia, it is evoked by discussion of "provocation" and "victim behavior." And this phenomenon is observable at the KCCM. The KCCM's crisis hotline director explained that men who called the hotline did not speak of domestic violence but of "family conflicts," and that the center counseled the men that (violent) family conflicts are a "symptom of a complex of psychological problems" at least partially caused by "victim behavior."[56] This allowance for the victim's responsibility for domestic violence resonates too easily with the dominant understanding that denies that domestic violence is a problem. When victims are blamed, even partially, the psychological frame reinforces the gender ideology in which women are held much more accountable for their behavior than are men.

A Working Group: Negotiating New Frames of Domestic Violence

Regardless of the differences between the organizations' frames of domestic violence, all three entities do sponsor new frames of domestic violence, calling for more attention to the issue and contesting the postcommunist gender ideology. In Barnaul more than in most other Russian cities, there has been a multiplication of frames of domestic violence sponsored both by organizations that identify as women's and by state institutions that focus on men.

This multiplication of frames and the commitment of their sponsors created an unusual opportunity realized in a working group organized in March of 2001 within the Altai *krai* administration. This group was officially titled a "working group of specialists-coordinators for the solving of the problem connected with the growth of violence in the family against women and children, an organization for the systematic struggle with violence in the *krai*."[57] The working group includes social workers; administrative, health, and education officials; the head doctor of a private hospital; the head of the youth commission; the deputy director of the *krai* administration of internal affairs; and

Natalia Sereda (as director of Women's Alliance) and Maksim Kostenko (as director of the KCCM).

The creation of the group was spearheaded by N. S. Remneva, the director of the department of medical-social and family-demographic problems of the administration of the *krai*. Remneva, who has described herself as a "militant feminist" (*boevaia feministka*—an identification that contradicts the common wisdom that Russian women are allergic to feminism), was a member of the national commission on women.[58] The police became more amenable to the working group when they accompanied members of the militia and of the four Altai *krai* crisis centers to Los Angeles as part of a U.S. government–funded Russian Association of Crisis Centers for Women project. The police were surprised to see the way that U.S. police worked with the community (as well as interested in the possibility of foreign assistance) and now were apparently more open to collaboration with the crisis centers. The various individuals, organizations, and state institutions were brought together through the patronage networks common in the *krai*, a phenomenon that, although problematic for the creation and sustainability of an autonomous civil society,[59] was useful in this case. Most of the participants and the supporting politicians in this midsize Siberian outpost already knew each other.

Sereda says that her goal in the group was to facilitate the negotiation of a common frame of the problem of domestic violence. At the first meeting of the working group, each of the members was asked to describe their understandings of the problem of violence in the family, an exercise that produced quite different understandings. For example, the police argued that victims were poor and that the problem was related to alcohol or drug abuse, indicating a sociological or psychological frame of domestic violence. Sereda, on the other hand, claimed that victims of domestic violence exist across class lines and that occurrences are often unrelated to substance abuse. She pointed out that, according to their statistics, only 2 to 3 percent of those who call the Women's Alliance go to the police. As a result of this disconnect, Sereda told me she has decided to be strategic in her use of language. She explained that she talks about domestic violence as a "family" problem—using the sociological frame —when she speaks to the police, because they always want to focus attention on the woman-victim instead of the perpetrator. Similar to many others in the women's crisis center movement, Sereda has begun to adapt the radical feminist frame to fit the Post-Soviet context.

As a consequence of their agreement on the frame of domestic violence, the group has designated a goal of facilitating coordination among the different disciplines, in contrast to earlier periods, when there was only competition over spheres of influence. The group anticipated training psychologists, doctors, and police to respond to domestic violence. They also expected to spread this training from the capital Barnaul out to the other nineteen *krai* municipalities. The plan was to develop a regional-level law on the prevention of "violence in the family" that will institutionalize collaboration.

In sum, a decade after the fall of the Soviet Union, the multiplication of frames of domestic violence led to an opportunity for NGOs in Barnaul to renegotiate the dominant understandings of domestic violence and gender. While the criminal-legal system remains troubled by both weakness and over-reliance on coercion, the working group has laid the groundwork for increasing the state's responsibility for protecting women from domestic violence.

Further, the Russian struggle to renegotiate gender contrasts with the transnational antiviolence movement that has been de-radicalized into sponsoring service-providing NGOs and legitimating the privatization of the response to violence against women.[60] It also contrasts with the overreliance in the U.S. on criminal justice responses to the problem. Instead, the working group on domestic violence suggests responsibility shared between women's organizations, social service providers, healthcare providers, law enforcement, and state administrators. Their approach most closely resembles the kind of coordinated response that is called for in the radical feminist frame of domestic violence. As described by Donna Coker,

> In a coordinated response, criminal sanctions are accompanied by strong supports for battered women. Prosecutors craft their strategies so as to maximize victim safety; police provide victims with information about rights as well as referrals to services including shelters; courts routinely order victim compensation; and detectives and prosecutors follow up with victims to monitor threats or intimidation tactics of the batterer. In addition, the justice system works closely with service providers to assist women in safety planning and advocacy with other systems, such as public assistance, child protective services, and employers, and also to encourage support from victims' family and friends.[61]

As described, the coordinated community response is a collaboration between the criminal justice system, social services, and the women's shelter (or crisis center). There are punishments for the violators as well the social support necessary for the victims to regain control over their own lives.

Conclusion: The Postcommunist Opportunity

Beginning in the mid-1990s, there were new domestic violence and gender politics in Barnaul. Partially, this opportunity arose because of the unique personalities involved, who have extensive energy and a deep commitment to their work, but other, less idiosyncratic factors also played a role. First, the incomplete political and economic transition in the region—where liberalization has allowed autonomous organizations to emerge but politics and the economy remain dominated by communist elites through patronage networks —allowed these remarkable individuals to create new mechanisms to address domestic violence. Protecting the family from violence also resonated with the residual communist values of providing social support, especially as the communists have added nationalist and conservative elements to their ideology.

Experiencing the benefits of "transnational advocacy networks,"[62] these activists and the politicians who gave their support were also strongly influenced by the availability of foreign assistance, which supplemented the often meager support available from the state. Foreign assistance also supported international exchanges for the activists and for key law enforcement officers to observe Western models of older crisis centers and effective collaboration between crisis centers, law enforcement, and state social services. Because of these remarkable individuals and the support of the global women's movement, domestic violence politics in Barnaul escaped some of the risks of that often emerge with such a "statist" type of civil society.[63]

Since 2002, developments in Barnaul confirm the transformation in local policy makers' understanding of domestic violence. In 2004, the Altai governor announced the establishment of a state crisis center for women designed to provide "specialized social assistance to women," especially those living with violence.[64] Illustrating how far their understanding had come, the administration invited Natalia Sereda to direct the center, which opened in January 2005.[65] She draws upon the experience and staff of the Women's Alliance (which still exists as a semi-separate entity). Though the new center receives relatively limited government funding for a few specialists and the rent, the regional government has institutionalized a feminist response to domestic violence. The men's crisis center has expanded to the regions and continues to challenge ideas about masculinity that contribute to domestic violence, for example, running a summer 2005 seminar on responsible fatherhood for social workers who work with men.

These reforms in Barnaul are remarkable, but not unique. Other strong crisis centers remain in Moscow, St. Petersburg, Saratov, Ekaterinburg, Izhevsk, and Petrazavodsk, and many have initiated state-society collaborations (as of 2005). In Kazan in the ethnic Republic of Tatarstan, the women's crisis center informally shares an office with a local social service agency, whose director had become sympathetic to women suffering from domestic violence. In Arkhangelsk, the women's crisis center collaborates with the school for social work, providing a practicum for students in exchange for space. In Khimki, a suburb of Moscow, the local government established a women's shelter. All of these collaborations illustrate that by mid-decade the Russian authorities were taking on new responsibilities to address domestic violence and that there was an opportunity for the transformation in the dominant gender ideology across Russia.

That there have been many significant reforms is not to say that the lives of women living with domestic violence have improved since the Soviet Union's demise. Shelters and prosecution for domestic violence are rare. The underfunding of social services, the economic depression, and the ways that poverty has been feminized have left many women more economically dependent on their intimate partners than before.

What had changed was that, in some cases, local authorities were attending to the social consequences of socialism's collapse, sometimes even recognizing and undermining gender inequality. Although the resurgence of traditional ideas about women and men demonstrated that the emergence of new gender ideologies is often problematic for women, these changes illustrate that a kind of state feminism, at least in some places on some issues, has also transpired. The question is whether these reforms supported by current leaders are just whims or whether the postcommunist opportunity for gender transformation will be institutionalized.

NOTES

A version of this paper was first presented at the annual meeting of the American Association for the Advancement of Slavic Studies in Pittsburgh, November 22, 2002. I want to thank Al Evans, Carol Nechemias, Julie Hemment, Serguei Oushakine, Jean Robinson, and our anonymous reviewers for their thoughts and suggestions. I am especially grateful to Natalia Sereda and her family and to the International Research and Exchange Board for the short-term travel grant that facilitated this research.

1. Tat'iana Iu. Zabelina, ed., *Rossiia: Nasilie v Sem'e—Nasilie v Obshchestve* [Russia: Violence in the Family—Violence in Society] (Moscow: UNIFEM, UNFPA, 2002).

2. Human Rights Watch, "Russia—Too Little, Too Late: State Response to Violence against Women," *Human Rights Watch* 9, no. 13 (1997): 1–51.

3. Marina Pisklakova (founding director of Moscow crisis center ANNA), interview by the author, Moscow, Russia, June 21, 2002, and Marina Regentova (director of Russian Association of Crisis Centers for Women), interview by the author, Moscow, Russia, July 7, 2002.

4. R. Amy Elman, *Sexual Subordination and State Intervention: Comparing Sweden and the United States* (Providence, R.I.: Berghahn Books, 1996), 3. Problem recognition is only an initial step toward responsiveness, which is the first stage in developing a policy that is effective. As explained by S. Laurel Weldon, *Protest, Policy, and the Problem of Violence against Women: A Cross-National Comparison* (Pittsburgh: University of Pittsburgh Press, 2002), effectiveness refers to the impact of policy, requiring the systematic analysis of victims' reports about their experiences in shelters and with the criminal justice system.

5. Robert D. Benford and David A. Snow, "Framing Processes and Social Movements: An Overview and Assessment," *Annual Review of Sociology* 26, no. 1 (2000): 613.

6. Ann Swidler, "Cultural Power and Social Movements," in *Social Movements and Culture*, ed. Bert Klandermans and Hank Johnston (Minneapolis: University of Minnesota Press, 1995).

7. For example: Nanette Funk and Magda Mueller, eds., *Gender Politics and Post-Communism: Reflections from Eastern Europe and the Former Soviet Union* (New York: Routledge, 1993); Barbara Einhorn, *Cinderella Goes to Market: Citizenship, Gender and Women's Movements in East Central Europe* (New York: Verso, 1993); Rosalind Marsh, ed. *Women in Russia and Ukraine* (New York: Cambridge University Press, 1996); Sue Bridger, Kathryn Pinnick, and Rebecca Kay, eds., *No More Heroines?: Russia, Women and the Market* (New York: Routledge, 1996); and Kathleen Kuenhast and Carol Nechemias, eds., *Post-Soviet Women Encountering Transition: Nation-*

Janet Elise Johnson

Building, Economic Survival, and Civic Activism (Washington, D.C.: Woodrow Wilson Center Press/Johns Hopkins University Press, 2004). See also Janet Elise Johnson, "State Transformation and Violence against Women in Postcommunist Russia" (Ph.D. diss., Indiana University, 2001), and idem, "Privatizing Pain: The Problem of Woman Battery in Russia," NWSA *Journal* 13, no. 3 (2001): 153–68.

8. Susan Gal and Gail Kligman, eds., *Reproducing Gender: Politics, Publics, and Everyday Life after Socialism* (Princeton, N.J.: Princeton University Press, 2000), and Susan Gal and Gail Kligman, *The Politics of Gender after Socialism* (Princeton, N.J.: Princeton University Press, 2000).

9. My approach is constructivist and thus begins with the assumption that the way problems are understood is socially constructed, not exogenous. Problems are not simply given or knowable. They shift over time and across societies. Not just the state response to problems is politically contested, but also the interpretation of what problems are even worthy of attention. My approach assumes that it is not unproblematic who gets to decide whose problems are considered worthy of attention. Public discourse tends to promote the recognition of problems of dominant social groups while disguising or rejecting the problems of subordinate or oppositional groups. See Nancy Fraser, "Struggle over Needs: Outline of a Socialist-Feminist Critical Theory of Late-Capitalist Political Culture," in *Women, the State, and Welfare*, ed. Linda Gordon (Madison: University of Wisconsin Press, 1990), 199–225.

10. Michael McFaul, *Russia's Unfinished Revolution: Political Change from Gorbachev to Putin* (Ithaca, N.Y.: Cornell University Press, 2001). Observers of Russian civil societies who have noted the exceptional nature of the women's crisis center movement include: James Richter, "Evaluating Western Assistance to Russian Women's Organizations," in *The Power and Limits of NGOs: A Critical Look at Building Democracy in Eastern Europe and Eurasia*, ed. Sarah E. Mendelson and John K. Glenn (New York: Columbia University Press, 2002), 54–90; Lisa McIntosh Sundstrom, "Women's NGOs in Russia: Struggling from the Margins," *Demokratizatsiya* 10, no. 2 (2002): 207–29; and Sarah L. Henderson, *Building Democracy in Contemporary Russia: Western Support for Grassroots Organizations* (Ithaca, N.Y.: Cornell University Press, 2003).

11. A *krai* is one of the 89 subnational units in Russia, each of which has a different federal status. In general, a *krai* has less autonomy than a republic, but more than most other kinds of subnational units.

12. Since the collapse of Soviet rule, Barnaul—and the region of Altai of which Barnaul is the capital—has been transformed from a military-industrial center to an economically depressed region that must rely on financial subsidies from the federal government. This is typical of most subnational units in Russia and is in contrast to Moscow. My understanding of Barnaul was informed by personal communication with Serguei Oushakine, an anthropologist from the *krai* who also writes about the *krai*. See Serguei Alex Oushakine, "The Fatal Splitting: Symbolizing Anxiety in Post-Soviet Russia," *Ethnos: Journal of Anthropology* 66, no. 3 (2001): 291, and "The Politics of Pity: Domesticating Loss in a Russian Province," *American Anthropologist* 108, no. 2: 312–23.

13. For another interpretation of this data, see Janet Elise Johnson, "Public-Private Permutations: Domestic Violence Crisis Centers in Barnaul," in *Russian Civil Society: A Critical Assessment*, ed. Al Evans, Laura Henry, and Lisa McIntosh Sundstrom (Armonk, N.Y.: M. E. Sharpe, 2005), 266–83.

14. Frances Elisabeth Olsen, "Feminism in Central and Eastern Europe: Risks and Possibilities of American Engagement," *Yale Law Journal* 106 (1997): 2215–57.

15. Rebecca Kay, "Meeting the Challenge Together? Russian Grassroots Women's Organizations and the Shortcomings of Western Aid," in *Post-Soviet Women Encountering Transition*, 241–61; Julie Hemment, "Global Civil Society and the Local Costs of Belonging: Defining 'Violence against Women' in Russia," *Signs: Journal of Women in Culture and Society* 29, no. 3 (2004): 815–40.

16. For example: Tat'iana Klimenkova, *Zhenshchina kak fenomen kul'tury: Vzgliad iz Rossii* [Women as a Phenomenon of Culture: View from Russia] (Moscow: Pre-obrazhenie, 1996); Marina Pisklakova and Andrei Sinel'nikov "Mezhdu molchaniem i krikom" [Between Silence and the Scream], in *Nasilie i sotsial'nye izmeneniia* [Violence and Social Change], ed. Tsentr ANNA (Moscow: Tacis, Caritas, 2000); and Zabelina, *Rossiia: Nasilie v Sem'e—Nasilie v Obshchestve*.

17. Uma Narayan, "Through the Looking-Glass Darkly: Emissaries, Mirrors, and Authentic Insiders as Preoccupations," in *Dislocating Cultures: Identities, Traditions, and Third World Feminism* (New York: Routledge, 1997).

18. Michele Rivkin-Fish, "Gender and Democracy: Strategies for Engagement and Dialogue on Women's Issues after Socialism in St. Petersburg," in *Post-Soviet Women Encountering Transition*, 288–312.

19. My classification is based on the taxonomy by Elizabeth M. Schneider, *Battered Women and Feminist Lawmaking* (New Haven, Conn.: Yale University Press, 2002).

20. Lisa Granik, "The Trials of the Proletarka: Sexual Harassment Claims in the 1920s," in *Reforming Justice in Russia, 1864–1996: Power, Culture, and the Limits of Legal Order*, ed. Peter H. Jr. Solomon (Armonk, N.Y.: M. E. Sharpe, 1997), 131–67.

21. Lynne Attwood, " 'She Was Asking for It': Rape and Domestic Violence against Women," in *Post-Soviet Women: From the Baltic to Central Asia*, ed. Mary Buckley (Cambridge: Cambridge University Press, 1997), 107–108.

22. Louise Shelley, "Inter-Personal Violence in the USSR," *Violence, Aggression and Terrorism* 1, no. 2 (1987): 41–67, and Valerie Sperling, "Rape and Domestic Violence in the USSR," *Response to the Victimization of Women and Children: Journal of the Center for Women Policy Studies* 13, no. 3 (1990): 16–22.

23. Johnson, "Privatizing Pain."

24. Bridger, Pinnick, and Kay, *No More Heroines?*

25. Human Rights Watch, "Russia—Too Little, Too Late," and Human Rights Watch, "Russia: Neither Jobs Nor Justice: State Discrimination against Women in Russia," *Human Rights Watch* 7, no. 5 (1995): 1–31.

26. Johnson, "Privatizing Pain"

27. Anastasia Posadskaya, ed., *Women in Russia: A New Era in Russian Feminism*, trans. Kate Clark (New York: Verso, 1994).

28. Margaret Keck and Kathryn Sikkink. *Activists beyond Borders: Transnational Advocacy Networks in International Politics* (Ithaca, N.Y.: Cornell University Press, 1998).

29. Valerie Sperling, *Organizing Women in Contemporary Russia: Engendering Transition* (Cambridge: Cambridge University Press, 1999); Rebecca Kay, *Russian Women and Their Organizations* (New York: St. Martin's Press, 2000); and Anastasia Posadskaya-Vanderbeck, personal conversation, New York City, June 17, 2004. See also Norma Corigliano Noonan and Carol Nechemias, eds., *Encyclopedia of Russian Women's Movements* (Westport, Conn.: Praeger, 2001).

30. Lisa McIntosh Sundstrom, "Foreign Assistance, International Norms, and NGO Development: Lessons From the Russian Campaign," *International Organization* 59, no. 3 (2005): 419–49.

31. For discussions of this movement, see Tat'iana Zabelina, "Sexual Violence towards Women," in *Gender, Generation and Identity in Contemporary Russia*, ed. Hilary Pilkington (New York: Routledge, 1996), 169–86; Johnson, "Privatizing Pain"; and Hemment, "Global Civil Society and the Local Costs of Belonging."

32. N. I. Abubikirova, et al., *Directory of Women's Non-Governmental Organizations in Russia and the NIS* (Moscow: Aslan Publishers, 1998), 9.

33. Regentova, interview. Since officially registering with the Ministry of Justice, the name of this organization has been changed to Association Ostanovim nasilie (Stop Violence).

34. Elena Shitova, "Women's Alliance," *Bradley Herald* (2002): 1, 7.

35. Ibid.

36. Ibid.

37. Dianne Post, interview by the author, Moscow, Russia, Febuary 23, 1999. See also Dianne Post, "Russian Women, American Eyes: The Rebirth of Feminism in Russia" (draft manuscript prepared for the Kennan Workshop on Women in the Former Soviet Union, 2002).

38. One tool she brought was the concept of post-traumatic stress disorder. In contrast to what Azra Hromadzic found in the application of this psychological concept to war rapes in Bosnia (see chapter 8), Post was not applying the concept to an entire population, but proposing that PTSD might help explain what is often seen as bizarre behavior of some victims of domestic violence (such as retracting complaints or refusing to testify). I would also argue that Hromadzic and I are talking about different stages in the policy process and different levels of imposition. Proposing alternative explanations (even when based on Western experiences and knowledge) in contrast to the explanations already existing in a society can help reveal gender injustice, such as when domestic violence and rape are explained as women's own fault. I agree with Hromadzic that there needs to be a place for women in this society to then consider and describe their own experiences.

39. Post, "Russian Women, American Eyes."

40. Evan Stark, "Mandatory Arrest of Batterers: A Reply to Its Critics," *American Behavorial Scientist* 36, no. 5 (1993): 656.

41. M. P. Belousova et al., *Gender: Obshchedostrupnyi Slovar'-Spravochnik* [Gender: Popular Dictionary-Directory] (Barnaul, Russia: AKZhOO "Otklik," 2001).

42. Over the last few years, there has been a lot of discussion about the role of "democracy assistance" in fostering low-quality and ephemeral NGOs in Russia and across the region. For book-length discussions, see Janine R. Wedel, *Collision and Collusion: The Strange Case of Western Aid to Eastern Europe* (1998, repr. New York: St. Martin's Press, 2001); Sarah E. Mendelson and John K. Glenn, eds., *The Power and Limits of NGOs: A Critical Look at Building Democracy in Eastern Europe and Eurasia* (New York: Columbia University Press, 2002); and Henderson, *Building Democracy in Contemporary Russia.*

43. Belousova, et al., *Gender.*

44. Ibid.

45. Ibid., 90–91.

46. Ibid., 32–33.

47. Zabelina, *Rossiia: Nasilie v Sem'e—Nasilie v Obshchestve.*

48. In the mid-1990s, there was a men's project affiliated with Moscow-based crisis center ANNA, and in the late 1990s, a men's organization affiliated the Murmansk crisis center. Saarinen, Aino, Olga Liapounova, and Irina Drachova, eds., *NCRB: A Network for Crisis Centres for Women in the Barents Region (Report of the Nordic-Russian Development Project, 1999–2002)* (Arkhangelsk, Russia: Pomor State University, 2003). For another detailed study of the center, see Rebecca Kay, "Working With Single Fathers in Western Siberia: A New Departure in Russian Social Provision," *Europe-Asia Studies* 56, no. 7 (2004): 941–61.

49. The brochure, simply titled "Altai Krai Crisis Center for Men," was given to me by the director, Maksim Kostenko, on July 2, 2002.

50. For example, he presented a paper on domestic violence offenders at a November 2001 conference of the Network for Crisis Centers for Women in the Barents Region.

51. The status of the KCCM is quite complicated. Affiliated with the KCCM is the NGO "Man's Conversation." Like many emaciated state institutions, the KCCM appears to also represent itself as an NGO in order to receive foreign grants for "democracy assistance." Otklik also has some roots within state institutions, in this case, a university. I discuss these complications in Johnson, "Public-Private Permutations."

52. Maksim Kostenko, "Work with Batterers in the Altay Regional Centre for men," in *NCRB: A Network for Crisis Centres,* 143–49.

53. Ibid, 145.

54. See http://www.yaj.ru/bulletin/1999/bull_40.ru.shtml (accessed Nov. 16, 2002).

55. There is complicated and mixed evidence in studies in the United States. For a summary, see Stark, "Mandatory Arrest of Batterers." While there is no agreement on what is the most effective strategy, there seems to be agreement that the best types of response have significant consequences, especially if immediate.

56. In response to my question to Sereda about the differences between her and KCCM's understanding of domestic violence, she called the hotline to ask how they counseled callers (Barnaul, Russia, July 1, 2002).

57. This is from the official list of the participants of the working group signed by the deputy head of the administration of the *krai*, Ya. N. Shoichet, given to me by Natalia Seredia, Barnaul, July 1, 2002.

58. Natalia Sereda, interview by the author, Barnaul, Russia, July 1, 2002.

59. Johnson, "Public-Private Permutations," and Alexei Yurchak, "Entrepreneurial Governmentality in Postsocialist Russia," in *The New Entrepreneurs of Europe and Asia,* ed. Victoria Bonnell and Thomas Gold (Armonk, N.Y.: M. E. Sharpe, 2002), 278–317.

60. Hemment, "Global Civil Society and the Local Costs of Belonging."

61. Schneider, *Battered Women and Feminist Lawmaking.*

62. Keck and Sikkink, *Activists beyond Borders.*

63. Johnson, "Public-Private Permutations."

64. "V Altaiskom krae sozdano novoe gosudartvennoe uchrezhdenie sotsial'nogo obsluzhivaniia—'kraevoi krizisnyi tsentr dlia zhenshchin'" [In the Altai *krai*, a New State Social Service Institution, 'the *Krai* Crisis Center for Women,' Has Been Created], *Altai Daily Review,* http://www.bankfax.ru/ (accessed June 28, 2004).

65. Sereda, e-mail message to author, June 30, 2005.

PART II.
DENYING GENDER

three

The Abortion Debate in Poland

Opinion Polls, Ideological Politics, Citizenship, and the Erasure of Gender as a Category of Analysis

Anne-Marie Kramer

Reproductive policy and politics have surfaced as topics of debate across Central and Eastern Europe since 1989. In Romania, the liberalization of abortion was one of the first initiatives proposed by the provisional government,[1] while in East Germany questions around access to abortion threatened the future of unification with West Germany.[2] In the former Yugoslavia, international and domestic attention was focused on the use of rape as a weapon of war.[3] Nowhere else in Central and Eastern Europe has experienced such sustained media and parliamentary discussion of reproductive policy as Poland, where debate around access to abortion has been ongoing since before the first semi-free elections in 1989.

Why have reproductive policies been the focus of so much attention across postcommunist Central and Eastern Europe since the demise of state socialism? Some initial attempts have been made to characterize and explain these developments. Gal and Kligman identify four ways in which "reproduction makes politics": first, in the way debates about reproduction "contribute to recasting the relationship between states and their inhabitants"; second, in the way that "narratives of nationhood rely . . . on reproductive discourses and practices to make and 'remake' the category of 'nation' and its boundaries"; third, for the ways in which "debates about reproduction serve as coded arguments about political legitimacy and the morality of the state"; and fourth, for the ways in which "such debates constitute women as a political group."[4] From this perspective, contestations around reproductive policy are arguments about the proper shape of postcommunist states, political arrangements, and civil society. Debate around reproduction serves as a substitute issue where wider concerns and anxieties around the proper ordering of the reconstructed postcommunist polity, (gendered) citizens, and nation/state are played out, and where the legitimacy of political authority is articulated and contested. Despite their real and material effects, postcommunist abortion debates are more about the nature of democracy than simply about reproduction.[5]

Johnson and Robinson note in their introduction to this volume that postcommunist Europe has borne witness to the retiring of the communist party state, seeing the emergence of other domestic sources of power that sponsor competing gender ideologies. This context has provided a new space for what Johnson and Robinson call "gender multiplication." If the abortion debate is a key site where arguments about democracy are played out, then opinion polls on abortion in Poland, as one such domestic source of power, assume a central role as methodology or evidence of democratic procedure in this debate: opinion polls have played a key role in substantiating both pro-life[6] and pro-choice[7] claims to speak for the Polish "public."

Opinion polls play a key role in postcommunist Poland in the context of moving from a discredited authoritarian state socialist regime, in which so-called public opinion was dictated from above, to an ideal of a democratic and representative state.[8] In the latter, members of formerly state socialist societies have both the right and the responsibility to influence and determine public policy, and public opinion polling necessarily assumes a central function in maintaining lines of communication between political elites and the rest of society.[9] In the Polish context, gathering public opinion—and acting on this information—plays a vital role in justifying and legitimating the desirability of legislative reform and of choosing among competing political projects. Indeed, opinion polling performs the function of legitimating politics itself by mandating and reinforcing the authority of the Polish parliament to determine public policy. Opinion polls are therefore central to the project of democratization under at least one conception of democratization as representation.[10]

Taking up Johnson and Robinson's argument, this chapter examines opinion poll bulletins on abortion as one such domestic source of power and as a site through which Polish national identity and gender ideology is constructed and critiqued. Adopting a constructionist approach to opinion polls, which is interested in opinion polls as discursive, communicative "cultural forms"[11] rather than as tools of psychological measurement,[12] this chapter analyzes how Polish national identity, citizenship, and democratic practice are constructed through opinion polling on abortion. After offering a brief chronology of the Polish abortion debate and a description of opinion poll methodology, I analyze the polling practices of the Public Opinion Research Center (hereafter, CBOS) bulletins on abortion in relation to gender. I argue that opinion polling on abortion constructs a form of knowledge that institutionalizes democracy in gendered ways by ignoring (or suppressing) gender as a category of analysis. I then analyze the ways in which the poll bulletins construct abortion as symptomatic of ideological clashes between the modernist, secularist (postcommunist) left and the neotraditionalist, Catholic right, arguing that while gender underpins both these nationalist projects, that dimension is consistently suppressed in the bulletins. Finally, I assess how opinion poll bulletins comment on the motives of political parties or factions participating in abortion debate. I suggest that the conceptions of the role of the (paternal) state thus advanced construct abortion as an issue through which individuals and factions can increase their political capital at the expense of women. Throughout, I argue that the gendered dimension of the abortion debate is consistently suppressed in the CBOS opinion poll bulletins.

A Chronology of the Abortion Debate in Poland

In the early 1990s, the abortion debate in Poland initially revolved around attempts to introduce legislation restricting access to abortion.[13] After the successful passage in 1993 of the *Law on Family Planning, Legal Protection of the Fetus, and the Conditions of Permissibility of Abortion*, which prohibited abortion for social and economic reasons,[14] various legislative attempts were made to widen women's access to abortion.[15] These finally culminated in the passage of the liberalization amendment in 1996, which widened access by again allowing abortions under the "socio-economic conditions" clause[16] and removing the notion, which had informed the 1993 "anti-abortion" law, of life beginning at conception.[17] After being referred to the Constitutional Court, the liberalization amendment was pronounced unconstitutional in May 1997, and the original, restrictive 1993 law was reintroduced as a result. In February 2005 a bill on "responsible parenthood" was deferred for discussion in the Polish Parliament. At the time of writing there is some debate over whether abortion legislation will resurface in the near future.[18]

The moment under analysis here is rather a series of related moments around the passage of the 1996 liberalization amendment through the Polish legislature. This point in the abortion debate has usually been overlooked in analysis. This is for three reasons: first, the liberalization of access was immediately undermined by the patchy application of its measures after opposition from the medical establishment. Therefore, while abortion liberalization was effected in law, in reality its provisions were never enforced as the Polish legislature had intended. Second, the liberalization legislation was almost immediately overturned by the Constitutional Court. Again, as liberalized access to abortion was enforced only for a matter of months, its overall significance remains limited. Third, the contents of the liberalization bill did not reflect campaigns articulated around women's choice, but merely added another option to the list of restrictive conditions enshrined in the 1993 law. At the same time, the provisions of the liberalization amendment limited access to abortion in other ways, by allowing abortions for social or legal reasons only within a twelve-week time limit, and by introducing a three-day mandatory "waiting period." All of these elements could be advanced as reasons for the lack of interest in this "moment" in the abortion debate. The liberalization amendment represented a measure of success for the pro-choice camp as it did widen access to abortion, however temporarily and problematically.

Opinion Poll Methodology

The issue of abortion has surfaced repeatedly in CBOS opinion polls since 1989, reflecting continuing media and parliamentary debate on the issue.[19] From 1989 to 1995, a total of nine bulletins were published relating to abortion, an average of two per year.[20] In 1996, the year under consideration here, a total of five bulletins specifically considered the question of public attitude toward abortion—a particularly high number, reflecting increased parliamentary and media debate on the question at this point.[21]

Despite this connection between politics and polling, throughout the opinion poll bulletins the process of opinion polling is represented as being *outside,* or rather *above,* the political process. Bulletins do not reflexively analyze the nature of the role being played by opinion polling in policy debates, nor do they analyze how "public opinion" comes to exist through the practice of public opinion polling. Polls describe dialogue between political elites and the "public,"[22] and between pro-liberalization and anti-liberalization campaigners, but nowhere is the role played by the pollster in enabling or representing dialogue between political elites and the "public" discussed.[23] This has the effect of making opinion polling look apolitical and divorced from functions of the state.

Although CBOS has existed and carried out opinion polls since 1982,[24] it is as if opinion polls started anew in 1989: there are no references to opinion poll bulletins before 1989 within the post-1989 bulletins. In a similar vein, reproductive policies during the state socialist period are never flagged as relevant to current policy debates over abortion. In this way, the practice of opinion polling is marked by a complete disjuncture from the lived and documented experience of state socialism, demonstrating CBOS opinion polling to be "untainted" by the previous experience of state socialism, despite its foundation in this period. By extension, this makes CBOS polling look "democratic," and its classification of data by respondents' sex, age, wage level, and the like further guarantees its "representative" function. Stressing CBOS's neutrality and professionalism further enhances the democratic credentials not only of the practice of opinion polling but also of the pollster itself.

Thus, the practice of opinion polling is underpinned by notions of its role as a guarantor for a democratic state through its contribution to opening and maintaining channels of information and communication between the mass of society and political elites. This feedback and evaluation of policy is seen as a direct "democratic guarantee." However, the categorization and sorting of individual respondents' opinions on individual questions into "public opinion" is neither objective nor disinterested. The practice of opinion polling is not a neutral instrument of the people, since CBOS is itself state-mandated, and as such is part of the machinery of government and is intrinsically linked to the democratic and political processes of state. Any such institution is therefore bound to consider the political dimension to be the key and defining feature of the abortion debate.

The practice of opinion polling remains political, not just in the manner and method of categorizing and translating individual respondents' opinions into "public opinion," but also in the fact that as mediator between "politics" and the "people," the opinion pollster (in this case, CBOS) performs the role of *translator*. This function may include explaining and summarizing to respondents the significance of the abortion debate, relating abortion to other key issues to be potentially posed in a referendum, or explaining and contextualizing the importance of the abortion debate for developments in Polish politics more generally. These processes of translation remain, for the most part, invisible.

The practice of opinion polling, therefore, itself contributes to political debate not simply by representing true/factual "public opinion" but by *creating such a category as public opinion* in the first place. Inevitably this has significant repercussions for the ways in which the practice of opinion polling comes to structure and frame the significance of the issue of abortion in the political arena. This is particularly relevant to the displacement of women as interested parties in the abortion debate and the claiming of abortion as an issue that is fundamentally not about gender.

Gender and Opinion Polling Practice

Gender is notable by its absence in the CBOS opinion poll bulletins. Despite or perhaps because of this absence, gender becomes represented in the methodology and practice of opinion polling in a particular way.

The practice of opinion polling presumes a gender-neutral citizen.[25] Citizenship is the primary identification of the CBOS opinion poll respondent; variables, such as sex, age, wage level, and so on, remain secondary.[26] In practice, however, it is only because CBOS opinion polling (in this instance at least) does not consider lived experience that attitudes toward abortion can be considered gender-neutral. Only women can have experience of abortion, but their views as women are not deemed significant. By suppressing lived experience as a form of knowledge, male "expertise" (as evidenced through their participation in opinion polling as respondents) is legitimated.[27]

Because no gender differentials seem to determine attitude to abortion, women are described as not having a "special interest" in abortion, and the issue of "public opinion" on abortion is claimed to be "gender-neutral." For example, on the question, "In your opinion, in the current situation, is it necessary to change the currently valid law on abortion?" one opinion poll bulletin notes:

> The changing of the law was approved by a somewhat larger proportion of men (55%) than women (50%), although those against the changes were more often women (32%) as opposed to men (25%), although the [overall] variations were not large.[28]

The bulletin claims here that gender does not "determine" attitude to abortion, since attitudes to abortion are similar between men and women. Therefore, it is claimed, abortion is not a gendered question. In other words, the discovery that women do not support liberal access to abortion in greater numbers than men is translated into the supposition that women aren't especially interested in the issue. The fact that men and women might have very different reasons for their attitude to abortion does not receive attention, reflecting the quantitative focus of the practice of opinion polling. Nor is attention paid to differences between women, nor to why it is that women as a group don't support abortion any more than men do. I would speculate that women's lack of overwhelming support for abortion might result from a desire not to be seen as "extreme" or associated with the implicit negative connotations of feminism. Or it might result from women's reluctance to admit the possibility that abortion has formed part of their own life experience, given the context of mass underground abortions and abortion tourism.[29]

CBOS opinion poll bulletins on abortion simply are not interested in the question of the relation between women and abortion, other than as a simple demographic category as a poll respondent. They are much more concerned with the significance of abortion for the status of the Polish Parliament. Consequently, the liberalization of abortion receives detailed attention in terms of the issue's (party) political dimension, such as its influence on voter support in the next election.[30] The liberalization amendment is not critiqued in terms that might center women in the abortion debate: there is no mention, for instance, of the vigorous and ongoing feminist project to improve women's access to abortion. Debate is located by CBOS purely at the (party) political level.

At the same time, the ways in which "opinion" on abortion is collected *are* gendered. For example, the opinion polls ask whether abortion should be allowed "in certain cases." These include the following: "danger to the mother's life"; "danger to the mother's health"; "if pregnancy was the result of a crime," including rape or incest; if it is "known that the child will be born disabled"; and finally, if the "woman is in a difficult material situation."[31] This hierarchization of abortion according to "degree of permissibility" serves as an abstraction that works to obscure debate around women's right, as citizens, of access to abortion. This is the only place in the opinion poll bulletins where fetal-maternal conflict is broached, and "public opinion" on the issue sampled. Broadly representative of existing and potential abortion legislation, this hierarchy of "permissible cases" offers the possibility that the mother/woman may not have sufficient justification to seek and obtain an abortion. In fact, CBOS opinion polls repeatedly note that respondents rate some cases (such as danger to the mother's life or health) as being more justifiable than others (such as difficult socioeconomic conditions).[32] Framed in this way, abortion rights are constructed as contingent only: listing "reasons" for abortion in this way does not admit the possibility that women should be allowed access to abortion on demand and without need of a justifiable "reason."

Respondents in opinion polls throughout the 1990s were asked whether abortion should be allowed without limit; allowed but within certain limits; banned, but with certain exceptions; or banned completely. The options allowing abortion without limit or else banning abortion without exception were labeled "extreme," with the majority of support being expressed for the middle options (that is, abortion allowed "within certain limits" or else banned "but with certain exceptions"). This matches but does not replicate the legislative options available since the dissolution of state socialism. The identification of "certain limit" to abortion, together with the lack of specification of what such "limits" might entail, ensures that limited access to abortion is presented as the majority opinion in Polish society. Noting that in fact there has been a falling away of support for what it calls "extreme" or "radical" options is extremely significant in the postcommunist context.[33] The concept of abortion "without limits" is associated with the state socialist regime, where abortion was available virtually "on demand" and where abortion was widely used as a form of contraception. A drop in support for the "extreme" options thus signifies a lack of popular sympathy either with the radical sex equality ideology of state socialism or with the ideology of the Catholic Church, which supports the total prohibition of abortion ("abortion [to be] banned without restriction"). Presenting limited access to abortion as the "majority" and representative opinion in Polish society labels both pro-choice and pro-life positions as marginal and "extreme."

Gender and the Ideological Shape of the State

Discussion concerning the state's ideological shape has constantly accompanied the processes of the introduction of economic reform. . . . There have been drawn two contrasting options—a state of "neutral world-outlook" or a state "respecting Christian values." The symbol of the conflict

> between these two options has been discussion concerning the legal regula-
> tion of the problem of abortion.[34]

In this bulletin extract, abortion is described as absolutely crucial in terms of marking the difference between two competing state-building projects: the perspective of "neutral world-outlook" versus the "respecting [of] Christian values." The word "neutral" (which I could also have translated as "non-aligned") is used to represent those opposing (or at the very least uninterested in) the construction of a Polish nation-state based on Christian morality and teaching.[35] What is significant here is that the abortion debate symbolically demarcates lines of division within Polish politics and society. In fact, the abortion debate is itself considered "the symbol of the conflict" between the two positions, with "Christian values" opposed to "neutral," for which read secular, values. In this context abortion assumes a significance far beyond its legislative implications, being identified as part of a wider ideological clash about the future direction of the state and the nation and about the purpose of reform. The abortion debate is explicitly harnessed to broader debates around the role of religion and Catholic belief in ideologically determining the con-tours of the newly reborn Polish state, as well as individual policies within it. Debate around abortion is thus affiliated with both competing versions of the nation/state-building project, but the gendered aspect of it is consistently suppressed.

That ideological conception that favors the state's "respecting Christian values" defines Poles as believers first and citizens second. Moral obligation and responsibility are therefore prioritized over, or are a prior condition of, the exercise of citizenship. In the case of abortion policy, this means that women's reproductive capabilities take precedence over any individual claim to bodily self-determination (through having an abortion, for example). The opinion poll bulletins consistently suppress the gendered dimension of such a conception of the ideological shape of the state.

At the same time the opposing "worldview," which presents a secular state capable of operating rationally, constructs an apparently gender-neutral cit-izen (as embodied in the opinion poll respondent, for example). Moreover, the opinion poll bulletins describe the liberalization of abortion (supported by this "secular" worldview) as enacted "above all in order to help women not having the appropriate conditions to give birth to and bring up a child."[36] The lan-guage and wording used is significant here: women are described as having "special" access to welfare because of their biological (and presumably eco-nomic) burden as child-carriers and child-rearers. The paternalistic state is thus presented as competent to offer help to vulnerable women, aiding women "in a difficult material situation": a paterfamilias role writ large. Despite dis-courses around the gender neutrality of the citizen, and in common with the alternative "Catholic" project, CBOS notes that the secular worldview at-tributes agency to the state rather than to individual women. Here the emphasis is on the rights and privileges of citizenship granted to women by the state, rather than on the agency of women themselves as citizens. Meanwhile, the agency of the individual as a component of "public opinion" is attributed to her status as "Pole-citizen," rather than as a specifically interested and affected party such as "woman" or "potential mother." Thus we can see that both nation-building projects, variously Catholic and secular, are crucially underpinned by gender ideologies.

The question of abortion is also constructed as symptomatic of ideological conflict around the "proper" rate of social transformation in the postcommunist context. Polling attitudes toward abortion, by linking it with other "key political issues" such as unemployment or privatization, places it in the wider context of determining and measuring "public satisfaction" with the rate and scale of postcommunist reform.[37] It is thus linked to the "liberal transformation" of the state after state socialism. In this way, abortion policy and debate "measures" the rate and scale of postcommunist state reform: abortion thus becomes emblematic of Polish transformation and democratization.

Assessing the Motivations behind the Abortion Liberalization Amendment: Self-interest versus Paternalism

The opinion poll bulletins also offer commentary on the motives of those participating in the abortion debate, particularly by evaluating "public opinion" on politicians' motivation in sponsoring the liberalization proposal. The poll poses questions about the motivations of, and electoral prospects for, parties involved in the liberalization legislation. It is in this context that a certain degree of skepticism is voiced toward the timing of the liberalization proposal:

> [T]hree years after the elections, the *Sejm* [lower house of the Polish Parliament] has carried out changes including adding social [factors] to the list of situations in which abortion is legally permitted. The fact of carrying out these changes to the strict regulations at this [particular] moment is sometimes attributed by commentators to the political context, [including] the desire to connect with voters through the fulfillment of one of their election promises, and at the same time, to provide an unofficial start to the campaign for the next parliamentary elections. The perspectives of respondents on the theme of motives directing the initiatives of the amendment are mixed, although there is a somewhat larger number of people who are not persuaded of a political subtext in the *Sejm*'s decision, instead persuaded of the opinion, that the changing of the regulations is above all in order to help women not having the appropriate conditions to give birth to and bring up a child.[38]

Investigating party manifesto pledges and voter support ties the abortion issue into the broader party political contest. The liberalization of the abortion law is equated with the loyalty of the postcommunist left toward their voters, "fulfilling a promise." So the successful passage of abortion liberalization legislation is seen to guarantee voter satisfaction with those parties, as well as to offer "help" to women in difficult living conditions who choose not to give birth to and bring up a child. This position assumes that the (paternal) state should compensate women for their biological function. Here a position of "compassionate realism," of assisting the "poor unfortunates" (in other words "women not having the appropriate conditions to give birth and bring up a child"), is assumed of those proposing abortion liberalization.

Following the successful passage of abortion liberalization legislation, a further poll bulletin suggests that public opinion is increasingly skeptical about deputies' motives in proposing such legislation.[39] This skepticism is complemented by a rise in the number of people believing that the drive for abortion liberalization legislation was motivated by the desire for those parties supporting the legislation to increase their "political capital" for the upcoming elections, and "not in reality because of concern for the fate of women finding themselves in a difficult material and living conditions."[40] In other words, "helping women" is presented as the correct reason for proposing and supporting such legislation, and skepticism seems to have increased precisely because (a certain portion of) the electorate felt that gritty political realities such as voter support, rather than compassionate realism, in fact motivated the legislative initiative. Hinting that the motives of politicians are strategic (and thus a little dubious), and that the liberalization of abortion was advanced principally to increase electoral support in the forthcoming elections, also suggests that the abortion issue has been "muddied," with the result that it is no longer possible to treat it separately from the balance of political power.

Similarly, another poll bulletin notes that certain groups have used debate around abortion strategically to advance their political manifestos:

> it seems that the existence of continual legislative changes [in regard] to the question of abortion is being attributed to the Church, or [politicians and political parties] taking advantage [of the abortion question] in political games.[41]

Here CBOS demonstrates awareness that the struggle over abortion legislation assumes a greater value and significance than a simple struggle over the terms of women's access to abortion: it symbolically marks the territory of division between political factions, and it is an arena in which the Church also stakes a claim as primary definer. Moreover, debate over access to abortion represents a critical and crucial arena in which politicians, political parties, and the Church can "take advantage"; in other words, bolster their authority and support within Polish society by taking part in debate. The subtext implies that participation in the abortion debate raises political profiles and allows a wider "public" engagement with politics than is otherwise the case. At the same time, this wording ("taking advantage") also suggests somewhat unscrupulous activity on the part of those involved in the scramble for heightened publicity and profiles.

Conclusion

Opinion polls are both a mechanism and a methodology of democratic practice and as such are crucial to the legitimization of Polish politics. Throughout the opinion poll bulletins, the pollster "voice" attempts to sound disinterested, dispassionate, and objective in order to reinforce its professionalism and enhance its credibility. We have seen that the CBOS opinion poll bulletins claim a gender-neutral space: while the respondents to opinion polls are broken down according to sex, the "voice" of the bulletins claims gender neutrality. This can be deduced by a marked lack of reference to the issue of gender in the questions addressed to respondents, as well as by the fact that the bulletins pitch questions to a hypothetical, gender-neutral respondent whose primary identification is as a citizen of Poland. Here the additional complications of gender, sexuality, class, location, and the like remain secondary to the primary identification of the respondent as "citizen." Where gender is raised as a secondary identification, the bulletins claim that gender does not "determine" attitude to abortion, since attitudes to abortion are similar between men and women; therefore, according to poll results, abortion is not a gendered question. The terms of debate thus militate against women's voices being heard *as women*. Women are displaced from the abortion debate in their own right: their participation in the abortion debate as pro-choice or pro-life activists, or their lived experience of abortion, disappear from view.

At the same time, and despite claims of gender neutrality, the ways in which public opinion is collected and categorized *is* gendered. The hierarchizing of abortions according to their "justification" constructs abortion rights as contingent only: there is no room here to claim abortion as a universal human/women's right. The privileging of consensus, meanwhile, labels abortion "on demand" as an extreme and a marginal position, which further delegitimates a feminist, "pro-choice" position at the same time that it delegitimates a total ban on abortion.

Simultaneously, and as we have seen, the poll bulletins recognize that women are a "special" kind of citizen that need protection, as evidenced by the fact that politicians can have "improper motives" or can "take advantage" in order to obtain political capital. Women are described as the subjects/objects (and the responsibility) of the paternal state. So while citizenship is described as a gender-neutral identity, with gender-neutral outcomes, the poll bulletins code citizenship as *male* and fraternal: women's biological capabilities render them outside this model and in need of "special measures." Citing Yuval-Davis, Tricia Cusak has noted that

> masculine hegemony in the modern state has frequently been maintained by social networks based on male bonding. While women are thus given a special symbolic status in relation to the nation, they are distanced from ac-

tive membership of the polity: consequently they are constructed as "other" to men in the nation: "they are often excluded from the collective "we" of the body politics, and retain an object rather than a subject position.[42]

In line with Cusack's analysis, I suggest that the model of democratic practice extended and exemplified through public opinion polling contributes to the association of masculinity with the exercise of citizenship. The terms on which democracy is being constructed thus work to exclude women. It remains a matter for discussion whether this represents change or continuity: as Johnson and Robinson note in their introduction to this volume, "The Soviets understood the 'woman question' as how to accommodate women's innate differences to the ideal of the New Soviet Man."[43] Thus while state socialism coded women as equal citizens to men, this meant women "becoming" men, rather than a radical re-visioning of the division of productive and reproductive labor constructed along gender lines. We might further speculate that the coding of citizenship as male is something new as well as something old: the democratic transformation of Polish society is after all widely understood as an ungendered or a "gender-neutral" process, reflected in the fact that most "transition" theorists have neglected gender as an axis around which transformation is being discursively effected. I would suggest, then, that the coding of citizenship as male, and the awkward inclusion of women as "male-citizens" with "special" biological responsibilities, as manifested in the opinion poll bulletins on abortion, results both from the gendered legacy of state socialism and from the gendered transformative futures being constructed along Western liberal democratic lines.

Fundamentally, the CBOS opinion polls are interested in abortion as a political issue. The abortion debate comes to stand as a symbol of ideological conflict between two competing nation-building projects: those of the modernist, secularist, postcommunists and those of the (neo)traditionalist, right-oriented Catholics. Despite the bulletins' claims to the contrary, gender remains integral to the ideological shape of the state, whether in the "Catholic option," whereby women's biological capabilities supersede their citizenship rights, or in the "rational, secular state option," whereby the paternal state confers special citizenship rights on women because of their biological vulnerability. Both of these positions are based on a particular conception of gender relations, either "traditional" and authentic or "progressive" and European. Thus although both positions are predicated on and determined by gender ideology, the CBOS opinion polls' focus on the party political dimension of the debate fosters the assumption that gender is in no way implicated in either of these political projects.

We can see then that in the Polish context at least, and as Gal and Kligman have indicated, reproduction is absolutely central to the reconstitution of political authority: the recurrence of abortion debate in Poland bears testament to the fact that "reproduction makes politics." However, and at the same time, the CBOS opinion poll bulletins make clear that although the abortion debate (and therefore, reproduction) is recognized to be a debate about politics, it is never considered to be a debate fundamentally about gender.

NOTES

I would like to acknowledge the UK Economic and Social Research Council for their provision of a research studentship and a postdoctoral fellowship, which have enabled me to carry out this research.

1. Gail Kligman, *The Politics of Duplicity: Controlling Reproduction in Ceausescu's Romania* (Berkeley: University of California Press, 1998).

2. See Rachel Alsop and Jenny Hockey, "Women's Reproductive Lives as a Symbolic Resource in Central and Eastern Europe," *European Journal of Women's Studies* 8, no. 4 (2001): 454–71, and Ewa Maleck-Lewy and Myra Marx Ferree, "Talking about Women and Wombs: The Discourse of Abortion and Reproductive Rights in the GDR during and after the Wende," in *Reproducing Gender: Politics, Publics and Everyday Life After Socialism*, ed. Susan Gal and Gail Kligman (Princeton, N.J.: Princeton University Press, 2000), 92–117.

3. See Wendy Bracewell, "Rape in Kosovo: Masculinity and Serbian Nationalism," *Nations and Nationalism* 6, no. 4 (2000): 563–90, and Lisa Price, "Sexual Violence And Ethnic Cleansing: Attacking the Family," in *Thinking Differently: A Reader in European Women's Studies*, ed. Gabriele Griffin and Rosi Braidotti (London: Zed Press, 2002), 252–66.

4. Susan Gal and Gail Kligman, *The Politics of Gender After Socialism* (Princeton, N.J.: Princeton University Press, 2000), 15–16.

5. Ibid., 30.

6. I am using this term loosely to describe those groupings in favor of the 1993 "anti-abortion law," which restricted abortion access to certain specified conditions.

7. I use "pro-choice" in this context to describe those groupings seeking to overturn the 1993 law in favor of more liberal access to abortion, such as those campaigning to include socioeconomic conditions as grounds for abortion, for example.

8. Here I am taking Nick Moon's definition of public opinion polls: "the definition of an opinion poll is more broad than voting intention, and less broad than any topic under the sun [. . .] the opinion in public opinion polls must be about political or social topics [. . .] they must be about matters that are in the general public interest" and "to count as a opinion poll rather than a random collection of anecdotal information, there must be some form of scientific approach." See Nick Moon, *Opinion Polls: History, Theory and Practice* (Manchester: Manchester University Press, 1999), 2–3.

9. For an understanding of how opinion polling functioned under the state socialist regimes in state socialist Europe, see Matt Henn, "Opinion Polling in Central and Eastern Europe under Communism," *Journal of Contemporary History* 33, no. 2 (1998): 229–40.

10. See Matt Henn, "Polls, Politics and Perestroika: The Emergence of Political Opinion Polling in Central and Eastern Europe," *European Business and Economic Development* 1, no. 5 (1993): 11–17, and Matt Henn, "Polls and the Political Process: The Use of Opinion Polls by Political Parties and Mass Media Organizations in European Post-communist Societies (1990–1995)," *Journal of Communist Studies and Transition Politics* 13, no. 3 (1997): 127–47.

11. Justin Lewis, "The Opinion Poll as Cultural form," *International Journal of Cultural Studies* 2, no. 2 (1999): 204.

12. Lisbeth Lipari, "Toward a Discourse Approach to Polling," *Discourse Studies* 2, no. 2 (2000): 187–216.

13. From 1956 the provisions of the Abortion Admissibility Law had allowed the termination of pregnancy for medical reasons, in case of rape or incest, or in the case of a woman's "difficult living conditions." These provisions had been interpreted liberally to include abortion on socioeconomic and therapeutic grounds. See Françoise Girard and Wanda Nowicka, "Clear and Compelling Evidence: The Polish Tribunal on Abortion Rights," *Reproductive Health Matters* 10, no. 19 (2002): 22–30.

14. The so-called "anti-abortion law" severely restricted access to abortion. Abortion was allowed in the following specified cases: danger to the mother's life or health; damage to the fetus; or pregnancy resulting from a crime. Meanwhile, the law declared its aim was to protect the health and life of the fetus from the moment of conception.

15. In 1994 the Parliamentary Women's Group attempted to add "social reasons" to the list of permissible abortions in order to widen access to abortion. After the rejection of this abortion bill in the upper house of Parliament (the Senate), the lower house of the Polish Parliament (the *Sejm*) was unable to reach a sufficient majority to overturn the Senate's ruling. The bill then passed to President Lech Wałęsa, who promptly vetoed the bill, ensuring its failure. In 1995 the Labor Union party (UP) attempted to put the matter of abortion to a referendum as it was widely believed that public opinion supported the liberalization of abortion legislation. However, this initiative once again failed.

16. Despite the similarity of provisions, there are significant differences between the 1956 Abortion Admissibility Law and the 1996 liberalization amendment. The liberalization amendment specifies a twelve-week time limit for abortions performed for social or legal reasons; there is a mandatory consultation and a waiting period of three days for the woman seeking an abortion; and there are harsher penalties for illegal abortions after twenty-four weeks. All of these provisions marked the 1996 amendment as less liberal than the 1956 law. See Eleonora Zielińska, "Between Ideology, Politics, and Common Sense: The Discourse of Reproductive Rights in Poland," in *Reproducing Gender*, 23–57.

17. Girard and Nowicka, "Clear and Compelling Evidence," 22–30.

18. So far, abortion legislation has changed after every election in Poland since 1989. The 1993 restriction of abortion followed the 1991 semi-free elections, where post-Solidarity parties won 65% of seats; the 1996 liberalization of access followed the resurgence of the postcommunist left (SLD and PSL) in parliamentary elections; the 1997 parliamentary ratification of the Constitutional Tribunal Ruling on abortion followed the election of Solidarity Election Action (AWS), an alliance of center and right-wing parties into government. The landslide victory of the postcommunist left (SLD and UP) in 2001 has borne witness to a further unsuccessful attempt to liberalize abortion law.

19. Monthly opinion polls are conducted by CBOS to satisfy the needs of Polish public administration bodies and wider society, as well as various other interested institutions, including local government, the press and television, industry, and advertising agencies. Founded in 1982 under martial law, CBOS is currently funded by a grant from the state and mandated with a responsibility to state and to society to determine public opinion on significant issues of the moment. Surveys are made on a

nationwide representative 1,000- or 1,200-adult population random-address sample, and CBOS is professionally verified for the quality of its questions, and is to some extent relieved of commercial pressures by virtue of its grant from the state.

20. These included the following bulletins: *Opinia publiczna o przerywaniu ciąży* [Public opinion on abortion], CBOS Opinion Bulletin (Warsaw: CBOS, June 1989); *Młodzież o przerywaniu ciąży* [Young people on abortion], CBOS Opinion Bulletin (Warsaw: CBOS, July 1989); *Opinia publiczna o przerywaniu ciąży* [Public opinion on abortion], CBOS Opinion Bulletin (Warsaw: CBOS, June 1990); *Prawo o aborcji w opinii społeczeństwa* [Law on abortion in the opinion of society], CBOS Opinion Bulletin (Warsaw: CBOS, March 1991); *Prawo o aborcji w opinii młodzieży* [Law on abortion in the opinion of young people], CBOS Opinion Bulletin (Warsaw: CBOS, June 1991); *Opinia publiczna o prawie do przerywania ciąży* [Public opinion on the abortion law], CBOS Opinion Bulletin (Warsaw: CBOS, April 1992); *Opinia społeczna o przerywaniu ciąży* [The opinion of society on abortion], CBOS Opinion Bulletin (Warsaw: CBOS, November 1992); *Społeczne konsekwencje ustawy o warunkach dopuszczalności przerywaniu ciąży* [Social consequences of the law on the conditions under which abortion is permitted], CBOS Opinion Bulletin, (Warsaw: CBOS, November 1993); *Stosunek do prawnej dopuszczalności aborcji i ewentualnej zmiany ustawy* [Attitude to the legal permissibility of abortion and eventual changes to the law], CBOS Opinion Bulletin (Warsaw: CBOS, June 1994).

21. These include the following: *Kwestie ideologiczne: prywatyzacja, bezrobocie, aborcja, Konkordat* [Ideological questions: Privatization, unemployment, abortion, Concordat], CBOS Opinion Bulletin (Warsaw: CBOS, January 1996); *Zakres tematyczny Referendum* [Thematic territory of a Referendum], CBOS Opinion Bulletin (Warsaw: CBOS, January 1996); *Stosunek do prawnej dopuszczalności aborcji i ewentualnej zmiany ustawy* [Attitude toward regulation permitting abortion and the eventual change of the law], CBOS Opinion Bulletin (Warsaw: CBOS, April 1996); *Stosunek do aborcji wobec liberalizacji przepisów jej dotyczących* [Attitude toward abortion in light of the liberalization of regulations concerning it], CBOS Opinion Bulletin (Warsaw: CBOS, November 1996); *Nowelizacja ustawy antyaborcyjnej i jej konsekwencje* [Amendment of the anti-abortion law and its consequences], CBOS Opinion Bulletin (Warsaw: CBOS, November 1996). All of the 1996 bulletins report on public attitudes toward abortion; however, some do so in the context of wider framing issues, such as possible topics for inclusion in a referendum, or the relationship between attitude to abortion and attitude to the Concordat, privatization, and unemployment. The remainder of the bulletins report on attitudes toward abortion in the narrower but perhaps more immediate context of then-current legislative attempts to liberalize abortion policy.

22. For example, one opinion poll states in its introduction that it sets out to chart the dynamic influence of the abortion debate on public opinion: "Similarly to two months ago, we asked respondents about the characteristic of their opinion of the method of legal regulation of abortion. This made it possible to trace how the current ongoing substantial debate around the amendment to the anti-abortion law has affected on public opinion" (CBOS, *Nowelizacja ustawy antyaborcyjnej*, 2).

23. Both Lipari and Lewis note that authorship in mainstream polling is deeply suppressed.

24. This is true for all of the CBOS public opinion abortion poll bulletins I have examined, not just the 1996 abortion poll bulletins. Of course, the reliability of opinion poll data obtained in the 1980s is questionable.

25. For a feminist critique of citizenship, see the following: Mary Dietz, "Context Is All: Feminism and Theories of Citizenship," in *Feminism and Politics*, ed. Anne Phillips (Oxford: Oxford University Press, 1998), 378–400; Ruth Lister, "Citizenship: Towards a Feminist Synthesis," *Feminist Review* 57 (Autumn 1997): 28–48; and Nira Yuval-Davis, "Women, Citizenship and Difference," *Feminist Review* 57 (Autumn 1997): 4–27. For an introduction to how these debates have been extended to the process of democratization and economic transformation in East Central Europe, see Barbara Einhorn, "Gender and Citizenship in the Context of Democratization and Economic Transformation in East Central Europe," in *International Perspectives on Gender and Democratisation*, ed. Shirin M. Rai (Basingstoke: Macmillan, 2000), 103–24, and Barbara Einhorn, *Cinderella Goes to Market: Citizenship, Gender and Women's Movements in East Central Europe* (New York: Verso, 1993).

26. There is little investigation of the "gender" variable as feminists might understand it. Instead the opinion pollster simply asks and notes only whether the respondent is a man or a woman. This book starts from the premise that gender is both constantly changing and culturally specific. However, this definition is not in operation in the opinion poll bulletins. The male/female distinction employed in the bulletins is rather more to do with "sex," meaning a biological definition that is both unchanging and universal. This must in part stem from the fact that in common with many European languages, the Polish language does not have separate words for sex and gender.

27. For an introduction to feminist epistemology and a discussion of feminist critiques of "malestream" epistemology see Alessandra Tanesini, *An Introduction to Feminist Epistemologies* (Malden, Mass.: Blackwell, 1999).

28. CBOS, *Stosunek do prawnej dopuszczalności aborcji*, 3.

29. It is very difficult to estimate the number of abortions performed illegally in Poland or abroad. On the basis of their research, the Polish Federation for Women and Family Planning has estimated that the number of illegal terminations of pregnancies may have reached 80,000 to 200,000 abortions a year (Federation for Women and Family Planning, 2000).

30. The 1996 CBOS opinion poll bulletins repeatedly frame abortion attitude in relation to parliamentary politics. One such bulletin measures voter support in the light of the forthcoming liberalization of abortion (CBOS, *Stosunek do aborcji*).

31. This question and these possible answers recur throughout all the opinion poll bulletins on abortion. Such a hierarchy of permissible abortions is also common in international surveys on abortion.

32. Again, analysis of opinion by these categories recurs throughout all the opinion polls on abortion.

33. CBOS, *Stosunek do prawnej dopuszczalności aborcji*, 3.

34. CBOS, *Kwestie ideologiczne*, 5.

35. Of course, such "neutrality" will have its own values and political vision: such "neutral" views are similarly subjective and just as political as those expressed by those in support of a state based on Christian morality and teaching.

36. CBOS, *Stosunek do aborcji*, 11.

37. One 1996 poll investigates the degree of public support for "liberal transformation" in the areas of privatization, unemployment, the Concordat, and abortion, further gauging public opinion on the "ideological shape of the state" (CBOS, *Kwestie ideologiczne*).

38. Ibid.

39. CBOS, *Nowelizacja ustawy antyaborcyjnej*, 5.

40. Ibid.

41. CBOS, *Stosunek do aborcji*, 8.

42. Tricia Cusack, "Janus and Gender: Women and the Nation's Backward Look," *Nations and Nationalism* 6, no. 4 (2000): 544.

43. CBOS, *Stosunek do aborcji*, 8.

The Gendered Body as Raw Material for Women Artists of Central Eastern Europe after Communism

Ewa Grigar

The suppression and limitation of creative expression during the rule of communist regimes catalyzed a rebellious voice among some Polish, Czech, and Slovakian women artists. The dramatic appearance of explicitly gender-related art since then is a sign that new opportunities for women artists have emerged. I argue that these opportunities are shaped by the challenges of finding the appropriate artistic execution for women artists' ideas and ideals.

The first step for women artists after communism was to reclaim the existence of an individual identity within postcommunist society. Performance art, installation, video, and photography became some of the most important channels of visual communication with the audience. Since the early nineties, women artists have continued to take up media such as projection, video installation, and video sculpture as a fresh means to explore the social position of women. As Dorota Monkiewicz, curator of the National Museum in Warsaw, observed, "Seeing that painting took a lead throughout most of the twentieth century, perhaps it came easier to women to strike out for independence in an arena that was, in certain sense, second-rate and less densely colonized by competitive, ambitious men."[1] In addition, an easier and more affordable access to the new computer technology and increased funding of the work coming from the institutions outside of their native countries allowed these women artists for greater field of their artistic productivity.

The opening of Eastern European borders was followed by the exposure of the art of this region to Western eyes, which for over fifty years had been viewed primarily within the boundaries of the Eastern bloc countries. Although at times there had been periods of more artistic freedom and movement, and thus of more appreciation by Western critics and audiences, generally the consequence of the isolation meant that many in the West regarded Polish, Czech, and Slovak art as artistically unproductive and uninteresting. Criticism of the newly emerging art was that it was not a product of the stylistic progress of the countries' own artistic movements, but rather an appropriation of Western styles. Unfortunately, the work of women artists, many of which first flourished in the postcommunist period, has been particularly hard hit by this criticism.

My intention in analyzing some of the issues of postcommunist women's art, specifically Central Eastern European gender concerns, was provoked by debates about the perspective and place of women's art—how was it rooted in historical as well as sociopolitical events that either consciously or unconsciously affected the creative environment of the women's visual arts? I argue that for Central Eastern European women artists, their art is a form of communication not only within their own nations, but also to nations outside those borders. They are concerned not only with their place as women artists within new capitalist republics, but also with issues, such as globalization or consumerism, whose presence became increasingly evident after the fall of communism. Furthermore they are concerned with working out the various meanings and implications of being female in these new contexts.

Tracing the Sociopolitical Context

Poland, the Czech Republic, and Slovakia share a common element of struggle with communist regimes. However, although positive in terms of uniting and activating people against these repressive regimes, the struggle also relegated issues of gender to the unaddressed margins. Martina Pachmanova remarked that because resistance to the regimes united people regardless of gender, issues specifically important to women were considered to be an unnecessary "adornment" of the politics and culture of former communist countries.[2]

Still, the position of not only women artists but women in general in this former collective life was subsumed under a shrewd tactic of the communist leaders. What the system offered its citizens was mandated equality: the gender equality of the labor force. In reality, as Belinda Cooper observed, a state-imposed equality did not offer a public dialogue about the changes in women's roles; thus sexism and discrimination persisted, in both public and domestic spheres.[3]

Despite the "social equality" offered to women by the communist govern-ment, which gave them access to high-level education and workplace support, their true social position was masked by covert governmental manipulation. The official state propaganda claimed to have emancipated women through education, work, and childcare, but in reality, it failed to achieve its goals. Overburdened with domestic and occupational tasks, women came to resent the very notion of "women's rights" as exploitative and ideologically biased.[4]

According to Piotr Piotrowski, a renowned Polish art critic and historian, the communist regime tried to disguise its anti-woman policies through a variety of shams in accordance with the tradition established by the "fathers of Bolshevism." It was only on the surface that woman appeared to play a signifi-cant role in the political, cultural, and national arenas. Women's lives were ostensibly shaped by the ideology of liberation and equal rights.[5] But women artists railed against this myth of homogenous culture. The mutinous voice was especially strong in Poland in the seventies, when artists such as Natalia LL, Ewa Partum, and Maria Pinińska-Bereś tried to incorporate elements of feminism in their work. Unfortunately, their messages seemed not to find any resonance in the Polish art discourse of their time.

Women's position in Poland was further complicated by the Catholic Church. As opposed to the former Czechoslovakia, where the Catholic Church did not play as distinctive a role in the social reactions against the communist regime, in Poland the Church stood out as a supporter of the struggle for political freedom. And yet at the same time the Church was a powerful and archly conservative voice for a traditional role for women. Izabela Kowalczyk, a Polish feminist writer and art critic, in her essay on feminist art in Poland, called attention to the special attribute that the Polish Catholic Church historically assigned to women: "Woman according to this tradition was repre-sented as a 'pathetic' Mother Pole, who nevertheless looked after the Polish home and was a guardian of national values. In this way the Polish Church strengthened the model of a traditionally passive woman, who can realize herself only in her home and family."[6]

Since the Catholic Church did not develop a powerful voice in the Czech Republic and Slovakia, women artists there have not engaged in aggressive polemics on the subject of the Catholic Church, as they have done in Poland. Rather, if religious symbolism has a presence there, it is usually as a critical tool censuring fundamentalism in faith more generally, or a way of describing messages, as in the Renaissance art, by using the language of Christian iconol-ogy. Such an iconological revision of Catholicism can be seen in the works of Slovakian artist Dorota Sadovská (b. 1973).

Sadovská's interest lies in the attraction of the religious language for the international public. In 1999, at the Gallery Priestor in Bratislava, she ex-hibited an installation with forty-nine paintings of saints represented in a shortened perspective on the sidewalls and ceiling of the exhibition space, which was enclosed within an enormous box. By reducing the naked figures of

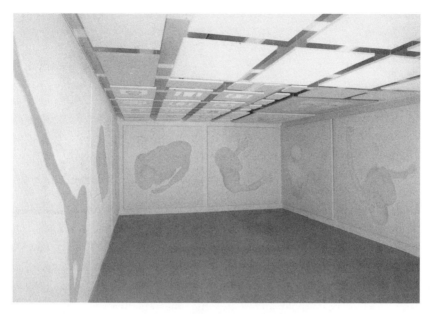

Dorota Sadovská, *In the Yellow Box*, 1999, detail of ceiling

Dorota Sadovská, *In the Yellow Box*, 1999, installation of paintings

Katarzyna Górna, *Madonnas*, 1997

saints to a pure yellow color and, at the same time, retaining the symbolic hand gestures, Sadovská shifted the established codes and meanings, whose rhetoric could be changed by only slight shifts in form. Her intention, as she stated in one of her interviews, was to provoke the spectator to search for new meaning for herself/himself, as the painting can work as a mirror of thoughts, or, in the language of psychology, as a projective test.[7]

Conversely, in Poland, the art employing a religious imagery—mostly a Catholic one—was often used by artists to voice their criticism toward the politics of the Catholic Church and its effect on the citizens of the postcommunist Poland. Being a strong supporter of the Solidarity movement during communism, the Catholic Church won hearts and the complete trust of Polish people and, as a result, reserved a secure spot in the process of shaping the new Republic. In a discourse on the role of women within a postcommunist society, the term *Matka Polka* (Mother Pole) is often used to describe a certain model of woman propagated both by the government during communism and, currently, more vehemently by the Polish Catholic Church. *Matka Polka* is seen as a symbol of woman submitted to a strict role of breeding new Polish citizens and, therefore, is bereft of her own individualism. She has been often compared with the image of Mother Mary, as in the photographic works of Polish artist Katarzyna Górna (b. 1968). Górna's "Madonny" (Madonnas), from 1997, is a cycle of three photographs representing the maturation of Mary: as an adolescent girl whose first step into womanhood is indicated by menstrual blood dripping down her leg, as a canonical Mother Mary with baby Christ, and as a mature Madonna in a pose reminiscent to the Pieta.

The metaphorical reference embedded by the artist refers to the dichotomy of women's roles in the Polish reality. Thus in reading the last part of

Górna's photographic cycle, one may conclude that it is not Jesus, represented here as a being alive and closely hugging Mother Mary's body as a helpless child, but Mary herself who is a true savior; a critical affront referring to the creation of the myth of Mother Pole. Simultaneously, the artist is interested in searching woman's true identity and corporality, which is often displaced, or lost, when one is deprived of its individuality.

Individuality has become a central focus for artists after communism. So too the quest for a gendered or gender-neutral art has elicited profound interest among many emerging artists. The changes born out of the fall of communism and the opening of the Eastern borders to the West evoked a self-questioning of their identities, still strongly connected to their social surroundings. For artists in Poland, the Czech Republic, and Slovakia, the ultimate goal has been to regain their voice and identity—an identity that had been lost when the individual artists were submerged within the working masses, and an identity that now, it is claimed, solemnly belongs to the individual artist. Individual artists, as the Polish art critic and curator Aneta Szyłak points out, have immersed themselves in the redefinition of their personal and national identities, and in the process they have explored social, political, and cultural issues that had scarcely been investigated in the recent past—issues such as the roles of religion (predominantly in Poland) and of education in the daily life of the individual and of the nation.[8] The sociopolitical changes during the postcommunist decade led toward a critical reexamination of the present reality, in an attempt to forge conditions for Central Eastern Europe that mediate between modernity's sense of belonging to a postcommunist aesthetic and the postmodernity of the present time. Piotr Piotrowski interestingly equated modernist mythology to universalism. In reference to the model of communist culture, he observed:

> Modernism did not differentiate art according to sex, race, origin. Art was one. This did not require individual negotiations, individual acceptance of one's position according to sex, race or origin. Indeed no negotiations with the existing reality were necessary. One's declaration was sufficient. But now it is no longer possible. The fall of the totalitarian point of reference resulted in the pluralization of the subject and a feeling of its individuality.[9]

This new socio-aesthetic shift allowed for the growth of interest in and a possibility of the articulation of gender issues. Whereas few women or men artists had used their sex as a medium of gender expression during the communist regime, after 1989, men and women artists became heavily interested in using their gender as way either of expressing their sociopolitical concerns—as in the work of Zbigniew Libera, from Poland—or of exploring alternative gender and sexual imagery.

The Concept of Individuality: On Gender Neutralization

Being a woman and "being" an artist is a relation with the self; perpetually asking yourself a question of self identity. Is this me, or maybe a certain code, inculcated model or psychological script where I try to find myself . . .

Anna Baumgart

The communist inculcation of false ideas of "equality" combined with the deprivation of one's individuality cultivated a strong need for a postcommunist resurfacing of individual identity. The recognition of "gender identity" in Central Eastern European countries, however, even in the postcommunist decade, has created discomfort among women artists. Being an artist, rather than a "woman artist"—that is, being gender-neutral—is highly preferred by some artists of Central Eastern Europe.[10] Such a stance is conditioned by the frightful repression of women by postcommunist sociopolitics as well as by the polemics of both official and unofficial art within Central Eastern Europe. Jana Gerzová, a Slovakian art critic, offers an insightful remark about the risk that the unofficial art of the communist decade carried along into postmodernity; it was its own defense mechanism. "One of these mechanisms was the forced need to reinforce homogeneity of the social and civic attitude of unofficial artists. This feeling of civic solidarity pushed back any need for emancipation based on generation, opinion, or gender. It helped to create an illusion of homogeneity even where a clear differentiation was present."[11]

Political changes throughout Central Eastern Europe may have brought a new promise for improving the exteriority of individual existence organized around one's bodily functions, but they did not necessarily allow enough room for the serious liberation of open expression of gender identity. I agree with Izabela Kowalczyk, who states: "Contemporary women artists often avoid qualifying their art or labeling themselves as 'feminist,' since they are afraid of the pejorative connotations of the term."[12] In Central Eastern Europe the pejorative sense is deeply rooted in a definition shaped during communism, which identified a "feminist woman" as one possessing more masculine than feminine features, thus being a deviation of nature—the "other." The change of the political system did not change the public attitude toward feminism. Unfortunately, present criticism of the issue only extends the social bias toward the gender identity of the feminine woman confined within the social sphere of imposed roles.

Do women artists see their environment differently than do men? Shall we categorize art based on artists' gender? These questions will always follow gender-related discussions. It is not about categorization itself, I contend, but about having the unrestrained choice for those who wish to make it. And in the present repressed state of social trauma in the countries of the former Soviet bloc, there is a continuing lack of such a choice.

Griselda Pollock declared that we are searching for ways to acknowledge "spaces of femininity" and their subjective temporalities in the rhythms of women's lived experience within and against the hierarchies of sexual difference that are configured in complex social formations of class, race, and sexuality.[13] The search for woman's own identity as an individual is relevant to Pollock's geographically universal statement on woman's condition. Indeed, an identification and critical unmasking of woman's condition is a prominent subject matter of women's art after communism.

For Polish artist Zuzanna Janin (b.1964), investigation of art based on gender or social strata is an anachronism. In an interview, she stated: "The fact that I was born a woman, was not my choice. The fact that I am an artist was solemnly my choice. . . . I do not tell 'feminine stories,' as I do not understand the meaning of 'feminine stories' because they never interested me."[14] This attitude of the "gender-neutral" positioning of some "new generation women artists" is, I argue, related to a unique identification as a "neutered victim of a social stance." Being a woman artist does not identify or imply a predilection to make a specifically feminine art, but rather, in postcommunist society, it accents the need to establish one's freedom of interpretative choice based on the goals and aspirations of the artist herself. And since this choice is not yet present in this geopolitical sphere, the argument is that we should strive for its presence, not sustain its absence.

Still, it is evident for the viewer of Janin's works that the artist herself had to be aware of women's issues, especially with her piece *Sweet Girl*, from 1997. The work, resembling a girl's silhouette made out of copper wire and cotton candy, was shown at the all-woman exhibition *Maskarady*, the IX Festival Inner Spaces, in September 2001 in Poznań, Poland.[15] Ironically, the show itself propagated the idea of exposing various stereotypes associated with women. The leading agenda of the exhibition, to which Izabela Kowalczyk made reference in a review of the exhibition, transcends a question posed by Judith Butler on distinguishing specific features for either man or woman. If there is a sphere for woman in Janin's work, which specifically deals with embodying stereotypical ideas of woman's exteriority, her role is to be a sweet girl. The use of cotton candy, a material lacking substance or permanence, renders unavoidable any escape from the passage of time. A sweet girl is the artist's transparent implication of the "external" self-portrait suspended in the surrounding space.

In a similar sphere of claimed gender neutrality is artist Jana Žáčkova (b.1961), Slovakian born, now living in Prague.[16] For Žáčkova, there is no difference between the art of men and of women.[17] The artist disregards sexual difference as a factor indicating potential characteristics assigned to the specific gender. Yet the external world—a world existing outside of the object and its artist—assigns a particular role to each sign. Thus, it is rather problematic to view Žáčkova's video from 1992, titled *Meditation*, displaying various shots of kaleidoscopic images of woman's lips that are rather highly eroticized and turned into an "object of desire."

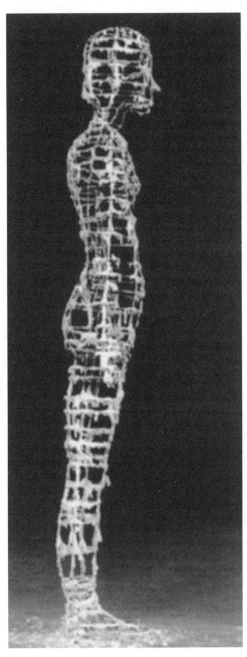

Zuzanna Janin, *Sweet Girl*, 1997

Intentionally or not, Žáčkova's choice of subject matter does not ask to be classified as "feminine," yet at the same time, it revolves around "the feminine." Hence, I perceive the artist's rendering of the woman's lips to function semiotically, to be read within the cultural ideology of patriarchal society as a symbol of sensual, erotic, or sexual representation. For that matter, the gender of the artist becomes diffused because the subject begins to function on its own—as a sign.

To describe this gender neutrality, Martina Pachmanova introduced the term "muzzled identity," from the title of a show of six Czech and six German women artists in Prague in June 1994. Pachmanova stated that "*muzzle* is used as a metaphor for various power and ideological mechanisms whose aim is to restrain feminist consciousness among contemporary Czech women artists and to control their socially and culturally 'inappropriate' gestures that could disturb the dominant patriarchal order."[18]

The term can be used as an informal definition of the gender neutrality not only of Czech women artists, but of all those artists from the Eastern bloc who claim this position. Moreover, these artists allow themselves to be manipulated by social views, or to be "muzzled," and this conscious awareness is as disturbing as the process of manipulation itself. Self-marginalization, as I would call this approach, only allows a continuation of the existing biased foundations. Through neutralization, certain women artists take an easier approach, but ultimately, I argue, a foolish one, for displaying their art in the male-dominated environment.

The Issue of Women's Identity

Representation of the female body occupies a great portion of the art created by Central Eastern European women. The increased interest in the female body can be attributed to the changing sociopolitical climate in recent years. In Poland, the work of Katarzyna Kozyra (b. 1963), who is representative of the younger generation of women artists, revives a discussion of issues of identity, female biology, and physicality, in order to erase the preexisting social framework of homogenous Polish culture.

Most of Kozyra's works oscillate around exploitation of the reality of the contemporary body living within a visualization of the present social culture. The pondering of one's relation to her or his own body, its subjectivity, and the social debates evoked by the visual dissimilarity of the presented bodies are notorious in the works of this artist. Her critical juggling of the social and cultural norms of "difference" and their acceptance and place within the surrounding reality have earned her reputation as a "controversial" artist.

One of Kozyra's critical pieces with gender-related implications is *Olympia* of 1996. The work comprises three photographs and a videotape. Adopting the prototype of Edouard Manet's *Olympia,* from 1863, which evoked a huge scandal due to a realism of a subject matter rather than nudity, Kozyra's piece similarly manifests a conflict of a sociopolitical nature, this time directed toward the politicization of an individual. Kozyra's figure of Olympia, as opposed to Manet's representation of an "anonymous" model, is a representation of the artist herself—a self-portrait of a transformative construction. The first image comments upon the social construction of identities of women in society, as with Manet's courtesan. The second portrait is an artist's parody of an "original" idea, implemented by an auto-bibliographical note. The representation of a healthy female body is substituted by a sick body that was affected by chemotherapy, which the artist herself had to undergo while she was struggling with cancer. The third picture from the sequence, *Olympia-Old Lady,* refers to the issue of time, to the history of an individual as it exists within the norms of society.

The artist confronts the viewer with an analysis of the body, dependent upon natural factors of age and sickness. She calls attention to the issue of viewer's gaze and questions its modes of perception. Is a viewer comfortable with looking at the raw representation of the bodily experience of the repugnant, rather then idealized, beauty of a female body? It is Kozyra's comment on the stereotype of woman's body in our culture as a source of visual satisfaction to fulfill the needs of a male gaze, a gaze to which the artist pays specific

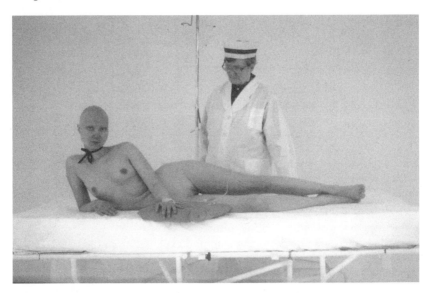

Katarzyna Kozyra, *Olympia*, 1996. Through kindness of artist and the Zachęta
National Gallery of Art.

Katarzyna Kozyra, *Olympia*, 1996. Through kindness of artist and the Zachęta
National Gallery of Art.

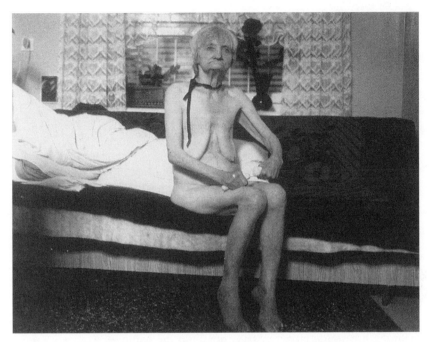

Katarzyna Kozyra, *Olympia*, 1996. Through kindness of artist and the Zachęta National Gallery of Art.

attention. In her essay "Whose Body? Whose Desire?" Leonida Kovac commented on Kozyra's intention that the model's gaze constitutes the principal visible link between the private and the public space, between the two zones separated by bourgeois ideology though sharing a common territory, or rather, object of exchange: a woman's body.[19]

Jana Zelibská (b.1941), a prolific woman artist from Slovakia, successfully creates powerful statements about the oscillation of woman's role within her society. In the video installations *Sisters I* (1997) and *Sisters II* (1999) the artist turned her attention toward a psychological study of the relationships between women. Taking into account a process of growing up, Zelibská defined a psychological picture of mutual relationships among young girls. A strong emphasis placed on the reactions among these young girls, meticulously exposed by video close-ups of their mimicking faces, indicates the artist's call for a return to the honest body language of young girls. Going back to the roots of our childhood memories will allow us to understand our own shaping processes; it will detect the core of the fear and anxiety imprinted upon the mind of a grown-up woman. For Zelibská, this exploration of childhood makes the claim that identity is constructed by the sociocultural ideals that are deeply

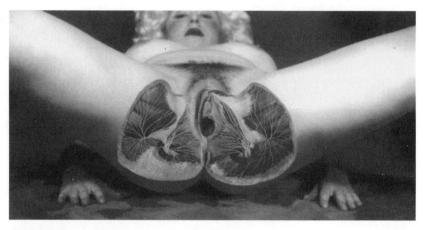

Veronika Bromová, *Views*, 1996

imbued within the internal structure of every society. Zelibská's representation in the video recording of spontaneous dialogue about intimate experiences between two young girls inevitably questions the nature of women's vulnerability and submission to social traditions, as well as gender stereotypes, a subject that had not been often present in the works of Slovak women artists before the fall of communism.

The issue of women's identity occupies a great number of works by Veronika Bromová (b.1966). Bromová belongs to a group of first-generation artists of the new Czech Republic who routinely use computer animation as an artistic tool in their creative process. She creates her artistic dialogue with the viewer through computer-assisted photomontages as well as installations. Her use of figures of deformed corporeal forms as well as her own tormented body is meant to represent a condition of the human being within an often questionable identification of reality.

In 1996, Bromová presented a cycle of digital photographs titled *Views*. Here the artist displayed an interest in the theme of pornography and voyeurism. The female crotch, exposing muscles and tendons, demonstrates the interiority of a woman's body as an essential part of the exterior veil that is the object of the sexual desire. "I just allowed myself to uncover its physical reality of which we do not know anything. I de-eroticised it."[20] This physical reality was portrayed by Bromová through the literal employment of the human body. Deconstructed to its internal ingredients, the body would no longer serve as an object of desire, as it is brought into a basic form of its own being, which might then repulse the notion of sexual fantasy.

In the postcommunist artistic discourse, woman's body has been used more often than in the previous decades as a cipher for the search for individual identity. Women artists engage critically by questioning the various social mechanisms, which have influenced the shaping of their gender. The new postcommunist condition has allowed more opportunities for artists to voice their criticism (of course, it was still censored, but not to as great an extent as during communism), and at the same time has engendered more debates about women's identity.

The Politics of Food: The Female Body as Consumer and Object of Consumption

The changes after 1989 in Central Eastern Europe awakened a specific awareness among women artists regarding a woman's body as an object of consumption as well as a consumer itself, controlled by the imposed norms of the newly emerging consumer culture. This awareness was greatly influenced by Western globalization that brought with it something that had been unknown under the communist dictatorship: consumerism.

Women artists of Central Eastern Europe probably became preoccupied with the artistic battle against consumerism because they had been aware of the danger of the consumer politic; for instance, a consumptive culture sees the body itself as an element for manipulation. Women became the most vulnerable victims of these schemes, since expectations about their appearance are always induced by the cultural canons of a scopophilic society. Paradoxically, women even allow themselves to be engaged in such activities. Thus, I agree with Kaja Silverman, who observed that "Most of the time, we desire what our culture tells us we should desire. As Heidegger would say, we are absorbed in the 'they,' displaced in relation to our subjectivity."[21]

In September of 2000, renowned Polish art curator Anda Rottenberg organized an exhibition titled *Postindustrial Sorrow*. Among the artists exhibiting on the theme of a "global supermarket" was Joanna Rajkowska. Born in 1968, Rajkowska belongs to the most engaging group of women artists to appear on the Polish art scene in the second half of the nineties. Her video installations, as well as cans containing "the essences" of the artist's body, aim to intellectually awaken the audience to a heightened sense of human existence, an awareness of self and others. These 0.33 liter cans, resembling cans of soda but filled with the artist's own body secretions, were presented in the show under the title *Satisfaction Guaranteed*.

Rajkowska's cans were displayed—just as their counterparts in the store—in a refrigerated case lent by the Norcool company. Ironically, the Coca-Cola company refused to allow its refrigerators to be used in Rajkowska's project, thus confirming a lack of support for critical art. Or perhaps Coca-Cola thought the artist's cans might be a successful marketing rival for their own mass-consumed soda? Among the cans containing fluids from different parts of Rajkowska's body is one batch of cans titled *Kok*, embellished by a picture of a young girl's crotch and containing coconut milk, which is supposed to evoke erotic stimulation.

Joanna Rajkowska, *Satisfaction Guaranteed*, 2000

Joanna Rajkowska, *Satisfaction Guaranteed*, 2000, detail of *Kok*

One of the important aspects of the artist's project was the active participation of viewers, who were able to purchase and drink the displayed cans. Indeed, the juxtaposition of commonly consumed product with its "unusual" content serves as a psychological game in which, unfortunately, the loser is a consumer. Rajkowska unmasks here the destructive evolution of cultural consumption, which ultimately leads to the insipid consumption of one's own body. In this consumption society, the boundaries between the consumer and the object of consumption are blurred. Woman, represented here as an object of consumption, is particularly vulnerable to becoming a victim. Her culturally assigned role as man's prey allows her to dissolve into a product of visual and consumptive digestion. Moreover, Rajkowska's cans are metaphors for an awareness of the exploitation of the female body.

Slovakian women artists also responded to the theme of consumption with great zeal. Jana Zelibská, using video as an interpretative tool, executed a work about the social construction of the beauty myth in *On Diet*, 1997. Food and diet are the artist's central subjects, exposing a constructed norm induced by social stereotypes, aggressively implemented by the emerging consumer in a capitalist society. Rosemary Betterton observed that a specific tension between repression and release is inscribed especially on the bodies of women through eating—the use of food as opposed to alcohol is for her still clearly gendered. Femininity and the consumption of food are intimately connected, and being fat is taken to signify both loss of control and a failure.[22] This loss of control is represented in Zelibská's piece through depicting bulimia. The artist juxtaposed in her installation piece two video projections: one on a small screen and another on a large wall, directly above a pile of food. The young girl presented in the video deliberately overeats and repeatedly throws up, to invoke an ironic trauma of the body, which becomes a focus of cultural anxiety. Maud Ellman asserts that "It is through the act of eating that the ego establishes its own domain, distinguishing its inside from its outside. But it is also in this act that the frontiers of subjectivity are most precarious. Food, like language, is originally vested in the other, and traces of that otherness remain in every mouthful that one speaks—or chews."[23]

In the Czech Republic consumerism and globalization have also been widely represented by Kateřina Vincourová (b.1968). Her installation pieces comment upon a crisis of the individual's identity, manipulated by the growing power of the media, which dictates the values for society. Vincourová's work *Call* (1999), a pneumatic construction made out of textile and PVC, comments ironically upon globalization's growing effect on our everyday lives. *Call* refers to a collapse of the borders between the public and the private spheres of human existence and the resultant crisis of identity. This concept has a very special societal resonance within the countries of the former Eastern bloc. The long-awaited fall of communism, a system that negated one's sense of individuality, was supposed to promise a rebirth of new and less constrained identity. Paradoxically, the sociopolitical changes only brought an unexpected epidemic of consumerism, which contributes to isolating an individual from others, and denies individuality. The motto of the politics of consumerism, "the more one possesses, the freer one can be," is only a systematic tactic for self-enslavement. As a result, our self-identity will become a product of simulated reality.

On Family Values

For the women artists of the Central Eastern European sphere, the family, or the problems of socially constructed family values, is a topic more broadly addressed than by their sisters in the West. Many women do not feel any anticipated change in their role within a family. Thus the importance of artistic articulations by women artists arose from the need to expose physical and psychological abuse present within the circle of one's own family. The subject of children, the relationships between spouses, and women's traditional role within their families often constitute the subject matter of their works. These subjects were rarely touched by such a strong criticism in the communist decade. It is not to say that women in the past had not been exposed to domestic abuse, but rather they were unable to openly voice their

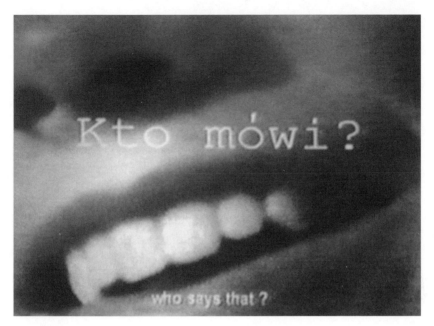

Anna Baumgart, *Who's Talking?* 1998

concerns without being seen as "poisoned" by socially and politically unacceptable Western ideologies, that is, feminism.

For Polish-born Anna Baumgart (b.1966), artistic broaching of this subject is confined to the various representations of woman. Baumgart explores the role of woman-lover or of woman-mother and her relationship with a daughter. What is the role of the mother in the process of her child's development? Who shapes the psyche of the child: the mother or society? These are some of the questions that Baumgart addressed in her 1998 video titled *Who's Talking?* The child—a little girl—is perpetually asked about her love for her mother. "Do you love your homeland as much as your mother who nourished you?" is a question raised in the video, which rhetorically refers to the insinuation of the system of values imposed on the child through social institutions, such as school.

This process is rather problematic for Baumgart, who recognizes that the interference of systems coming from the outside may intrude on the equilibrium of family relations. Thus, this psychological entrapment of the child's perception may cultivate a barrier that will separate the child from the influence of its family. Moreover, the system, which will become a surrogate parent for the child, will shape that child according to its set schematics. As a result,

Ewa Grigar

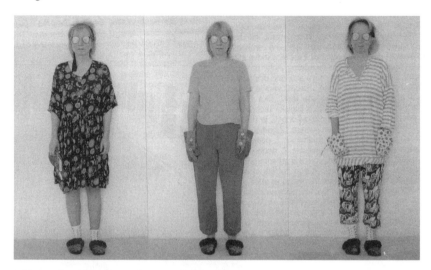

Mila Preslová, *Woman in the Household*, 2000

the child will join the circle of "perfect" citizens—deprived of his/her own individuality.

The Czech artist Mila Preslová (b.1966), through a direct deployment of context in her own photographic installation, focuses on the socially assigned roles of women within their domestic environment. *Woman in the Household* (2000) is a series of photographs representing a woman dressed according to her household tasks.

Preslová displays the woman as a target of social objectification, exposing the role of the woman within her family. Woman is portrayed as mother, worker, lover—slave of her mundane duties. The artist gives particular attention to her hands, either wearing or holding gloves, as well as her meticulously chosen attire, whose unkempt appearance reinforces the representation of the image of a housewife.

The role of a housewife as mother has been explored by Slovak artist Anna Daučikova (b. 1950). Apart from her other works concerned with the subject of self-identification as the *femme*, the artist is intensely involved in rendering the family as a subject. In her *Untitled* piece from 1999, Daučikova portrays the potential "family picture" of an already inscribed role of both sexes essential for the ideal functioning of the family. Through a simple sketch overlapping the central photographic image, Daučikova implies social establishment of a schematic for the perfect example of the family.

This comparative overview reflects Amelia Jones's assertion that the female body expressing itself in the rhetoric of the pose is inclined to absorb meaning from the outside because of the passivity imposed by the conventionality of social roles.[24] Jones's view challenges the problem of social insinuation, targeting the vulnerability of women based on the traditional politics of sexual identity. The problematic stance for Central Eastern European women was consistent denial of the allegedly existing social pressure. Thus, with the passage of time, woman's body increasingly became an instrument of social manipulation. For this reason the direction taken by women artists of the postcommunist decade toward self recognition was a way of discovering their true social identities as well.

Defining Attitudes of the West toward Central Eastern Europe

In the early thirties, Jan Mukařovský, a member of the Prague Linguistic Circle, observed that in order to adequately analyze a linguistic or visual sign one has to take into consideration a specific code or "social fact," which cannot be separated from the work of art itself. Moreover, the key to understanding the work of art must be sought not in its internal organization but in the relation of this organization to the underlying code.[25] The process of tracing this code has to be regarded in relation to specific external impulses coming from the surrounding environment of the artist. It can often take the form of myths and memories, either personal or collective. Understanding this notion will allow the viewer to appreciate more fully the value of a work of art. Unfortunately, this conception appears to be problematic not only for viewers or critics from "outside" the borders of the cultural sphere of Central Eastern Europe, but also for those from within the region itself.

Do works of art by women artists from the postcommunist countries share identifiable aspects with their counterparts from the West? The answer to this question is not a simple one. Inevitably, certain formal and aesthetic aspects can be traced as common, just as the continuing fight for woman's emancipation is a global one. It is not the intention of any of these women artists to produce works of a nationally inbred sentiment, but rather to expose broader aspects of the social injustices related to gender. Hence, using globally understood language is imperative to the success of global conversation. On the other hand, the elements that differentiate "Central Eastern European" aspects from the "West," are, as I prefer to call them, *conditional elements*—residing in both the consciousness and the unconsciousness of the artist's mind—that navigate the social symbolism of the work. These *conditional elements* are socially derivative; they are the essential distinguishers of the East-West difference.

How different is the approach of contemporary women artists to the issue of gender and feminism within the sphere of Central Eastern Europe as opposed to the West? In contrast to the United States, where it often appears that feminism does not have to be political anymore, since it has attained a defined and even institutionalized cultural if not political power, Central Eastern European feminism is presently in the state of sociopolitical turmoil. It is not to say that works of art by contemporary American women artists are not political at all, but, I will argue, the attention is being directed to woman's singular identity as an individual human being rather than a representative of a collective; personal experiences often dominate the visual rhetoric of work by Kiki Smith or Nan Goldin. On the other hand, when it comes to visual representation of a culture politic, both Eastern and Western women artists share similar views on ruinous aspects of globalization and social injustice. The issue of race within the works from Central Eastern Europe does not appear in the same context as in the United States. Rather, religious affiliation holds a place in Central Eastern Europe similar to the place race holds in America.

Although Central Eastern Europe recently embarked upon its journey concerning the subject of feminism, it should not be forgotten that earlier but unsuccessful attempts had been made. Traditionalism and misconception of the term "feminism," deeply rooted within the Central Eastern European art world of the 1970s and 1980s, did not allow female artists to visually express their thoughts on gender. Indeed, even some bleak attempts undertaken by Natalia LL, from Poland, to address the subject of gender were discussed without using the word "feminism." The body and character of the works of art by Central Eastern European women artists in the postcommunist decade have less subjective and more objective thematic quality, circumscribing the sociopolitical essence of their living environment.

A significant value of these artworks is that they serve as the emblem of a universal struggle for a stabilized nation finally freed of a painful burden carried from the past. Hence, the attempt of women artists of this sphere is to become "internationalized"—to become universal rather than national. Let us hope for their voice to be heard, as well as understood.

NOTES

1. Dorota Monkiewicz, "A Panoramic View: Art by Women, Feminine and Feminist Art in Poland After 1945," in *Architecture of Gender: Contemporary Women's Art in Poland,* ed. Aneta Szyłak (Warsaw: National Museum in Warsaw, 2003), 23.

2. Martina Pachmanova, "The Muzzle: Gender and Sexual Politics in Contemporary Czech Art," *ArtMargins,* Jan. 27, 2000, http://www.artmargins.com/content/feature/pachmanova2.html (accessed Dec. 2001).

3. Belinda Cooper, "Building Feminism from the Ground Up," *Civnet's Journal for Civil Society,* 1, no. 3 (1997), http://www.civnet.org/journal/issue3/cfbeco.htm (accessed Oct. 2001; URL no longer active).

4. Elżbieta H. Oleksy, "Plight in Common? Women's Studies in the New Democracies," *Outskirts: Online Journal* 3 (Nov. 1998), http://www.chloe.uwa.edu.au/outskirts/archive/VOL3/commentary1.html (access restricted).

5. Piotr Piotrowski, "The Old Attitude and the New Faith," in *Beyond Belief: Contemporary Art from East Central Europe,* ed. Laura J. Hoptman (Chicago: Museum of Contemporary Art, 1995), 41.

6. Izabela Kowalczyk, "Feminist Art in Poland Today," N. *Paradoxa International Feminist Art Journal* 11 (1999): 1.

7. Dorota Sadovská, interview by Jan Gerzová, "The End of Geography?" *Praesens* 2 (2002): 7, http://www.praesens.net/szamok_en.php?d_id=9 (accessed June 2002).

8. Aneta Szyłak, "The New Art from the New Reality: Some Remarks on Contemporary Art in Poland," *Art Journal* (Spring 2000): 55.

9. Piotr Piotrowski, "Sztuka Wedlug Polityki," in *The Negotiators of Art*, ed. Bożena Czubak (Gdansk: Centre of Contemporary Art Łaznia, 2000), 33.

10. Here, as an example, I would refer to the statements made on this subject by Polish artist Zuzanna Janin or Czech artist Jana Žáčkova.

11. Jana Gerzová, "Art and the Question of Gender in Slovak Art," N. *Paradoxa International Feminist Art Journal* 8 (August 2001): 76.

12. Kowalczyk, "Feminist Art in Poland Today."

13. Griselda Pollock, *Generations and Geographies in the Visual Arts: Feminist Readings* (London: Routledge, 1996), 8.

14. Excerpt from an interview by Przemysław Jedroski, "Patrze Na Swiat Jak Patrze" [I Look at the World as I Look] *Arteon* 18, no. 10 (2001): 34.

15. Other artists who participated in the show were: Katarzyna Kozyra, Anna Baumgart, Elzbieta Jabłońska, Paulina Olowska, Dorota Podlaska, Joanna Rajkowska, Jadwiga Sawicka, Julita Wüjcik, and Monika Zielinska.

16. National identity is a new dilemma which appeared after the split of Czechoslovakia into the Czech Republic and Slovakia in 1993. Since many artists born in Slovakia moved to the Czech region, I will always refer to them as Slovak working and living in Prague.

17. An opinion expressed in the inquiry published in *Revue Labyrint*, no. 1–2 (1997): 118.

18. Pachmanova, "The Muzzle."

19. Leonida Kovac, "Whose Body? Whose Desire?" N. *Paradoxa International Feminist Art Journal* 6 (2000): 23–24.

20. Tereza Bruthansová, interview, "Worlds Temptingly Marked 'Top Secret,' " in *On the Edge of the Horizon*, exhibition catalog (Prague: Prague City Gallery), 7.

21. Kaja Silverman, interview by Martina Pachmanova, *Věrnost v Pochybu* [Loyalty in a Movement] (Prague: One Woman Press, 2001), 62.

22. Rosemary Betterton, *An Intimate Distance: Women Artists and the Body* (London: Routledge, 1996), 131.

23. Maud Ellman, *The Hunger Artists: Starving, Writing and Imprisonment* (London: Virago, 1993), 53.

24. Amelia Jones, *Body Art: Performing the Subject* (Minneapolis: University of Minnesota Press, 1998), 121.

25. John Burbank and Peter Steiner, eds., *Structure, Sign, and Function: Selected Essays by Jan Mukařovský* (New Haven, Conn.: Yale University Press, 1978), xvi.

PART III.
TRADITIONALIZING GENDER

five

Birthday Girls, Russian Dolls, and Others

Internet Bride as the Emerging Global Identity of Post-Soviet Women

Svitlana Taraban

Twenty-one-year-old Olga from Ukraine writes in her online ad: "I am a calm, even-tempered lady. I love children, home comfort, and stability. I also like music, movies, and sports. I adore children. I'm looking for a kind, honest man, who dreams to create a strong family." This personal ad written in awkward English is rather unremarkable when taken on its own. However, the fact that one can find thousands of similar advertisements on the Internet written by women from Ukraine, Russia, and some other countries of the former Soviet Union suggests that it is more than one woman's quest for love. Rather, it is a large-scale phenomenon embedded in a complex web of gender ideologies, economic exchanges, romantic fantasies, and mobility/migration strategies.

On the international marriage market Olga is considered an Internet bride. Her online ad, accompanied by a sexualized photo, can be seen as a typical way to initiate transnational courtship and romance with a Western man. Like hundreds of thousands of women from Ukraine and Russia, Olga is part of the new phenomenon known as *Internet-nevesty* (Internet brides).

During the last five years, the image of the Internet bride has frequently appeared in Western popular discourses and is almost invariably linked to women from the countries of the former Soviet Union. It was in mid-1990s that the term *Russian bride*, which is used to refer broadly to all Russian-speaking women from the Post-Soviet countries, was coined in the global cultural economy. Today the descriptor *Internet bride* is commonly used to describe Slavic women from Post-Soviet states who seek Western husbands via the Internet. Russian and Ukrainian Internet brides appear in internationally circulated magazines with a predominantly male readership (e.g., *Maxim* and *Playboy*), in fiction and nonfiction writing (*The Internet Bride* by Gregory Ward, *Leaving Katya* by Paul Greenberg, *Russian Women and Marriage: Love Letters from Russia* by Weston Rogers, and *My E-mail Order Bride: A Trip to Feodosia, Crimea, Ukraine* by Robert Herbst), in films (the American *A Foreign Affair* and *Birthday Girl*, the Australian *Russian Doll*, and the Swedish *Lilja 4-ever*) and in numerous media accounts featuring stories of individual mail-order brides.

Unfortunately, there is little credible data on the number of Post-Soviet Internet brides advertised on the Internet every year or of the number of Post-Soviet women who succeed in marrying Western men after meeting them online. One study, by American scholar Donna Hughes, examines 219 out of the estimated 500 marriage agencies advertising women from the former Soviet Union as Internet brides in 2001 to suggest that there were at least 250,000 Post-Soviet brides being advertised, approximately one-half from Russia and one-quarter from Ukraine (with a population about one-third of Russia's).[1] As the Internet becomes more available in Post-Soviet countries and as marriage agencies expand the repertoire of their services online (e.g., video clips featuring women, immigration assistance) and offline (e.g., romance tours to Post-Soviet countries), it is unlikely that the numbers of Post-Soviet women advertised as brides will decline any time soon.[2]

This Internet industry advertises Post-Soviet women to Western men, capitalizing on the myth of a traditional woman in order to attract new clients. Thus, a new gender phenomenon—Post-Soviet Internet brides and their Western grooms—suggests that a particular construction of the relationships between Western men and Post-Soviet women is evolving. With their promises of traditionalism and sexual pleasures, Post-Soviet women emerge as top candidates for the roles of wives or companions of Western men. These intimate transactions via the Internet are facilitated by several factors: reconfiguration of gender practices in Post-Soviet countries, differential positioning of Post-Soviet women and Western men in the global economy, and the development of new technologies, especially the Internet, that make a transnational search for love and marriage possible.

Yet, given that the ascendance of the Internet bride and the explosion of the Internet bride market are linked to the advancement of digital opportunities and proliferation of the Internet, it is ironic that so many Internet brides are from the former Soviet Union,[3] where the proportion of the population having a PC at home and regularly using the Internet is rather small. This is especially true of Ukraine, where some 400,000 women under the age of thirty left between 1995 and 2000.[4] Ukrainian researchers found that two-thirds of young Ukrainian women want to go abroad, and many dream of marrying a rich Westerner who will provide for them.[5] Given that legal labor migration from Ukraine to Western countries is rather limited due to difficulties in obtaining visas, it is logical to conclude that many Ukrainian women view marriage to a Westerner as a viable route to achieve their dream of a better life abroad. Indeed, the data on the attitudes of Ukrainian women toward migration and marriage to foreign nationals supplemented by actual rates of female migration from Ukraine suggests that seeking a Western husband via the Internet is increasingly being viewed, at least by the female population of Ukraine, as a popular path to marriage and migration. Internet-based marriage agencies, which charge their male clients membership fees as well as fees for women's addresses, ensure a constant supply of Post-Soviet Internet brides on their Web sites and assist women in becoming Internet brides. With the help of marriage agencies operating online, Ukrainian women—regardless of age, fluency in English, and experience with the Internet—are offered an opportunity to gain a new identity of an Internet bride and to initiate online contact with Western men.

What are the reasons behind the presence of Ukrainian and other Post-Soviet women online in the role of Internet brides? What do they hope to achieve through the online strategy of husband-seeking, which is rather novel, not to mention quite unorthodox, for Ukraine? To answer these and other questions related to the Internet bride phenomenon, I will use the insights afforded by recent works on gender and new technologies to examine this rapidly growing terrain of cyberspace—the global market of Internet brides, where women market themselves to the best male bidder.

My data are drawn from English language Web sites of the marriage agencies where Ukrainian women advertised themselves to men from North America, Western Europe, and Australia in the summer of 2002.[6] I found these Web sites using a keyword search of "Ukrainian women" and "Ukrainian brides," yielding hundreds of Web sites, from which I selected ten. The criteria for selection were: (1) the Web site must contain at least one hundred profiles of Internet brides from Ukraine, and (2) the Web site must target men primarily from North America. Paying special attention to occupational and age diversity, I then selected two hundred profiles of Internet brides from Ukraine. I used content analysis methodology to identify the ways in which Ukrainian women presented themselves in electronic texts posted on the matchmaking Web sites. Following the standard procedures for conceptual analysis, electronic profiles of Internet brides were coded manually for existence of self-descriptions that use vocabulary derived from the (neo)traditional gender ideology. In addition to the primary data that I collected from the Web sites, I also used media pieces on Ukrainian women and reports related to Ukraine published by the United Nations agencies and Ukrainian and international NGOs.

In this chapter, I draw on Johnson's and Robinson's argument (see the introduction to this volume) about gender multiplication and negotiation that characterize the Post-Soviet space in order to show that contemporary Ukrainian Internet brides attempt to negotiate multiple roles and identities while moving between several different gender ideologies. First, Ukrainian women are confronted with a traditional gender ideology inherited from the Soviet state and reinforced by current nation-building discourses that emphasize women's nurturing and mothering role in the rebirth of a nation.[7] Secondly, the sexualization and commodification of Post-Soviet women in global circuits requires Ukrainian Internet brides to define their position in relation to the images of Russian-speaking women as sex objects that are circulated in popular discourses[8] and on the Internet.[9] From here stems Internet brides' persistent self-portrayal of themselves as domesticated potential housewives and mothers. On the other side of the spectrum are various gender ideologies brought forth by globalization and the growing exposure to the West, which allow women to imagine more egalitarian family relationships and the possibility of economic mobility and advancement.

In the rapidly growing economy of Internet brides, Ukrainian women emerge as "marketable" and in high demand due to the male perception of them as docile and devoted wives as well as "submissive and sexually willing"[10] subjects with low expectations of men. For an Internet bride, her chances of finding a foreign husband depend on her ability to sustain the male fantasy of herself as a pre-feminist and hyper-feminine subject. To accomplish this task, women capitalize on Western men's fantasies of perfect wives in order to have access to global opportunities and choices associated with migration to the West. As Internet brides, Ukrainian women feed into Western men's fantasies of perfect brides, with a view to initiate online romance leading to an entrance visa to one of the Western countries.

As stated, in order to land a foreign husband, Ukrainian Internet brides strategically deploy the male-authored rhetoric of the bride market and capitalize on its image of "traditional" women untainted by feminism. In actuality, the oversimplified portrayal of a modern Ukrainian woman as a traditional woman does not accurately capture the recent changes in Ukrainian women's lives and identities and the complexity of their relationships with traditional gender ideologies. By looking at social experiences of Ukrainian women as well as their views on family and work, one can see that outside the parameters of the online bride market Ukrainian women are actively exploring new gender spaces and renegotiating their roles in all spheres of society.

Indeed, socioeconomic changes in the Ukrainian society and the need to adapt quickly to a rapidly changing environment propelled shifts in women's perceptions and attitudes, including increased tolerance of nontraditional relationships, participation in the new forms of economic activities, and growing mobility and resistance to domesticity. Therefore, the recourse of Ukrainian women to gender traditionalism within the parameters of the online bride market can be understood as a representational strategy and as a discursive move for obtaining a marriage contract and improving their life situations through migration to the West. As I will show later, in the context of the evolving gendered and sexualized economy of the virtual bride market, the strategic use of neotraditional gender imagery and language not only allows Ukrainian Internet brides to become sought-after candidates for wives of Western nationals, but also permits them to reverse, to a certain extent, their discursive position as victims and passive receivers of the male-catered and male-regulated economy of the virtual bride market and to obtain entrance visas to one of the Western countries.

The chapters in this collection offer many examples of how gender performances and behaviors of Post-Soviet and Eastern European women work to confirm and defy gender ideologies endorsed by the state, the market, and religious and cultural institutions. This chapter adds to this analysis by mapping the sources of gendered identities and behaviors of Post-Soviet, and specifically Ukrainian, women, which originate not only within but also beyond the borders of the postcommunist nation-state. My goal is to take a closer look at the workings of the local and global gender ideologies in the production and consumption of the Russian-speaking Internet brides by exploring the ways in which neotraditional discourse is embraced by the global Internet bride market.

Women's Identities in Cyberspace

The development of computer-based information and communication technologies (ICTs) has led to profound transformations in virtually every sphere of modern society. Not only have new technologies altered established frames of knowledge, conventional social practices, and local and global political and economic transactions, but they have emerged as a new site for the construction and performance of gendered identities. Opportunities for forging transnational identities, finding translocal friendship and romance, and forming online communities have propelled people across the globe to further explore the opportunities of the new landscape known as cyberspace.

The emergence of new technologies also signaled the beginning of new academic and popular debates as to how gender, along with other markers of identity, is being constructed, imagined, and performed in cyberspace. The preoccupation with the absent female bodies in cyberspace has provoked heated debates on the relationship between women and ICTs that drew on previous theorizing on (female) bodies. Earlier writings in different disciplines explored various (non-virtual) sites related to the performances, practices, histories, and articulations of (female) bodies.[11] In response to criticism of some theories of the body as being too abstract and general, a number of authors have advocated a more nuanced and material reading of the construct of body.[12] Other important insights developed in the scholarship on the body include understanding it as a social rather than biological construction,[13] analysis of multiplicity and diversity of bodies,[14] and critique of techniques used to control and regulate bodies.[15] With the proliferation of new technologies, theorizing on the body shifted toward discussions of the interrelations between bodies and cyberspace.[16]

Current diversity of stances and opinions with regard to the question of gender performance in cyberspace suggests that at present there is little consensus as to how the intermingling of women's cyber-bodies and new technologies might be interpreted and represented. Many scholars and activists have made claims about the liberating potential of the Internet in terms of erasing traditional identifications of the self/other through the categories of race, gender, ethnicity, and age.[17] The virtual persona that inhabits cyberspace, the argument goes, does not carry the characteristics of a biological body. Therefore, it is capable of transgressing gender/race/sexuality divides (for instance, by gender-switching in online communication).

On the other side of the spectrum are scholars who appear more skeptical toward the possibility of disembodiment in cyberspace.[18] As Bell points out, "what we find in cyberculture are *techno-bodies*, rather than *tech-nobodies*."[19] A large amount of scholarship in North America has defined the relationship of women and new technologies as somehow problematic.[20] Some believe that gender emerges as the most important category of identity on the Internet.[21] Sharpe argues convincingly that the "liberating variety of imagined embodiments" promised by cyberspace has been only marginally incorporated into the contemporary cyberculture.[22] Moreover, insistence on certain kinds of visibility (race, gender, age) becomes increasingly normalized within the cyberspace, suggesting that "we continue to seek to regulate bodies and thoughts on the Net in the same ways we do in RL (real life)."[23]

Departing from the view of technology as a tool of women's oppression and control, recent writings by academics and civil society activists began to conceptualize ways to think about new technologies as an advocacy tool that promotes gender equality and women's empowerment.[24] However, the question of the digital divide in general, and the digital gender divide in particular, was understood until recently in terms of disparities between the developed countries of the North and developing countries of the South. The entire Commonwealth of Independent States (CIS)[25] and Central Eastern Europe region became excluded from the discussions on gender and ICTs—a concern that has been recently voiced by feminist scholars embarking on the study of gender and ICTs in transition countries and echoed by the UN agencies (UNIFEM, UNDP).[26] Not surprisingly, gender-disaggregated data for the countries of the former Eastern bloc is scarce since most CIS countries do not have data on women's use and knowledge of new technologies. Further, newly formulated national ICT policies in postcommunist countries do not integrate gender. This lack of attention on the part of policy makers, academic community, and civil society groups in CIS/CEE region to the question of gender and the Internet is puzzling given that women from postcommunist countries, especially the former Soviet Union, serve as a reference point for new sexualities in cyberspace. I will return to this point later during my discussion of the presence of female bodies of Post-Soviet women on the Web sites of marriage agencies and online sex industry.

In Ukraine, the examples of ICT use to promote gender equality and to empower women are rare. At the same time, sex tourism and marriage agencies that operate through the Internet are increasingly being used "to sell women to a global market of men mostly from industrialized countries."[27] Geographically, the majority of women whose bodies, at first virtual and then real, are used to attract the male gaze come from postcommunist and developing countries. In the following section I will set the stage for discussion of the identity of Ukrainian Internet bride by exploring the reasons behind the presence of Ukrainian women as Internet brides and by situating Ukrainian women in social and geopolitical context of Ukraine after the fall of communism.

Becoming an Internet Bride

The mail-order bride is not a new phenomenon, at least in North America. In the U.S., mail-order marriage is "an inseparable part of North American history and the settlement of the United States,"[28] says the report by the U.S. Immigration and Naturalization Service (INS), referring to the long-standing tradition of bringing wives, primarily from Asia, by American men. For a long time, Western popular discourses portrayed a generalized Asian bride[29] (originally from Japan and Korea and then from Philippines and Thailand), as an ideal choice for marriage. The stereotyped Asian bride has symbolized (and continues to symbolize) docility and traditionalism, which were highly valued by American men looking for marriage. Today, the same imagery is used to construct the collective identity of Post-Soviet women, who are portrayed as exotic, sexual, and docile. In other words, perfect traditional wives for Western men.

It appears that while geographies of mail-order bride export might change over time, the quest of Western males for the female Other that embodies sexual pleasures, femininity, and traditional values remains unchanged. Whereas in the past opportunities to find foreign brides were limited to bride-order catalogues and marriage agencies, the international bride market is now rapidly moving online. Marchetti observes that "although the under-age Philippine 'pen pals' and Post-Soviet mail-order brides have been part of the transnational exchange of sex in the postcolonial and post-cold War marketplace of desire before the digital age, the Internet had accelerated these transactions."[30] Available national data on female marriage migration in some countries supports this claim: according to the INS report in the U.S., each year four thousand to six thousand marriages take place between American men and foreign-born women who met through matchmaking agencies.

Why might Ukraine/former Soviet women enter the cyberspace as brides? The most apparent explanation of the popularity of the Internet bride identity among Ukrainian women lies in the economic decline associated with the transition from the planned to a market economy and the worsening living conditions among the majority of the country's population, especially women. Post-Soviet economic reforms hit the majority of Ukrainian women hard: of Ukrainians who have lost their jobs since the collapse of the Soviet Union in 1991, more than 80 percent are women.[31] The absence of legitimate local opportunities to pursue meaningful careers, along with a large-scale deprofessionalization of Ukrainian women, has had direct consequences on women's decisions to seek opportunities elsewhere. As a result, Ukrainian women have developed a broad arsenal of survival strategies, all of which were meant to improve their economic situation. A marriage to a man from an affluent society is seen as an opportunity for a Ukrainian woman to restore a lost sense of financial security and to improve her material conditions.

The economic motive alone, however, cannot account for the presence of Ukrainian women on the international bride market. Many Ukrainian Internet brides live comfortably—at least by local standards—and do not experience severe economic hardships. This is particularly true for young educated women and women attending universities, who constitute a significant proportion of Ukrainian cyber-brides.

Another factor contributing to the choice of Ukrainian women to become Internet brides has to do with the strong migration sentiment among the Ukrainian population. Over 2 million Ukrainians left the country for permanent residence abroad between 1991 and 1999.[32] The findings of the research on the emigration of the Ukrainian population conducted by the National Institute for Strategic Studies (NISS) in Ukraine suggest that the country has experienced significant demographic losses due to the outflows of its citizens over the past decade. Lack of data on the nature and types of migration of Ukrainians during the Post-Soviet period is a fundamental constraint in assessing the numbers of Ukrainian women who married Western men after meeting them online. According to NISS, "until [the mid-1990s], emigration was not characteristic to the Ukrainian society and therefore was silenced. There were no adequate migration statistics."[33]

The popularity of the Internet bride option in Ukraine is sustained not only by socioeconomic realities but also by stories about Ukrainian women who married Westerners and the glamorized images of living in the West, which Ukrainian girls and women consume through media and Hollywood movies. The fantasies of happy marriages with wealthy Western men and utopian ideas about life in the West sustain women's desire to marry a Westerner using online Web sites. However, despite the narratives of transnational marriages as a happy picture of women's lives abroad, virtually no empirical evidence exists showing what happens to former Ukrainian Internet brides once they relocate to the West.

Indeed, the stories of happy marriages with Western men do not say anything about the extent to which Ukrainian women who emigrate as wives or fiancées might become dependent—both financially and psychologically—on their new husbands, about the social exclusion and psychological adjustments associated with migration, and about the language barrier and professional downgrading experienced by many women. Olga Makhovskaya, Russian psychologist and writer, who conducted one of the first studies of female marriage migration from Russia to the West, states that 80 percent of marriages between Russian women and American men end in divorce after two to three years of marriage.[34] One of the reasons for the high divorce rates, explains Makhovskaya, is the age difference and the fact that after receiving permanent residence in the U.S., much younger Post-Soviet brides are ready to move on and start a new life.

Nonetheless, the numbers of international marriages between Western men and foreign women seem to be increasing. As shown by Hughes, Makhovskaya, and other scholars studying the phenomenon of female marriage migration and online marriage agencies, Ukrainian and Russian women constitute a large percentage of Internet brides worldwide. It is therefore reasonable to assume that a significant number of women who are granted fiancé or spouse's visas each year come from one of the Post-Soviet countries. Seeking to escape economic hardships, instability, and lack of choices to pursue meaningful relationships, Ukrainian women further dissociate themselves from the local marriage market and turn their attentions to foreign males, who could both improve their shaken material conditions and fit their image of an ideal husband.

When it comes to the gendered global linkages involving Ukrainian women that have transpired over the past decade, the ascendance of the Internet bride phenomenon reveals only one scenario of how Ukrainian women are implicated into the global economy. Since the mid-1990s, many Post-Soviet women have found work as domestics, maids, and sex workers in Western countries, alongside women from the developing countries.[35] Even more alarming is the rise of sex trafficking of Ukrainian and other Post-Soviet women.[36] The evidence on trafficking from Ukraine suggests that Ukraine has become one of the main source countries in the global sex traffic. According to the reports by international organizations, many young Ukrainian women have become easy prey for the transnational sex industry.[37] American scholar Donna Hughes, who has written extensively on the trafficking of women from Ukraine and other Post-Soviet countries, states that "in the sex industry markets today, the most valuable and popular women are from Ukraine and Russia."[38] In 1998, the Ukrainian Ministry for the Interior estimated that four hundred thousand Ukrainian women had been trafficked in the past decade, although Ukrainian NGOs and researchers believe the numbers to be higher. The situation has improved little since the late 1990s: the Trafficking in Persons Report–2005 released by the U.S. Department of State indicates that Ukrainian government did little to curb the trafficking of Ukrainian women and that existing anti-trafficking programs in the country are operated by NGOs with virtually no support from the government.[39]

In some ways, the distinction between the Internet bride phenomenon and the sex industry is blurred: a romantic trip to Ukraine undertaken by a Western man to meet his online bride (usually more than one at a time) resembles, in the words of Victor Malarek, the author of a popular press book, *The Natashas: The New Global Sex Trade,* "a sex vacation extravaganza."[40] The women who do get chosen by Western men and who receive visas to join their husbands are still at risk of mistreatment and abuse by their husbands.[41]

While recognizing possible similarities between the sexual exploitation faced by Ukrainian women on the global sex market and some Ukrainian Internet brides, I think it is important to note the difference between Ukrainian Internet brides who choose to migrate as wives or fiancées of Western men and those Ukrainian women who are being trafficked abroad either involuntarily or under false promises of employment. Many Internet brides are attracted by the appeal of a family-forming migration and a fulfilling marriage. Unlike trafficked women, Internet brides know which country they are going to, some are fluent in English, and others have contacts with Ukrainian women who emigrated there earlier or with Post-Soviet diasporas in the country of destination. Thus, Internet brides, if only in theory, have more flexibility in accepting or rejecting a men's offer (marriage proposal). Most importantly, they bring with them expectations of a proper treatment on the part of their Western husbands, which suggests that they would be less likely to tolerate mistreatment, abuse, or gender violence.

Internet Brides in the Context of ICT Development in Ukraine

To grasp the phenomenon of the Internet bride, it is important to understand the ways in which Ukrainian Internet brides engage new technologies, most importantly the Internet, when advertising themselves to potential husbands from the West. Do the high numbers of Ukrainian Internet brides in cyberspace indicate that Ukrainian women are benefiting from new digital opportunities? Do Ukrainian Internet brides engage the Internet the same way as women in developed countries who use the Internet to meet their informational, professional, and social needs? Finally, is an Internet bride phenomenon a part of a broader trend of wide-scale use of ICTs among Ukrainian women?

The data on the proportion of Internet users and on the level of ICT infrastructure development in Ukraine suggests that despite a significant increase in the number of users, the country still lags behind Western countries in terms of the ICT production and use. According to the Internet World Stats, with the population of 47 million, Ukraine has only 2.8 million Internet users (as of March 2005).[42] In fact, the number of Internet users in Ukraine is low not only compared to Western countries, but even compared to other Eastern European countries. Neighboring Poland, for example, which has a population of 38 million, has 10.6 million Internet users (almost 28 percent of total population), while Czech Republic which has a population of 10 million, currently has 3.5 million Internet users (or 34.5 percent of total population).

According to the Information Society of Ukraine (ISU), over half of Internet users in Ukraine reside in the capital city of Kiev, and nearly all users are based in urban centers. As stated earlier, the lack of gender-related indicators on ICT access, use, and knowledge in the newly independent states make it difficult to understand the relationships between women and ICTs in post-communist countries. Ukraine, according to the United Nations Economic Commission (UNECE), is the only CIS country that has gender-disaggregated data on use and knowledge of computers. Whereas worldwide studies suggest that women globally are increasingly active in using electronic communications,[43] the survey conducted in Ukraine shows that only 4.9 percent of Ukrainian women have access to a computer at home.[44]

This data suggests that cyberspace dating and husband-seeking via the Internet entail certain challenges for Ukrainian women. Most basic is the issue of access and affordability: the majority of Ukrainians find the Internet beyond their reach. While in some countries, most notably the countries of the Asian Pacific realm and Western Europe, the numbers of women online have increased significantly,[45] it appears that only a small number of women in Ukraine enjoy regular access to the Internet. The majority of women who go online do so from work or from increasingly popular Internet cafes, known in Ukraine as computer clubs. While only 5.3 percent of the Ukrainian population has access to a computer at home, 14 percent of population has access to computers at work. The percentage of women with a computer at work is slightly higher (15.4 percent) than of men (12.1 percent). The data on student population in Ukraine suggests that close to 34 percent of students have computer access (36 percent of men and 32 percent of women).[46]

Considering that many Ukrainian Internet brides mention *student* as their occupation in their online profiles and that very few Ukrainian women have a computer at home, it is possible to assume that Ukrainian women—especially young and educated—advertise themselves as Internet brides from places of work or study, which are more likely to have Internet access. In addition, women in large- and medium-size cities might turn to local marriage agencies, who would create the woman's identity as an Internet bride without her ever going online. Whatever the case might be, it certainly takes a great deal of resourcefulness and persistence on a woman's part to maintain regular online contact in the conditions of low Internet access in Ukraine. This makes the presence of large numbers of Ukrainian Internet brides in virtual space particularly striking.

Aside from the access problem, limited computer literacy poses another challenge for Ukrainian women. Lack of computer skills coupled with limited proficiency in English, the lingua franca of the Internet and the global bride market, means that many women in Ukraine face an array of challenges in negotiating their entrance into the global Internet bride market. At the same time, this lack of experience with technology, especially among older women, allows online marriage agencies to turn their ventures into a multimillion-dollar industry. The majority of Internet brides in Ukraine do not access the online bride market from their PCs at home. Instead, their entrance into the bride market is mediated by professionals from online-based marriage agencies, who make large profits on one of their best-selling items—"traditional" Slavic women from Post-Soviet states.

Performing Gender Online: The Portraits of Internet Brides

In the past decade, Web sites advertising Ukrainian brides have mushroomed. Most of the sites offer, free of charge or for a nominal fee, an opportunity for women to create their digital identities as brides. For a woman, marketing herself as a bride at the virtual bride market involves some gender moves that are determined by the gendered cultures of the ICTs. Several studies on the relation between globalization, ICTs, and gender addressed the ways in which new technologies are used for the delivery of sexuality, sexual performances, and sexualized violence (e.g., cybersex, online prostitution, sex shows, online stripping, and sex tour advertisements).[47] The difficulties of controlling and censoring information channeled through the Internet lead to the proliferation of overtly sexist and exploitative texts and images that represent women as sexual commodities to be bought, used, and abused by men.

It is important to note that the Internet is embedded within larger discourses of representation, including the material/non-virtual social realities as well as other forms of information and communication, such as mass media. Thus, the analysis of the Internet bride phenomenon can benefit from the investigation of the ways in which bodies, biographies, and aspirations of Internet brides are being regulated both in and out of cyberspace.[48] Understanding the interconnection between these different discourses can shed some light on how the prescriptive and sexualized gender ideologies and representations of women are being transferred into the cyberworld, thereby reproducing the sexualized and gendered discourses that exist outside of the virtual space. Further, future studies on this topic should analyze how male-dominated commercialization and sexualization of women online and the sharp rise of online pornography and sexual exploitation on the Internet affect offline behaviors and attitudes of men toward women.

Although the virtual bride market is a relatively recent phenomenon, it has already established gendered norms that regulate the process of taking up a virtual identity. Thus, the body of an Internet bride is symbolically constructed using two components: E-introduction (text) that speaks to a Western man looking for traditional wife and the accompanying visual image (photo) that displays the physical characteristics of the "absent" material body. E-introduction (usually very brief and with little variations in the choice of self-describing vocabulary) speaks to unknown Internet (male) communicators and serves two main purposes: (1) to describe what the digital body is (I am . . .); and (2) to describe what the digital body wants (I am looking for . . .). In what follows, I explore the question of how Ukrainian Internet brides as inhabitants of virtual space construct their identities and are, at the same time, being constructed by the gendered discourses of the ICTs.

Gendered and sexualized cultures of information technology mediate the actions of the Ukrainian women who enter it for the purpose of finding a spouse. As a result, women are required to follow the established parameters of the sexual economy while creating their virtual portraits and virtual bodies in cyberspace. On one hand, the Ukrainian Internet brides are looking for "serious" men who will be willing to invest their time and money in order to bring them into their countries and for relationships that would culminate in marriage. Therefore, in presenting their virtual selves through this technology, Internet brides attempt to dissociate themselves from Internet representations of women as sexual commodities that are easily accessible to the male consumer. In order to counter the images circulating on the Internet that portray Post-Soviet women as sexually permissive and readily available, Ukrainian brides need to construct their identities as "virtuous women" who "believe in a lasting marriage and a happy home."[49]

To accomplish this goal, Ukrainian brides routinely present themselves as good potential wives and mothers, emphasizing such qualities as nurturance, docility, and family orientation:[50]

> I'm very kind, soft, calm and tender. I like to cook for my close people. And I love my work. I'm fond of house keeping. My house is always full with hospitality and coziness. I like to spend evenings reading some interesting book or watching intellectual shows on TV. (Hairdresser, 23)

> I'm merry, kind, labor-loving. I like to knit, to embroider, to listen to music. (Accountant, 34)

> I am faithful, tender, kind-hearted, sociable, caring, and passionate. I have a good sense of humor, I am sensual. I like music, sports, am fond of foreign cultures and languages. (Student, 20)

In their claim to be taken seriously by prospective husbands, Ukrainian women refer to the traditional female roles and responsibilities that defined women in Ukraine for several centuries: child rearing, cleaning, cooking, sewing, and so on. Internet brides strategically eschew representations of themselves as educated, intelligent, self-reliant, career-oriented, resourceful, and independent. They downplay certain characteristics and biographical details that might portray them as too strong or liberated in the eyes of Western men, thereby avoiding carefully any parallels with an image of a modern

Western woman. Not surprisingly, the word *feminist* is taboo in the vocabulary of Internet brides.

In their online ads, Ukrainian Internet brides accentuate the qualities and attributes that portray them as prefeminist, vulnerable, and docile. The sentiments in the representations of Ukrainian Internet brides are framed around the traditional wife fantasy, which revolves around the image of a woman who is beautiful, feminine, and devoted. Although the profiles of Internet brides do not have explicit references to and comparisons with the images of Western women, it is not hard to tell that their representations are meant to be read vis-à-vis (stereotypical) images of Western women, who are seen as career-oriented, selfish, opinionated, and unfeminine. Internet brides want to reassure their potential husbands that, unlike Western women, they are easygoing and forgiving and therefore are unlikely to cause marital problems:

> I am an easy going young woman concerning feelings of other people. I am sociable, quiet girl. I do not like to give false promises and I appreciate the same qualities in people. Career and money play some role in my life, but it's not my goal. I prefer to arrange home coziness to my friends. My hobbies are: walking with my dog outside, reading good books, listening to good music and enjoying movies. (Economist, 36)

Ukrainian Internet brides' descriptions of what they are seeking in a husband also portray the women as devoted, mature, and family-oriented. Women claim that age or financial situation of their prospective husbands is of minor significance. Instead, Internet brides' representations of the desired husband are routinely constructed around an idealized image of a mate who can appreciate what Ukrainian women have to offer:

> I would like to find a partner who is family-oriented, a natural person, who likes activity and sees us as a team, a man who is my "one and only." (Student, 19)

> Most of all in people I appreciate moral qualities. I want to meet the man of my dream: clever, serious, kind, decent, intelligent, and reliable. The financial position of the man is not the most important thing for me; I want just to meet the really good person. Because I want to have more children in my future marriage and I need the strong family-oriented person with a kind and loving heart by my side. (Editor/Bookkeeper, 27)

> I'm looking for a decent, kind, reliable, family-oriented, caring, loving, thoughtful, and faithful, with a sense of humor and without bad habits man. (Accountant, 22)

> I would be fine to meet a kind man with careful character. His own child would be welcomed. (Hairdresser, 23)

> I can fall in love with a man who is decent, kind and honest. Actually, appearance does not matter a lot, though I adore beautiful athletic built. I want him to be cheerful, tender, passionate, romantic. Besides, he must be

steady, and, the main thing, loving husband and father for his future wife and children. All the other small shortcomings I can forgive. (Entrepreneur, 26)

Many Ukrainian women, especially those in their twenties, often evoke well-known love motifs and images in order to increase the emotional impact of their words on the (male) communicator. The following quotes from Web sites featuring Ukrainian women aptly illustrate this point:

I am very romantic. I enjoy mountains, beautiful beaches, seeing sunsets and spending the time with my friends on nature or at home in front of the fireplace. (Nurse, 25)

I think that paradise is right here near us on Earth. (Economist, 27)

I am Juliet . . . Does Romeo exist? (Secretary, 23)

I want to build a Palace of Love and to raise our child in it. (Designer, 22)

I want to create a family that would have an ocean of love. (Unemployed, 23)

The recourse to the "biological"—or what this volume refers to as neotraditional—discourse is a defining feature of self-presentations among Internet brides who represent themselves in "natural" roles as mothers and housewives:

I will be a perfect wife. (Student, 22)

I will be an excellent mother and wife. (Teacher, 27)

One of the sources for the neotraditional gender imagery employed by Internet brides can be traced to the nation-building discourses in Ukraine that emerged as important sites of identity construction after communism. In her study of gender debates in postcommunist Russia, Haldis Haukanes points out that the tendency to "biologize" women became even more widespread in the aftermath of socialism.[51] In the Ukrainian context, this tendency is manifested primarily in the state- and nation-building discourses that construct an identity of a Ukrainian woman around an image of a "strong empowered woman as a supporter of the state-building process."[52] In political debates and within the Ukrainian women's movement, the iconography of the Ukrainian matriarchal culture is appropriated in order to construct an identity of a contemporary Ukrainian woman. In national imagination, the newly born Ukrainian state is being construed as needing female protection and nurturing. Taken collectively, the state-building ideologies that emphasize a "special mission" of Ukrainian women perpetuate "traditional women's roles of mother, carer and housekeeper as 'natural' and 'vitally important' for society."[53] In this ideological framework, women's needs and concerns are seen as subservient to that of the new Ukrainian nation-state. Further, nation and family (the latter traditionally associated with women) are seen as cornerstones of a new Ukraine. Ukrainian scholar Tatiana Zhurzhenko maintains that "in the framework of Ukrainian neo-traditionalism the solution of family problems is being linked to the revival of the Ukrainian nation, and vice versa—the revival of the nation starts within the family."[54]

Another representational move that transpires in profiles of Ukrainian Internet brides directly relates to my earlier discussion on the sexualized culture of ICTs and (Western) men's fantasies of a sexy and beautiful wife. Online profiles of Internet brides are characterized by almost obsessive detailing of characteristics of absent female bodies that serve to expose women and make them available for men's perusal. All brides' profiles contain information about their age, weight, height, body structure, eye color, and the like. Most Web sites even allow searching brides' profiles by their physical characteristics. The expectation to make the body of the Internet bride visible, which leads to the exposure and vulnerability of an Internet bride, inevitably evokes parallels with online prostitution, with its emphasis on women's sexual visibility and men's complete anonymity.[55]

To reinforce the visual impact on male visitors of bride Web sites, the photos that accompany brides' profiles portray them through the lens of eroticism, sexuality, and physical attractiveness. Looking at the photo images of Ukrainian women, one might easily see the parallels with the colorful covers of the Western magazines that are now widely available in Ukraine. Wearing revealing clothes, taking sensual poses, and stressing their sex appeal, Ukrainian brides-in-waiting resemble the images of the cover girls from the popular magazines sold in Ukraine. Malcolm Waters's notion of symbolic exchange is helpful for understanding the ways in which the symbol produced in one part of the world begins to circulate in transnational spaces. According to Waters, "Symbolic exchanges liberate relationships from spatial referents. Symbols can be produced anywhere and at any time and there are few resource constraints on their production and reproduction. Moreover, they are easily transportable."[56] Adopting the hyper-feminine and overly sexual code of self-presentation, Ukrainian women learn to play with (neo)traditional gender construct and to assume multiple gender identities both in virtual and in physical space.

Symbolic exchanges of the traditional gender imagery circulating in the global landscape have accelerated the processes of exporting Western canons of beauty and desirability across the globe. In Ukraine, the process of transforming the appearance of the female's body to align it with the Western ideals of beauty cuts across the broader gendered discourses that regulate social behaviors of Ukrainian women in the wake of globalization. The emergence of so-called image schools and model schools in Ukraine, where young women are taught how to dress, walk, talk, and act, not only invites a gendered definition of success but also sends a message that a woman can advance only if she uses her feminine qualities and sexuality.

Indeed, there is a number of parallels between the ways in which Ukrainian women perform their gendered identities on- and offline. In cyberspace, revealing clothes and seductive poses are a necessary part of attracting the gaze of a male viewer. Outside of cyberspace, female bodies continue to be regulated by male-dominated discourses and practices. According to the report *Women's Work: Discrimination against Women in the Ukrainian Labor Force* (2003) prepared by the Human Rights Watch, Ukrainian women face discrimination in the labor market based on appearance, age, and marital status.[57] Explicitly gendered and sexualized job advertisements are common in Ukraine, and so are the incidents of sexual harassment at the workplace and professional segregation between men and women.[58] Male employers seek to hire educated and attractive women between the ages of eighteen and twenty-five. This suggests that to Ukrainian Internet brides, the gendered imagery and gendered etiquette of online communication are not new phenomena. In fact, Ukrainian women come prepared to create their virtual selves in accordance with all-too-familiar to them traditional gender imagery.

Problematizing Traditional Woman in the Postcommunist Context

To what extent do the portraits of the Internet brides reflect social experiences and biographies of Ukrainian women following the end of communism? To answer this question, I suggest we take a closer look at social experiences and life choices of Ukrainian women in the new market economy. Tanya Rands Lyon's chapter in this volume shows that Post-Soviet women often lean toward egalitarian practices in their marriages, even if they view themselves as traditional. In the study of young Russian females between the ages of fifteen and twenty-five, Kotovskaya and Shalygina (1996) found that "free experimentation in sex-role behavior"[59] appears to be a common practice among young Russian women. A recent study by Hilary Pilkington describes the ways in which modern Russian women use their sexuality and physical attractiveness in order to improve their lives and achieve the desired lifestyle.[60] Taken together, these ethnographies suggest that the view of marriage is being reformulated by the young generation of Russians around the logic of marketization and consumerism. Within the new social economy of Post-Soviet space, marriages to local *nouveau riches*, as well as transnational marriages to Western men, can be viewed as part of the broader arsenal of gendered strategies used by women seeking a different, perhaps a better, future.

Indeed, the majority of Post-Soviet women can hardly be considered traditional when it comes to the views on family and marriage: in the survey *Women 2000: An Investigation into the Status of Women's Rights in Central and South/Eastern Europe and the Newly Independent States*, the International Helsinki Foundation for Human Rights found that the number of common-law marriages in Ukraine has been increasing substantially since 1991, along with a decrease in the number of registered marriages.[61] Further, this survey found that Ukrainian women are more liberal in their attitudes toward common-law unions than are their male counterparts. According to the same source, 36 percent of Ukrainian women answered *yes* to the question "Do you approve of a woman who wants to have a child without having fixed relations with a man?"

This data is at odds with representations of Ukrainian Internet brides that portray them as dependent, vulnerable, and docile subjects who lack a sense of agency. Overall, Ukrainian women appear more liberal and open to alternative lifestyles, family arrangements, and career choices than suggested by their representations on the Internet bride market.

I am in no way arguing that strategic deployment of different gender ideologies (and sometimes overt manipulation of gender discourses and practices) by Ukrainian Internet brides is necessarily liberating for Ukrainian women. Despite the claims of the Internet marriage agencies about the prospects of successful unions between Ukrainian Internet brides and their Western grooms, the reality of economic imbalances between this group of women and men as well as the pressure on the Internet brides to perform gender traditionally hardly make the gendered encounters online empowering and liberating for Ukrainian women. However, playing upon the cult of beauty, femininity, and fantasies of a traditional woman, Ukrainian women seek to escape lack of choices for marriage and career that are available locally. Instead, they look with hope and optimism toward the liberal democracies of the West with their stable economic environment, meritocratic ideologies, and gender egalitarianism. In fact, some Ukrainian Internet brides who married Westerners by posing as traditional women did receive a chance to start a family and find new educational and economic opportunities in Western countries.

In conclusion, the persistent equation of a collective identity of Ukrainian women with that of a traditional woman and sexy beauty produces a somewhat misleading representation of these women in global circuits. Living in transient and rapidly changing Post-Soviet states with competing gender constructions and ideologies, women in Ukraine, Russia, and other neighboring countries construct their local and global biographies in ways that exceed the rigidly ascribed qualities of a traditional woman. Numerous strategies developed by Post-Soviet women in order to negotiate the processes of change and continuity in their lives give hope that they will be able to resist the forces of neotraditional ideology and to imagine alternative futures—both locally and globally.

NOTES

This research was partly supported by a grant from the Department of Gender Studies, Central European University, Hungary. The critical commentary offered by Jean Robinson, Janet Johnson, and Roz Galtz allowed me to clarify and strengthen some of the arguments. I want to thank Jason Gordon for his help with language and editing of the manuscript.

1. Donna Hughes, "The Role of Marriage Agencies in the Sexual Exploitation and Trafficking of Women from the Former Soviet Union," *International Review of Victimology* 11, no. 1 (2004): 49–71. Hughes focused on the Web sites of 219 marriage agencies that she saw were representative of the Web sites advertising Post-Soviet women. After the profiles of women were catalogued and entered into the database to exclude double counting, there were almost 120,000 women counted on these sites, with the majority of Internet brides being from Russia (62,605 women) and Ukraine (31,837 women). Given that the number of agencies selected for the study represented only half of the total number of agencies featuring Post-Soviet brides, it can be concluded that there are at least 250,000 Post-Soviet women advertised as Internet brides annually. Note also that while small Internet-based marriage agencies feature a limited selection of women, established agencies offer hundreds of women's profiles to choose from. The most popular Internet-based marriage agencies (i.e., Foreign Affair) advertise thousands of Post-Soviet women annually.

2. Of these advertised women, the actual number of brides who marry and emigrate appears relatively small. In the U.S.—one of the primary destination countries—282 fiancée visas were issued to Ukrainian women, and 747 to Russian women in 1997 (ibid). Unfortunately, there are no global data to estimate the scope of female marriage migration from Post-Soviet states to the West. Further, if the data on the number of female marriage migrants does exist, it does not say how many of the women who married Westerners met them online.

3. See the U.S. Immigration and Naturalization Service's report titled *International Matchmaking Organizations: A Report to Congress* (1999). According to the report, the majority of Internet brides are women from Philippines and the newly independent states of the former Soviet Union. The full report can be viewed at http://uscis.gov/graphics/aboutus/repsstudies/Mobrept_full.pdf (accessed August 12, 2003).

4. Donna Hughes and Tatiana Denisova, "Trafficking in Women from Ukraine" (study conducted as part of the U.S. Ukraine Research Partnership, 2002), http://www.ncjrs.org/pdffiles1/nij/grants/203275.pdf (accessed Feb. 23, 2006). This number includes women who married Western nationals, migrated for work, and were trafficked abroad.

5. Ibid., 49.

6. The data for this research were collected from the following Web sites: http://www.women.kiev.ua; http://www.ukrainian-women.com; http://www.ukrainladies.com; http://ua-dating.com; http://www.fairylove.kiev.ua; http://www.ukrdate.com; http://eliteagency.net; http://www.eleo.com.ua; http://www.aukrainelady.com; and http://www.charming-lady.net.

7. See Marian J. Rubchak, "Christian Virgin or Pagan Goddess: Feminism Versus the Eternally Feminine," in *Women in Russia and Ukraine*, ed. Rosalind Marsh (New York: Cambridge University Press, 1996), 315–31; Tatiana Zhurzhenko, "Ukrainian Feminism(s): Between Nationalist Myth and Anti-Nationalist Critique," *IWM Working Paper* No.2 (Vienna: 2001), http://www.iwm.at/publ-wp/wp-01–04.pdf (accessed June 10, 2002).

8. In Turkey, for example, Russian-speaking women are known as "Natashas" and are commonly associated with prostitution, immoral behavior, and a threat to traditional values (Ildiko Bellér-Hann, "Prostitution and Its Effects in Northeast Turkey," *European Journal of Women's Studies* 2, no. 2 (1995): 219–35). In the U.S., popular discourses associate Russian-speaking women with "sex, crime and murder" (Tatiana

Osipovich, "Russian Mail-Order Brides in U.S. Public Discourse: Sex, Crime, and Cultural Stereotypes," in *Sexuality and Gender in Postcommunist Eastern Europe and Russia,* ed. Aleksandar Štulhofer and Theo Sandfort (New York: Haworth Press, 2004). In Israel, women with the Russian accent, most of whom arrived in the country as ethnic migrants or spouses of Post-Soviet Jews, experience sexual harassment, street harassment, and hostility not only from Israeli men but also women (Larissa Remennick, "'Women with a Russian Accent' in Israel: On the Gender Aspects of Immigration," *European Journal of Women's Studies* 6, no. 4 (1999): 441–61).

9. The Internet, which features a large number of pornographic images involving Post-Soviet women and Internet-based prostitution businesses offering photographs and videos of these women, sex shows, and erotic tour packages to Post-Soviet countries, aggressively promotes the image of Post-Soviet women as sexual commodities. For an excellent analysis of trafficking in images of sexual exploitation and the use of new technologies for the sexual exploitation of women, see publications by Donna Hughes available at http://www.uri.edu/artsci/wms/hughes/pubtrf.htm.

10. Matthew Tabbi, "Russian Girls," *Playboy,* November 2000, 109, 154–55.

11. Barbara Brook, *Feminist Perspectives on the Body* (New York: Longman, 1999).

12. Simon J. Williams and Gillian Bendelow, *The Lived Body: Sociological Themes, Embodied Issues* (London: Routledge, 1998).

13. Anthony Synnott, *The Body Social* (London: Routledge, 1993).

14. Brook, *Feminist Perspectives on the Body.*

15. Susan Bordo, *Unbearable Weight: Feminism, Western Culture, and the Body* (Berkeley: University of California Press, 1993).

16. Anne Balsamo, *Technologies of the Gendered Body: Reading Cyborg Women* (Durham, N.C.: Duke University Press, 1996); Elizabeth Grosz, *Architecture from the Outside: Essays on Virtual and Real Space* (Cambridge: Massachusetts Institute of Technology Press, 2001); Donna Haraway, *Simians, Cyborgs, and Women: The Reinvention of Nature* (New York: Routledge, 2001); and Gail Kirkup et al., eds., *The Gendered Cyborg: A Reader* (London: Routledge, 1999).

17. David Bell, "Bodies in Cyberculture," in *An Introduction to Cyberculture,* ed. David Bell (London: Routledge, 2001), 137–62.

18. Balsamo, *Technologies of the Gendered Body,* 140.

19. Bell, "Bodies in Cyberculture."

20. For an excellent compilation of resources on women and technology, refer to the database of the Center for Women and Information Technology, University of Maryland, http://www.umbc.edu/cwit/ (accessed Feb. 23, 2006).

21. Jodie O'Brien, "Changing the Subject," *Women and Performance: A Journal of Feminist Theory* 9, issue 17, no. 1 (2000), http://www.ucm.es/info/rqtr/biblioteca/ciber espacio%20gltb/CHANGING%20THE%20SUBJECT.pdf (accessed Feb. 22, 2006).

22. Christine Sharpe, "Racialized Fantasies on the Internet," *Signs: Journal of Women in Culture and Society* 24, no. 4 (1999): 1089–96.

23. Ibid., 1092.

24. Jennifer Light, "The Digital Landscape: New Space for Women?" *Gender, Place and Culture* 2, no. 2 (1995): 133–43.

25. The Commonwealth of Independent States is a loose alliance, formed in 1991, of twelve of the fifteen former Soviet Republics: Armenia, Azerbaijan, Belarus, Georgia, Kazakhstan, Kyrgyzstan, Moldova, Russia, Tajikistan, Turkmenistan, Ukraine, and Uzbekistan.—Eds.

26. See for example, Lenka Simerska and Laterina Fialova, *Bridging the Gender Digital Divide: A Report on Gender and ICT in Central and Eastern Europe and the Commonwealth of Independent States* (Bratislava, Slovak Republic: UNDP/UNIFEM: 2004). See also Kristina Mihalec and Nevenka Sudar, *Women and Internet: Croatian Perspective* (Zagreb, Croatia: B.a.B.e., 2004).

27. Donna Hughes, "The 'Natasha' Trade: The Transnational Shadow Market of Trafficking in Women," *Journal of International Affairs* 53, no. 2 (2000).

28. U.S. Immigration and Naturalization Service, *International Matchmaking Organizations.*

29. Lynn Thiesmeyer, "The West's 'Comfort Women' and the Discourse of Seduction," in *Transnational Asia Pacific: Gender, Culture and the Public Sphere,* ed. Shirley Geok-lin Lim, Larry E. Smith, and Wimal Dissanayake (Urbana: University of Illinois Press, 1999).

30. Gina Marchetti, film review of *Writing Desire* by Ursula Biemann, *Women Make Movies Catalog,* 2003, http://www.wmm.com/filmcatalog/pages/c537.shtml.

31. Tatiana Zhurzhenko, "Free Market Ideology and New Women's Identities in Post-Socialist Ukraine," *European Journal of Women's Studies,* 8, no. 1 (2001): 24–49.

32. Hughes and Denisova, "Trafficking in Women from Ukraine."

33. National Institute of Strategic Studies, "Emigration of the Ukrainian Population: Socio-Economic Aspects and Potential Consequences" (National Institute of Strategic Studies, 1993), http://www.niss.gov.ua. As a result of scarce statistics on migration from Ukraine, it is also difficult to ascertain the number of Internet brides who left the country to join their husbands. The major receiving countries, such as the United States, Germany, and the countries of Western Europe, also appear to lack information as to the numbers and places of origin of mail-order brides who arrive on their territory. With reference to the U.S., Konstantin Palchikoff states: "Reliable statistics on the number of foreign-born mail-order brides are not available. The Immigration and Naturalization Service estimated in 1999 that there were 4,000 to 5,000 such women in the United States." (Kim Palchikoff, "Unregulated Internet Matchmaking Trade Booms," *Women's eNews,* March 2, 2001, http://www.womensenews.com).

34. Olga Makhovskaya, interview, "Zamuzh za Ameriku" [To Marry America], *Radio Svoboda,* April 26, 2003, http://www.svoboda.org/programs/rt/2003/rt.042603.asp (accessed June 27, 2005).

35. See the edited volume by Barbara Ehrenreich and Arlie Russell Hochschild, *Global Woman: Nannies, Maids, and Sex Workers in the New Economy* (New York: Metropolitan Books, 2003). Although the case studies in this volume do not include Post-Soviet women, analyses of the multitude of ways in which women from developing countries are implicated in the global economy (as mail-order brides, nannies, domestics, and sex workers) offer useful analytical tools to think about the less-researched experiences of Post-Soviet women in transnational spaces who increasingly find themselves in similar roles.

36. For a detailed investigation into the factors contributing to trafficking in women from the former Soviet Union, the methods of trafficking, transit, and destination countries, see research reports on trafficking in women from Ukraine and Russia prepared by Donna Hughes. All reports are available on her website: http://www.uri.edu/artsci/wms/hughes/pubtrfrep.htm.

37. International Organization for Migration, "Information Campaign against Trafficking in Women from Ukraine—Research Report" (Geneva, Switzerland, 1999),

Svitlana Taraban

http://www.iom.int/DOCUMENTS/PUBLICATION/EN/ukr_traf_wom_res_rep.pdf.

38. Hughes, "The 'Natasha' Trade." See also Donna Hughes, *The Impact of the Use of New Communications and Information Technologies on Trafficking in Human Beings for Sexual Exploitation: The Study of Users* (Strasbourg: Council of Europe, 2001), http://www.uri.edu/artsci/wms/hughes/study_of_users.pdf (accessed August 28, 2005).

39. U.S. Department of State, *Trafficking in Persons Report* (Washington, D.C.: 2005), http://www.state.gov/g/tip/rls/tiprpt/2005.

40. Victor Malarek, *The Natashas: The New Global Sex Trade* (Toronto: Viking, 2003).

41. Michelle J. Anderson, "A License to Abuse: The Impact of Conditional Status on Female Immigrants," *Yale Law Journal* 102, no. 6 (1993): 1401–30; Lewis Kamb and Robert L. Jamieson, "Mail-Order Bride's Dream of a Better Life Ends in Death," *Seattle Post-Intelligencer*, February 2, 2001, http://seattlepi.nwsource.com/local/brid02.shtml (accessed Feb. 23, 2006).

42. Internet World Stats: Usage and Population Statistics (data as of March 2005), http://www.internetworldstats.com/europa2.htm#ua (accessed June 23, 2005).

43. United Nations Division for the Advancement of Women, "Women and the Information Revolution," *Women 2000*, no. 1 (October 1996), http://www.un.org/womenwatch/daw/public/w2cont.htm (accessed March 8, 2002).

44. Angela Me and Marie Sicat, "Statistics on Women and Men and ICT: The ECE Region" (paper presented at the Regional Symposium on Mainstreaming Gender into Economic Policies, Geneva, Switzerland, January 28–30, 2004), http://www.unece.org/oes/gender/documents/ICT%20paper.pdf?OpenAgent&DS=ENERGY/GE.1/2001/1&Lang=E (accessed July 2, 2005).

45. Paul Hediger, "3% Increase in Internet Users in Austria in Last 3 Months," *Europe Media*, 2000, at http://www.civilrights.org/issues/communication/details.cfm?id=9687 (accessed Feb. 23, 2006); L. Sang-Chul, "Digital Divide Cannot Be Solved by One Nation," *Korea Times*, June 26, 2002, http://www.hankooki.com (accessed July 20, 2003).

46. Me and Sicat, "Statistics on Women and Men and ICT," 11.

47. In addition to many works by Donna Hughes mentioned above, see also Jeff Hearn and Wendy Parkin, *Gender, Sexuality and Violence in Organizations* (London: Sage, 2001).

48. See Sharpe, "Racialized Fantasies on the Internet."

49. Ursula Biemann, *Been There and Back to Nowhere: Geschlecht in Transnationalen Orten* [Gender in Transnational Spaces] (Berlin: B—books, 2001).

50. All women's texts from the Web sites are quoted exactly as they appear online and are not edited for syntax or style. This was done in order to preserve the originality of women's writing.

51. Haldis Haukanes, "Anthropological Debates on Gender and the Post-Communist Transformation," *NORA—Nordic Journal of Women's Studies* 9, no. 1 (2001): 5–20.

52. Zhurzhenko, "Free Market Ideology and New Women's Identities in Post-Socialist Ukraine," 4.

53. Ibid, 4.

54. Ibid, 6.

55. Donna Hughes, *Prostitution Online,* http://www.uri.edu/artsci/wms/hughes/prostitution_online.pdf (accessed July 20, 2005).

56. Malcolm Waters, *Globalization* (London: Routledge, 1995).

57. Human Rights Watch. "Women's Work: Discrimination against Women in the Ukrainian Labor Force" (2003), http://www.hrw.org/reports/2003/ukraine0803 (accessed June 15, 2004).

58. United Nations Development Program, "Gender Issues in Ukraine: Challenges and Opportunities" (2003), http://www.undp.org.ua/?page=documents (accessed June 15, 2004).

59. Mariia Kotovskaia and Natal'ia Shalygina, "Love, Sex and Marriage—the Female Mirror: Value Orientation of Young Women in Russia," in *Gender, Generation and Identity in Contemporary Russia,* ed. Hilary Pilkington (London: Routledge, 1996).

60. Hilary Pilkington, " 'Youth Culture' in Contemporary Russia: Gender, Consumption and Identity," in *Gender, Generation and Identity in Contemporary Russia.*

61. International Helsinki Foundation for Human Rights, *Women 2000: An Investigation into the Status of Women's Rights in Central and South-Eastern Europe and Newly Independent States* (Helsinki, Finland: International Helsinki Foundation for Human Rights, 2000).

Does the Gender of MPs Matter in Postcommunist Politics?

The Case of the Russian Duma, 1995–2001

Iulia Shevchenko

In postcommunist Russia, the problems that women face as women have for the most part been ignored.[1] In this new situation, the problem of representation of women's interests in top government institutions becomes of utmost importance. Can the Russian political elite be responsive to women's interests? If so, which segments of the elite may be especially supportive of women's issues? This study assesses whether female legislators of the State Duma (the lower house of Russia's national parliament) are more likely to promote women's concerns than male legislators are. Although much feminist research suggests that a "critical mass" of female politicians is needed before blocking women-unfriendly policies might become possible,[2] there is also contestation over the claim that mirror representation—that is, women representing women in this case[3]—is necessary in order for interests to be addressed legislatively.

The effect of mirror representation is unlikely to be seen anytime soon in Russia, or in any political system. Indeed, in Russia, women tend to be underrepresented within elected bodies, and the cumulative effect of women politicians upon Russian government policies is limited. Therefore at present, the more appropriate question is, does the presence of women in the Russian

Duma make a difference in women's lives? Do women politicians promote more women-friendly policies, that is, policies that take into account women's interests?[4] If the number of women in the Duma increases, will they be willing and able to induce policy changes that give women more control and enable them to make more choices? I argue that increasing the number of women in the legislature is unlikely to have positive effects on women's issues unless women politicians' policy priorities are indeed women-friendly. In other words, increasing the numbers of Russian women legislators will matter only when they promote policies that go beyond the neotraditional views of contemporary Russian political parties.

Answering these crucial questions requires analyzing the effects of postcommunism in a Russian context. This study analyzes the impact of postcommunism-related factors upon female legislators' willingness and capacity to act together across ideological lines to support various women's issues. These factors pertain to new institutional practices, including the inchoate democratic institutions and competitive politics, early postcommunist electoral experience, and neotraditional gender ideology. In order to test relations between postcommunism and women politicians' behavior, I examine roll call votes for the 1995 and 1999 Dumas.

I find that gender is only a weak claimant on women parliamentarians' voting in the second half of the postcommunist decade in Russia. Women deputies tend to support only what can be argued to be women-friendly policy positions when the issues are less partisan (or when there is less partisanship in the Duma) and when these issues can be framed in terms of neotraditional gender ideology (such as issues pertaining to the family and children). The findings show that there is a limited space for women to advocate in the Duma by deploying neotraditional gender ideology, but almost no opportunity for non-essentialist feminist arguments.

Postcommunism and Neotraditionalism

In order to understand the actions of women deputies in the Duma, it is important to place postcommunism into a wider, historical context of Russia's gender politics. As argued in the introduction to this volume, the Soviet party-state monopolized control over the politics of gender in order to make it consonant with the political and economic needs of socialism. Official Soviet propaganda claimed the "woman question" was solved because women and men were declared to enjoy equal rights. Hence, women were required to participate like men in labor. But when sex differences could not be ignored, women were quickly reminded that they had "natural" responsibilities involving performing housework, taking care of children, and creating a good family atmosphere. As a result, women were frequently employed in lower-paid and lower-status positions.[5]

The late 1960s and the 1970s witnessed a limited discussion about how women could best combine their roles in production and reproduction. The discussants, however, quickly accepted the conservative views that demanded women place the family at the center of their lives. The main political organization dealing with women's issues, the Soviet Women's Committee, which could have challenged this gender traditionalism, failed to be critical of the predicament of Soviet women. The committee was generally viewed as an apologist for the regime, reinforcing the Communist Party's power.[6] With the accession of Mikhail Gorbachev to power in the Soviet Union, women's issues began to receive greater attention. However, Gorbachev's understanding of women's problems appeared to be reactionary, similar to that which had been voiced in Russia since the mid-1970s. He encouraged women to return to their "purely biological mission" involving housework and bringing up children.[7]

Although the end of Soviet rule increased women's individual freedom, postcommunism also has given rise to neotraditional attitudes toward women's "destiny."[8] As Rosalind Marsh observes, "it is now clear that democratization in Russia has not entailed the gaining by women of a political voice, since the balance has shifted even further to male dominance of the arenas of formal politics."[9] The current neotraditional gender ideology may be rooted in communist gender ideology, but it has adapted to postcommunist reality.[10] Similarly to traditionalism, neotraditionalism privatizes women's lives, but at the same time, it "justifies" its claims with reference to socioeconomic conditions that are specific to postcommunism. Postcommunist society has been affected by crisis-level unemployment, but women suffered more job losses because both state officials and employers regard them as less desirable and less efficient members of the workforce.[11]

Postcommunist policy makers have produced legislation and executive decrees stressing women's reproductive roles as crucial to survival not only of the society, but also of the nation and ethnic community.[12] Seeking to implement a pronatalist policy, the federal government offers such incentives as paid maternity leave, child allowance, and a variety of benefits in public services and housing for families with at least three children. Some of the material support provided to enable women to both work and have children might have served to increase women's rights. However, the failure at the same time to invest in sexual education and contraception makes these pronatalist social welfare policies coercive and manipulative.

Gender neotraditionalism is also bolstered by the resurgent nostalgic nationalism and religious revivals that seek to confine women to the home.[13] Negative demographic trends—declining life expectancy and birth rate, numerous abortions, late marriage, and a high divorce rate—provoke a nagging sensation of "a dying nation" and a reemphasis on women's reproductive functions. This postcommunist gender discourse limits the ability and willingness of female politicians to protect nontraditional women's interests, because by accentuating these issues, women politicians may alienate themselves from the mainstream political process.

Early Postcommunist Electoral Experience

The collapse of the Soviet party-state led to not only the rise of neotraditionalism, but also the emergence of competitive political space and, as Johnson and Robinson argue in the introduction, the greater opportunity to experiment with a broader array of gender ideologies. Greater political openness gave women more options and choices in their lives, and this change affected Russia's elite. In the late 1980s, the Soviet Women's Committee adopted a more critical stance toward women's issues, facilitating a transformation of the agency into the organizational core of the new women-based political movement called Women of Russia. A leader of the movement, Ekaterina Lakhova, served as an advisor to President Boris Yeltsin, and also chaired a special commission dealing with women and family that was attached to the president's office.

In the 1993 national legislative elections, Women of Russia won 8.1 percent of the vote and formed its own faction in the 1993–1995 State Duma. In the 1995 parliamentary elections, the movement garnered only 4.6 percent of the vote and, failing to cross the five-percent threshold, lost parliamentary representation in the Duma.

The programmatic message delivered by the movement was ambiguous. On the one hand, Women of Russia sought to sustain the image of a "moderate" party.[14] Toward that end, the leaders of the movement publicly denied that there was anything "feminist" about them, and the movement's electoral programs were generally conformed to gender neotraditionalism. The strategy of adherence to neotraditionalism, which has been popular among Russians regardless of their sex, did not make the movement's electoral base more heterogeneous. Survey research has demonstrated that up to 90 percent of Women of Russia's voters were female.[15] In the Duma, Women of Russia stressed that it was not close to any political party and had no political orientation. Its members occasionally collaborated with various Duma parties, depending on the issue under consideration.[16] On the other hand, the movement did go beyond asking for price ceilings on basic goods, including baby food. The movement (and especially its radical wing, including Ekaterina Lakhova) actively supported the Federal Family Planning Program that significantly expanded the availability of contraception and access to sexual education and family planning counseling across the country.

The attempt to combine both centrist image and feminist ideas resulted in the lack of a recognizable ideological profile, which probably was the most important cause of the movement's failure in 1995. Although abortion has been the major method of birth control for many Russian women, there is strong opposition to family planning methods. A large segment of Russian government and society has been extremely suspicious of family planning, which it sees as a direct cause of low fertility in the country. Complicating these matters is strong resistance, dating from communist days, to formal education on sexuality.[17] The hostility of many Russians toward new gender issues, such as birth control and family planning, suggested that feminism could not be an electorally advantageous strategy in Russia. At the same time, adherence to centrism could not help the movement to reenter the Duma. Many other parties, which shared the centrist component of Women of Russia's policy agenda, had better chances to gain representation in the national parliament, which apparently discouraged strategically thinking voters from supporting the movement.

How did the early postcommunist electoral experiences influence the actions of women deputies in the 1995 and 1999 Duma? First, Women of Russia's failure to develop a consistent gender-based ideology meant that "women's issues" continue to be understood in terms of women's traditional roles. (There are Russian feminist groups that define women's issues more widely, but these groups are politically marginal.) In this context, if mainstream women politicians were to band together to support women's interests, one can safely predict that these issues would not go beyond traditional women's concerns. If proposed policies contravene neotraditionalism, women are likely to split over them. As a result, women politicians play a predominantly defensive role.

Second, the electoral failure of the Women of Russia political movement apparently convinced contemporary female politicians that stressing the "gender component" in their political stances may not be politically advantageous. They may easily neglect not only new but also traditional issues if political context encourages them to do so. Thus, strong commitment to women's issues has not developed. In sum, the early postcommunist experience, while paradoxically characterized by the first successful women's party in the world, has weakened gender as a motivator of women politicians' actions.

Theory of Parliamentary Practices and Women Politicians' Voting

Both postcommunist political discourse and electoral experience have discouraged attention to the new problems of women. What is the role of recently established democratic institutions, such as political parties, themselves also a product of postcommunism, in the process? Women's political representation shriveled after 1989 when rubber stamp parliaments were transformed into loci of real power. In the Duma elected in 1995, only 46 of 450 deputies were women (10.2 percent). In the Duma elected in 1999 the number of women dropped to 34 (7.7 percent).[18]

The number of women legislators may affect policy output because the political priorities of female legislators are found to differ from or even conflict with those of male legislators. Studies of Western parliaments have revealed that legislatures with higher percentages of female representation pass more bills pertaining to women's issues than do those with lower percentages of women.[19] However, an increase in the number of women legislators does not necessarily lead to a legislature devoted to women's issues.[20] Globally, political party affiliation has proven to be the most prominent divider among representatives. In a legislature with cohesive political parties, female legislators respond to cues provided by their party, even when voting on women's issues.[21] It is in these systems that female representatives' ability to cross party boundaries to protect women's interests is most problematic. In presidential systems such as Russia, on the other hand, female legislators are less restricted in their activities since there is no institutionalized need for party cohesion.[22] While regime type provides the general institutional framework within which a legislature's internal structure develops, studies also show how the political and electoral context can also shape the structure of a legislature and thus influence female legislators' autonomy from their parties.

The "gender gap," the manifestation of different perspectives between women and men, also varies across different types of women's issues. The prominence of gender-based voting by women legislators depends on the cohesiveness of party voting, which can vary across issues. Party voting is most cohesive on issues that divide party electorates and thus reinforce the dominant partisan conflict.[23] Women's-issue bills vary in the degree to which they can be related to partisan competition. Studies demonstrate that if a bill fits into a partisan conflict, legislative voting on this bill is driven by party rather than gender. But as soon as a bill ceases to match the partisan dimension, voting may be influenced by socially constructed gender.[24]

In the rest of this chapter, I investigate the ability of female deputies in the Russian Duma to address different types of women's concerns by voting together across party lines.[25] Voting patterns will be analyzed in several policy domains: social protection and health issues, neotraditionalist protection for women, and new gender issues. In the specific social, historical, and cultural context of postcommunist Russia these issues can be defined as "women's issues," although in a global context, some of them may not be essentially women's issues. The chronological scope of the statistical part of the study is 1995–2001. It encompasses the life span of the 1995–1999 Duma and the first half of the term of the Duma elected in December 1999. Based on these studies of women parliamentarians' behaviors, I hypothesize that the likelihood of women deputies to support women's issues depends upon the legislative contexts and issue profile.

The Legislative Context of the 1995 and 1999 Dumas

The Duma elections of 1995 resulted in victory for the left-wing opposition to President Yeltsin, but also a weak party structure within the legislature. The left wing of the Duma, represented by the Communist Party (CPRF) and its close allies, held slightly less than a legislative majority, while Our Home Is

Russia (OHIR), the only Duma party clearly associated with the government, gained less than 15 percent of Duma seats. To cope with the situation of divided control, Russian executives minimized partisan appeal and curried the favor of some opposition legislators. The inter-branch conflict was successfully managed at the expense of party cohesion and legislative discipline.

Another factor weakening parties after the 1995 election was the presence of competing centers of power. To perform its law-making function, the Duma has developed a system of strong and specialized committees to serve as centrifugal forces that counter the centripetal tendencies of parties. Furthermore, Russia is a split electoral system, meaning that only half of the 450 Duma deputies are elected through a party-list proportional representation system.

How were women deputies represented in the Duma's organizational structures? In contrast to the previous Duma elected in 1993, the failure of the Women of Russia political movement to surpass the proportional representation threshold meant that women deputies did not form a gender-based faction. Women were, however, represented in parliamentary leadership: Svetlana Goriacheva, a CPRF leader, was a deputy chair of the Duma, and women chaired Duma committees on women, family, and youth, and on ecology. But these committees occupy rather low positions in the informal Duma committee hierarchy, dealing with budget-poor social issues. Thus, chairmanship appointments marginalized women against a male majority that addressed such matters as budget affairs, economic policies, industry, and privatization—issues that were widely regarded as "more important."

Since 1993, the general institutional design of the Russian state has remained relatively unchanged; however, the legislative contexts of the 1995 and 1999 Dumas were substantially different. The 1999 Duma elections were held in the period when Yeltsin's successor, Vladimir Putin, was experiencing a dramatic increase in popularity. On this wave, a new, overtly pro-governmental electoral association called Unity emerged as the second-runner in the races and formed the core of the pro-presidential legislative coalition. As a result, inter-branch relations changed. After the 1999 election, the executive could afford to maximize partisan appeals and disregard the interests of the opposition or of those legislative parties that it considered situational opponents. Members of the pro-presidential camp, especially Unity, were aware that their standing required greater legislative discipline.

Several other factors also facilitated party power in the 1999 Duma. The committee reconfiguration that occurred in 2000 undermined the accumulation of personal expertise on policies and, hence, the personal resources that would enable deputies to counter the impact of electoral associations. Moreover, the pro-presidential coalition possessed less legislative professionalism, and its members were less able to operate independently of party leaders. In the 1999 Duma, therefore, party voting was more cohesive than in the previous Duma.

Although overall female representation dropped between 1995 and 1999, women deputies were more widely represented in the legislature's steering body and organizational structures in the 1999 Duma. Liubov' Sliska, a Unity member, was the first deputy chair of the Duma, while Irina Khakamada, a leader of the right-wing (pro-reform) Union of Right Forces, was one of the deputy chairs of the legislature. Women chaired three committees: on women, family, and youth; on the problems of the North and Far East; and on ethics. As it was in the 1995 Duma, women tended to chair committees with less power. Indeed, the committees on women and on North and Far East affairs were the least sought-after among Duma legislators: as few as six legislators initially decided to participate in each of the committees. In comparison, the budget affairs committee was preferred by fifty-one deputies. Thus, the distribution of committee chairmanship demonstrated that there was a consensus within the Duma's male majority regarding "appropriate" women's interests: family, youth, ethics, ecology, and concern for people living in distant territories of Russia were amongst them. From this perspective, women were viewed as caretakers of the society as a whole and, specifically, inhabitants of the socially and economically deprived distant areas of the country.

Legislation Concerning Women: The Set of Variables

Because, as I described above, issue profile also impacts the role of gender in determining parliamentarians' voting, this study examines three sets of issues for which gender-based differences are likely to emerge: protection of society as a whole, neotraditional women's concerns, and some of the non-material well-being concerns. While the first and second types of issues deal with budgetary investments in respective social sectors, the third policy domain addresses more general aspects of life quality. All three types of issues are gendered, although to varying extent. From the dominant male perspective, the "importance" of these issues depends on the extent to which they tap into the partisan conflict. Most partisan issues are regarded as "most important."

The first dependent variable is an index of roll call votes on social protection bills.[26] This domain includes such issues as social security programs, unemployment compensation, aid to agriculture, and the like. These issues correspond to a "soft" version of neotraditionalism that portrays women as caretakers of the society as a whole. At the same time, these issues define partisan conflicts as well. The construction of the index includes two steps. First, Duma deputies' votes on each of the bills are ascribed dummy values: left-wing and right-wing positions are coded as 1 and 0, respectively. If a deputy abstained from voting on a given issue, this position is coded as 0.5. Second, the average of these values is calculated for each legislator. To compare voting results for the 1995 and 1999 Dumas, two different sets of indexes are calculated. The total numbers of bills analyzed for each of the Dumas are eighteen and sixteen, respectively.[27] For the 1995 Duma, only legislators who voted on at least fifteen of the eighteen bills are included in the study. For the 1999

Duma, I include only those legislators who voted on at least thirteen of the sixteen bills. I analyze roll call votes for different periods of the Dumas' term rather than for one particular session.

With women cast as the caretakers of the home, children and family matters are often constructed as women's issues. Thus, the second dependent variable is an index of roll call votes on these neotraditional women's issues, such as child care and child support, benefits to citizens with children, pregnancy benefits and pregnancy leave, and reduced taxes for families with many children. These bills also fit into partisan cleavage since all of them deal with protectionist measures. However, they divide party electorates to a lesser extent than do social protection bills. This happens because neotraditional women's issues are in the line with Russia's pronatalism, which is popular among both elites and "ordinary" people. Paternalistic expectations regarding family and child protection remain strong even among those Russians who are neoliberal-minded in other respects. An index of roll call votes on the domestic issues is constructed similarly to the first dependent variable. Positions supportive of and opposed to protection for women in the domestic space are coded 1 and 0, respectively. The total numbers of bills analyzed for the 1995 and 1999 Dumas are fifteen and eleven, respectively. The votes of only those legislators who voted on at least twelve of the fifteen bills and nine of the eleven bills are examined in the study.

The next two dependent variables relate to nonmaterial aspects of life. There were few bills with such profiles that related specifically to the women's agenda. Some of these bills matched a partisan dimension, while others did not. For the 1995 Duma, the selected bills were aimed at "protecting women's dignity" by enhancing governmental control over the circulation of pornographic materials. Some scholars believe that articulating what could be seen as pornography gives us something to set against the increasing masculinization of sex.[28] However, feminist opposition to pornography stresses women's sexual subjugation through pornography.[29] Pointing to pornography's specifically gender-based harms as well as its more general, community-based harms, the proponents of censorship propose to channel legal power to regulate pornography.[30] Some believe that women in Russia are denigrated by the representation of women in pornography as sex objects.[31] As Johnson and Robinson argue, this sexualized gender ideology is the flip side to neotraditionalism. Therefore placing pornography under strict control can be seen as an important step toward de-masculinization of the Russian society. The pro-censorship position is ascribed value 1. From an opposite perspective, legal power cannot be used to protect public morality. This position is coded 0.

The last dependent variable pertains to the environmental health of the society. Eco-feminists argue that there is a link between the violation of nature and marginalization of women.[32] Cast as caregivers in the society, women might be expected to place a priority on ecological aspects of life quality.[33] (At the same time, this supposition relies on essentialist arguments not unlike those of neotraditionalism.) At the least, ecology concerns did not bother the 1999 Duma's male majority: the legislature adopted two anti-environmental bills permitting the import of spent nuclear fuel onto Russian territory. Votes for and against these bills are assigned dummy values 0 and 1, respectively.

There are four independent variables in the study. The first variable is the sex of a legislator. It is coded 1 for women and 0 for men. Second, to investigate statistically the diversity of political differences among women, I introduce a control variable that reflects the effect of constituency connection. The impact of constituency is similar to that of gender: it should become more relevant if party power declines. One of the most important bases of legislators' constituency support is ideological congruence between representatives' attitudes and constituents' political preferences. Therefore to measure the impact of constituency connection, I use the share of the votes gained by the CPRF in a region in the 1995 and 1999 Duma elections by party lists. Deputies on party lists (from the half of the Duma elected through proportional representation) are assigned the share of the vote gained by the CPRF in the federal district: 22.3 and 24.3 percents in the 1995 and 1999 Duma elections, respectively. Legislators elected from single-member constituencies are assigned the share of the vote received by the CPRF not in the given constituency but in the region as a whole. This reduces the distorting effects of candidates' personal popularity.

The third and fourth independent variables identify factors that counter the impacts of gender and constituency upon legislative voting. One of these variables is legislative party ideology. For the 1995 and 1999 Dumas, it is coded 1 for the left-wing parties and 0 for the other Duma parties, including independents. The last independent variable indicates the link between a legislative party and the government. While the Duma does not take part in the formation of the government, members of pro-presidential parties are often appointed to government positions, which creates what will be further referred to as "government linkage" (although government members must give up their legislative seats). This variable is coded 1 for OHIR and Unity members, and 0 for other legislators.

This study offers three hypotheses specifying interrelations between legislative contexts, issue profiles, and women legislators' voting patterns. These include:

1. Women legislators do not band together to support social protection issues because these issues are strongly defined by partisan conflict. Rather, women legislators split into ideologically diverse subgroups and vote in accordance with their party's ideology. Or in other words, party trumps gender.

2. Women may vote together on neotraditional issues because such issues polarize the Duma to a lesser extent. However, as legislative parties become stronger, they do not allow legislators to cross party lines. In other words, the impact of these issues' profile, which gen-

erally facilitates cross-party women's coalitions, is overwhelmed by the legislative context.

3. Women from different parties may vote in favor of some of the non-material well-being concerns, as long as these issues do not match the principal partisan dimension. However, if these non-economic issues tap into the partisan conflict, gender differences disappear. Even in a less partisan legislative context, voting on such issues is determined by party rather than gender.

Findings: Women's Votes in the 1995 and 1999 Dumas

The goal of this section is to investigate statistically whether female representatives in the Duma are more supportive of women's issues than are their male colleagues. Multiple regression analysis was used to determine if sex of legislators has a statistically significant effect in the presence of other important influences on representatives' voting behavior.[34] Table 6.1 presents the results of the regression analysis for the 1995 Duma. Model 1 shows that party ideology is the major driving force of the vote on the social protection issues. The government linkage variable affects legislative voting to a significant but lesser extent. The impacts of local political preferences as well as gender are insignificant. Hence there is no uniform women's position on the social protection issues. Rather, different subgroups of women display varying voting behaviors. These behaviors are determined by both party and personal ideological priorities.

Do female legislators in the Duma address women's concerns in the domestic sphere? In the Russian context, the neotraditional concerns tend to unify party electorates, thus reducing the intensity of partisan conflict. According to Model 2, although party ideology substantially influences legislative voting on the domestic issues, its impact is not as strong as on the social protection issues. The analysis reveals that the left-wing legislative parties that traditionally advocate protectionist state measures appear to be most supportive of these women's issues. Opposition leaders repeatedly express concerns about the effects the negative demographic trends may have on the development of the national economy—for example, how a shrinking working-age population will support a growing number of elderly citizens. The opposition depicts population decline as the direct outcome of market reform and even as a conspiracy aimed at destroying the Russian state. Therefore measures aimed at boosting fertility rates, particularly, through increasing state support of family and children, are strongly welcomed by the communists.

At the same time, the statistical evidence confirms that gender moderates the effect of party on legislative voting on domestic women's issues. Female legislators tend to support neotraditional policies irrespective of their party's ideology. Even the right-wing women downplayed their ideological preferences by supporting paternalist expectations regarding family protection. This

Table 6.1. Determinants of legislative voting in the 1995 Duma.

Independent variables	Model 1 / social protection issues	Model 2 / traditional women's issues	Model 3 / new gender issues
Gender	0.004 (0.015)	0.035** (0.015)	−0.01 (0.04)
Party ideology	0.25*** (0.01)	0.14*** (0.01)	−0.38*** (0.03)
Government linkage	−0.20*** (0.01)	−0.02* (0.01)	0.04 (0.04)
Constituency connection	0.001 (0.001)	0.002*** (0.001)	0.004** (0.002)
Intercept	0.65*** (0.02)	0.73*** (0.02)	0.77*** (0.05)
Number of cases	414	413	413
Adjusted R-squared	0.78	0.43	0.38

Note: OLS regression analysis with unstandardized beta coefficients. Standard errors are in the parentheses. *** - sig p. 0.00; ** - sig p. 0.05; * - sig p. 0.1

is not to say that all women in the Duma voted in support of the neotraditional policies. But among the female segment of the parliament, voting in favor of these issues occurred much more frequently than among the male majority. Male legislators demonstrated greater party loyalty and, as a rule, voted in accordance with their party ideology. The 1995 Duma's less partisan context allowed female legislators to transcend party boundaries to view women as a specific constituency whose needs are to be addressed. Similar to many other women politicians, female deputies to the Duma gave higher priority to their constituency needs. Duma women's responsiveness to local concerns is facilitated by these legislators' greater personal resourcefulness. To be elected, a female candidate must often display substantial electoral superiority over her male rivals. Thus very unequal electoral conditions serve as a filter for the most politically experienced and resourceful women.[35]

Model 3 of Table 6.1 reveals that the anti-pornography bills sharply divide women deputies. Party ideology is the best predictor of legislative voting on these issues. While the right-wing parties were strongly supportive of the bills, the communist opposition was opposed even to placing them on the legislative agenda. The communists' shift toward an explicitly nationalist ideological stance reinforced their moral traditionalism that viewed the Russian nation as firmly adhered to family values, which left no space for such things as pornography. From the left-wing perspective, the adoption of these bills would propagandize rather than restrict pornography. The communists preferred to close their eyes to the violation of the rights of Russian women, who are constantly abused by the open circulation of pornography, for the sake of preserving the traditionalist image of the society.

The statistical results show that constituency connection substantially affects legislative voting on moral issues. At the same time, the results reveal a tricky tendency: the higher the local support of the CPRF, the more likely it is that the region's representatives support these bills. To account for this finding, it may be noticed that economics feeds into Russians' electoral behavior. To a certain extent, the support of the CPRF is justified with reference to bad economic conditions in a region. The poorer the management of the regional economy, the more it is likely that the censorship problem is perceived as one of the most important. As a CPRF male representative supportive of the bills put this, "thousands of people are forced to work in the evenings, work in additional jobs, while their neglected children watch television. But you prefer to stand for supreme morality and do nothing to at least partly eliminate this disgrace."[36] Thus some of the communists realized that their party's moral traditionalism conflicted with their constituents' interests. The less partisan legislative context allowed legislators to take into account not only their party's ideological position but also constituency needs, even if these factors contradicted each other.

While constituency connection proves to be an influential factor affecting voting attitudes on morality issues, gender plays no role in determining a legislator's position. In other words, there is an ideological conflict between different subgroups of women. A few female members of the CPRF not only strongly supported the anti-pornography bills but also actively sponsored them. However, the majority of the left-wing women were similar to their male counterparts in their position on the pornography problem. It cannot be said that the left-wing women readily disregarded women's interests. But they tended to understand these interests in terms of left-wing ideology. As a left-wing female legislator argued, "today in our country there is no circulation of these [pornographic] materials; as soon as the bill will be adopted, we will introduce the circulation."[37] Another communist woman also saw the problem in strictly partisan terms, insisting that "the true reason [of pornography] is the unruliness of *glasnost'*, the propaganda of depravity . . . with the direct participation of the authorities."[38]

This finding reveals that women's solidarity in voting on the traditionalist bills should be taken with a grain of salt. Uniform voting is a positive sign showing that women politicians, in principle, can come together to protect common interests. But when women's cooperation is confined to the protection of their domestic interests, it reinforces rather than challenges neotraditional gender ideology. In other words, it is not that the support of such neotraditional policies as child allowances conflicts with women's interests. It is that such policies are insufficient for the advancement of women's rights without social welfare and protection of women's dignity in the mix.

Could the 1999 Duma's women address women's interests? Table 6.2 presents the results of the regression analysis for the 1999 Duma. Model 1 confirms that party ideology is the strongest predictor of legislative voting on the social protection issues. The government linkage is also a significant indicator of how the legislators in this study voted on the social protection bills. In

Table 6.2. Determinants of legislative voting in the 1999 Duma.

Independent variables	Model 1 / social protection issues	Model 2 / traditional women's issues	Model 3 / ecology protection issues
Gender	0.009 (0.014)	0.001 (0.015)	0.19** (0.07)
Party ideology	0.38*** (0.01)	0.07*** (0.01)	0.07 (0.05)
Government linkage	0.33*** (0.01)	0.04*** (0.01)	0.39*** (0.05)
Constituency connection	0.000 (0.001)	0.001 (0.001)	0.005 (0.004)
Intercept	0.44*** (0.02)	0.87*** (0.02)	0.32*** (0.09)
Number of cases	431	431	431
Adjusted R-squared	0.91	0.17	0.12

Note: OLS regression analysis with unstandardized beta coefficients. Standard errors are in the parentheses. *** - sig p. 0.00; ** - sig p. 0.05.

comparison with the 1995 Duma, the impacts of both variables appear much stronger. At the same time, the impact of constituency diminishes markedly. Indeed, there is no room for Duma women's individualistic behavior. The statistical results demonstrate that gender does not influence legislative voting on the protectionism issues. The results of Model 2 reveal that the strong partisan context of the 1999 Duma did not allow female legislators to transcend party boundaries even to vote in favor of women's domestic interests. In fact, many of the neotraditional policies debated by this Duma were adopted. Indeed, by the end of the 1990s, social climate in Russia became more conservative and pronatalist than previously.[39] For instance, concerns about Russia's low fertility rate and population decline prompted the Duma to discontinue federal funding for family planning services in 1999, which significantly reduced access to contraception and reproductive counseling.[40] Women legislators were deprived of any possibility to either express their opinion on neotraditional policies or reverse the Duma's decision to cancel the Family Planning Program.

These findings suggest that gender did not make a difference in the 1999 Duma. But as soon as policy issues cease to fit into the one-dimensional left-right space, the picture changes drastically. The statistical results of Model 3 show that party ideology did not influence legislative voting on the environmental bills. Indeed, Duma debates on these issues demonstrated that while right-wing deputies were against the importation of spent nuclear fuel into Russia, Unity and its allies were strongly in favor of the shipment of the waste. Unity's position was also supported by the communists: the direction of the sign of the coefficient for the party ideology variable indicates that left-wing parties tended to support anti-environmental bills. The results indicate that the crucial role in determining legislators' positions regarding these bills was played by government linkage: Unity members clearly rallied around the president and his government on these votes.

Insofar as different Duma camps failed to reach an ideological consensus regarding these issues, voting was not strictly regulated by party ideology. Therefore deputies gained an opportunity to behave more independently. This was a critical test for women legislators' policy priorities. The statistical results confirm that female deputies proved able to transcend party boundaries to vote against the anti-environmental policies. Gender strongly influenced legislative voting on these issues. As studies from a comparative perspective have shown, female deputies, who often perceive support from environmentalists as a constituency group,[41] give priority to environmental issues.[42] This tendency is also characteristic of women deputies to the Duma. Questions of the non-economic quality of life cannot gain substantial political support in Russia while the country is experiencing economic hardship. But even in such unfavorable conditions, the Duma's female minority has become a specific political group able to give priority to environmental issues. The political implications of this finding are of crucial importance. It may be plausibly speculated that if the share of female representatives in the Duma were greater, these anti-environmental bills would face much stronger opposition on the floor. At the same time, as with the domestic protection bills, the ecology bills are also consonant with the neotraditional vision of women as caretakers.

Conclusion

This study investigates the impact of postcommunist realities upon the political behavior of female legislators in the 1995 and 1999 Russian State Dumas. The study shows the weakness of gender as an explanation of the votes of Duma deputies. The finding is explained with reference to the fact that postcommunism has created unfavorable conditions for women's political representation. This happens not only because the number of women within elected bodies has dropped. Another important factor is the strengthening of neotraditional views toward women that penetrates Russian society from masses to elites. The early postcommunist electoral experience has also contributed to the relative insignificance of women's issues for female politicians. Although the Women of Russia movement did make women's voice louder, if only temporarily, in the national parliament, the neotraditionalist tendencies were not reversed. In addition, the strengthening of political parties into a source of power in the Russian parliament tends to mitigate the impact of gender upon legislative voting.

My study shows that such factors as legislative context and issue profile can affect the relevance of gender to legislative voting. Although the less partisan 1995 Duma context facilitated the active representation of women, the level of female politicians' commitment to women's issues depended on issue profile. Such policy questions as social protection and control over pornography sharply divided female deputies into different subgroups. Only neo-traditionalist issues dealing with children and family matters tended to downplay partisan preferences. Women banded together to vote in favor of these interests irrespective of their party ideology. This study suggests that if party power continues to increase, as it did in the 1999 Duma, female legislators will be even less likely to support women's traditional issues, and more likely to vote in accordance with their party ideology. Legislators are subjected to party discipline that wipes out the gender gap. However, the gender plays a substantial role in determining legislators' votes on bills that do not tap into partisan cleavage, such as ecology issues. In sum, the comparative analysis of the two Dumas reveals that there are at least two policy domains that may catalyze a gender gap in legislative voting: family protection and nuclear safety. Both policy domains, however, closely relate to the neotraditionalist gender ideology. Therefore the current Russian parliament is unlikely to pioneer de-feminization and de-masculinization of the society.

NOTES

Research for this paper was supported by the Research and Writing Initiative of the Program on Global Security and Sustainability of the John D. and Catherine T. MacArthur Foundation, Grant # 01-68437-000. I would like to express my deep gratitude to Yulii A. Rybakov for his help in data collecting. I would also like to thank Karen Dawisha, Grigorii V. Golosov, and anonymous reviewers for their valuable comments on the draft of the manuscript. None of these persons is responsible for the views expressed.

1. Sue Bridger, Kathryn Pinnick, and Rebecca Kay, *No More Heroines? Russia, Women, and the Market* (London: Routledge, 1996).

2. See, for instance, Michael B. Berkman and Robert E. O'Connor, "Do Women Legislators Matter? Female Legislators and State Abortion Policy," *American Politics Quarterly* 21, no. 1 (1993): 102–24, and Sue Thomas, *How Women Legislate* (New York: Oxford University Press, 1994). However, the question of the exact size of the "critical mass" remains unanswered. Some studies use the 15 percent cutoff, while others conclude that it should be closer to 30 percent of legislative corps. See Rosabeth M. Kanter, "Some Effects of Proportions on Group Life: Skewed Sex Ratios and Responses to Token Women," *American Journal of Sociology* 82, no. 5 (1977): 965–90; Mark Considine and Iva Ellen Deutchman, "Instituting Gender: State Legislators in Australia and the United States," *Women and Politics* 16, no. 4 (1996): 1–19.

3. Anne Phillips, *Politics of Presence* (Oxford: Clarendon Press, 1995); Iris Marion Young, *Justice and the Politics of Difference* (Princeton, N.J.: Princeton University Press, 1990); Jane Mansbridge, "Should Blacks Represent Blacks and Women Represent Women? A Contingent 'Yes,'" *Journal of Politics* 61, no. 3 (1999): 628–57; Jane Mansbridge, "Rethinking Representation," *American Political Science Review* 97, no. 4 (2003): 515–28; Robert E. Goodin, "Representing Diversity," *British Journal of Political Science* 34, no. 3 (2004): 453–69.

4. Kathleen B. Jones, "Citizenship in a Woman-Friendly Polity," *Journal of Women in Culture and Society* 15, no. 4 (1990): 781–812.

5. Ol'ga A. Khasbulatova, "Obzor opyta sovetskoi gosudarstvennoi politiki v ot-noshenii zhenshchin" [A Review of the Experience of Soviet State Policies toward Women], in *Gendernaia rekonstruktsiia politicheskikh sistem* [Gender Reconstruction of Political Systems], ed. N. M. Stepanova and E. V. Kochkina (St. Petersburg: Aleteiia, 2004), 397–421.

6. Mary Buckley, "Adaptation of the Soviet Women's Committee: Deputies' Voices from Women of Russia," in *Post-Soviet Women: From the Baltic to Central Asia*, ed. Mary Buckley (Cambridge: Cambridge University Press, 1997), 157–85.

7. On Russian women during perestroika see Gail Lapidus, "Gender and Restruc-turing: The Impact of Perestroika and Its Aftermath on Soviet Women," in *Democratic Reform and the Position of Women in Transitional Economies*, ed. Valentine M. Mogha-dam (Oxford: Clarendon Press, 1993), 137–61.

8. Tat'iana Klimenkova, "What Does Our New Democracy Offer Society?" in *Women in Russia: A New Era in Russian Feminism*, ed. Anastasia Posadskaya and trans. Kate Clark (London: Verso, 1994), 14–36.

9. Rosalind Marsh, "Women in Contemporary Russia and the Former Soviet Union," in *Women, Ethnicity, and Nationalism: The Politics of Transition*, ed. Rick Wilford and Robert L. Miller (London: Routledge, 1998), 101.

10. Anastasia Posadskaya, *Women in Russia*; Valerie Sperling, "Gender Politics and the State during Russia's Transition Period," in *Gender, Politics and the State*, ed. Vicky Randall and Georgina Waylen (London: Routledge, 1998), 143–66.

11. Vitalina Koval, "Women and Work in Russia," in *Women in Contemporary Russia*, ed. Vitalina Koval (Providence: Berghahn Books, 1995), 17–33; Lynne Att-wood, "The Post-Soviet Woman in the Move to the Market: A Return to Domesticity and Dependence?" in *Women in Russia and Ukraine*, ed. Rosalind Marsh (Cambridge: Cambridge University Press, 1996), 255–66.

12. Among them there were: federal program "Safe Maternity, 1995–1997" (1994); presidential decree "On Basic Directions of the State Family Policy" (1996); the State Duma's resolution "On Urgent Measures Improving Health of Women and Children in Russia" (1999); governmental resolution "The Concept of Russia's Demo-graphic Development until 2015" (2001); and also many laws.

13. Rebecca Kay, "Images of an Ideal Woman: Perceptions of Russian Woman-hood through the Media, Education, and Women's Own Eyes," in *Post-Soviet Women: From the Baltic to Central Asia*, ed. Mary Buckley (Cambridge: Cambridge University Press, 1997), 77–98.

14. Laura Belin and Robert W. Orttung, *The Russian Parliamentary Elections of 1995: The Battle for the Duma* (Armonk, N.Y.: M. E. Sharpe, 1997).

15. Wendy Slater, " 'Women of Russia' and Women's Representation in Russian Politics," in *Russia in Transition*, ed. David Lane (New York: Longman, 1995), 76–90; Grigorii V. Golosov, "Political Parties, Electoral Systems, and Women's Representation in the Regional Legislative Assemblies of Russia, 1995–1998," *Party Politics* 7, no. 1 (2001): 45–68.

16. Buckley, "Adaptation of the Soviet Women's Committee," 169.

17. Michelle Rivkin-Fish, *Women's Health in Post-Soviet Russia: The Politics of Intervention* (Bloomington: Indiana University Press, 2005); A. Popov and Henry P. David, "Russian Federation and USSR Successor States," in *From Abortion to Con-traception: A Resource to Public Policies and Reproductive Behavior in Central and Eastern Europe from 1917 to the Present*, ed. Henry P. David (Westport, Conn.: Green-

wood Press, 1999), 223–77; Julie DaVanzo and Clifford Grammich, *Dire Demographics: Population Trends in the Russian Federation* (Santa Monica, Calif.: RAND, 2001).

18. Data sources: *Vybory deputatov Gosudarstvennoi Dumy 1995: Electoral'naia statistika* [The 1995 Elections of the Deputies of the State Duma: Electoral Statistics] (Moscow: Ves' Mir, 1996), 237–40; *Vybory deputatov Gosudarstvennoi Dumy Federal'nogo sobraniia Rossiiskoi Federatsii 1999: Electoral'naia statistika* [The 1999 Elections of the Deputies of the Federal Assembly of the Russian Federation: Electoral Statistics] (Moscow: Ves' Mir, 2000), 235.

19. Debra L. Dodson et al., *Voices, Views, Votes: The Impact of Women in the 103rd Congress* (New Brunswick, N.J.: Center for the American Women and Politics, 1995); Susan J. Carroll, Debra L. Dodson, and Ruth B. Mandel, *The Impact of Women in Public Office: An Overview* (New Brunswick, N.J.: Center for the American Women and Politics, 1991); Thomas, *How Women Legislate*; Michelle A. Saint-Germain, "Does Their Difference Make a Difference? The Impact of Women on Public Policy in the Arizona Legislature," *Social Science Quarterly* 70, no. 4 (1989): 956–98; Elizabeth A. Segal and Stephanie Brzuzy, "Gender and Congressional Voting: A Legislative Analysis," *Journal of Women and Social Work* 10, no. 1 (1995): 8–23.

20. Considine and Deutchman, "Instituting Gender."

21. Pippa Norris, "Women Politicians: Transforming Westminster?" *Parliamentary Affairs* 49, no. 1 (1996): 89–102.

22. Michele L. Swers, "Are Women More Likely to Vote for Women's Issue Bills than Their Male Colleagues?" *Legislative Studies Quarterly* 23, no. 3 (1998): 435–48.

23. Paul Allen Beck, *Party Politics in America*, 8th ed. (New York: Longman, 1996), 323–25.

24. Political scientists who study legislative behavior often use the term "gender" when, as we understand it, they are referring to sex.—Eds.

25. An earlier interpretation of some of this data was published in Iulia Shevchenko, "Who Cares about Women's Problems? Female Legislators in the 1995 and 1999 Russian State Dumas," *Europe-Asia Studies* 54, no. 8 (2002): 1201–22.

26. In this study, the term "bill" includes not only federal laws but also legislative resolutions, which are an important component of the Duma's legislative activity.

27. The reason for selection of the eighteen and sixteen social protection issue bills is purely methodological. To make comprehensive inferences regarding voting on social protection and women's issue bills, it is necessary to analyze comparable numbers of both types of floor votes. Only a few women's issue bills were considered by both Dumas, and the majority of these bills are included in the study. Hence the limited but comparable numbers of bills dealing with protectionism.

28. Alison Fell, "Language and the Body," *Critical Quarterly* 37, no. 4 (1995): 60–65; Alan Soble, *Pornography: Marxism, Feminism, and the Future of Sexuality* (New Haven, Conn.: Yale University Press, 1986).

29. Chilla Bulbeck, "'Women Are Exploited Way Too Often': Feminist Rhetorics at the End of Equality," *Australian Feminist Studies* 20, no. 46 (2005): 65–76.

30. Lynn Mills Eckert, "The Incoherence of the Zoning Approach to Regulating Pornography: The Exclusion of Gender and a Call for Category Refinement in Free Speech Doctrine," *Georgetown Journal of Gender and the Law* 4 (Summer 2003): 863–87; Ronald J. Berger, Patricia Searles, and Charles E. Cottle, *Feminism and Pornography* (New York: Praeger, 1991).

31. Marsh, "Women in Contemporary Russia and the Former Soviet Union," 105; Attwood, "The Post-Soviet Women in the Move to the Market."

32. Petra K. Kelly, "Women and Power," *Earth Island Journal* 9, no. 1 (1993/1994): 38–40.

33. T. Jean Blocker, "Gender and Environmentalism: Results from the 1993 General Social Survey," *Social Science Quarterly* 78, no. 4 (1997): 841–58; Ruth Liepins, "'Women of Broad Vision:' Nature and Gender in the Environmental Activism of Australia's 'Women in Agriculture' Movement," *Environment and Planning* 30, no. 7 (1998): 1179–96; Manjusha Gupte, "Gender, Feminist Consciousness, and the Environment: Exploring the 'Natural' Connection," *Women and Politics* 24, no. 1 (2002): 47–62.

34. Multiple regression is commonly used for studying the effects of gender on legislative voting. See, for instance, Swers; Michele A. Barnello, "Gender and Roll Call Voting in the New York State Assembly," *Women and Politics* 20, no. 4 (1999): 77–93.

35. Iulia Shevchenko and Grigorii V. Golosov, "Legislative Activism of Russian Duma Deputies, 1996–99," *Europe-Asia Studies* 53, no. 2 (2001): 239–61.

36. See the records for the Duma meeting of February 20, 1997 (the first reading of the bill). Data Source: http://www.cir.ru/.

37. See the records for the Duma meeting of April 7, 1999 (the second and third readings of the bill). Data Source: http://www.cir.ru/.

38. See the records for the Duma meeting of February 20, 1997 (the first reading of the bill). Data Source: http://www.cir.ru/.

39. Elena B. Kochkina, "Politicheskaia sistema preimushchestv dlia grazhdan muzhskogo pola v Rossii (1917–2002)" [Political System of Advantages for Citizens of the Male Sex in Russia (1917–2002)], in *Gendernaia rekonstruktsiia politicheskikh sistem*, 477–523.

40. *Izvestiia*, Sept. 11, 2003.

41. Beth Reingold, "Concepts of Representation among Female and Male State Legislators," *Legislative Studies Quarterly* 17, no. 4 (1992): 521–22.

42. Thomas, *How Women Legislate*, 65; Irene Diamond and Gloria Feman Orenstein, eds., *Reweaving the World: The Emergence of Ecofeminism* (San Francisco: Sierra Club Books, 1990).

PART IV.
NEGOTIATING GENDER WITHIN NATIONALISMS

Romanian Women's Discourses of Sexual Violence

Othered Ethnicities, Gendering Spaces

Shannon Woodcock

In December 1989, Romanian citizens of all ethnicities revolted against the socialist dictatorship of Nicolae Ceauşescu and demanded radical change. Among the first legislative revisions was the reversal of the oppressive pronatalist policies that had denied Romanian women the right to abortion and contraception in the interests of "the nation." Socialist rhetoric of gender and ethnic equality was replaced by that of a "return to Europe," which often meant an attempted return to contemporary perceptions of presocialist Romanian experience. As in other postcommunist societies, the right not to work was presented as a natural freedom for women as reproducers, even as economic pressures forced more women into the flailing job market. I argue that attempts of women and ethnic minorities to find work in new capitalist markets were perceived by Romanian men as a threat not only to their incomes, but to the nation itself. The public sphere as a naturalized frame for the masculine ideal and the private as frame for the feminine became contested sites requiring regulation. This chapter takes gender and ethnicity as the twin constitutive discourses of society, and explores how subjects are articulated in relation to their "places."[1] While discourses of gender mask their construction by claiming to be manifest in the body, they are in fact dynamic and, as the introduction of this book argues, constantly negotiated and policed.

As an Australian, Romanian-speaking woman in Bucharest, I inhabited an unusual position, perceived by locals as vulnerable and requiring education as to the dangers of Bucharest's public space. Between 1997 and 2002, in informal and formal meetings, in bars, universities, and private homes, female Romanian friends, colleagues, and strangers repeatedly performed a series of explanatory warnings about how a woman needed to behave in the city.[2] I call this a prescriptive discourse because it was pervasive and identifiable as a kind of warning, prescribing behavior. The prescriptive discourse was initiated with the statement that a woman should not walk alone in the city at night because it is dangerous. In response to the question of why, the answer was Ţigani, a pejorative reference to the ethnic group that self-identifies as Roma. As I was a foreigner likely to be ignorant of the implicit gamut of stereotypical discourses conjured by the name of the ethnic Other, women were patient enough to answer my further question of why with the word "rape." (There is an assumption that Ţigani are thieves as well.) This prescriptive discourse was also enacted for Romanian women new to Bucharest, and reiterated in response to specific situations. Even among long-term Bucharest inhabitants, this discourse was regularly used as a reminder of necessary precautions, invoked, for example, when a woman mentioned that she intended to travel home alone. I would describe the discourse as a series of signposts to wider discourses of danger in public space.

The striking uniformity and repetition of this prescriptive discourse raises various questions concerning the unstated discursive links between the various terms of engagement (danger-Ţigani-rape) and concerning the place of women in Romanian postcommunist society more broadly. There seemed to be a disjunction between the high value placed by women on being recognized as sexual objects and embodiments of the feminine ideal and the daily fear of this recognition, equated with sexual harassment in public space. Although violence against women in private spaces was understood as a fact of life in Romanian society, Romanians felt that as a foreigner, I needed to be explicitly warned about dangers to women in public spaces. I asked why one form of violence didn't need comment, but another did. And though I was well acquainted with the extent of racism against Roma identified as Ţigani in postcommunist Romania, the fact that it was the Ţigan man who supposedly posed the threat of rape led me to question the intersections of ethnicity and gender in experiences and perceptions of sexual violence.

Romanian anthropological studies, especially those undertaken by scholars at Babeş-Bolyai University in the multiethnic Cluj-Napoca, focus on how women articulate their experiences of sexuality and violence, most often experienced within the family structure. Although these studies, primarily those by Enikő Magyari-Vincze, analyze the intersections of ethnic and gendered identity, they concentrate on Hungarian and Romanian stereotypes and experiences of each other, and, being located in the home, do not mention the Țigan Other of public space in any capacity.[3] This study focuses on Bucharest rather than the more multiethnic cities of regional Romania solely as a means of limiting the research project, although there is evidence that the Țigan Other functions similarly throughout the whole of Romania.

Incisive critique of the stereotypical construction of a fantastic Țigan Other is absent from scholarly discussion: I argue that these stereotypes are not simply "facts" exaggerated to debatable extents from factual communities. Those studies that do address these stereotypes merely measure their occurrence, or presume that they relate to a "real" problem of Țigan mafia/ sexual violence/ primitive culture. I limit this chapter to an examination of how ethnic Romanian women utilize the gendered Țigan Other in *only* one particular discourse. Since the Țigan is not exaggerated from but often "pinned" to self-identified Romani individuals, there is no additional value to be gained from extending this study to Roma women's discourses of Țigani over Hungarian women's discourses. Such a study of how Romani women relate to constant attempts at identifying them as the feminine Other of the Țigan is a very different topic to that which we are exploring here. This chapter focuses on discourses of the primary Other projected from within the majority ethnic community, the community with the most discursive power in Romanian society.

Contrary to what one might hope from the significant number of contemporary Romanian feminist writers, they are deafeningly silent on the role of the Țigan as ethnic Other in how Romanian women claim social positions and rights. On occasion, established and influential feminists have themselves projected the masculine Țigan Other as threat to an ideal Romanian feminist subject.[4] These texts are vital to an analysis of how "the Romanian woman" is articulated and policed in society through the Țigan rapist discourse but also, unfortunately, as examples of the discourse of the Țigan Other as sexual threat. In tandem with discursive silence, there is an absolute lack of institutional support such as shelters or counseling services. These factors must be situated in the context of Romanian postcommunist patriarchal society, which relies upon creating and maintaining gendered spaces for its perpetuation.

To explore these issues, I designed an open-ended interview structure using Romanian surveys and studies of women's experiences of violence, which I then used for individual and group surveys in the summer of 2002.[5] A sample of forty-five ethnic Romanian respondents aged eighteen to thirty-five (including eleven men, the majority in group interviews), recruited through social and professional networks and the involvement of the history department of Bucharest University, took part in interviews lasting approximately one hour.[6] The interview questions were open-ended, and sessions were conducted informally to encourage respondents to use their own language. The first question always asked was which areas of the city the respondent considered dangerous, so that while setting the frame as urban public space, there was no prompt as to ethnic signifiers. The structure created a conversational setting in which respondents were free to articulate their perceived position in relation to the interviewer (me).

As a Romanian-speaking foreign woman connected to respondents through distant social or academic networks, I observed that respondents used language suitable for a local Romanian speaker, and yet were careful to explain their meanings at length to ensure that I understood specific inferences. Respondents were patient in answering questions for an inquisitive Australian, while a level of trust was gained through shared language and culturally specific knowledge as well as sometimes through the assumption of shared experiences of gender.

Due to the qualitative nature of the interviews and the sample size, I claim no results in terms of generalizable conclusions. This chapter seeks to frame an analysis of postcommunist Romanian society, which is organized through the intersections of gendered and ethnic identities, regulated and dominated by the heterosexual ethnic Romanian masculine ideal subject. I use the interviews to reflect upon the range of discourses used by a sample of Romanian women to articulate their experiences of the place of gender in encounters in and of public spaces in Bucharest. While understanding and addressing the prescriptive discourses of Romanian women as a form of agency, this chapter also briefly discusses the (im)possibility of agency for the Roma subject identified as Țigan in such prevalent discourses of sexual violence.

Roma and Țigani: A Note on the Power of Naming

The presence of Roma ethnic groups was first recorded in the Romanian lands of Wallachia and Moldova in the fifteenth century, where they were immigrant slaves owned by the state, the church, and private landlords. Stereotyped by Romanian peasants as uncivilized, uneducated, nomadic, and enslaved (named Țigani), Roma were "unslaved" in 1856 as a benevolent act to consecrate the formation of the United Principalities of Romania as a modern, civilized European nation.[7] After emancipation, Roma continued to be stereotyped at all levels of society as inferior to ethnic Romanians. Roma were economically, socially, and politically marginalized as the Țigan ethnic Other under democratic, fascist, and socialist rule in Romania.

Since 1989, the "Roma issue" has exemplified the tension between an intensification of Romanian ethno-nationalism on one hand and discourses of civil society, from Roma and non-Roma non-governmental organizations (NGOs) and the European Union, on the other. The political and intellectual elite of postcommunist Romania must negotiate between an exclusively Romanian ethno-national identity and a Romania that identifies itself as EUropean,[8] a vital project for economic integration in the European Union (EU). Accession to the EU requires a series of economic, judicial, and social reforms, but while the necessity of equal opportunities for Roma has been heeded in the elite discourses of government officials, mainstream society remains dominated by negative stereotypes against Țigani. In response to international and Roma group pressure, the Romanian government agreed to replace the term Țigan with *Roma* in official documents in 1996. Romanian parliamentarians, intellectuals, nationalists, and the media protested that this spelling was unacceptably similar to the Romanian language term *Românii* for individuals of Romanian ethnicity.[9] In 2000, the Romanian government adopted the suggestion made by Roma groups in 1994, and decided that the official documents would refer to *Rromi*, with an extra, silent "r" to dispel possible confusion.[10]

The name Țigan continues to be used in mainstream Romanian discourses to refer to Roma, and the government-decreed term is mobilized as a tongue-in-cheek reference to what is widely considered a EUropean dictate that betrays the ethno-national Romanian cause. The intellectual newspaper *Dilema* recently published an article entitled "Just between Us, Rromi Are All Țigani," highlighting the intense investments of identity and the disparity between elite (EUropean) and mainstream Romanian discourses of national identity, and the significance of a name.[11] It is important to note, therefore, that Țigani exist through Romanian discourses, although this group often corresponds to self-identified Roma.

Public Space Encounters of the Other Kind

Encounters with Others in physical space and time are powerful because the individual must deal with the unpredictable power of unknown actors to participate in the encounter.[12] Individuals use dynamic stereotypical discourses in order to cope with the ambivalent relationships between the self and Others that can be confronted and must be negotiated in everyday public space encounters. Individuals invest heavily in claiming a fixed origin of identity, a claim to inhabit a stable set of personal characteristics defining "who they are," and at the same time individuals fix Others in stereotypes embodying essentialized characteristics. An ethnic Other, for example, is very often stereotyped as lazy and unemployed, a stereotype that may be usually applied to beggars in public space. A single stereotype, however, can never account for every aspect of an Other's behavior in public-space encounters, and so the self must successively apply different stereotypes. Often stereotypes of Others are even contradictory, for example a Roma woman seen from a distance in the subway may be assumed to be begging; however, upon recognizing that the woman is actually selling phone cards, a Romanian viewer may stereotype this Other with the common, albeit contradictory, discourse of Țigani as mafia-like black-market business dealers. Through this stereotype, the Romanian subject can retain their position as morally superior to the Țigan Other, if not as hard worker (in opposition to beggar), then as legal (as opposed to illegal) worker. The dynamics of encounters in public space thereby require the mobilization of multiple (and often contradictory) stereotypical discourses in the effort to maintain privileged identifications.

Shannon Woodcock

In addition to being the physical location of encounters, places exist as discursive frames for Others. In both Europe and America, for example, underground subway stations discursively frame begging, aggressive, and homeless Others, while marketplaces may frame groups such as female shoppers, produce marketers, and ambient traders. As Alaina Lemon notes in her study of discourses of national identity in the Moscow metro, such "narratives achieve forceful validity not only because they seem to be grounded in concrete spaces but also because they intersect familiar discourses and images depicting authority, culture and belonging."[13] To explore the constitutive role of gender in public spaces and encounters, therefore, it is useful to take what we know about the functioning discourses of gender in postcommunist Romania and combine that knowledge with evidence of how Romanian women frame their experiences in public places. Discourses of the Other in and through public space reflect the power of public space encounters with the Other and create a "grammar of surfaces" through which intense negotiations of ethnic and gendered identities are performed.[14]

The Place of "Woman" in Postcommunist Romania

Since the fall of Ceaușescu, new hybrids of national, ethnic, and gendered identities have been under intense renegotiation. This process is often masked as a "retraditionalization" to pre-regime values. This masking of contemporary gender roles goes hand in hand with the normalization of gender performance as supposedly essential to bodies, so that women are once again "allowed" to assume their (biologically) "natural" roles as child bearers rather than career women.[15] Elite (government and intellectual) support for the discourses of the European Union thus stands in tension with the postcommunist mainstream project of defining gender through "traditional" values as constructed in the Romanian patriarchal matrix. Unlike the categories of ethnic minorities, trade, and industrial production, however, the European Union category of "gender mainstreaming," which requires that Romania show "political will" to incorporate a "gender equality perspective" in all policies, has been largely ignored even by the Romanian state.[16]

European Union funding has enabled the development of a network of NGOs attempting to identify and deal with issues facing women in Romania. These organizations have produced a significant number of surveys and studies highlighting the alarming rate of violence against women in the home. To some extent, the focus on gendered violence in the private sphere reflects the assumption that the place of women is in the home; in this naturalized site of reproduction, women can claim a right to safety within the institution of marriage that is not extended to them in the public sphere.[17] A recent European Union funded survey concluded that 73 percent of respondents had experienced domestic violence.[18] The right of men to "discipline" women who fail to inhabit the feminine ideal (for instance, by being too assertive or not physically attractive enough) is pervasive, as is blaming the female victim.[19]

Legislation against violence in the home was initiated in the Romanian parliament in November 2001, was adopted two years, and has yet to be tested.[20] Even though rape within marriage can now be considered a criminal offense, police routinely refuse to intervene when called into "matters between the husband and his family," and violence between partners (or ex-partners) in the street is also considered a "private" matter.[21] "Private" space is thereby constituted by gender rather than by physical location.[22]

Given this context, it is noteworthy that the single Romanian NGO that uses the term "feminist" in its name, the Society for Feminist Analysis (ANA), has, from its inception, prioritized issues of women in relation to public space. Laura Grunberg, one of the founders and a leading Romanian feminist, explained in the organization's journal that "for a long time ANA was considered a kind of infant which needed to be thrown into the fight against the authorities, the poverty, the pollution, the street dogs and the *Ţigani* of the area."[23] This description locates the feminist fight in public space, specifying the ethnic Other alongside animal and chemical threats to a vulnerable feminine (albeit feminist) subject.

Media reports of women being bashed and raped in public and private space are detailed in narratives similar in style to pornographic prose, describing the victim's body and providing the victim's address, school, and age. Initials usually replace the victim's name, a useless form of privacy protection that is also characteristic of the unnamed pornographic object.[24] The function of these reports as social discourses of sex crime bears a striking resemblance to those addressed by Jane Caputi in *The Age of Sex Crime*.[25] Caputi argues that the adult men's press valorizes sex crime as active and that patriarchal identification with the perpetrator "correspondingly demands that women play along by identifying with the sexual victim."[26] "Mass responses of titillation . . . and expressions of envy or amusement" among men regarding sex/violent crimes against women have been documented by numerous scholars.[27] Indeed, Denise Roman notes in her study of postcommunist Romania that "rape is always sensational news . . . designed to stir laughter and not compassion."[28] In this way, "all instances of sexual terror serve as lessons for all women," and pervasive social discourses of violent sexual crime against Romanian women serve to construct the public sphere as dangerous.[29]

The familiar theme is, of course, that women who are outside their "natural" boundaries invite sexual violence from men. In theory, the private sphere offers sisters, wives, and mothers of men protection from rape, a protection in the "traditional" place of women as reproducers. The terror of sexual violence in public space compounds the need for a safe private sphere, explaining to some extent the disparities in postcommunist Romanian discourse between the importance of "catching a man" and real experiences of married life.

Despite the introduction of new models of femininity since 1989, these models still require subjects to exceed the ideal of the feminine subject. The stereotypical career woman, for example, remains primarily a sexual object and site of reproduction; being recognized as an intelligent individual depends first upon fulfillment of the feminine ideal. The woman who is not only feminine (beautiful, reproductive) but also successful in the public sphere is the "superwoman," while the woman who chooses a career over family is deemed unnatural, an aberration of femininity. "Superwomen" are accepted as modern versions of the traditional woman who raises the family at home as long as they are perceived as effortlessly taking on the public role only in addition to the primary task of motherhood and private care. The absence of any accepted subcultures of femininity in contemporary Romania, such as women who may choose to live alone or with another woman, or those who do not raise children, reflects the dominance of the patriarchal ideal in society.

The Romanian feminine ideal is a sexual object for men, yet victims of sexual violence are held responsible for attracting the desire of men. In this construction, women who fulfill the feminine ideal in public space suffer sexual violence. The place of women in postcommunist Romania is therefore a double bind that discursively chains women to the terror of sexual violence in the location of the feminine ideal. Private space is the safe place for the reproducer/sexual object that is protected by the patriarchal claim extended in marriage. In this construction, domestic violence becomes what may be termed a lesser or necessary evil in face of the dangers to women outside the institution of marriage or the family home.

Women's Prescriptive Discourses:
Placing Danger within the Patriarchy

As discussed earlier, the prescriptive discourse performed by Romanian women frames sexual violence as something committed by Țigan men in public space, yet there is a distinct lack of information specifically about public space and violence against women in Romania. This section draws on qualitative interviews with Romanian women about their experiences and perceptions of violence in order to explore how these women negotiate gendered places in public space.

I began each interview with the question of which places in Bucharest the respondent considered dangerous. While some respondents primarily answered that everywhere was equally dangerous, the vast majority named suburbs of Bucharest where they did not reside.[30] When prompted with "why?" approximately 70 percent of respondents answered that these places were dangerous "because of Țigani," while the remaining minority identified potential threats in general terms for men such as *baieții de cartier*, culturally translated as "boys in the 'hood" and connoting young men capable of criminal activity. Expanding further on why Țigani, or men in general, posed a danger, respondents detailed a variety of scenarios including having their pocket picked on public transport, being talked to or asked out on the street, being touched by men, and being raped.

If the threat of sexual violence in public space is primarily a means of constituting women as sites of reproduction in the ways discussed above, it is little wonder that there is no explicit name for sexual harassment in public space.[31] Respondents most often articulated verbal harassment as "a kind of stress," and, consistent with media and social discourses, never used the term "sexual harassment." This lack of a name for a commonly occurring and feared practice reflects, in this case, its normalization. "Pretend not to notice" was presented by respondents as the general rule for how a woman should react to being approached by men on the street, because "a response will just provoke them" or "if you answer it means you want him to touch you."[32] Respondents thereby situated verbal harassment in a series of possible actions, and placed responsibility for physical approach on the object of attention. Many women interviewed placed responsibility for rape on the victims themselves, guilty of inciting the action by their performance of the feminine ideal. The Romanian woman who fulfills her supposedly natural role of sexual object, therefore, is also considered responsible for defending herself against men fulfilling the patriarchal masculine ideal through acts of sexual aggression in public space. Numerous respondents said that only women who wanted to be touched were assaulted, even while citing cases that did not conform to this theory.

One respondent explained that she always wore jeans and no makeup in public space to avoid attention from men, and then recounted a recent experience of having being groped in the street by two "younger and weaker" male children about thirteen years of age.[33] This respondent began her story by pondering whether she had attracted these boys because she looked "too girly," illustrating the pervasiveness of interpreting harassment as an issue rooted in the appearance of women and their role as sexual objects for men. A postgraduate respondent spoke at length of the way that men in groups laughed while addressing sexual comments to a passing woman, noting that "a real man can make a woman afraid in front of his friends."[34] These men perform for one another rather than for the sexual object, corroborating Caputi's insights into how social discourses of sexual violence are a point of masculine identification (often expressed in laughter) that simultaneously identifies the passing woman as potential victim.

Indeed, respondents consistently elaborated on the fact that they were always afraid of sexual violence in public space. One young woman described the feelings of a friend who had to walk home alone at night after work: "nothing has ever happened to her but she can't relax . . . she doesn't think 'oh, it will be ok,' no, every night she is still stressed even if nothing has happened, my friend can't relax at night, you never know when something will happen."[35] Night was considered more dangerous than daytime, possibly due to the perception that "normal people" are then at home with their families as much as to the issue of darkness. The fear of sexual violence, perpetuated through events and their extensive media coverage and evidenced in social discourses of sex crimes, is of a threat located anywhere and anytime in public space.

The question of whom female respondents would approach for help in public space received a variety of responses, all variations on the theme of masculine ideal. A Romanian man who "looked nice" was the most common answer. One respondent reckoned "not the police, they work with the criminals . . . a man, a Romanian man . . . not a woman—what could a woman do?"[36] One group of women collectively concluded that they would find a shop space with a policeman or a security guard. Each of these responses illustrates the nature of safe space for the feminine gendered subject as a space claimed by the ethnic Romanian masculine subject.

Just as rape was presented in the prescriptive discourse as the threat facing women in public space, the interviews suggested that respondents held rape to be the most severe in a trajectory of acts of sexual violence that includes various forms of verbal and physical harassment (although there was no commonly accepted term for sexual harassment). One of the leading Romanian feminists, Mihaela Miroiu, considers widespread sexual harassment on Romanian streets as part of a "socialization for rape."[37] Sorina Neculaescu, another local activist, terms sexual harassment "mini-rape."[38] Romanian feminist academic understandings of the role of sexual harassment thereby also situate such acts as stages linked clearly to rape. The utterance of this most severe manifestation of sexual violence in the prescriptive discourse fits with the aim of educating women as to the dangers of public space in Bucharest.

While the first interview question about dangerous places in Bucharest consistently led to discourses of gendered violence in public space, no respondent raised the issue of domestic violence. I led respondents through a series of questions as to whether they believed domestic violence took place in their area, on their block, and among their family and friends. Only three of twenty-six individual women interviewed said that they had *not* witnessed or experienced violence in their personal life from partners or family; all twenty-three other respondents volunteered that they had experienced violence at the hands of male partners and family members. In every case the perpetrator of the violence was of Romanian ethnicity.

While such a high ratio of respondents had experienced violence at the hands of Romanian men in the private sphere, none had experienced rape by Ţigani or Roma men. Furthermore, not all of the sexual harassment experienced by those who identified the perpetrators as Ţigani was necessarily perpetrated by Roma men. Actual statistics are impossible to calculate due to severe underreporting of rapes, lack of prosecutions, lack of available crime statistics (including ethnicity of perpetrators), and disproportionate incarceration rates of Roma men across the board.[39] We must not confuse the utterance Ţigan, invoking a range of historically and culturally specific stereotypical discourses, with real Roma men, although individuals of this group are inarguably affected in the process. Why is it, then, that Romanian women ethnicize the masculine threat of sexual violence in public space?

Ţigani Others and Bucharest Spaces

Avtah Brah provides an interesting model for mediating the intersections of gendered discourses of ethnic Others in her study of an English community in the midst of post–World War II immigrations.[40] Noting women's use of discourses that marked the "intruder" as a "form of aggressive masculinity," Brah considers that this is a discourse of male aggression displaced onto the ethnic Other through a transmutation of the formerly colonized Other into colonizer. By articulating the ethnic Other as aggressive masculinity, "the discourse converts the transgressed against into the transgressors."[41]

The Ţigan Other has been constructed as the transgressor of Romanian ethno-national identity throughout history. When literally enslaved, the Ţigan Other was described in popular pre–twentieth century folktales and proverbs as constantly controlling or dominating the ethnic Romanian peasant, and even as Ţigani were actively marginalized from agricultural collectives under socialism, they were labeled enemies of the people.[42] After 1989, the flood of consumer goods into Romania and the shock of capitalist trade were symbolized by the Ţigan bişniţari.[43] The Ţigani trader remains the scapegoat for market fluctuations.[44] In each of these stereotypes, the Ţigan Other is simultaneously lazy and uneducated but cunning, deceptive, and controlling. The evidence is located in the visibility of Ţigani, usually in the public spaces of the markets and streets. The Ţigan Other functions as the primary Other of the ethno-national Romanian self in postcommunist society, the transgressor that threatens (and explains) changing economic, social, and political factors.

Public transport in postcommunist Bucharest is one of the primary sites through which the Ţigan Other is discursively framed and constructed. As Lemon's study of the Moscow Metro shows, public transport and narratives thereof play an everyday role in the lives of urban city dwellers, as a real space in which the Other is (or may be) encountered. Stereotypical, physically recognizable ethnic identities (including that of the self) are utilized in discourses of public space as a means of navigating localized issues of economics, politics, and cultural identity.

Bucharest's public transportation system, and specifically its buses, is a public space medium that frames representations of ethnic Romanian oppression and Ţigan transgression in pervasive Romanian discourses. Pickpockets on buses are referred to as Ţigani, and the stereotypes of Ţigani as uncivilized, violent, and vengeful are utilized to explain why when someone is robbed on a crowded bus, no one should protest.[45] Romanians (Roma can be included in this category also) thereby render themselves powerless in the face of supposedly Ţigan criminals. This discursive construction of public space and its control by ethnic Others not only creates a fixed "grammar of surfaces" for real space encounters, but uses this essential grammar to explain, justify, and strengthen Romanian ethnic control as a "necessary" defense in postcommunist society.

My informants' prescriptive discourse intersects both ethnic and gendered matrices. By identifying sexual violence from men as the threat against Romanian women, the discourse fixes women as sexual objects, and by identifying the threat as existing in public space, the discourse locates the natural safe place of the feminine ideal in the home. Presenting the Ţigan male as the greatest threat invokes danger specifically to the Romanian feminine subject, the site of reproduction of the ethno-nation.

The prescriptive discourse, as noted earlier, identifies the vital danger points as danger-Ţigani-rape, and so the question is what kind of threat the masculine Ţigan poses to Romanian women. The discourse presents as worst-case scenario an encounter in which the Ţigan (the ethnic subaltern) utilizes his power of the masculine to claim the feminine subject, thus overriding the naturalized ethnic hierarchy in which Ţigan is supposed to be subordinate to Romanian. I have posited that the construction of the feminine subject is the site of (ethno-national) reproduction in postcommunist Romania. Thus this encounter places the Romanian woman outside the protection extended to her within the Romanian gendered and ethnic matrix. At the same time, by fulfilling and fixing the dominant Romanian gender roles, the Romanian woman earns the right to be protected by the Romanian masculine subject. Invoking the ethnic Other is the basis for a claim of ethnic defensiveness in order to protect the Romanian feminine subject. Siding with the Romanian male subject of the gendered and ethnic matrices and locating all threat and danger in the ethnic Other then becomes the only valid way of claiming protection within the ethnic matrix. The preference among my respondents for turning to Romanian men for help in public space is an expression of this strategy for survival.

Social discourses of sex crime create public space as the sphere where women (especially those who inhabit the feminine ideal) face the perpetual danger of sexual violence. By this logic, it is in the private sphere of marriage that the Romanian feminine ideal is safe, claimed within the dominant Romanian heterosexual matrix as vital site of ethno-national reproduction. The small number of extensive surveys about women's experiences of domestic violence highlight that despite high incident rates, women discursively construct violence in the home as a result of women's provocation or failure to "deal with" the particularities of violent male behavior.[46] The fact that respondents experienced the most violence in the supposedly safe private sphere at the hands of the ethnic Romanian subject that claims to protect them highlights the power imbalance intrinsic to the function of the patriarchal social body and raises questions concerning the nature of agency claimed by Romanian women's discourses.

Women's Discourses and the Question of Agency

Women in postcommunist Romania constantly negotiate and contest gendered identities in order to avoid physical violence against them as women. The prescriptive discourse explored in this chapter illustrates one way that women strategically interact with their environments, and we can assume that the aim of the discourse is to protect women from the perceived dangers of sexual violence in public space. The agency of this discourse, however, is not a radical break with or subversion of the place of women in the gendered matrix of the social body; rather it fixes the feminine subject as by nature in the private sphere and attempts to claim the promise of patriarchal protection. The spatial and gendered categories distinguishing private and public and Romanian and Ţigan spaces in the women's discourse seem even more problematic when one considers the lack of discourses amongst women about active strategies to prevent (rather than to lament or deal with) domestic violence as a threat to women. While there are numerous new surveys and reports about the high incidence of domestic violence, these same reports highlight that women have limited practices for dealing with the problem. The following discussion teases out some of the effects of the gendered discourse.

The ethnicization of the masculine threat in public space places women in the privileged and vulnerable place of the Romanian feminine ideal (site of national reproduction and sexual object) and mobilizes the hegemonic Romanian ethnic discourses in the service of the feminine subject. Romanian women are thus enabled to claim the protection of the Romanian masculine ideal against the ethnic threat of the Ţigan Other. This movement constitutes and consolidates the private sphere (secured through the institution of marriage) as the safe place of the feminine subject, in contrast with the masculine threat outside. The definition of naturally gendered spatial spheres complicates the possibility of articulating violence within the "safe" place of the home as being *un*natural.

The ethnicization of the masculine threat as Ţigan also allows Romanian women to communicate the prescriptive discourse without fear of being policed by Romanian men, as scapegoating the ethnic Other would not draw the negative attention of Romanian men. Invoking Ţigani displaces attention from the specifically gendered nature of the threat. At the same time, naming the masculine threat as Ţigan hides the fact that ethnic Romanian men *are* complicit in sexual violence against women in public space. In the long term, recognition of this fact is necessary for women to be able to critique how legal and media discourses perpetuate and encourage masculine identification with sexual violence. The fact that Romanian society relies upon sexual violence to maintain the private domestic sphere as the safe place for women cannot be approached while masculine aggression is disassociated from ethnic Romanian masculinity. In addition, the scapegoating of Ţigan men as threats to

Romanian women intensifies stereotypical discourses of the Other and contributes to the severe marginalization of Roma individuals and communities identified as Țigani. This precludes an interrogation of how the Romanian gendered matrix relies upon ethnic Others to strengthen and normalize its own hegemony.

The imperative structure of the discourse (you must/should not go out alone) circumscribes activity and places the responsibility for sexual violence on the feminine subject who fails to inhabit the feminine ideal as located in private space. The discourse is thereby effective as an educational strategy for the safety of women, but it perpetuates the myth of the safe private sphere, ignores the realities of sexual, physical, and psychological violence women suffer in the home, and leaves unacknowledged the fact that the masculine ideal never fulfills its promise of protection. It seems that the threat of the Țigan Other warns women against transgressing the feminine ideal by placing themselves in public space, while everyday experiences of violence at the hands of Romanian men in the home are blamed on the failure of women to fulfill the feminine ideal in private space.

There are few agency-enhancing aspects to the ways Romanian women frame their perceptions of violence. A possible direction for further research is the question of whether Romanian women manifest on a societal scale the much noted propensity of victims of domestic violence to internalize the rationale of the aggressor and blame themselves.[47] Perhaps the banal centrality of violence in the home looms so large in women's experiences that blaming one's own failure to inhabit the proper place of the feminine subject is a tactic for psychological survival. Considering that women (as child bearers inhabiting the feminine ideal) are often economically reliant on male support, the discourse is a component of material as well as psychological and social survival. The prescriptive discourse, which displaces aspects of lived experiences of violence onto the ethnic Other and public space, remains an expression of the desire to address the issue of violence against women, and this Othering enables expression within the matrix regulated by Romanian men. Needless to say, the discourse makes no moves to create a supportive network for victims of violence; rather it places the responsibility for avoiding or incurring violence upon women themselves.

Despite these questions of agency and effect, the prescriptive discourse is a clear example of how a number of Romanian women in a particular period of postcommunist Bucharest negotiate the violence of everyday spaces by strategically mobilizing discourses of ethnicity in the patriarchal matrix.

Subaltern Agency and the Ethnic Other

Having discussed the agency of the Romanian women who perform the prescriptive discourse, it is important to ask what space for agency is available to Roma men identified as Țigani. It is a minority of men of any ethnicity who rape strangers, and there is no doubt that intense and widespread Romanian racism against Roma is mobilized and perpetuated in women's discourses of sexual violence. As previously mentioned, Roma receive harsher punishments for crime and are grossly overrepresented as criminals in the Romanian press.

Still, this does not mean that individuals identified as Ṭigani are not agents. On the contrary, encounters between gendered and ethnic Others in public space hold great potential for discursive manipulation, strategy, and agency. Stereotypes of the Other claim to be fixed forms of knowledge that relate (often in opposition) to fixed forms of knowledge of the self; the identi-fication of an Other in a stereotypical discourse simultaneously chains the identifier to a discursively conditioned response. The Other holds the power to display a particular stereotypical characteristic (through language, actions, clothes), and mobilize a particular chain of stereotypical discourse. A simple example is the agency of a Roma child to invoke the stereotypes of primitive Ṭigan exploitation of children in order to beg for money or food from a Romanian stranger in the street. This agency may reinforce stereotypical dis-courses of Ṭigani on the larger scale, but enables small gains for individuals in the short term.

A relevant example to my exploration is the stereotype of pickpockets in public transport as gangs of vengeful, violent Ṭigani. As previously described, this stereotype is so strong that witnesses of acts of theft on buses refuse to respond for fear of revenge, despite their numerical superiority. In qualitative research with Bucharest commuters, I found that the prime signifier of Ṭigan thieves on buses was not skin color, but language, and not fluent Romanes (the Roma language), but a simple vocabulary of words common as street slang among young people of every ethnicity in the suburbs.[48] In theory, signifying oneself as Ṭigan in this context is an act of agency that draws upon the image of thieves as violent and vengeful, and thereby fixes witnesses as threatened and passive, allowing pickpockets to steal with little risk of reproach. In practice, pickpockets (of all ethnicities) do just this, by sharpening their small pocket knives at the bus stop and by using a street slang of mixed Romanian and Romanes.

While this example shows how petty criminals are agents who can inhabit the stereotypes of the Ṭigan Other to mobilize the fear of the Romanian majority, the scapegoating of Ṭigani as criminals and rapists has negative effects predominantly on real Roma people. The anxieties of the Romanian community that can be mobilized to the subaltern's advantage do not disap-pear, but are channeled into increasingly aggressive discourses of the ethnic Other deployed to police the ethnic Romanian nation.

My focus on Romanian women's discourse of ethnicized sexual violence elides issues of sexual violence faced by Roma women as well. While Ṭigan slaves faced a punishment of death for raping a Romanian woman prior to 1856, Romanian men were free to rape Roma women, who were considered naturally lascivious, without fear of punishment. The stereotype of Roma women as seductive, deceptive, and promiscuous remains prevalent in post-communist Romania. In addition to being victims of domestic violence in the home, Roma women face even greater hurdles than Romanian women in access to the Romanian legal system, resulting in severe underreporting of violent crime among this community. The inaudibility of Roma women's experiences in Romanian women's discourses reflects their circumscription from the imagined (gendered and ethnic) community of Romanian women.

Conclusion

Despite the dominance of a historically and culturally specific patriarchal ideal in postcommunist Romanian society, dynamic discourses of gender and ethnicity, such as the prescriptive performance examined in this chapter, are performed. The ethnic Romanian feminine ideal, as site of national reproduction and sexual object, constitutes the private space. Discourses of sexual violence in society regulate the gendered division of spaces to make public space not only unnatural, but dangerous for women *as* women. In this way, the actual experiences of women facing violence in the private sphere are discursively overpowered, constructed as natural, individual experiences of violence.

The prescriptive discourse warning women not to go out at night for fear of rape at the hands of Ţigan men evidences the intersections of gendered and ethnic matrices in Romanian women's ways of understanding public space and sexual violence. The ethnicization of the masculine threat as Ţigani disavows Romanian masculine complicity in sexual violence and simultaneously claims protection for the Romanian feminine subject within the naturalized gender roles of the hegemonic ethnic group. While the effects of this discourse may consolidate the dominance of Romanian masculinity, its existence illustrates a dynamic strategy for the negotiation of gender and its places in everyday life among women in Bucharest. As campaigns for gender equality gain stride among Romanian proponents of a European civil society, women's discourses that recognize the vulnerability of the gendered and ethnic subject within patriarchal society may prove to be the link that enables widespread and critical debate about gendered bodies in postcommunist Romanian social spaces.

NOTES

1. Gender is defined in this work as a series of acts and gestures that are "performative in the sense that the essence or identity that they otherwise purport to express are fabrications manufactured and sustained through corporeal signs and other discursive means." Judith Butler, *Gender Trouble: Feminism and the Subversion of Identity* (New York: Routledge, 1990), 136.

2. I was aware of this discourse through 1997–2002 and in 2000 began making notes of each occasion it was presented to me. Rarely did a new female acquaintance *not* perform this discourse.

3. Enikő Magyari-Vincze, ed., *Femei şi Bărbaţi în Clujul Multietnic*, vols. 1–3 [Women and Men in Multiethnic Cluj] (Cluj-Napoca: Editură Fundaţiei Desire, 2001), and *Diferenţa care conteaza: Diversitatea social-culturală prin lentila antropologiei feministe* [Differences That Matter: Socio-cultural Diversity through the Lens of Feminist Anthropology] (Cluj-Napoca: Editură Fundaţiei Desire, 2002). One exception to these fields and their silences is Lorena Văetişi's recent postgraduate dissertation that studies how self-identified Roma adolescents perceive themselves as gendered and ethnic subjects in Romanian society (*Discursuri identitare şi intersectoralitate: O analiză privind identitatea de gen şi identitatea etnică în cazul femeilor rrome* [Analysis Concerning Gendered and Ethnic Identity in the Case of Romani Women], M.A. thesis, Babeş-Bolyai University, Cluj-Napoca, 2004.

4. The feminist movement in Romania, as in other parts of the world, works with sexuality before ethnicity issues in Bucharest; Bucharest feminist organizations are strong allies of organizations for gay rights such as ACCEPT but not of any Romani organizations. This is not the case with feminist movements in the multiethnic centers of Cluj-Napoca and Timişoara, but highlights again the Bucharest focus of my research. It is Bucharest which claims the "real Romanian" identity and from which many media discourses are produced.

5. This research was conducted as part of my Ph.D. studies at the University of Sydney. The design of the survey benefited from surveys conducted by Romanian organizations. See the report of Asociatia pentru Promovarea Femeii din Romania [Association for the Promotion of Women in Romania], a project of the "Centrul de Informare, Educaţie si Consiliere Timişoara pentru femeile si feţele victime ale violenţei domestice şi abuzului sexual" [For the Women and Girl Victims of Domestic Violence], a survey of opinions conducted July 5–7, 2002, financed through the PHARE-ACCESS program (July 2002); Laura Grunberg, "Povestiri din vremea cand am incercat sa fiu o buna Foisoreanca" [Stories from the Time I Tried to Be a Good Neighbor], AN*Alize: Revista de Studii Feministe* 5, no. 16 (1999), http://www.ana saf.ro/romana/index(rom).html; and Tatiana Olteanu, *Studiu de opinie privind violenţa asupra femeii in familie*, manuscript published online, 1998, http://www.pitesti.ro/grado/studui_ro.html (accessed August 5, 2002).

6. No ethnic Roma women or men were interviewed in this research, and research into discourses of sexual violence in these communities is a valuable area to be researched in the future.

7. See Mihail Kogalniceanu, "Dezrobirea Ţiganilor, Ştergerea privilegiilor boiereşti, emanciparea Ţăranilor" [The Unslaving of the Ţigani: The Erasure of Boyar Privileges, and the Emancipation of the Peasants], speech given at the Romanian Academy, April 1, 1891, in *Scrieri Literare* (Bucharest: Editura 100+1, undated); Viorel Achim *Ţiganii in Istoria României* [Ţigani in the History of Romania] (Bucharest: Editura Enciclopedica, 1998); and Ian Hancock, *The Pariah Syndrome: An Account of Gypsy Slavery and Persecution* (Ann Arbor: Karoma, 1988).

8. This representation of EUrope signifies the uniqueness of the contemporary aim to identify common values throughout European nation-states in the EU.

9. Lucian Boia, *Romania: Borderland of Europe* (London: Reaktion Books, 2001), 219.

10. Petre Roman, "Termeni folositi pentru denumirea etniei romilor/tiganilor" [Terminology for the Naming of the Ethnicity of Roma/Ţigani], memorandum of the Minister of External Affairs, February 29, 2000.

Shannon Woodcock

11. Cristian Ghinea, "Intre noi fie vorba, rromii tot Țigani sînt" [Just between Us, Rromi Are All Țigani], *Dilema* 19, no. 3 (2001): 3.

12. Homi K. Bhabha, *The Location of Culture* (London: Routledge, 1994).

13. Alaina Lemon, "Talking Transit and Spectating Transition: The Moscow Metro," in *Altering States: Ethnographies of Transition in Eastern Europe and the Former Soviet Union*, ed. Daphne Berdahl, Matti Bunzl, and Martha Lampland (Ann Arbor: University of Michigan Press, 2000), 14.

14. Ibid, 28.

15. See the introduction to this collection, and also Adriana Baban, "Women's Sexuality and Reproductive Behaviour in Post-Ceausescu Romania: A Psychological Approach" in *Reproducing Gender*, ed. Susan Gal and Gail Kligman (Princeton, N.J.: Princeton University Press, 2000), 225–56.

16. Council of Europe, *Gender Mainstreaming: Conceptual Frameworks, Methodology and Presentation of Good Practices; Final Report of the Group of Specialists on Mainstreaming* (Strasbourg: Council of Europe, 1999).

17. A recent issue of the intellectual newspaper *Dilema*, no. 530 (May 30–June 5, 2003), http://www.algoritma.ro/dilema/530), for example, chose domestic violence as its theme. The majority of contributors (all women) began their articles by stating that violence in the home was most damaging because it is the natural place of women.

18. See the report of the Asociatia pentru promovarea femeii din România.

19. Forty-six percent of respondents in a study by a Romanian women's organization stated that in cases of domestic violence both the victim and the aggressor were responsible for the attack (ibid.). I understand this statistic as indicating the extent to which violence in the home is considered normal and not a result of power imbalance or gender-specific behavior.

20. Alina Bărbulescu, "Violența intrafamilială și neliniștea justiției" [Intrafamilial Violence and the Restlessness of Justice], *Dilema*, no. 530.

21. Daniel Ciumăgeanu Mugur, "Vorbele bune" [Good Words], *Dilema*, no. 530, and Stela Serghiuță "Violența domestică—în lume și în Romănia" [Domestic Violence —in the World and in Romania].

22. Note that the section of the penal code that could be applied to domestic violence in public space would be Article 200, which applies to "public scandal." This is the article that is used to prosecute both organized prostitution (when it suits) and, primarily, gays and lesbians. Gays and lesbians can and have been charged throughout the 1990s for associating in public space (the *potential* to create public scandal violates Article 200), while heterosexual persons are not arrested for "public scandal." See the Human Rights Watch International Gay and Lesbian Human Rights Commission report *Public Scandals: Sexual Orientation and Criminal Law in Romania* (New York: Arta Grafica, 1998). Sexual harassment and violence in public space are not addressed in legislation. Together these factors plot the construction of gendered spaces and places in Romanian society.

23. Grunberg, "Stories from the Time I Tried to Be a Good Neighbor," 16.

24. See Lindsey Rose, "From Atrocity to Data: Historiographies of Rape in Former Yugoslavia and the Gendering of Genocide," *Patterns of Prejudice* 36, no. 4 (2000): 59–79.

25. Jane Caputi, *The Age of Sex Crime* (London: Women's Press, 1987).

26. Ibid, 47.

27. Ibid, 46.

28. Denise Roman, *Fragmented Identities: Popular Culture, Sex, and Everyday Life in Postcommunist Romania* (New York: Lexington Books, 2003), 105.

29. Caputi, *The Age of Sex Crime*, 47.

30. The most cited 'dangerous' suburbs were, in order of frequency, Ferentari, Rahova, Pantelimon, and Cringaşi. This articulation of "new" (socialist period, post-1970) suburbs and city as dangerous in opposition to the old "authentic" center of Bucharest is in keeping with postcommunist discursive articulation of Ceauşescu's "new city" as corrupt, and the pre-Ceauşescu city as genuine. C. Buica, M. Popescu, and O. Tomescu, "Bucureştiul vazut de Bucureşteni; reprezentari speciale ale spaţiului urban" [Bucharest as Seen by Bucharesteans: Special Representations of Urban Space], *Revista de Cercetari Sociale* [Journal of Social Research] 13 (1995): 111–15.

31. I will use the term "sexual harassment" to mean any unwelcome verbal or physical sexual approaches in public spaces, such as the street and on public transport. For more about sexual harassment and its history as a term in postcommunist societies see Krassimira Daskalova, "Women's Problems, Women's Discourses in Bulgaria" (337–69), Malgorzata Fuszara, "New Gender Relations in Poland in the 1990s" (259–85), and Laura Grunberg, "Women's NGOs in Romania" (307–36), in Gal and Kligman, *Reproducing Gender*.

32. J. 7/3/02, E. 7/3/02.

33. E. 7/3/2002. Note that the respondent's articulation of her harassers as "weaker" indicates the rupture of discourses that conceal feminine "weakness" as a biological trait.

34. J. 7/3/02.

35. Group Interview A 7/12/02.

36. L. 6/30/02.

37. Mihaela Miroiu, "Experienţele Femeilor" [Experiences of Women], in *Gen şi Societate* [Gender and Society] (Bucharest: Alternative, 1997), 81.

38. Sorina Neculaescu, "Corpul Femeii—Trofeu al Dominaţiei Masculine" [The Female Body: Trophy of Masculine Domination], AN*Alize: Revista de Studii Feministe* (September 2000): 15–16.

39. For further information on Roma and the penal system, see Romani Criss si Argentia de monitizoare a presei [Romani Crisis and the Agency for the Monitoring of the Press], *Prezentarea romilor in presa româneasca* [Representation of Romani People in the Romanian Press], report (February–August 2000). For insight into Romanian police mechanisms of "keeping tabs on" the Roma community, see Tudor Amza, *Fenomenul infractional în rindul ţiganilor: Activitaţi specific Poliţiei Române pentru protenjarea etniei si prevenirea faptelor antisociale* [The Infractional Phenomenon amongst the Ţigani: Specific Activities of the Romanian Police for Protection of the Ethnicity and Prevention of Antisocial Factors] (Bucharest: Academie de Politiei Alexandru Ioan Cuza, 1995).

40. Avtah Brah, "The Scent of Memory: Strangers, Our Own and Others," in *Hybridity and Its Discontents: Politics, Science Culture*, ed. Avtah Brah and Annie E. Coombes (London: Routledge, 2000), 272–90.

41. Ibid, 277.

42. See Michael Stewart, "Gypsies, the Work Ethic and Hungarian Socialism," in *Socialism: Ideals, Ideologies and Local Practice*, ed. C. M. Hann (London: Routledge, 1993), 187–203, and Shannon Woodcock, *How to Be a Real Romanian: Articulations of Țigani Others and the Construction of Ethno-National Romanian Selves*, Ph.D. diss., Sydney University, 2003.

43. *Bisnița* is an adaptation of the English word business; *bisnițari* refers to people who conduct business. See Katherine Verdery, *What Was Socialism and What Comes Next?* (Princeton, N.J.: Princeton University Press, 1996), 98.

44. Woodcock, *How to Be a Real Romanian*.

45. Ibid. It is important to stress here that the ethnic identity of convicted pickpockets is irrelevant, as Țigani is not legally considered an ethnic category, and self-identifying Romani individuals are not recorded as such. The fact is that anyone who pickpockets on a bus is identified and labeled as Țigan; this is how the Țigan Other functions in Romanian society. The inability to frame the fantastic and projected Țigan Other in formal surveys regarding women and violence is evidenced in the 2003 Gallup survey, where women's responses regarding violence in public space (which occurred at a much lower rate than experiences of violence in private space) were not published with any mention of "Țigan" infractors. The Țigan other cannot be recognized as an existing objective category of individuals. Gallup Organization Romania Survey, "Violenței împotriva femeilor" [Violence against Women], conducted April 12–23, 2003, Bucharest (May 27, 2003).

46. For example, 46% of respondents stated that in cases of domestic violence both the victim and the aggressor were responsible for the attack in the survey of the Asociatia pentru Promovarea Femeii din Romania [Association for the Promotion of Women in Romania], a project of the "Centrul de Informare, Educație si Consiliere Timișoara pentru femeile si fețele victime ale violenței domestice și abuzului sexual" [For the Women and Girl Victims of Domestic Violence], a survey of opinions conducted July 5–7, 2002, financed through the PHARE-ACCESS program (July 2002). See also the Equal Chances for Women Foundation 1998 Survey of Women Victims of Domestic Violence, http://www.proiectns.org/archives/000050.html.

47. This is not to say that Romanian women do not discuss domestic violence with friends, family, or health workers. My discussion relates to the lack of a widespread prescriptive discourse that deals with the most common form of violence experienced by the respondents in my research. How Romanian women articulate their experiences of domestic violence among family and friends is a separate and important question.

48. Woodcock, *How to Be a Real Romanian*.

eight

Challenging the Discourse of Bosnian War Rapes

Azra Hromadzic

*The more one possess power or privilege, the more one is marked as an
individual, by rituals, written accounts or visual reproduction.*

Foucault, *The Archeology of Knowledge and the Discourse on Language*

This chapter challenges the existing discourses on the Bosnian war rapes
by capturing nuances that have been omitted in many, especially earlier,
analyses.[1] When I use the word "discourse," I use it in Foucault's sense, desig-
nating "practices that systematically form the objects of which they speak."[2]
These discourses have formed the object of the *powerless raped Bosnian
women,* and they have framed the domain and knowledge of this object. I
group these discourses into three types: *ethnic and gender group approaches,
postcolonial approaches,* and *medical approaches.*

I argue that there is a need to *challenge, individualize,* and *heterogenize*
the category *powerless raped Bosnian women,* which is casually employed in
the existing discourses and analyses of the Bosnian war rapes. Earlier analyses
of the war rapes overlooked the nuances of suffering, coping, and resistance
that were part of individual women's experiences. I argue that women's suffering, coping, and resistance must be seen against the complex interrelation
among women's multiple identities, such as religious, ethnic, urban or rural,[3]
generational, educational, and personal—a point also overlooked in most previous analysis. In order to begin to rethink the discourses of the Bosnian war

rapes, we must look at the individual women's accounts, consisting of testimonies and interviews. Only in doing this can we begin to capture the ways in which individual women sought to overcome the rapes they were subjected to. Not doing this results in denying the agency of every individual woman who suffered.

I proceed by, first, identifying my position as a Bosnian and a U.S.-educated scholar. Second, I outline the international attention paid to the Bosnian war rapes, which contextualizes the discourses. Next, I critically present the discourses themselves. I then undermine these discourses by contrasting them with women's testimonies.

Notes on Research and Method:
From the Position of a U.S.-Educated Bosnian

My suggestion that there is a need to look afresh at the testimonies and interviews stems from my own experiences and education. I lived in the small northwest Bosnia town of Bihac prior to and during the war (1992–1995). After the war ended, I moved to the United States in order to receive further academic training. My complex identity, as a native of Bosnia and Herzegovina, a secular Muslim,[4] a woman, a war survivor, and an academic educated in the United States, gives me an unusual opportunity to explore the gaps that exist between the experiences (mine and those of others around me) of the Bosnian war and the scholarly writings about it. Here I attempt to close some of the gaps between the spheres of discursive knowledge and my experience.

I was sixteen years old when the war in Bihac started in May of 1992. My memories of the first summer under siege (Bihac was besieged between 1992 and 1995) are pregnant with the pictures of Bosnian Muslim refugees coming to my hometown from surrounding areas under Serb control.[5] Thousands of people came to the town from the woods, side roads, and mountains, to escape torture and death. Most of these refugees came from places such as Donji Vakuf, Orasac, Bosanska Krupa, Sanski Most, and Prijedor, all small towns located in northwestern Bosnia. Several of the refugee families moved into my building and occupied the apartments of mostly Serb families who had left their homes a few days prior to the beginning of the siege. The demography of my hometown changed overnight. From a multiethnic environment in which Muslims, Serbs, and Croats coexisted, Bihac was transformed into a predominantly "Muslim town." During the war Bihac was surrounded by Serb forces, but it remained under the control of the Bosnian government until the end of the war. Refugees came to Bihac with no personal belongings but with numerous memories and narratives. These were stories of displacement, torture, concentration camps, and rape. I spent much time talking to the refugees in the basement of my apartment building as we hid from the constant shelling from the surrounding hills.

The refugee stories are at the heart of my project to begin to develop new, more adequate discourses for the analysis of the Bosnian war rapes, discourses that allow these stories to be heard. In the terms of Johnson and Robinson's argument about opportunities for negotiating gender after communism, I "bring into relief that each of us has multiple identities to draw from and that people can negotiate within and among these identities." Women who suffered rape in Bosnia had varied experiences and used various strategies of coping and resistance. This struggle sometimes liberated women from oppression. In other contexts, however, to resist meant to suffer greater constraint, sometimes even death.

My method for collecting and analyzing testimonies and interviews is informed by Rose Lindsey's criticism of the casual use of survivor testimony by numerous academics.[6] In various scholarly analyses "the testimony of the informant is cut off and edited, out of context, and thus only partial, so that the voice of the survivor is never entirely heard."[7] To counteract that kind of casual testimony, I carefully collected and researched the existing testimonies (a total of sixty-three) from Bosnia and the United States (diaries, tapes, films, and accounts) and other archives of rape in the Bosnian war. I also consulted over forty interviews conducted in 2001 and 2002 with a group from the region of Bihac, and I watched multiple times the movie *Calling the Ghosts*, which portrays the stories of two women victims of sexual violence. I chose the stories and interviews that appear in this chapter after examining numerous narratives such as Bosnian women's memoirs and witness accounts published by the Center for Research and Documentation of the Bosnian and Herzegovinian Concentration Camp Survivors in a book entitled *Molila sam ih da me ubiju: Zlocin nad zenom Bosne i Hercegovine*, as well as accounts collected by Seada Vranic in her book *Breaking the Wall of Silence*. Both works are politically motivated; the victims are Muslim women, and the rapists are *chetniks*,[8] or simply "the Serbs." It is important to stress that the existing data on the sexual violence during the Yugoslav wars supports the claim that the Muslim women were raped in a significantly larger number than the women of other ethnic groups.[9] It is unacceptable and unscholarly, however, to portray Muslim women as the only victims and the Serb men as the only rapists. This attitude lessens the complexity of the war situation, and it diminishes the credibility of otherwise informative works.

The International Focus on Bosnian War Rapes

European Union investigators calculated that in 1992 alone, twenty thousand Bosnian women were raped, and that by the end of the war the number was between thirty thousand and fifty thousand.[10] The numbers were extremely important for human rights activists, journalists, and feminists, who were all trying to bring Bosnian rapes to the attention of the international community. This international situation created a new forum, crucial for the political and scientific treatment of rape in the last decade (1990–2000). For the first time in the midst of the events themselves, "gender" was widely recognized to be of political and strategic importance in situations of armed conflict; "women demanded that their voices be heard, they requested their suffering to be acknowledged, and they sought punishment for the perpetrators of the crime."[11]

In reaction to the systematic rapes in the conflict in Bosnia, women's and human rights groups produced and exercised enormous pressure, ultimately creating a new debate on rape. This resulted in changes in international law, particularly in the treatment of rape in war as a crime against humanity. The organized pressure by women and antiwar and human rights groups eventually initiated an international investigation into the degree of rape and its purposes in the Bosnian war. On 27 June 1996, the International War Crimes Tribunal announced the indictment of eight male Bosnian Serb military and police officers on charges of raping Bosnian women.[12] As a consequence of a widespread, long-term effort on the part of activists, feminists, and human rights groups, this was the first time in history that rape was treated as a separate crime in war.[13]

The political discussions on the Bosnian war rapes in the international arena strongly influenced the ways in which scholars' and activists' interest in this topic developed.[14] One consequence of the great interest in the Bosnian war rapes was that it revealed competing interests and diverging agendas, as evinced in the speculation about the actual numbers, character, and circumstances of rapes of Bosnian women. As Vesna Kesic argues, the numbers were initially exaggerated (e.g., some women's groups set the number at 120,000) and rapes were characterized as "genocidal."[15] Kesic suggests that the next stage was a "counterattack from the side that was allegedly wrongly accused, the Serbs. . . . Pointing at the exaggerated numbers, they protested that nothing 'really serious' had happened. Only a 'couple thousand' women were raped."[16] These politically charged hyperboles had a strong impact on the individuals who were raped as well as on the international public. In Kesic's view, this obsession with numbers is understandable because "war rapes and other forms of violence against women were so tightly enmeshed within the categories of nation and ethnicity, so they could be recognized as war strategy, subjected to indictments as war crimes, and juridically sanctioned—in short, taken seriously—only if they occurred in large numbers, if they were systematic and followed the pattern, and if they supported the claim of genocide or ethnic cleansing."[17] It was in this context that discourses on the Bosnian war rapes were applied.

Some Pitfalls of Analysis:
The Homogenization and De-Individuation of Women

In this chapter I look at the "Western" scholarship on the Bosnian war rapes. In the category "Western" I include not only those scholars and activists who come from the "Western" part of the world, but all scholars and activists, including the ex-Yugoslav ones, who rely on these paradigms in their analysis. "Western" feminist and human rights groups often rely heavily on the political ideology and discourse of *individual* self-determination, *individual* values, *individual* human rights, *individual* experience, and *individual* voice and value. But paradoxically, in their analyses these same groups deny that very individuality of the Bosnian women victims. The individual testimonies and voices of women victims were used by some scholars and activists in order to support their already established frameworks for analyzing rape in war. As mentioned, these frameworks can be divided into three main subgroups: (1) academic discourses, which I label as ethnic and gender approaches, (2) academic and activist discourses, which include postcolonial attitudes and feminist approaches, and (3) medical and psychosocial discourses. Of course, the three sets of discourses overlap to a large extent, and scholars and activists may use various combinations of these discourses when analyzing Bosnian war rapes. Most scholars, however, have in one way or another homogenized the diverse experiences of the women victims, thus creating a generic *powerless raped Bosnian woman* object of knowledge and discourse.

The Emphasis on Ethnicity and Gender

One of the most dominant approaches to the analysis of ethno-political conflicts is, of course, a focus on ethnicity. This approach is based on the idea that the conflict between ethnic groups is the main explicator for an understanding of the phenomena of war. Consequently, many analyses have the division between bounded groups at their core. In this context, the rapes of the women in Bosnia are analyzed as rapes of Muslim women by Serb men, or of Muslim women by Croat men, or of Muslim men by Serbs, and so on. This dominant approach emphasizes the group and ignores individual experiences of violence, because ethnicity and thus collective identity is what matters in this paradigm.[18] Only a few scholars, such as Korac, challenge this order of things and explain the "state-imposed divisions among women along and within ethnic-national lines" by contrasting these state policies with the women's lived experiences.[19]

One of the ways to break away from this "ethnic monopoly" in the analysis of the Bosnian war rapes is to introduce additional aspects of analysis that are omitted in the ethnic discourse. Some scholars, for example, use gender as the primary category in their analyses, and they explore the interplay between ethnicity and gender in times of war.[20] The main argument behind this approach is that "this so-called ethnic war was totally gendered."[21] These scholars argue that it is necessary to transgress the boundaries of the ethnic group approach and show the gender-specific sides of this crime. For instance, Olujic emphasizes how war rapes in the former Yugoslavia would not be such an effective weapon of torture if it were not for the concepts of female honor and shame and the peacetime meanings of sexuality that existed long before the war.[22] Similarly, Zarkov argues that in the discourse about the Bosnian war, ethnic hatred has intertwined with the discourse on male and female sexuality and their sexual bodies.[23]

The gender approaches, however, have to be critically applied and examined as well, since gender is an additional, not an all-encompassing, category of analysis. Gender approaches enable for a much more profound understanding of the role of rapes in the Bosnian war, but in these discourses the "raped woman" object is often imagined as an a priori, self-explanatory category of analysis. As a consequence of this level of analysis, the diversity and subjective experiences of women victims have been overlooked. In other words, these discourses (like ethnic group approaches) operate at the level of collective or group identity and omit the fact that there is more than one way of being a Bosnian woman and a woman victim of rape. Diversity among women victims has been ignored by the researchers who stress the shared gender identity of a victim. The advantages and disadvantages of this approach will be further discussed in the following paragraphs.

(Post)colonialism and Rape

There is a strong parallel between the way feminist groups in the "West" approach issues of women in the "Third World"[24] *generally* and the way these groups approach the Bosnian war rapes. In both situations there is a strong emphasis on "universal sisterhood/womanhood"—the idea that the "Western" women who have achieved some level of equality and power in their own societies need to export/disseminate this acquired knowledge and liberate the women in the "Third World."[25] I want to emphasize here that "Western" feminisms are complex historical products of the process of individuation of women (through civil rights and human rights) in the "West."[26] But when it comes to the "Third World," processes of individuation are either uncritically assumed or taken for granted by Western scholars and/or feminists. Chandra Talpade Mohanty, in her analysis of "Western" feminisms, points at this problem by observing the following:

> I would like to suggest that the ["Western"] feminist writings I analyze here discursively colonize the material and historical heterogeneities of the lives of women in the Third World, thereby producing/re-presenting a composite, singular "Third World Women"—an image which appears arbitrarily constructed, but nevertheless carries with it the authorizing signature of Western humanist discourse. Western feminisms appropriate and "colonize" the fundamental complexities and conflicts which characterize the lives of women of different classes, religions, and castes in these countries.[27]

Nevertheless, Talpade Mohanty emphasizes the importance of "Western" feminist discourse and action for "Third World" women. These "Western" feminists were the main actors in breaking the silence of "Third World" women and giving them a voice, and they forged international links between women's political struggles. Talpade Mohanty argues that "Western" feminists' work is essential for women around the world, but that differences (in attitudes, ethnicity, race, etc.) among women have to be emphasized as well. The complex cultural, political, and historical contexts in which women are situated and in which they participate have to be considered when building bridges between women's struggles across national and ethnic boundaries.[28]

Talpade Mohanty's criticism and my own criticism of the U.S. scholarship on the Bosnian war rapes are similar. Like Talpade Mohanty, I want to recognize the importance of "Western" scholars and activists in advancing women's position in the world. Their pressure was crucial in getting rape on the international political agenda and in making decision makers aware of the necessity of viewing rape as a crime against humanity. This work has led to some groundbreaking changes in the treatment of women and humanity in general. Bosnian war rape reports became essential for understanding and prosecuting rape in wars.[29]

However, many "Western" feminist groups saw Bosnian rapes through the lenses of their own agendas, and they treated Bosnian women accordingly. Under their Western-style "universal womanhood" and human rights discourses, the cultural and social complexities, subjective sufferings, and individual resistances of women victims all blended into one story of suffering. In other words, the object *powerless raped Bosnian women* was discursively formed as an already constituted and bounded a priori category. Female Bosnian war victims, as Talpade Mohanty found of Third World women, were "characterized as a singular group on the basis of a shared oppression . . . and . . . they were socially constituted as a homogeneous group identified *prior* to the process of analysis."[30]

Medicalization of Raped Women's Experiences

In numerous reports on the Bosnian war rapes, the rape-victim's suffering, if recognized, was immediately "psychiatrized." Many Western and local doctors and social workers, even with honest intentions to help the victims of rape, reduced the experience of war and rape to post-traumatic stress disorder (PTSD). Similarly, Malkki and Pupavac have shown how this was done to refugees in the past, who were routinely discursively formed and described as "traumatized," "psychologically scarred," "hopeless," "overwhelmed by grief," and so forth.[31]

The overuse of the PTSD diagnosis to explain the suffering of the women victims involves two main problems in the analyses of the Bosnian war rapes. First, even if it is statistically true that Bosnian raped women suffer PTSD, obviously one should not assume that each individual raped woman suffers PTSD. Such an inference clouds the significance of individual trauma and blurs individual difference, claiming that raped Bosnian women undergo the same psychological experience. Secondly, the medical/psychosocial approaches, by focusing exclusively on rape, lessen other traumas women victims experienced or are still in the process of experiencing.[32] Women experience not only rape in war, but other pain as well. For example, women lose parents, husbands, and children, become displaced, are driven into poverty, and so on. Yet, PTSD, by focusing on *post-rape* trauma, effectively reduces the victims' experience of war and postwar. It thereby creates a hierarchy in the memory of subjective suffering (i.e., rape becomes the main focus around which all other suffering and identities are organized). In other words, psychosocial and medical discourses do not take into consideration that individual victims suffer not only from rape-induced PTSD. Their experiences are shaped by a complex dynamic of "cultural countering of memory and historiography."[33] Recently, there have been some sophisticated critiques of the PTSD analysis and "other recuperations of traumatic memory whose fictive psycho-medical legitimacy"[34] has been challenged by scholars such as Young, Hacking, and Pupavac.

The three homogenizing discourses go to represent the category I am calling "powerless raped Bosnian women." Recently, a few scholars, such as Lindsey, Korac, Cockburn, and Walsh,[35] have hinted at some problems introduced by the homogenizing discourses and generalizations. These scholars have argued, each in her own way, for a more careful reading and use of the survivor's experiences, where additional attention is given to women's personal stories and accounts of war. Likewise, in what follows I turn to the individual testimonies and interviews in order to challenge the constructions of "raped women," "Bosnian women," and "powerless women."

Individualizing Women Victims: The Heterogeneity of Experience

I argue that the testimonies of women victimized by violence should be the starting point from which to challenge the existing top-down discourses. The top-down accounts are problematic because they cram survivors' testimonies into the already existing mold of theories of violence in war. These works habitually portray women as powerless recipients of violence, despite the fact that many of these women, as I am about to present, found various ways of coping and defying the violence that was inflicted on them. These forms of coping and defiance are subculturally specific and vary according to individual difference.

As a result of the abovementioned international attention, Bosnian women were invited to speak at The Hague Tribunal, and some decided to share their experiences. Many of those who agreed to speak had left Bosnia, but some women who had stayed in their Bosnian homes also decided to speak out. While some women victims felt better after giving testimonies, others experienced testifying as further suffering. Several women who had the courage to testify about sexualized violence were often forced to relive their traumas during the trial. In addition, "they risked being ostracized by their society for speaking out about something that is taboo."[36]

Women's "multiple and fluid identifications tend to disrupt the singular identifications"[37] of "raped," "Bosnian," and "powerless." The Bosnian women victims of violence became only secondarily "women": the term "raped" became their label and their identity. Many women victims found this treatment traumatizing, tasteless, and limiting. For example, Nusreta, a lawyer from Prijedor who was raped multiple times in the Omarska concentration camp and who is one of the two protagonists in a documentary film on the Bosnian war rapes (*Calling the Ghosts*), says: "[W]e cannot divide women into two categories: raped and not raped, as if they are some exhibits in the window . . . as if their only identity and characteristic are that they were raped . . . that sounds terrible, 'raped women' . . . we need to look for some other term, not so exclusive and limiting, maybe 'women victims of war,' or 'tortured women,' but not raped."[38] Nusreta's statement illustrates how the phrase "raped women" became like a mantra, casually used by journalists, politicians, activists, academics, and laymen.[39]

Another commonly used phrase is the expression "Bosnian women," which came to represent a homogeneous group of women. The interviews I collected, however, show that Bosnian women have developed different identities and cannot be subsumed under a general category of "Bosnian women." All informants I interviewed were overwhelmed when I asked them to describe or draw a "typical" Bosnian woman. One of the informants (I.A.) responded by saying that her answer depends on the region or the town we were discussing: "*Baksais* women are different from *Ozimice* women, and both groups are different from the refugee women, who are again different from [downtown] city women."[40] This informant described a "Bosnian woman" as a smelly, village type of woman, as well as a progressive, smart, ambitious, and creative woman.[41] This answer, which agrees with the other answers I received from my informants in the northwestern part of Bosnia, suggests the complexity and problematic use of the category "Bosnian women" in the numerous analyses of the war rapes.[42] There is no "typical Bosnian woman"; there are only Bosnian women who differ tremendously from one another and who represent different religious, ethnic, educational, historical-geographic, social, political, and age groups. Thus, apparently self-contradictory answers such as "the typical Bosnian woman is covered, obedient, weak, passive, strong, energetic, intelligent, successful, smart, limited, smelly . . ." make sense in the turbulent and colorful Bosnian history and in certain sociopolitical contexts. Bosnian women are extremely diverse among themselves, and in the analysis of the Bosnian war and postwar situations, these differences "divide" Bosnian society among many layers of identity. These different identities were important for the victims' coping attempts and strategies of resistance in war.

The third phrase that has subtly dominated our understanding of the Bosnian war rapes is the "powerless [raped Bosnian] women." Granted, the women were victimized, but, as with the other singular identifications, something here too is lost. In this case unique forms of resistance, however slight or great, are overshadowed by the discourse of "the victim." The following testimonies[43] show clear signs of empowerment in the midst of ethnic, gender, and political violence.

Enisa's story shows how the common portrait of the passive raped women is inaccurate. Enisa was a young teacher who was raped by her student in a rape camp near Prijedor:

> I decided to start singing and by singing to try to convince other women in the camp of my madness. The story spread around the camp that I lost my mind since I never stopped singing for days, even when the rapists would threaten me with knives and guns. I sang until the soldiers decided to take me out of the camp and dump me near the road that led to Croatia. Only after I made sure that I was in safe hands did I stop singing. I believe that the Serbs decided not to kill a mad woman because of their superstitious beliefs that suggest that the one who kills a crazy person will be visited by demons.[44]

Enisa resisted her captivity and devised a means to escape the torture and rape. She showed admirable creativity and some culturally specific forms of behavior. In order to purchase her freedom, Enisa relied on the cultural knowledge of the particular relationship between "madness, death, and demons" that was apparently held by her torturers. This strategic employment of cultural knowledge saved Enisa's life.

Other women used their physical power to resist the rapes. Senda, a young woman from Foca, testifies:

> The next night they came for me to take me to some Bosnia [Bosnian Muslim] house in Foca where they locked me into one room. In the room there was a bottle of *rakija* [domestic brandy] and some meat wrapped in the newspaper. Half-an-hour later, they brought in an older Serb civilian. He was more than 60 years old. He was drunk and he immediately started insulting me and my Muslim faith. In front of the room, there was a younger *chetnik*, to whom the older guy said: "Watch the door while this *bula* [Muslim girl/women who practices Islam] licks my whole body and sucks it [his penis]." He forced me to drink *rakija*, which I refused to do. Then he forced me to undress and dance in front of him. Then I jumped on him and started to strangle him, madly and desperately, without thinking about the consequences. We wrestled for a few minutes until he gave up. When he recovered, he got up and left. Leaving, he said to the *chetnik* outside that the *bula* gave herself to him [with no resistance].[45]

Some women prisoners tried to save other women from rape. Edita and her younger sister were both at the Center for Mentally Retarded Children in a town called Hadzici, not too far from Sarajevo, when the war started. At the very beginning of the war, some members of the Yugoslav People's Army entered the center and started to sexually abuse young girls. Edita's younger sister was only twelve years old when she was raped by one of the soldiers:

> One day the nurse Milena ran anxiously into our room, and told me to follow her, because *chetnik* Dragan came up to my sister and told her that

she has to come with him to the room with the central heating system. I ran out as fast as I could, entered the room, and after much struggle, I succeeded to save my sister from Dragan. Since then, I carry the scars on my hands and arms. I earned them from Dragan when he cut me with a knife while I was trying to rescue my sister. Luckily, Ranko Sajinovic from Doboj was there and he helped my sister and me. He cursed at Dragan for harassing a mentally retarded and unprotected child.[46]

Other women attempted to mask their feminine features in order to escape violence. Fatima, a young and pretty woman from Foca and a mother of a young child, was captured by the Serbs, together with a few dozen of people from her town, while trying to escape the town through the woods:

They asked us about the weapons—whose weapons we carried? No one said anything except for Meliha and Selma who complained that the Serb soldiers were beating us too hard. One of the soldiers come up to them and hit them again. He hit Selma twice on her injured head, and asked: "Why are you talking?" I pulled my child closer to my body, while he was walking towards me. He violently pulled my hair and said: "Look at this beauty. Shall we get married?" Another solder with a long hair pulled in a pony tail told him to leave me alone, because he saw me first, and wanted me for himself. Meanwhile, the whole group started to move again. While walking, secretly, I started to cover my arms and my face with mud and dirt, to make my skin darker not to look so beautiful and feminine.[47]

Aida's story shows how some women victims successfully used the strategy of befriending one of their rapists, in order to avoid gang rapes:

Once I was raped by Zoran Samardzic. He was monstrous—you cannot imagine something that terrible. After that I decided to ask "Roko" to come and sleep in my room and do nothing, just be there, because I was fed up with the gang rapes. He started to sleep in my room, and since then, other *chetniks* came less frequently. We women concluded that if one woman had "her own" *chetnik* next to her, she would be rescued from gang rapes and other extreme forms of violence.[48]

The story of Berina, a young woman from Visegrad who was raped for days by a soldier, Mikavica (Misa), illustrates a different kind of resistance. In the words of a friend:

One morning Berina whispered in my ear that she would bite his penis off if he makes her perform oral sex again. I begged her not to, to be strong. One night they came inside, walking over our heads, stepping on the women who were sleeping on the floor. Ratko took me, and Misa took Berina. I was raped for 30 minutes when we heard the scream coming from the room next door. The scream came out of Misa's mouth. Ratko stopped raping me and started putting his clothes on. Suddenly, Misa entered the room we were in, screaming and waving the gun in his hand. When he saw me on the bed he shot at me twice. Ratko stopped him and took his pistol away. He came closer to me, since I was bleeding. I was shot by two bullets; one ended up in my hip, the other one between my left shoulder and my breast. I was in the hospital for 10 days. Only after I came out I learned what had happen that night. Berina was dead. She did what she said she would. Misa tried to force her to kiss his penis. She bit him so strongly that she almost cut off his penis. He, while screaming madly and in terrible pain, got his gun and killed her at the place. Then he came to our room.[49]

Although Berina did not survive Mikavica's reaction to her resistance, her story demonstrates a choice not to remain a passive victim. In this case, the cost of the resistance was extremely high; it ended with Berina's death. Berina's story was told by another informant, her friend. This introduces additional questions regarding authenticity, memory, and representation in testimonies, and it further complicates the relationship between resistance, power, and agency. Does the resistance of an individual to violent oppression still constitute agency if it ends in death? If yes, what kind of agency is it? An attempt to answer these questions, however, is beyond the scope of this paper.

There are many more examples that show the resistance of the women victims. The failure to see such individual resistance limits our analysis and knowledge of gendered war violence and feeds the notions of the "passive and powerless raped women." The coping mechanisms and active acts of resistance to ethno-political inequalities and violence that can be found in individual testimonies point to the fact that women are taking an active stance contesting these discourses. These women suffered, coped, and resisted in individual ways, ways understood relative to the particular intersection of social, political, economic, regional, and cultural background in question.

Careful ethnographic fieldwork, interviews, and sociolinguistic analysis would index the differences among raped Bosnian women, and thereby enrich our knowledge about the scope of women's suffering from war rapes and the relationships between suffering and coping, memory and history, and victims' particular mosaic of social, cultural, and political identities. This kind of approach would eventually erode the common ways of portraying the *powerless raped women* in Bosnia.

Conclusion

In this chapter, I address the limitations of present-day academic and activists' analyses and discourses on rapes in ethno-political conflict. I argue that in order to enrich our knowledge about this violent practice, we need to pay attention to individual testimonies and interviews. By using this bottom-up approach, we are not blind to other aspects of the experience of rape in war, as well as the ways in which different individuals and subgroups of victims cope with these experiences.

One might wonder why many scholars and activists have not heeded the individual voices in their analyses and simply have applied the already existing "gender," "ethnic," and "medical" discourses and paradigms. Here are a few possible reasons. First, initial analyses of war rapes had to be produced quickly, because it was crucial for the international community and for scholars to enter into a discussion on what had happened; at that time, testimonies were not available, or scholars might not have had time to actually read these testimonies. Second, scholars and activists unfamiliar with the language of the testimonies may have overlooked linguistic differences that index regional, socioeconomic, educational, and religious identities among Bosnian women victims. In addition, much was lost in the translations of the testimonies from Bosnian into English or other languages.

Many would say that an individual-based analysis is too complicated and leads to multiple and scattered directions of inquiry. Additionally, some critics may point at the small number of testimonies that I use to support my arguments. My aim, however, is not to present a statistically valid and general argument, but to illuminate the weaknesses in the existing theories of war rapes, which often favor numbers and general categories over individual voices. The voices of women, located in the testimonies and interviews, encompass enormous creativity and individual capacity for coping with violence in highly profound and subculturally specific ways. These diverse aspects of survival and suffering deserve a stronger emphasis in our analyses if we are to understand how women cope with gender and ethnic violence both during war and in postwar situations.

The differences in identities among women victims are crucial for our understanding of the culture of rape and the use of rape as a war strategy. Attention must be paid to both group and individual experiences. One might wonder what we can learn about rape as a war strategy if we focus on the individual victims. I would argue that we cannot forget that rape is, even in war, *also* an individual act. However, our task does not stop with the individual. To be sure, first we need to find the individual voices within the scholarship on rape. After the (re)discovery of individual voices and testimonies, we can reconstruct these patterns of experience and behavior in order to shed new light on what happened in Bosnia between 1992 and 1995.

NOTES

An earlier version of this paper was published as "Kriegsvergewaltigungen in Bosnien: Alte und neue Erklaerungsansaetze" [War Rapes in Bosnia: Old and New Approaches], in *Gender, Identitaet und kriegerischer Konflikt: Das Beispiel des ehemaligen Jugoslawien* [*Gender, Identity and Armed Conflict: The Example of the Former Yugoslavia*], ed. Ruth Seifert (Muenster, Germany: Lit Publishers, 2004), 112–30. This research was supported by a grant from the Solomon Asch Center for Study of Ethnopolitical Conflict at the University of Pennsylvania. Aaron Vlasak deserves special mention for his intellectual contribution to this chapter. In addition, I wish to express my gratitude to the editors of this volume for their valuable suggestions. I also gratefully acknowledge the help of Helen Cunningham, Heather Michel, Genevra Murray, and Lakshmi Ramarajan in regards to various parts and versions of this chapter.

1. Exceptions to this trend include Rose Lindsey, "From Atrocity to Data: Histo-riographies of Rape in Former Yugoslavia and the Gendering of Genocide," *Patterns of Prejudice* 36, no. 4 (2002): 59–78; Cynthia Cockburn, *The Space between Us: Negotiating Gender and National Identities in Conflict* (London: Zed Books, 1998); Maja Korac, "Refugee Women in Serbia: Their Experiences of War, Nationalism, and State Building," in *Women, Citizenship, and Difference*, ed. Nira Yuval-Davis and Pnina Werbner (London: Zed Books, 1999); and Martha Walsh, "Mind the Gap: Where Feminist Theory Failed to Meet Development Practice; A Missed Opportunity in Bosnia and Herzegovina," *European Journal of Women's Studies* 5, no. 3–4 (1998): 329–43.

2. Michel Foucault, *The Archeology of Knowledge and the Discourse on Language* (New York: Pantheon Books, 1972), 48.

3. For an analysis on the gap that opened between rural and urban women see Maja Korac, "Prisoners of their Sex," M.A. thesis (Belgrade: Institute for Sociology, Faculty of Philosophy, University of Belgrade, 1991).

4. Muslim here stands for ethnicity, not religion.

5. The legal term for these people is Internally Displaced Persons (IDPs). However, I will use the term "refugee" when referring to these individuals since this is the term they used to describe themselves, and it was also a term that other people in my town used when talking about them. Displaced populations are the consequence of a coerced displacement of persons *within* the borders of their countries, while refugees live, as consequence of a coerced displacement, outside the country of their former habitual residence.

6. Lindsey, "From Atrocity to Data," 59.

7. Ibid., 63.

8. *Chetniks* are the members of the Serb paramilitary forces with a long history of violence, massacres, and extreme nationalism during WWII and the recent wars.

9. See Beverly Allen, *Rape Warfare: The Hidden Genocide in Bosnia-Herzegovina and Croatia* (Minneapolis: University of Minnesota Press, 1996); Joanne Barkan, "As Old as Rape Itself: Rape in Foca," *Dissent* 49, no. 1 (2002); Cockburn, *The Space between Us*; Swanee Hunt, "Silovannje" [Rape], in *Molila sam ih da me ubiju: Zlocin nad zenom Bosne i Hercegovine* [I Begged Them to Kill Me: Crimes against Women of Bosnia-Herzegovina] (Sarejevo: Centar za istrazivanje i dokumentaciju Saveza log-orasa Bosne i Hercegovine, 1999); Ruth Seifert, "War and Rape: Preliminary Analysis," in *Mass Rape: The War against Women in Bosnia-Herzegovina*, ed. Alexandra Stigl-mayer (Lincoln: University of Nebraska Press, 1994); Stiglmayer, *Mass Rape*; Seada Vranic, *Breaking the Wall of Silence: the Voices of Raped Bosnia* (Zagreb: Izdanja Antibarbarus, 1996); and Dubravka Zarkov, "Gender, Orientalism and the History of Ethnic Hatred in the Former Yugoslavia," in *Crossfires: Nationalism, Racism and Gender in Europe*, ed. Helma Lutz, Ann Phoenix, and Nira Yuval-Davis (London: European Forum for Left Feminists, 1995).

10. Cynthia Enloe, *Maneuvers: The International Politics of Militarizing Women's Lives*. (Berkeley: University of California Press, 2000), 141.

11. Barkan, "As Old as Rape Itself," 64.

12. In 1993 the United Nations voted the International Crime Tribunal for ex-Yugoslavia (ICTY) into existence. The precedent for this court was the existence of the international war crimes tribunals at Nuremberg and in the Far East after WWII. See Barkan, "As Old as Rape Itself," 62.

13. Ibid.

14. Cockburn, *The Space between Us*, 170.

15. Vesna Kesic, "Muslim Women, Croatian Women, Serbian Women, Albanian Women . . ." in *Balkan as Metaphor: Between Globalization and Fragmentation*, ed. D. Bjelic and O. Savic (Cambridge, Mass.: MIT Press, 2002).

16. Kesic, "Muslim Women," 317.

17. Ibid.

18. See Roy Gutman, *A Witness to Genocide* (New York: MacMillan, 1993); Beverly Allen, *Rape Warfare: The Hidden Genocide in Bosnia-Herzegovina and Croatia* (Minneapolis: University of Minnesota Press, 1996); Vesna Nikolic-Ristanovic, *Women, Violence, and War: Wartime Victimization of Refugees in the Balkans* (Budapest: Central European University Press, 2000); Seifert, "War and Rape"; Robert M. Hayden, "Rape and Rape Avoidance in Ethno-National Conflicts: Sexual Violence in Liminalized States," *American Anthropologist* 102, no. 1 (2000): 27–41.

19. Korac, "Refugee Women in Serbia," 192.

20. See, for instance: Zarkov, "Gender, Orientalism and the History of Ethnic Hatred in the Former Yugoslavia"; Rada Boric, "Against the War: Women Organizing across the National Divide in the Countries of the Former Yugoslavia," in *Gender and Catastrophe*, ed. Ronit Lentin (New York: Zed Books Ltd., 1997); Ruth Seifert, "Der weibliche Koerper als Symbol und Zeichen: Geschlechtsspezifische Gewalt und die kulturelle Konstruktion des Krieges" [The Female Body as a Symbol and a Sign: Gender-Specific Violence and the Cultural Construction of War], in *Gewalt im Krieg* [Violence in War], ed. Andreas Gestrich (Muenster, Germany: Lit Verlag, 1996); Ruth Seifert, "The Use of Women and the Role of Women in the Yugoslav War," in *Gender, Peace and Conflict*, ed. Inger Skjelsbaek and Dan Smith (London: Sage Publications, 2001); Catherine A. MacKinnon, "Crimes of War, Crimes of Peace," in *The Aftermath of Rape: Women's Rights, War Crimes and Genocide*, ed. Elenor Richter-Lyonette (Ancien College: Coordination of Women's Advocacy, 1995); Maria B. Olujic, "Embodiment of Terror: Gendered Violence in Peacetime and Wartime in Croatia and Bosnia-Herzegovina," *Medical Anthropology Quarterly* 12, no. 1 (1998): 31–50; Hunt, "Silovannje"; Julie Mostov, "Our Women, Their Women: Symbolic Boundaries, Territorial Markers, and Violence in the Balkans," *Peace and Change: A Journal of Peace Research* 20, no. 4 (1995); Julie Mostov, "Sexing the Nation/Desexing the Body: Politics of National Identity in the Former Yugoslavia," in *Gender Ironies of Nationalism: Sexing the Nation*, ed. Tamar Mayer (London: Routledge, 2001).

21. Cockburn, *The Space between Us*, 207.

22. Olujic, "Embodiment of Terror," 33.

23. Zarkov, "Gender, Orientalism and the History of Ethnic Hatred in the Former Yugoslavia," 113.

24. The phrase "Third World Women" is itself problematic because it is both colonizing and homogenizing. However, I use it here for lack of a better term.

25. Chandra Talpade Mohanty, "Under Western Eyes: Feminist Scholarship and Colonial Discourses," in *The Postcolonial Studies Reader*, ed. Bill Ashcoft, Gareth Griffiths, and Helen Tiffin (London: Routledge, 1995), 259–63.

26. I am grateful to Ruth Seifert for helping me think through this idea.

27. Talpade Mohanty, "Under Western Eyes," 260.

28. Ibid.

29. See Kesic, "Muslim Women."

30. Talpade Mohanty, "Under Western Eyes," 262.

31. Vanessa Pupavac, "Pathologizing Populations and Colonizing Minds: International Psychosocial Programs in Kosovo," *Alternatives: Global, Local, Political* 27, no. 4 (2002): 489. See also Liisa H. Malkki, "Refugees and Exile: From 'Refugee Studies' to the National Order of Things," *Annual Review of Anthropology* 24, no. 1 (1995): 495–523.

32. Cockburn, *The Space between Us,* 180.

33. Allen Feldman, "Strange Fruit: The South African Truth Commission and the Domestic Economies of Violence," *Social Analysis* 46, no. 3 (2002): 263.

34. Ibid., 236.

35. Lindsey, "From Atrocity to Data"; Korac, "Refugee Women in Serbia"; Cockburn, *The Space between Us*; and Walsh "Mind the Gap."

36. Kvinna till Kvina, *Report on Testifying about Sexualized Violence in War* (Stockholm: 2003).

37. Korac, "Refugee Women in Serbia," 200.

38. From the movie *Calling the Ghosts.*

39. I thank the anonymous reviewers for this remark.

40. Baksais and Ozimice are two parts of the town of Bihac, which has 70,000 inhabitants.

41. Interview with I.A., 8/21/01.

42. The responses to the same question given to me by informants in Herzegovina (Bileca) greatly contrast the answers I received from women in the same age group in northwestern Bosnia (Bihac).

43. I translated all but one of the following testimonies from Bosnian into English. When the names of the women victims were not available, I used common Bosnian female names.

44. Vranic, *Breaking the Wall of Silence,* 103.

45. *Molila sam ih da me ubiju,* 391.

46. *Molila sam ih da me ubiju,* 172.

47. *Molila sam ih da me ubiju,* 388.

48. *Molila sam ih da me ubiju,* 166.

49. *Molila sam ih da me ubiju,* 208.

Deficient Belarus?

Insidious Gender Binaries and
Hyper-feminized Nationality

Anna Brzozowska

Belarus did not yield to the wave of nationalism that swept across the former Soviet bloc states in the late 1980s and early 1990s. The country regained its independence in 1991 and, in contrast to the neighboring states overwhelmed by ethnic and nationalistic tensions, remained peaceful. At first open to the national resurgence symbolized by Zianon Pazniak and the Popular Front, the population of Belarus seemed to have ultimately chosen the "old" through their vote for Aleksandr Lukashenka (in 1994) and the approval of the policy of close integration with Russia.

In the understanding of many political scientists, these choices demonstrate the lack of national sentiment. They indicate that it was a weak identity that made Belarus seek reunification with Russia.[1] This chapter, trying to understand this classification of Belarus, offers an in-depth analysis of the discourse of Belarusians. I attempt to make sense of the kind of identity that has been (re)constructed in Belarus since the collapse of the Soviet Union, posing the question if, indeed, it cannot be called a national one.

I draw upon the literature that examines the "gendering" of national identification and that observes that portrayals of nations frequently invoke feminine symbolism and feminine metaphors.[2] This literature argues that imagining the nation as predominantly female can contribute to the creation of concrete individual subjectivities that orient people's behavior in specific situations.[3] Depending on the symbolism through which a nation is constructed, its people may be deployed in the world in a particular way, prone to take certain actions and reluctant to take others. "Nation" and "gender," although both culturally constructed, exert powerful control over attitudes and preferences. These constructs influence decisions, making some things natural while labeling others as deviant or not allowing them even to be imagined.

Although the nation is predominantly represented as feminine, this very representation is possible only if there exists a masculinity against which femininity is contrasted. Engendering, then, bases itself on the reference to binary oppositions. "Masculine-feminine" forms the most powerful and basic pair of oppositions, and all other primary values, such as light/dark, up/down, reason/emotion, and culture/nature, tend to reinforce one or the other pole of it. Typically, one of the opposites is always seen as "positive" (usually masculinity) and the other as a "negative," or lacking (often femininity). At the same time, as the deconstructive work of Derrida demonstrates, oppositions are not stable, and there is always a space for "play" within them.[4] "Femininity" is consequently an overdetermined category, in the sense that it can be characterized in several plausible ways that do not exclude one another.[5]

Thus, "engendering" a nation may also mean its re-masculinization as in the ethnicity discourses or attempts to (re)gain control over reproduction. In newly reborn nation-states across Eastern Europe, for example, the ethnically informed accentuation of differences between masculinity and femininity has been a factor in anti-abortion debates.[6] As a result of the postcommunist derision of the socialist ideology of equality, women have been "othered" as main benefactors and implicit supporters of communism. Consequently, efforts have been made to discipline them and reduce them to their traditional roles.[7]

National discourse may marginalize women because, as Belarusian scholar Elena Gapova argued on the basis of her country's experience, this discourse is "not so much about the national belonging as about class interests."[8] It was constructed by one class—intellectuals—who used it while competing for scarce resources. The idea was used, she claimed, to justify the unfairness of new gender inequality and to obscure the real goal of female marginalization with noble slogans of national freedom.[9] In her more recent work, Gapova draws explicit comparison between national and class projects, both of which make use of symbolic references to feminine/masculine and demand concrete gender arrangements.'[10]

Interested in the intersection between gender and nation, I show how feminizing—and more broadly, gendering—has been incorporated into the reimagining of the Belarusian nation, and how this gendering may have contributed to the production of concrete subjectivities that orient Belarusians in everyday life. I argue that both the academic discourse in Belarus and the self-descriptions of Belarus by Belarusian citizens are strongly gendered, even hyper-feminized. This hyper-feminization means that imagining Belarus as an autonomous nation is hardly possible. It may be responsible for Belarus's weak position within an international system that predominantly links strength with masculinity.

I start my analysis by contextualizing within its political history the current process of reimagining of the Belarusian nation. I then describe my method of discourse analysis of extended, semi-structured, in-depth interviews with both Russian- and Belarusian-speaking elites. Next, I interrogate the literature on identity, gender, and nation. My findings look at the way Belarusian citizens perceive themselves. I am interested in whether/how they ascribe certain values, stereotypically marked as "female," to their identity. In conclusion, I argue that Belarusians' self-descriptions implicitly reproduce and reinforce the stereotypic female-male dichotomy, thus leading to discriminative classifications and (self)perceptions.

Belarus as a "Deviant" Case

Belarus, in spite of its long and troubled history and its location in the heart of the European continent, remains barely visible in international politics. In the Middle Ages, the territories of present Belarus belonged to the powerful Great Duchy of Lithuania, which also contained today's Poland, Lithuania, and part of Ukraine. Following the partitions of Poland in the eighteenth century, the majority of Belarusians became subjects of the Russian empire. One year after Belarus declared independence in 1918, the Bolshevik Revolution brought about the creation of the Belarusian Soviet Republic.

Under Soviet rule, the land and the people were severely tried. In the late 1920s and 30s, Stalinist purges of the intelligentsia robbed the country of its elite. During World War II, 25 percent of the population lost their lives. In the 1980s, Belarus's population suffered immense consequences of radiation in the fallout of the Chernobyl tragedy. Yet despite these and other injustices, the communist-era dissident movement was very weak.

Belarus became an independent state only in August 1991, following in the footsteps of the Baltic states and Ukraine. Unlike those of other former satellites, Belarusian leaders have been unwilling to engage in market reforms, and since 1995 the country's economic system has been described by President Aleksandr Lukashenka as "market socialism." The state continues to control prices and currency exchange rates and to intervene in private business via frequent inspections. Regulations have been constantly changing without any public consultation, while any sign of political protest or social unrest is nipped in the bud.

Also atypical for this region, Belarus has turned toward the Russian Federation in its foreign policy, signing a number of treaties with it.[11] The ultimate creation of a common political system was planned for and justified as a replication of the success of the European Union. In the early 1990s Belarus was a docile participant in the international arena. It gave away nuclear weapons without any negotiations,[12] before all the deadlines, and displayed considerable passivity, epitomized by such statements as the one made by Stanislav Sushkievich, speaker of the Parliament: "We are a small country; we will accept whatever Russia and Ukraine agree on."[13]

Yet, a national-democratic movement sprang up following the discovery of the mass graves filled with Stalin's victims in Kuropaty and followed the common Eastern-European pattern of national resurgence. In the mid-1990s, two competing camps emerged in politics. The national and democratically minded group saw Belarus as part of Europe and Western tradition and trusted the country would ultimately join European institutions. Competing with that vision of Belarus was one placing the country within the Russian sphere of influence and proud of the Slavic and Orthodox roots of the nation. The two discourses are fluid and at times even overlapping. Their central parts are, however, not compatible— one is informed by liberal, democratic, and individualistic philosophy, the other by communist nostalgia and egalitarian tendencies.[14]

Aleksandr Lukashenka epitomizes the latter version of Belarusian-ness. A former *sovkhoz* (state-owned farm) manager, Lukashenka knew how to address thousands of his compatriots who could not find their own way in the new reality. He came "from nowhere," and in 1994 his victory was a surprise for many, including Russian leaders who supported former prime minister Kebich. As soon as he was in power Lukashenka started to abuse his position— controlling media, fighting with the opposition, imprisoning uncomfortable or critically minded people, and tampering with electoral results. His success and ability to maintain his status need to be understood in a more complex context. It should be recognized that at least partly they result from Lukashenka's exploitation of the heavily gendered national discourse.

Narratives of Belarusian Nationality

To address the two central questions of this study—to what degree Belarus possesses a specific national identity and how or whether that identity is being feminized/gendered—I analyzed material collected during a series of extended, semi-structured interviews with about forty members of the Belarusian elite.[15] The interviewees comprised Belarusian and Russian speakers, women and men, and representatives of age groups between nineteen and fifty-four. The group included artists, businessmen, and people involved in politics. All the interviews were conducted between August 2000 and October 2001. In order to support my small sample, I compared their responses against press material; excerpts of textbooks, poetry, and fiction; radio broadcasts; opinion polls conducted by foreign and local independent institutes; and officially published texts of Lukashenka's speeches.[16]

I would like to emphasize that within this chapter I purposefully do not draw a distinction between the Russian and Belarusian speakers, the only exception being the section where I talk of Belarusians who are devoid of their own voice (language). This decision is dictated by the fact that while listening to both linguistic groups I noticed the same symbols and metaphors being reproduced, irrespective of the mother tongue. It seemed to me that drawing a linguistic or ethnic line between the two groups would be an incorrect choice. Many of my interlocutors described themselves as patriots—and yet did not speak Belarusian. During the general census they marked the Belarusian language as their native tongue, but they confessed during the interviews that they felt uncomfortable trying to use it as they could not express themselves fluently. Others stressed that although they speak only Russian (one interlocutor was born in Russia and came to study in Belarus, where he stayed), they are not less Belarusian than those who religiously use the Belarusian language in public and private life. Some of the interviewed stressed bilingualism. Finally, quite a few of them were openly hostile toward Russian. What I observed, however, notwithstanding those different reactions mentioned above, was a similarity of imagery that is the topic of this article. Thus, in the analysis, I refer to both Russian- and Belarusian-speaking citizens as Belarusians and reserve Russian for reference to the people of Russia.

Striving to collect information that was not self-censored or filtered by possible translations, I undertook efforts to prepare for the discussion of the most likely topics, not only in Russian, but also in Belarusian. This was dictated by my first interview experience, when I encountered hostility from some national movement activists while attempting to address them in Russian. Although those experiences ended up being rare, I asked a Belarusian native speaker to accompany me during the interviews to assist the communication should the need arise. My efforts and willingness to use Belarusian brought clear results as all interlocutors, after a couple of introductory sentences and exchanges, seeing that my spoken Belarusian was not fluent, switched of their own accord to Russian (which all Belarusians speak at native level) to guarantee better understanding of their arguments. As far as the analysis of textual material was concerned, I was fully capable of understanding written Belarusian to analyze it. I frequently checked my observations with the Belarusian colleagues (both scholars and people who did not have any contact with academia) to confirm the validity of my findings.

The fact that I am Polish played a role in the interaction. On the one hand, my interlocutors seemed to take more time to carefully explain the situation to me. On the other, a number of understandings and opinions were assumed or imputed to me (e.g., a concrete religious affiliation). My intentions were perceived in different ways too. The reactions at the outset of the conversation ranged from friendliness and appreciation to accusations (of imperialistic intentions of my country) and distrust. However, in general, the attitude was quite open: my interlocutors mostly felt that "the world" is not adequately interested in Belarus and wanted to "make me understand." Moreover, I believe that my authentic interest was communicated easily to those who spoke with me; ultimately, even in the few cases when interviews started off in a difficult way, none of them ended in the same manner.

Although my training is within the discipline of international relations, I employ here the rich theoretical heritage of literary theory and anthropology. The latter's influence is visible in my research techniques: extended interviews and repeated field trips to Belarus. The inspiration of literary studies is evident in my analysis of the material, especially in my sensitivity to metaphorical constructs and in the stress I place on the importance of representation and signification. Derrida's writings and particularly his analyses of binary, implicitly valorized oppositions are of particular significance for my investigation of this subject.

Identity, Gender, Nationality

I employ the concepts of identity, gender, and nation. As a construct devoid of essence or core, identity is open to modifications and restatements. It is forged, as feminist criticism proposes, by language.[17] Thus, people and organizations become what they are through the utterances they make and as a result of what is said about them.[18] Since the language used is gendered, it will translate into gendered behavior. The existence of "gendered discourse" has been generally acknowledged, at least since the beginning of the last century, and there is a plethora of studies on the gendering of everyday language.[19] Only recently has attention been paid to the gendering of academic concepts, and, more generally, of so-called objective and quantifiable knowledge.

Most classifications are highly contestable, and the definition of what constitutes "national identity" is a particularly difficult one. It requires the elucidation of two concepts, "nation" and "identity," each of which is individually problematic. While it is hard to catalogue the characteristics of nations, definitions of nationality predominately embrace the element of political will, the highest form of which is the creation of the nation-state.[20] Even if this political element is not explicitly mentioned, it is assumed that the nation is either the creator or the creation of the state.[21]

This understanding leads to a conflation of the concepts of state and nation and the loyalties developed toward these two elements. State and nation may be closely interrelated, as in the French case, or the two may be thought of independently, as in the German case.[22] It would be equally possible, however, to imagine a nation that does not aspire (apart from a small part of the elite) to completely autonomous statehood, as happens in the case of the nations within the United Kingdom.

Many authors appreciate the ideational character of nation as a function of people's self-perception rather than any tangible characteristics of nationhood.[23] Greenfeld derives national identity from the feeling of belonging, and Brubaker sees nations as groups that, instead of being stable products of developmental trends, are sometimes called to being as if "by accident."[24] Drawing from this literature, I propose that Belarus's unusual behavior on the international stage, for instance its willingness to unite with Russia, is not a sign of a weak national sentiment or a result of a lack of Belarusian identity. The problem consists rather in the fact that Belarusian identity is different from what we are used to in Central and Eastern Europe and that it cannot be simply pushed into the available intellectual compartments. This specificity of Belarusian self-imagining might be directly related to its heavy gendering.

Masculinization of Concepts via "Power" Component

The popular classification of Belarusians as possessing "no national identity" may be simply an effect of both academic and everyday language gendering. In this section I would like to expand on this claim. Although multiple femininities[25] and masculinities function within different discourses, and although both "male" and "female" categories are inherently ambiguous, in everyday life people tend to refer to the mainstream, easy, mythologized, and naturalized schemata of female- and male-ness. People perceive, interpret, and order the world via simplified mechanisms, such as stereotyping. Stereotypical views of what constitutes the feminine are reinforced through the implicit correlation between femaleness and "lack." Thus, "female" tends to be stereotypically compatible with weak or passive.[26] Strength and agency are typically reserved for the male principle. For many years, feminist critical texts[27] presented abundant evidence on how the tendency to dichotomize the world makes the categories of objectivity/subjectivity, reason/emotion, knowing/being, and public/private, replicate and reinforce the male/female opposition.[28] In spite of that, many academic texts continue to implicitly reproduce those constructs.

Nancy Hirshmann, speaking of knowledge construction, proposes that the presence or absence of power has been the essential difference between masculine and feminine constructs.[29] The stereotypical conceptualization of the state, for example, mimics the masculine individual in its drive for autonomy, singularity, and ability to defend the inside sphere and to expand through the military or cultural imposition. As the male-female dualism inscribed in epistemology deeply permeates perceptions of reality, alternative state behaviors that are not designated as "male" are automatically excluded. The dominant international relations (IR) paradigms of realism and liberal institutionalism reflect this engendered character of the construction of the knowledge about the world.[30]

In the light of the preceding discussion, I argue that Belarus is represented as not having a national identity because its self-description and behavior has been devoid of the "aggressiveness" associated with maleness. Active, "normal" behavior, stereotypically associated by IR with masculinity, is contrasted with Belarusian passivity. Binary categorizations governing both Belarusian self-description and academic vocabulary present the country as passive, mute, emotional, subjective, or associated with the private sphere, that is, as implicitly "feminized." The next logical step within the IR paradigm is the evaluation and diagnosis of its "deficiency," "lack," or "abnormality."

Self-Descriptions: Production of Lack

Contrary to the propositions of the IR literature, both textual and interview data (analyzed in the sections that follow) provide evidence of a Belarusian sense of common belonging and their self-perception as being "other" than neighboring nations.[31] In their responses, Belarusian citizens referred to stereotypes and presented their national characteristics in a series of binary oppositions, where the other pole was predominantly "Russia." Thus, if Belarusians are described as patient, Russians are portrayed as violent. While Belarusians focus on their neighborhood, cultivate their land, and care for their belongings, Russians are nomads who are always ready to leave, to "mount a horse, set fire to their own house and the one of their neighbor's"[32] and risk everything. Still, this certitude that "we" are "simply different, we are Belarusians"[33] is, in most cases, not charged with a strong political element. I believe that this depoliticization of national identity has led to the classification of Belarus as "denationalized."

Thus, it might be not due to the absence of concrete self-identification that Belarus was described as lacking national identity. Rather, a rigid definition of national identity, which stresses the indispensability of the political, conventionally "male" element, might be responsible for that status. It seems that the insistence on the political dimension of national identity is analytically limiting. After all, the legal claim to a territory does not necessarily have to coincide with the moral one. The latter is quite strong in Belarus and transpires in the interviews and the references to lands that were originally "theirs" and then "taken away."[34]

Consequently, the understanding of "nation" and "national identity" that I embrace and propose here is the one bracketing the "male" element of political aspiration and emphasizing instead cultural and territorial belonging of people. This understanding relies on the presupposition that there is a clear difference between the concepts of the state as a political entity and of the nation as a cultural (or moral) one. Belarusians repeatedly demonstrated throughout my interviews that they constitute a unique entity and referred to the feeling of territorial belonging.

Lack of Agency

Speaking about modern conceptions of identity in the Post-Soviet era, Verdery takes up the theme of agency. She observes how female, inactive objects are contrasted in the identity constructs with male, active subjects.[35] The characteristics repeatedly referred to by the Belarusians I interviewed are passivity, inaction, and victimization. Passivity—or "tolerance," as Belarusians prefer to call it—is rationalized in Belarusian discourse by the experiences of World War II and heavy population loss. Even in the victorious WWII narratives the heroism of Belarusians is somehow tainted by passivity; it is the heroism provoked by history. Belarusians are shown to be recipients rather than makers of history. They perceive themselves as constantly in the epicenter of conflicts due to their position between Russia and Europe. Their heroism is tragic and desperate, and its memory brings pain and feelings of injustice, as exemplified by a child-hero, Marat Kaziej, who was killed throwing bottles with petrol at German tanks.

This dominant war narrative, on the surface stressing the resistance, in fact portrays the nation as a victim of brutal terror. The blood-curdling war stories illustrated by the animated installations at the Minsk WWII museum are retold to every new generation, instilling the general feeling of suffering and loss. On the other hand, the WWII partisans are frequently evoked with pride, as they epitomize the Belarusian ability to offer life willingly for the country.

The central war narrative, speaking of the provoked agency of Belarusians, in reality justifies their present passivity or unwillingness to get involved in conflicts. In the words of a politician opposed to Lukashenka's reelection in 2001:

> the worst fear is conflict . . . war and [. . .] the value of a conflict free life is enormous. Ours is a conformist society, able to stand a lot and get used to it. [. . .] Fear of change. Better if things could stay as they are. [. . .] In 1995/6 we researched the level of fatalism in the society. People were saying, "never mind, we need to survive it, to take it as it is." For a Belarusian to be active is the very last possible step.[36]

Belarus is presented throughout history as a precious land that, like a female body, is the passive object of strangers' rapacious designs. It is indispensable and essential yet has no voice of its own. History seems to have its sources somewhere "outside" of Belarus, a sentiment expressed by references to geopolitics and the country's naturally given, problematic position on the map. Russians repeatedly try to grasp the Belarusian space as a road to the world, as the essential passage through which everything comes to Russia, both good and evil.

A number of interlocutors justified today's peaceful coexistence of Belarusians and Russians with the national quality of "tolerance." One of my interviewees stated that this particular Belarusian "tolerance" is the greatest source of pride for him as it is the value that the nation carried intact through all the postwas years and could now donate to the European community. Belarusian tolerance is painted as qualitatively different from that of Europeans, as "real" and "natural," containing an emotional component that the European community is devoid of. It is claimed that, in the case of the European community, there is more indifference than tolerance.[37]

It is often emphasized that Belarusians can boast of the fact that "they never took anything from anybody . . . [although others] took things from us and we just looked calmly at this."[38] The things taken away include, apart from their native land, Belarusians' symbolic values. The name of the country was taken away by Lithuanians, as were the coat of arms, heroes, and national history.[39] This theme of undeserved harm and deprivation returns in many variations throughout the material.

The nature of Belarusian nationalism is defined as a "good nationalism," devoid of aggression and expressed in the willingness to live in "this country in peace" and "to be happy." In spite of this, some Belarusians believe that their compatriots need to have a strong authority over them, something akin to "a lid" that would keep the "steam in the cauldron." The feminized conceptualizations of Belarusians appear with clarity when it is proposed that the people have to be *controlled* because they may not know what to do with their freedom.[40] The "need for control" theme is closely connected to a powerful metaphor of the nation as an immature child (another concept typically associated with femininity) that needs to be taken care of.

As a Child

Metaphoric understanding based on the transfer of a certain familiar experience to another, unknown domain is a very powerful means of constructing reality. Some particularly useful insights into the functioning of metaphor can be gained from the writing of Lakoff, who presented differences between Conservative and Liberal moral systems via the opposition between the Strict Father and Nurturing Parent metaphors.[41] I argue that both Lukashenka and his political opponents, in their communication with the Belarusian people, resort to what Lakoff defined as the Nation-Family metaphor in its Strict Father version. There are some obvious differences, though, in the two camps' interpretations. The Lukashenka group represents itself as keeping things in order, providing jobs, money, health, and education. It is a vision of a strict but good and just parent, leading the child by the hand, an image that was literally articulated in one of Lukashenka's speeches comparing Belarus to a little girl carried in his "manly arms."[42] Lukashenka, the Father (*Bat'ka*), demands that the children follow his orders in return for the provision of security. They should work and study in peace, never doubting the genuineness of his good intentions. Belarus, the child, is simply not strong enough to make its own decisions and therefore has to be protected from the insidious external influences.

Interestingly, the democratic opposition in Belarus sets itself in the Strict Father role as well. The parent here is equally stern and authoritative, but the child itself is no good; it does not appreciate what is done for it and does not pay back. It does not want to learn; it is not intelligent enough. It therefore must be strictly controlled. If it does not perform, it should be forbidden from speaking. This is exemplified by the proposition of a restrictive local voting system that is seen as appropriate because the "majority of people from the moral and logical point of view have no right to do it [i.e., vote]. This would be a normal route that Western countries traveled . . . everywhere there was a restrictive census in the very beginning, possessions or education were decisive."[43]

Lack of Voice

My interviewees' depiction of the role of Belarus in world politics emphasized invisibility and muteness. Belarus is presented as being denied the role of a speaker, which is another frequent trope in feminist analyses of gendered constructs.[44] Belarusians themselves make jokes about their ability to cope with difficulties without voicing protest or fighting back. In one of these, a Belarusian who is hanged between a German and a Russian survives the execution and then comments on his experience. In the beginning, he admits, it was hard but then he "got used" to it. In another joke, having sat on a pin, a Russian throws it away, a Ukrainian hides it in his pocket, and a Belarusian remains seated, because if the pin was there, it means that "for some reason it should have been this way." The ability to suffer patiently is commented on by many, but not always favorably. As one of the interviewees sarcastically put it, "Sisyphus is an archetype of the Belarusian" and "masochism is our national feature."[45]

Belarusians are speechless also due to the fact that their historical heritage of the Grand Duchy and its language was "stolen" from them by the Lithuania and Russia: They are not heard by the world as "we cannot speak of our history without using the words 'Lithuania (Litva) and Rus' but 'it is us, Belarusians, who appear in history as [i.e., under the contemporary names of] Lithuania and Rus.'" It is proposed, therefore, that it would be necessary to introduce new words to refer to Russians ("Rasejtsy") and Lithuanians ("Letuvtsy") and return to Belarusians their heritage and voice.[46]

On the other hand, the Russian-speaking Belarusians are disempowered by the national circles who do not want to recognize the legitimacy of Russian in the country. This produces a lot of tension as Russian speakers do not consider themselves lesser patriots than those speaking exclusively Belarusian. "We are Belarusians and we will not start to love our motherland, Belarusian land, songs and history less if we speak Russian (. . .) we think in Russian and our children speak Russian."[47]

Belarusian muteness is, therefore, multifaceted. It is related both to the inability to verbalize the complaints resulting from national "personality" and to the lack of means to do so, due to the linguistic dispossession or disputes over the legitimacy of the language used.

Smallness

Fear is an emotional state frequently attributed to femaleness,[48] and in the interviews the fear of conflict or change is a dominant theme. In the majority of cases the interlocutors led me, via the topic of fear, to the twin themes of domesticity and shelter, and to the traditional associations of home and safety, attachment and settlement.[49] Home is a central idea dominating the responses to inquiries about the highest "values" of life. Family happiness is the main life goal mentioned by the respondents. This may be a consequence of the sharp division between the private and public spheres that predominates in Belarus. The withdrawal from the latter is justified by its association with something dirty, dangerous, and destructive, something that is "likely to culminate in a personal tragedy."[50]

Belarusians see themselves as open and hospitable, which is quite typical for any nation's self-description. But in their self-portrayal they are also modest, naïve, weak, sincere, and satisfied with the little they have.[51] The quality to which they constantly point in their comparisons to Russians is their ability to work very hard and to look after their own household. Thus, they fence their land and plant trees and vegetables, unlike the Russians, who are prone to constant relocation. The difference is again explained in terms of geographic conditions: Belarusians imagine their land as being "small." In contrast, they speak of vast space as provoking Russian mobility.

The recurring topic of stillness, or life-as-it-always-was, is well illustrated by an interpretation offered by one of the interviewees. In her comments on the Belarusian state of mind she referred to the symbolic title of a novel by Ivan Melesh, *Ludzie na balotie* (People of a Marsh). The *boloto*, mud or mire, represents the place that is cut off from the rest of the world: nobody can reach it unless the water is frozen. This has two types of consequences. The "new" cannot reach this place, which remains eternally the same, stagnated and backward. Mud or swamp is also a site of physical sickness, of a bad, stale atmosphere. On the other hand, due to the isolation some archaic, traditional values that were lost elsewhere may be kept alive here, so it is a treasury of all things pure and noble.[52]

Lack of Strength—Eugenics

Female interlocutors, as a rule, made comments on the men in the population, who are, according to them, highly effeminate and unable to cope with life. Husbands are compared to children and described as an additional burden. They are seen as psychologically weak, prone to alcoholism and depression.[53] This, the women say, is the result of the war, the fact that so many men died and that the postwar generations were brought up by single women who shunned conflict and aggression. Thus, the task of "mending" lives being assigned to women in the aftermath of the war is seen as responsible for the passivity of the male population. According to one of the interviewees, the wars (starting with the Napoleonic) led to the death of the "heroes." The survivors are just weak and cowardly men, childlike and capricious:

> [D]uring the Stalin times a lot of people died, men died. They were liqui-
> dated. You see, now we have a problem with the autonomy of males in

Belarus. They are just older children. I think it is the effect of the fact that every fourth Belarusian died in the war. The upbringing of boys fell on the shoulders of women, solely women. Single mothers. Heroes died. The weaklings survived.[54]

On the other hand, enfeebled men also have the capability of manipulating women to do everything for them. They are not willing to compromise and discuss, are unable to listen and argue.[55] This visualization of males in terms of deficiency/lack is heavily reminiscent of the typical image of the female body as "seeping, and lacking form."[56]

The view that Belarusian nature is somehow defective in a biological sense is so predominant that we may find it in Belarusian academic pieces as well. For example, Zaprudnik implies that the present political developments result from Belarusian physical "fitness" having been impaired by Stalinism, WWII, and Chernobyl.[57] Another author diagnoses Belarusian society as inert and apathetic, while the leader of the Belarusian National Front, Pazniak, describes Belarusians as "seriously sick," heading toward either death or complete rebirth.[58] Finally, the writer Tkacou sees his countrymen as "genetically" pessimistic and cautious, "dominated by fear of any change making things worse than they are at present."[59]

Conclusion

In my investigation of Belarusian national identity and its postcommunist incarnations I focused on the consequences of the implicit perception of the world in terms of the binary oppositions organized around the principles of "female" and "male." Two aspects of this dichotomous conceptualization of national identity have been of particular importance to my investigation. First, I argue that political theory has incorporated the "masculine" principles of "agency" into its definition of "national identity." Second, I show that the language of self-description used in Belarus is permeated with the values that are implicitly gendered female, which has in turn led to the negative self-evaluation of Belarusians as a people.

The analyses of the interviews and their triangulation with opinion polls and other textual sources (press articles, literary pieces) indicate that Belarusians do define themselves in opposition to other nations. Sometimes this definition was in terms of an "indescribable sphere of feeling," but in most cases it was documented by the attribution of concrete features to "us" and "them." At the same time, while referring to their country's positioning in the world, Belarusians stress its vulnerability, passivity, victimization, muteness, invisibility, and smallness. This group of images for centuries has been stereotypically associated in European culture with the principle of "femaleness." For example, the fact that Belarusians describe themselves as "passive" and devoid of agency (and, therefore, implicitly "female") leads to their construction as deficient and lacking, a trend attested by contemporary social

science and international politics analyses. Their "docility" and ethnic tolerance (vis-à-vis Russians) is not seen as positive and valuable or as something to
be emulated by others. Instead, they are represented, even in their own discourse, as "abnormal" or "deviant." This tendency, I believe, originates in the
implicit reliance on binary oppositions of male and female and in the negative
valuation of experience that is traditionally labeled as female. This devaloriza-
tion of what is seen as female behavior does not allow Belarusians to feel
satisfied and proud of what they represent. Instead the self-depreciatory attitude is reinforced.

The case of Belarus demonstrates the consequences of the unreflective
way in which people tend to organize their experiences. The disempowering
self-description of post-independence Belarusians has been exploited politically for more than a decade. Belarusian passivity, weakness, and smallness
have been embraced by Lukashenka's discourse, offering fatherly "protection"
and pushing for a continued close relationship with a powerful neighbor.

NOTES

1. The "no-identity" claim is one of the most frequent explanations of Belarusian
specificity. It consists of stating that the international orientation of Belarus is a result of
the fact that Belarusians have no national identity. See. Kathleen J. Mikhalisko, "Belarus Retreat to Authoritarism," in *Democratic Changes and Authoritarian Reactions in
Russia, Ukraine, Belarus and Moldova*, ed. Karen Dawisha and Bruce Parrot (Cambridge: Cambridge University Press, 1997), 223–82. See also David Marples, *Belarus: A
Denationalised Nation* (Amsterdam: Harwood, 1999).

2. Due to the multiplicity of constructions of femininity—ranging from passivity
and subservience to untamed natural energy and destructiveness—nations may be
feminized in many ways.

3. Katherine Verdery, "From Parent-State to Family Patriarchs: Gender and Nation in Contemporary Eastern Europe," *East European Politics and Societies* 8, no. 2
(1994): 226.

4. Jacques Derrida. *Of Grammatology* (Baltimore: John Hopkins Press, 1976).

5. For example, femininity can be both associated with "nature" and transmitting
"culture," both docile and aggressive in an animalistic way, both birth-giving and
destructive.

6. See Susan Gal and Gail Kligman, *The Politics of Gender after Socialism*
(Princeton, N.J.: Princeton University Press, 2000) and Susan Gal and Gail Kligman,
eds., *Reproducing Gender: Politics, Publics, and Everyday Life after Socialism* (Princeton, N.J.: Princeton University Press 2000).

7. Verdery, "From Parent-State to Family Patriarchs," 251.

8. Elena Gapova, "On Nation, Gender, and Class Formation in Belarus and
Elsewhere in the Post-Soviet World," *Nationalities Papers* 30, no. 4 (2002): 652.

9. Ibid., 658.

10. Elena Gapova, "Conceptualizing Gender, Nation, and Class in Post-Soviet
Belarus," in *Post-Soviet Women Encountering Transition: Nation Building, Economic
Survival, and Civic Activism*, ed. Kathleen Kuehnast and Carol Nechemias (Wash-
ington, D.C.: Woodrow Wilson Center Press, 2004).

11. Skak argues that generally Post-Soviet states reject nonalignment strategies and tend to engage in what she called *Einbindung*. This happens because they fear abandonment and staying outside of European co-operation. Mette Skak, *From Empire to Anarchy: Postcommunist Foreign Policy and International Relations* (London: Hurst, 1996), 282. The difference is, then, not the willingness to ally and diminish sovereignty, but rather the direction of *Einbindung*.

12. Belarus never bargained, nor demanded concessions or security guarantees (unlike Ukraine). Taras Kuzio and Marc Nordberg, "Nation and State Building, Historical Legacies and National Identities in Belarus and Ukraine: A Comparative Analysis," *Canadian Review of Studies in Nationalism* 26, no. 1–2 (1999): 83.

13. In 1991, at Belovezhskaya summit, in Peter Rutland, "How the SU Ended," *EOMRI Analytical Brief*, no. 453 (November 11, 1996).

14. My intention would be to refrain from a rigid classification of particular groups that belong to a concrete version of the Belarusian discourse. Although one may find the national faction speaking on some issues in the same manner as one splinter of a communist party, this coincidence of opinion is not formalized by the creation of a brown/red coalition, as in Russia. The core values of Belarusian nationalists and communists are too distant—one group cherishing Belarus that is completely independent from Russia, the other seeing it as spiritually or even physically linked to this country. On the other hand, communists forming the anti-Lukashenka party were frequently of the same opinion as nationalists where the attitude to the president was concerned.

15. By "elite," I refer to people who may have some influence (official or not) on the formation of the views of general public (e.g., politicians, artists), and people whose opinions are in some way prominent and may influence the discussion in the public sphere. Therefore, elite for me included both members of the official apparatus and people working in the opposition. The interviews, in chronological order, include: September 2000: Tamara M (F/activist), ZaLi (M/professor); December 2000: Waclav Areshka (M/director of a historical archive), Minsk; January 2001: I. L. (M/historian, researcher), Minsk; May 2001:Vladimir Dorohov (M/journalist, Russian background), Minsk; August 28–30, 2001: V (F/Russian speaker, working for NGO), Irina (F/Russian speaker, employed by state institution), Tzwieta (F/working for a women's organization, Women's Reply), group of 3 female interviewees, 2 from Minsk and one from Brzesc (F/ballet dancer, a linguist and a housewife), all of them Russian speaking, A. S. (M/journalist, Belarusian speaking), Minsk, V. M. (M/radio journalist, Belarusian speaker), Minsk; and September 2001: D. H. (M/researcher), Minsk, Artiom (M/poet), Minsk.

16. The sources I consult include official texts of agreements between Belarus and Russia as published in the Russian Foreign Ministry's *Diplomatichesky Vestnik* and *Byulleten Mezhdunarodnykh Dogovorov*. I take into consideration official statements and addresses of Belarusian politicians as well as various indicators produced by international economic and political bodies (OSCE, IMF, World Bank, and EBRD), as well as the statistical data published by independent Belarusian agencies (mainly Novak and NISEPI). External views are obtained from *RFERL Newsline*, and everyday updates from the *Charter 97* (opposition) e-mail services and *Sovietskaya Belorusia* (presidential mouthpiece). I look at available issues of a number of Russian and Belarusian newspapers, starting from *Nasha Niva* through *Belaruskaya Delovaya Gazeta* to Russian-speaking pro-regime *Sovietskaya Belorusia*. Other titles include, among others: *Belorussiya, Belaruskaya Maladzyozhnaya, Belaruskaya Gazeta, Belaruski Rynak, Czasopis,*

Femida, Informatar, Krynitsa, Literatura i Mastatstva, Narodnaja Volja, and *Termopily.* These are supplemented by articles from the Russian press, as well as other foreign periodicals, including *Belarusian Review, Belarusian Chronicle* (English), and *Perspectives Biélorussiennes* (French). Interesting images and self-depictions are, similarly, derived from fiction and poetry. Finally, I review available historical textbooks and literature manuals.

17. Mary M. Talbot, *Language and Gender: An Introduction* (Cambridge: Polity Press, 1998), 144.

18. This stands in opposition to traditional sociolinguistic approaches. See Deborah Cameron, "Performing Gender Identity: Young Men's Talk and the Construction of Heterosexual Masculinity," in *Language and Masculinity,* ed. Sally Johnson and Urlike Hanna Meinhof (Oxford: Blackwell, 1997): 49.

19. See, for example, Anne Pauwels on the sexism in language in her *Women Changing Language* (London: Longman, 1998); Ruth Wodak, ed., *Gender and Discourse* (Oxford: Blackwell, 1996); Sara Mills, ed., *Language and Gender: Interdisciplinary Perspectives* (London: Longman,1995); Mary M. Talbot, *Language and Gender, An Introduction* (Cambridge: Polity Press, 1998).

20. John Stuart Mill claims that people constitute nationality when they desire to be under the same government, "governed by themselves" ("Considerations on Representative Government," *The Nationalism Reader,* ed. Omar Dahbour and Micheline R. Ishay (Atlantic Highlands, N.J.: Humanities Press, 1995), 98. K. Deutsch describes the modern nation as the bond between the state and the people; Weber describes it as a community that "normally" would tend to produce a state; Ernst Barker makes the state the maker of the nation; and A. Smith speaks of it as an "active ethnicity." T. K. Oommen, *Citizenship, Nationality and Ethnicity* (Cambridge: Polity Press, 1997), 49–55. I. Prizel offers a five partite typology of nationalism, but all categories are based on the existence of a polity, in *National Identity and Foreign Policy* (Cambridge: Cambridge University Press, 1998).

21. Barry Buzan, "The Idea of the State and National Security," in *Perspectives on World Politics,* ed. by R. Little and M. Smith (London: Routledge, 1996), 37.

22. Ole Weaver, "Identity, Communities and Foreign Policy: Discourse Analysis as Foreign Policy Theory," in *Between Nations and Europe: Regionalism, Nationalism and the Politics of Union,* edited by L. Hansen and O. Weaver (London: Routledge, 1999), 59.

23. Walker Connor, *Ethnonationalism: The Quest for Understanding* (Princeton, N.J.: Princeton University Press, 1994), 91. Connor states that self-view determines if a nation exists or not, and Seton-Watson refuses the possibility of an academic definition of a nation.

24. Rogers Brubaker, *Nationalism Reframed: Nationhood and the National Question in the New Europe* (Cambridge: Cambridge University Press, 1996), 24.

25. On the construction of different femininities, see Jennifer Coates, "Thank God I Am a Woman," in *Gender and Discourse,* 232–63.

26. For example, in adventure narratives, even if "active," women are described as "acting in subordinate capacity," http://www.sou.edu/ENGLISH/IDTC/Terms/terms .htm (accessed Dec. 2002).

27. For instance, the work of Evelyn Fox Keller, Sandra Harding, and Ann Tickner.

28. Ann Tickner, "A Critique of Morgenthau's Principles of Political Realism" in

International Politics, edited by Robert C. Art and Robert Jervis (New York: Harper Collins College, 1996), 17–29; Evelyn Fox Keller, *Reflections of Gender and Science* (New Haven, Conn.: Yale University Press, 1985); and Sandra Harding, *The Science Question in Feminism* (Ithaca, N.Y.: Cornell University Press, 1986).

29. Nancy Hirshmann, *Rethinking Obligation: A Feminist Method for Political Theory* (Ithaca, N.Y: Cornell University Press, 1992).

30. Marysia Zalewski and Jane Parpart, *The "Man" Question in International Relations* (Oxford: Westview Press, 1998), 76.

31. If anything, we may speak of competing versions of the national identity, one of which is represented by the anti-Soviet group and the other embracing the Soviet, pan-Slavic tradition. Both groups, however, state their differences vis-à-vis other nations. Moreover, the distinctiveness of Belarusians from both the groups mentioned is felt and reproduced in stereotypes about the world. It is, however, predominately apolitical.

32. Tamara M. (NGO activist, Belarusian speaker, originally Russian speaker), interview by the author, Minsk, Belarus, September 2000.

33. Vladimir Dorohov (journalist, Russian background, originally in Lukashenka's camp, Russian speaker), interview by the author, Minsk, Belarus, May 2001.

34. This is the opinion frequently voiced in the interviews, e.g., V.M. (Belarusian speaker), Irina (Russian speaker), Minsk, Belarus, August 2001, or M.A. (journalist), Minsk, Belarus, May 2001, and W.A. (director of a national [non-state] archive, Belarusian speakers), Minsk, Belarus, December 2000.

35. Verdery, "From Parent-State to Family Patriarchs," 248.

36. Swetlana Naumova (Russian-speaking journalist of *BDG*, member of the team of Goncharik, Lukashenks's contender in 2001 presidential elections), interview by the author, Minsk, September 2001.

37. W.A. (director of a national [non-state] archive), interview by the author, Minsk, December 2000.

38. V.M. (radio journalist, Belarusian [formerly Russian] speaker), interview by the author, August 29, 2001, Minsk, Belarus.

39. Unpublished article on Belarusian versions of history and heraldic, untitled, by Ihar Lalkov, historian, employed at the state research institute, version of December 2000.

40. Three women (two from Minsk and one from Brzesc, a ballet dancer, a linguist, and a housewife, all of them Russian speaking), interviews by the author, Minsk, Belarus, August 28, 2000.

41. George Lakoff, "Metaphor, Morality, and Politics, or Why Conservatives Have Left Liberals in the Dust," 1995, http://www.wwcd.org/issues/Lakoff.html (accessed April 18, 2005).

42. "Wmeste! Za silnuyu i protsvetayushchuyu Belarus!" [Together! For the Strong and Blossoming Belarus!], Program of the President of the Republic of Belarus, A. G. Lukashenka, *Sovetskaya Belorusia*, http://www.president.gov.by/rus/president/profile/progr.html (accessed Sept. 5, 2001).

43. Painter (Belarusian speaker), interview by the author, Minsk, Belarus, December 2000.

44. For instance, the research on the amount of space given to women in British quality newspapers shows the disproportion. Carmen Rosa Caldas-Coulthard, "Man in the News: The Misrepresentation of Women Speaking in News-as-Narrative-Discourse," in *Language and Gender, Interdisciplinary Perspective*, ed. Sara Mills (London: Longman, 1995): 226–39.

45. A.S. (journalist and lecturer, Belarusian speaking), interview by the author, Minsk, August 30, 2001.

46. Sergej Dubaviec, "Strona i Narod v zerkale publitsistiki" [The Country and the Nation in the Mirror of the Publicists], in *Beloruskaya Tragedia, 1986–1999* [Belarusian Tragedy, 1986–1999], ed. Semen Bukchin (Warszawa: n.p., 2000), 76.

47. Letter of 1992, signed by mothers from Pogachevo *oblast'* [region], published in *Narodnaja Gazeta* on June 9, 1992, reprinted in *Beloruskaya Tragedia*, 146.

48. Study on sexism by Louise Pusch, quoted in Anne Pauwels, *Women Changing Language* (London: Longman, 1998), 25.

49. Wendy Webster, *Imagining Home: Gender, "Race" and National Identity, 1945–64* (London: University College of London Press, 1998), ix.

50. Z. L. (linguist), interview by the author, Minsk, Belarus, Sept. 2000. Interestingly, the "home" theme is frequently connected with the positive evaluation of the Soviet Belarusian Republic.

51. TaM (Belarusian, formerly Russian speaker), interview by the author, Minsk, Belarus, Sept 2000; Artiom (Russian/Belarusian speaker), interview by the author, Minsk, Belarus, December 2000.

52. I.M. (Russian speaker), interview by the author, Minsk, Belarus, September 2001.

53. V. (Russian speaker, working for an illegal NGO organization and in the evenings as a phone operator), interview by the author, Minsk, Belarus, Aug. 29, 2001; Irina (Russian speaker, working for a state institution), interview by the author, Minsk, Belarus, August 30, 2001.

54. Tsweta (feminist organization leader), interview by the author, Minsk, Belarus, May 2001.

55. Tzwieta (staff at the women's organization "Women's Reply," Russian and Belarusian speaker), interview by the author, Minsk, Belarus, August 30, 2001.

56. Elisabeth Grosz, *Volatile Bodies: Towards a Corporal Feminism* (Bloomington: Indiana University Press, 1994), 203.

57. Jan Zaprudnik, "Development of Belarusian National Identity and Its Influence on Belarus Foreign Policy Orientation," in *National Identity and Ethnicity in Russia and the New States of Eurasia*, ed. R. Szporluk (Armonk, N.Y.: M. E. Sharpe, 1994): 131.

58. David Riach, "Nation Building: Identity Politics in Belarus," *Canadian Review in Nationalism* 27, no. 1–2 (2000): 58, and Z. Pazniak, "O russkom imperializmie i ego opasnosti" [About Russian Imperialism and Its Danger], *Narodnaya Gazeta*, no. 5–6 (May 1993).

59. Quoted by George Sanford, "Belarus on the Road to Nationhood," *Survival* 38, no.1 (1996): 135.

Fifteen Years of the East–West Women's Dialogue

Nanette Funk

Introduction

Since the 1989 breakup of the Soviet bloc, women from the region of the former Soviet Union, eastern, southeastern, and central European states (hereafter referred to as "the region") engaged in dialogue with each other and with women and feminists who came to the region, especially from Western Europe and the United States. The latter initially arrived in many capacities: as volunteers in newly set up women's centers and organizations, as young women looking for a new, exciting, inexpensive place to which they could travel, as academics doing research, as funders and supporters of new or expanding women's organizations, and as Western women's non-governmental organizations (NGOs) looking for partner NGOs in the region.

When I first started dealing with gender and transformation in the region, I was politically curious and fascinated but aware of the risk of feminist "imperialism." The dialogues and interactions that ensued in the region were diverse, but were often accompanied by tension and conflict, leading those involved to reflect on their roles, in both dialogue and joint action.

As I will elaborate, perhaps no concepts were more problematic than the Western feminist concepts of "gender" and "feminism." Reflections about concepts, discourse, power, and actions were necessary steps in this newest development of transnational feminism. Such feminist activity involves not only local action in one's own country, but sometimes cooperation, participation, and support from outside, sometimes from women's NGOs and journalists, interaction in journals and research, and learning from each other. It also involves participation in transnational networks, such as global social forums, the United Nations (UN) or European Union (EU) sponsored transnational or regional meetings of women.

But it would be a mistake to think that the East-West dialogues took place only in the region. Migration was part of the upheaval produced by the breakup of the Soviet bloc, and women were part of that migration. Flight from wars, ethnic cleansing, nationalism, and economic crisis, a desire to study and improve one's job possibilities, as well as marriage and trafficking in women led to temporary or permanent residence, asylum, or immigration to Western countries, including the United States. Some women from the region came to the United States as visiting scholars, enrolled in gender studies programs in the United States, especially at the New School for Social Research and Rutgers University, as well as several other universities. Some made U.S. second-wave feminism, feminist theories, and organizations the subject of their research.

But with the exception of the united Germany, little has been discussed of the relationships and ensuing dialogue within the Western countries themselves, or the moral and cultural conflicts and differences between women from the region and Western women. In what follows I first present an initial exploration of this underexamined aspect of East-West relations in the case of the United States. My discussion not only reveals differing attitudes toward gender justice, but also reveals moral conflicts more generally. Next I analyze the dialogue over the past fifteen years within the region between East and West women, the different forms of that dialogue, and the necessary conditions for an effective dialogue. I show that these forms of dialogue are similar to the forms of dialogue that East-West women outside the region engaged in.

My hypothesis is that self-reflective East-West dialogue must continue if there is to be a constructive, just transnational women's movement that includes East and West women. I understand a just transnational women's movement to be one founded on recognition and understanding of the other and the issues of importance to them while engaging the issues in the world, ever sensitive to their gendered nature. It is committed to gender justice consistent with the demands of justice in general and is a movement mutually supportive of the efforts of others, especially other women, where possible.

I discuss the difficulties in the East-West dialogue and the need to discuss the ever-present risks of inequalities of power East-West. It is also still necessary to have a dialogue about differences in meanings and concepts, including the concept of gender and the problems attached to an emphasis on gender identity. Such dialogues can also be transformative for all parties to the dialogue and bring problems to the surface, attempt to understand and confront them. Dialogues can change and develop both East and West gender theory and practice. I do not in this paper discuss the necessity for dialogue about the conflicts among women within the region and different countries of the region, but I assume its equal, if not greater, importance.

I do not assume that transnational feminist dialogue either requires or achieves agreement on gender issues, much less an absolute universalism. But I do assume that there is some moral minimum of a commitment to gender equality and justice. I make no general claims about dialogue for other instances of transnational feminism, but I presume an overlapping nature and necessity for dialogue to build transnational feminism anywhere. Sometimes these dialogues are foregrounded, other times subordinated to other concerns.

At this moment in the twenty-first century new forms of not solely state-based global governance are being proposed, are being organized, and exist, in part in response to economic globalization from above. It is important that transnational feminist networks participate in these new forms of fair and just global governance and even be a model for the possibility of other forms of non-state-based networks. To that end dialogue is also important. Transnational feminist cooperation has already been effective in the development of new international laws and concepts, such as recognition of rape in war as a war crime and a violation of human rights. This formulation of international law is itself one form of global governance.

Meanwhile, Back in the U.S.A. . . .

Since the early 1990s there has been extensive discussion on how women from the West benefited by building careers, got jobs with decent salaries, strengthened their own Western NGOs, and enhanced their reputations and status as power brokers who could make things happen in the region. But there are other impacts of meetings and discourse that took place in the United States in particular and that are not so often mentioned. After fifteen years of engagement in gender and transformation in the region, my own life changed in ways I had never imagined. Not only did I go to many meetings with women from the region who were in the United States, but my friendship circle was enriched by many long-term friendships, both in New York and in Europe, with interesting, smart, engaged women from the region, some of whom live in the United States, either permanently or temporarily.

My perception, understanding, and reaction to gender issues in the United States and at my own university changed, as did the moral issues I confronted. I always knew that daycare was a crucial issue for gender justice, but I had also become accustomed to middle-class academic women colleagues with children finding individual solutions—hiring African-American and immigrant women in their home to provide daycare or finding good, though expensive, daycare to which they sent their children. There were moral problems in these individual solutions, of white women making a career by hiring black women, and of the high financial costs of doing so but relatively low wages for those they hired. But these were the problems within individual solutions.

Then I changed. Suddenly, I experienced the lack of daycare at my own university through the eyes and moral assumptions of A, a woman faculty member from the region. She expressed a matter-of-fact moral disgust, verging on contempt, at the absence of what she regarded, not just as an unmet need, but as a moral minimum that any decent society, including its universities, ought to provide. "If you really care about gender issues in this country, how come there is no daycare for faculty at the university?" As a consequence of my colleague's perception, I in turn experienced this situation as a shameful, unjust, morally backward state of affairs. I also regarded the impact of the absence of daycare on my colleague's life and job possibilities as well as on the non-teaching staff at the college as deeply disturbing and a gross injustice. Because she had to spend so much time caring for her children and family, my colleague's writing of professional papers suffered, for which she was academically penalized.

My colleague had left her country because of the war and ethnic nationalism. The economic, psychological, and professional dislocations of moving to the United States in midlife meant she did not have the home, money, or family situation that could make possible a good middle-class individual childcare solution. A very smart, strong, and talented woman was caught up short by the problems of family and daycare. Of course, I had long known how difficult it was to get good affordable daycare in the United States and in my university in particular and that women had demanded it over the years, but this concern remained theoretical on my part.

But the "consciousness-raising" or change in my perception of my own university prompted by my colleague was transformative in that it moved me to act on this issue. I quite effortlessly wrote a forceful, clear, moral argument on why my university had to make affordable, good daycare available to faculty and non-teaching staff. I wrote with conviction on the discriminatory impact of the absence of daycare at the university and how it entrenched unequal gender roles in the home. I presented these arguments to the progressive feminist women's committee of my faculty union, and they adopted them and used them to successfully urge our union to make daycare a demand in the contract negotiations. My local union chapter also brought this topic and my arguments to the attention of our college president. When these were conjoined with the demands of many new faculty at the university for whom daycare was an important personal issue, things began to move, albeit slowly. Thus the strongly entrenched moral beliefs of my colleague from the region played a pivotal role in beginning a change not only in myself, but in my university.

From my earliest encounters with women in the region I faced moral issues I had never before confronted, and this continued in the United States. I disagreed with B, from the region, on whether it was morally acceptable to verbally accept an academic job offer, but continue looking for other jobs, and even accept a later job offer. We had a fierce moral argument. "You are just defending the capitalist contract," she said "while my whole future is at stake." But B seemed to be just "better dealing" the university, acting amorally out of pure self-interest. I argued B had an obligation to keep her word from which she wasn't excused by her career ambitions. Given her argument, no verbal agreement between an employer and prospective employee, or buyer and seller, should be morally binding. B's argument was overly general and unconvincing. But the intensity of the disagreement led me to think further, and I came to see a greater moral complexity to the case than I had initially realized. The university had the power to strategically make an early offer, binding the candidate before competition could surface; B did not have an equal power. But, still, it seemed that B could have refused the offer. But could she? B had finished her studies in the United States, and in an increasingly repressive U.S. state with unjust, harsh, and humiliating immigration laws and practices, B would have been forced to leave the United States within a few months unless she got another job offer, which she had no rational grounds to believe with certainty she would get. Her children studied and were married and living in the United States, and she had no other family. Back in Eastern Europe she would face long lines in front of the U.S. embassy just to get a visa to visit her children, with no certainty she would even be granted such a visa. If she did not verbally accept the first offer, she faced the risk of being unemployed, being forced to leave the United States, and losing a life with her family. The harm to the university if B accepted an offer she hoped not to keep was not comparably grave. If the stakes were so high did B have any choice but to accept the offer, doing all that anyone could be either expected, or morally required, to do? The university did not intend to coerce B, but in the circumstances was that offer in fact coercive, an offer B could not refuse? If so, then B could not be morally bound by her word, and was free to break her word and seek and accept a second offer. I came to realize both that one's immigration status had significance even in academic employment and that the ethics of academic job offers had a greater moral complexity than I had initially understood.

The explanation of our initial moral positions is surely complex; I wondered whether her being from a former state socialist country and my being from the United States explained our respective moral beliefs. I knew that in state socialism it was often a norm that one was free to act as one wished toward "them," the *nomenklatura*, or if one was from the *nomenklatura*, one was free to bend the rules to suit one's own interests. I was raised in a society with an ideology of individualism and the absence of class, but aware that the rich and powerful often bent the rules for their own self-interest. Neither of us was simply a representative of a system; we were rather particular individuals with particular differences. Those differences included the following: B was looking for a job while I was a secure tenured faculty member who had been on academic hiring committees; B was raised in a society in which a woman's gender identity included doing paid work and having close family ties while gender norms had changed in my lifetime and I had no children. How did our histories explain our moral positions? What were our histories? We did not ask, and I wondered whether this was still taboo territory. The explanation of our moral psychology would surely require a complex analysis.

There were other cases of conflicts between myself and women from the region. In several cases in the United States, I experienced what seemed to me insensitivity on the part of several women from the region. C, one of my dearest friends, strikingly compassionate and supportive in my drawn-out moment of crisis, suddenly disappeared with only a bare minimum of a few gruff words. D seemed to be oblivious to my moment of crisis. The American "being in touch with one's feelings" was confronted with what seemed to me to be an attitude of being strong, repressing feelings, hiding vulnerabilities, toughing it out, and, in some cases, expecting others to do the same—in short, what I experienced as a more male style. I knew my friends and colleagues from the region presently in the United States had their own needs and difficulties, in part due to the particular ways in which stresses in the region conjoined with the stresses of being temporarily or long-term in the United States, separated from family and support system. At the time I could not do much about their problems. The United States had also become a harsher, more denigrating place, more arbitrary toward noncitizens, not only those from the Middle East, Africa, or Latin America, but those from eastern Europe and the former Soviet Union as well. This could have partially explained some of these cases. I also learned that some of the same tensions I experienced in the United States with my friends from the region also surfaced between women in the region itself. Vesna Kesić, speaking of difficulties between women working in the Center for Women War Victims, wrote:

> In the male world of "heroes, shepherds, and outlaws"[in the Balkans] there was not much room for any subtle feeling, particularly for women's emotionality and its expression. In order to survive—either in the social hierarchy or in the world of intimacy and emotion—women of all cultures had to adopt the patriarchal behavior patterns that the male environment supported. . . . On the Balkans everything was a little more difficult and a little more crushing. In order to survive in these cruel social gullies the women had to suppress, conceal, and adjust. They themselves became inconsiderate, arrogant, cynical about the feelings of others and their own feelings, incapable of empathy, egotistical, aggressive, and—you know how we are. The specific Balkan form of patriarchy has made us insensitive and even more isolated in believing that each of us had to be able to deal with their own problems. The women from the Balkans do not dare identify with their shamed or roughened sisters or seek support among them.[1]

My own conflicts with C and D made me more aware of the significance of such phenomena and differences in gender identity and that they were yet another ingredient in understanding our conflicts.

Kesić shows both how patriarchy had an impact on relations between women and how male domination or patriarchy culturally existed alongside state provision of daycare, legal availability of abortion, and paid maternity leave. Her comments reveal that the question whether state socialist or capitalist societies are more feminist or patriarchal is much too simple a question. It presumes that there is only one question to answer, when in fact it is a complex question that needs unpacking. How feminist or patriarchal a given country is depends not only on the nature of the state and whether or not it was state socialist—and there were also many different forms of state socialism in the countries of the region—but also on the society, the influence of church, ethnicity, history, internalized norms, and family structure.

My examples are anecdotal but nevertheless important. I am not the only one deeply engaged with women from the region who has learned much from them about the United States or had theoretical knowledge turned into political practice. One of the editors of this volume recounted that it was her research in Russia in the 1990s that got her interested in feminism and domestic violence, rather than these being issues in which she was already interested when she came to Russia. In addition, women from the region presently in the United States were given support by U.S. women active in groups such as the Network of East-West Women. We listened, gave support and assistance, showed them the ropes in a strange new land when no one else did.

Post 1989 East–West Women's Dialogue in the Region

In the region after 1989, the context or circumstances for East-West women's dialogue, and the kind of dialogue, continually changed. Without an analysis of the problems of those dialogues, cooperation between women East and West can be threatened, unproductive, or inauthentic. There were three different circumstances in which dialogue took place.

Initiated by the West[2]

The earliest context was the early 1990s, with extensive face-to-face meetings in some countries in the region, less so in others. Some of these contacts were precipitated by Western women, especially from the United States, western Europe, and Canada, coming to the region, interviewing women from the region, and organizing and running conferences and "training" sessions in the region. They invited women from the region to these meetings. Most of these East-West women's encounters were thus ones in which Western women had greater power, both material and discursive. They had the theories and concepts for discussion of gender issues. They had the know-how, money, and contacts to get funding for future meetings and conferences.

Initial meetings were sometimes euphoric, often disorienting, irritating, and frustrating. The earliest and most explosive post-1989 East-West women's dialogue and conflict took place in Germany, especially in the newly united Berlin, prompted simply by the fall of Berlin Wall in November 1989 and German unification in 1990. As is well known, the initial dialogue was a dramatic failure. East and West German women spoke the same language, more or less, but their words still had different meanings; they had lived in different, competing post-1945 and post-1989 conditions. The political systems under which they had lived played different roles in their identity,[3] and there were differences in their power post-1989. The hostilities of the initial dialogues led to a breakdown of further dialogue for a long time, although there were certainly exceptions.

Meetings started in the early 1990s in the Czech and Slovak lands, Poland, Russia, Bulgaria, and Romania and some countries of the former Yugoslavia. These first dialogues were pre-reflective in that none of the parties were prepared for the misunderstandings, the impact of power differences, and the tensions that would occur. Some Western feminists who came to the region unreflectively, and without explaining themselves, used taken-for-granted feminist concepts. The latter had arisen in the United States or West Germany at a moment in those countries when identity politics, and especially a challenge to traditional gender identities, was one of the central forms of social change. Some assumed, with little self-reflection, that gender identity would be a central form of self-identification for women in the region in the 1990s as well. But women in the region had different histories, were in very different, often crisis-ridden situations of state formation, dissolution, war, corruption, and radical economic and political transformation. Different identity questions were paramount. In addition, Western women, in trying to understand what was happening, often made generalizations about the region. Such generalizations are important to making sense of what one is experiencing, but should be made with caution. Often this was not the case, and errors were made. Such a starting point caused conflict and criticism and was emotionally disturbing. Each challenged the other, often in destructive emotionally loaded terms. Women, more than men, confronted those disturbing emotions and differing claims in early East-West interactions both in face-to-face interactions between East-West women and in their writings. New issues continue to be added to the dialogue.

Dialogue also occurred in the contacts created by Western women's NGOs who worked in "partnership" with women's organizations in the region. Western women and their NGOs helped fund women's NGOs in the region. U.S. funders often required Eastern "partner" organizations for Western women's NGOs active in the region that they funded. The funders gave the decision-making power on projects, budgets, and salaries to the Western NGOs. Hence structurally Western women had the power to determine individual and organizational survival for active women in the region.

As might be expected, the dialogue misfired. Difficulties arose partly because of the failure to satisfy two premises that are necessary for a successful dialogue, as will be discussed below. This failure was especially important in a dialogue about gender and feminism—for which there were often not equivalent terms—and that was across cultures, languages, and political systems and was pervaded by power hierarchies.

Self-organization by Countries in the Region

The second context for the East-West dialogue was, as Hana Havelková stated, when women from the region organized and ran their own conferences, both national and international. They did not wait for Western women to invite them and were not dependent on an agenda or a language set by women from the West. It was an attempt to correct the power imbalances under which dialogue took place. Some women from outside the region were invited to these meetings, but their role was more marginal, and the concepts and choice of topics were made by women from the region. Such conferences occurred in Belgrade in 1994 and 1998, in eastern Berlin in the Independent Women's Association (UFV) in 1990, and at many other conferences thereafter organized by the Center for Interdisciplinary Women's Studies in Humboldt University in Berlin, in Russia with the first International Women's Forum in Dubna in 1991, in Liblice in the Czech Republic, and at meetings sponsored by networks of women from the former Yugoslavia across the new state boundaries, both during and after the wars. Other meetings were organized within the new countries making up the former Yugoslavia.

Those women who were active in gender organizations and conferences in the region, a relatively small number of women in each country, at that time turned away from focusing on the dialogue with Western women and being studied by Western women and decided to learn about themselves and their differences. They took action on the urgent issues in their country, from a gendered perspective, as did, for example, Women in Black in Belgrade and the Center for Women War Victims in Croatia. They focused on understanding the political and economic upheavals and transformations they were undergoing, including war, nationalism, dissolution of the state or ethnic cleansing, and their gendered nature. Some felt attention to the East-West dialogue was primarily of interest to Western women, eager to assuage their guilt arising out of their structural domination of the East-West dialogue and interactions. In some cases, as in Prague, which had been heavily inundated with Western visitors, this phase coincided with a withdrawal of intense face-to-face contact between East-West women, with fewer women from outside the region coming to the region. In other countries in the region, the number of women visitors reduced as well.

Institutionalization of Gender Studies in Countries in the Region

The third context for dialogue occurred after the establishment of gender studies in many universities or free standing centers in the region, usually in the mid-1990s, sometimes earlier. A new generation of younger women in the region took courses on feminist and women's literature and the history of women's movements in their own country in the nineteenth and early twentieth centuries. Feminist scholars and activists in each country retrieved and researched this material. They analyzed literature, the media, the law, employment, society, political power and participation, war, and ethnic nationalism from a gender perspective. Gender studies courses had good registration, and there was greater access to Western feminist writings in many countries in the region within the universities and outside. This included Serbia, Poland, Czech Republic, Croatia, Belarus, Russia, Ukraine, Slovakia, and eastern Germany. In eastern Germany, although there is a gender studies program in Humboldt University in eastern Berlin and in the University of Greifswald, there are unfortunately relatively few eastern German women teaching in those programs. Others from the region completed gender studies programs abroad in the United States, in western Europe, and at the Central European University in Budapest. Some argued that being "east" or "west," ever contested terms, were now much less meaningful, especially in the united Germany and with the accession of eight countries of the region to the EU in 2004 and Bulgaria and Romania accepted for accession in 2007.

"Binational" women originally from the region and living and studying abroad—such as many of the authors in this collection—became ever more active in the discourse; some returned to their region to do gender research, teach, or become politically active, while others remained abroad but did research on the region. They could claim to understand Western gender theories as well as gender experiences and developing gender issues in their country in the region, and avoid the mistakes of both East and West. By the late 1990s fewer U.S. women came to the region, fewer U.S. NGOs were active in the region, and funding for women's NGOs in the region began to dry up. But pressure to adopt Western language also began to come from "gender mainstreaming" requirements for accession to the European Union and even from the World Bank, that is, the consideration of gender in all aspects of state planning and policy. This was more appearance than real implementation. It thus remains to be seen how significant this will be for creating divisions between those former Soviet bloc countries in and out of the EU.

Presuppositions of a Successful Dialogue

The normative principles for dialogue, as Habermas among others has argued, are different than that for a subject/object relationship. A dialogue is predicated on the assumption that all participants are equally entitled to raise questions, challenge concepts and pose those they regard as relevant to the discussion, set the agenda, and challenge the premises of the discussion. Not only should each be encouraged to express their own experiences, but those experiences and the social realities in which they arise should equally be presuppositions of the dialogue. Such dialogue has always been the stated goal, only partially realized, for feminism generally, and transnational feminism in particular. As many have noted, the dialogue between women from the region and those from more Western countries, especially the United States, was studded with structural power inequalities that determined the lingua franca of the dialogue. The ensuing dialogue was distorted by differences in meanings of terms and in cultural and political assumptions, economic conditions, and history, both in general and in women's history in a particular country. Differences in East and West contexts, between those in which feminism was entrenched and in which it was not, were often ignored. A discourse under such conditions can succeed only when both parties are self-reflective and aware of their position, their use of language, the differences, and the structural inequalities in power and theory that pervade the discourse. Each has to minimally be prepared to explain their language to the other, why it should be adopted, and to be open to questions and disagreement and change in the taken-for-granted presuppositions of the dialogue. Only then can the dialogue be self-correcting and can inauthentic dialogue—that is, dialogue in which some only mimic the terms of the dialogue imposed by the other—be reduced. Otherwise, as was initially the case in the East-West women's dialogue, the discourse is subverted by mistaken claims, different assumptions and realities, different language leading to misunderstandings, biased starting points, and power that constrains what can and cannot be said, ensuring resentments, conflicts, and tensions. All this ensued in the dialogue in the early 1990s in the united Germany and in other countries in the region.[4] The breakdown of discourse in Germany, and the tensions elsewhere, did, to some extent, trigger both self-reflection and reflection about the other, which itself became part of that dialogue. But the inequalities in power and discourse continue, and it is thus important that this self-reflection continue.

Secondly, a principle of epistemic generosity should be assumed in transnational dialogue—a working assumption that until proven otherwise, when many others "arrive at beliefs conflicting with one's own" as Gerald Gaus has argued in a very different context, one should "consider their views closely to see if *you* [my italics] have made an error."[5] Instead, in the East-West women's dialogue there was often "epistemic chauvinism" (Gaus), a belief that because women from the region did not always share Western feminist beliefs, women from the region were assumed to be epistemically defective, that is, mistaken.[6] The power inequalities in the dialogue conjoined with epistemic chauvinism clouded the dialogue, provoking at best further reflection and self-reflection and at worst a temporary breakdown of that dialogue. Those women from the United States who exercised such epistemic generosity, recognizing their partners as often more knowledgeable than themselves, and who encouraged challenges, as well as acknowledging the particular present and historical context out of which their own discourse arose, had the most successful dialogues.

Reflective and Self-Reflective Forms of the Dialogue

The East-West discourses fell into three broad categories: descriptive, normative, and explanatory. All three forms were either self-reflective or reflective about the other; all are necessary for transnational feminist understanding and the building of transnational feminism.

My earlier discussion was both descriptive and normative, and hinted at explanations. It both was self-reflective and reflected on the practice of my interlocutors. In many cases in the region, especially in the earliest instance of the dialogue in Germany, descriptive and normative discourses arose contemporaneously between 1990 and 1994, but the relationship between these forms of the discourse varied by country. In the best cases this discourse reveals how conflict can be a constructive force in moral and cognitive transformation. Let us look at some of these discourses in more detail.

Descriptive Discourse

The early descriptive discourse included self-reflective experiential, phenomenological accounts by Western women and women from the region about their confusions, anger, and disturbing emotions produced by East-West women's meetings in the context in which dialogue took place. Women began to make such self-expressive claims as soon as contacts were initiated by the West. Some Western women described their sense of being overwhelmed by this vast reality that was new to them and that they didn't quite understand; they expressed fears of their Western feminist imperialism and doubts about the applicability of Western feminism in the region. They also described their irritation at women from the region. Hana Havelková described how Western women's challenges and interviews initially forced women in the region to describe their own experiences and histories, and provoked self-reflection and the realization they had something interesting to say.[7] Women from the region also expressed resentment at the criticisms made of them by Western women for not understanding or using the "correct" concept of gender, or for having "essentialized" or "naturalized" gender. They also described being overwhelmed by grand questions posed by Western women, for which no one had answers, creating pressure to invent answers on the spot.[8] They described the double duty of having to inform Western women and of having to speak one way at Western meetings and another way at home. Women from the region also described their own identity concerns resulting from the breakup of their country. Yugoslav women described being forced to no longer think of themselves as Yugoslav and Slovak women asked whether it was important to identify as Slovak. Such expressive, self-descriptive discourse was necessary, even if the accounts differed greatly, were disturbing, or caused resentment. There was not nearly enough space, however, for a democratic discourse that allowed each to honestly speak for herself and allowed each to become aware of the experiences and problems of the other and the underlying problems between them.

The descriptive discourse did continue in the first six years of the twenty-first century. A less angry, less personal descriptive discourse begun to develop as women in the region organized themselves. For example, Irene Dölling (eastern Germany) in 1995 and Ralitsa Muharska (Bulgaria) in 2005 describe women from the region playing the feminine role in the dialogue, speaking descriptively to "fill the information gaps with facts" about their country, while Western feminists played the masculine role of theorizing.[9] Muharska describes a kind of "parodic" speech by women from both the region and the West that at once mirrors but distorts. Western authors, she claims, give parodic generalized accounts that somehow manage to miss the mark in what they purport to describe. Women in the region use quasi-Western feminist categories to describe their situations, but the descriptions misfire given that the language isn't the right one to capture their experiences, or they don't say quite what they mean but rather what they think "Big Sister" wants or requires. Muharska argues that such parodies are actually subversive of the discourse in that they expose the differences and East-West misunderstandings.[10] Muharska is certainly right that such misfiring unintentionally reveals the "dirty little secret" that women from the region only pretend to accept Western feminist categories, and Western women only apparently understand the realities of gendered postcommunist societies. Her account might add that the listener, however, often reacts with spoken and unspoken critical normative judgments of the other. Both Miethe and Muharska also describe the unstated Western participants' assumption that the same circumstances and language prevailed elsewhere as had prevailed when gender discourse was adopted in their country or that the differences didn't matter. Šmejkalová-Strickland had similarly described the mistakes, confusions, and "misspellings" by Western authors.

Women from the region have also described how western European, West German, and U.S. feminists employed their own taken-for-granted concepts as the lingua franca without even explaining those terms, especially that of gender. Muharska describes assumptions made by editors of anthologies on the region even in the late 1990s that each individual author was representative of her country and that speakers and writers from countries in the region internalized that obligation to speak as representatives, even though those who spoke a feminist discourse hardly represented anyone in their country.[11] Miethe similarly describes West and East German women having reacted to each other in face-to-face meetings in the early 1990s as though they represented the whole hated system of the German Democratic Republic (GDR) or Federal Republic of Germany or West German feminists generally.[12]

Thus one can see that such descriptive discourse continues to be part of the East-West women's discourse, even after the formation of gender studies programs in some countries in the region.

Normative Discourse

Implicit or explicit normative claims can be either self-critical or critical of the other's practice and discourse. This discourse of critique and self-critique became a substantial literature throughout the region in the early 1990s in the first context discussed above.[13] West German women harshly criticized East German women for not being more politically active about the new abortion law developed in Germany between 1990 and 1995; they criticized East German women's use of language, for their "not understanding" feminism and for inviting men to their meetings. In some cases, they even criticized GDR women for having placed their children in full-time daycare and working full time outside the home. East German women harshly criticized West German women for their competition with East German women for jobs, for their arrogant, ignorant, and tutelary manner, their hostility to children, their degradation of East German women writers, and their "explaining" East German women rather than explaining themselves.

In other countries, women from the region criticized U.S. interviewers who came and went with hardly any follow-up, criticized Western feminists for their "feminist imperialism" in discourse and practice and for their confusions and misunderstandings of the region both in the topics they discussed and in those they omitted. In the early 1990s, some women criticized arrogant or ignorant young U.S. women volunteers working in newly founded women's centers in the region, such as in the Prague Women's Center. Western women were criticized for defining the terms of the discourse and subject matter at conferences or for calling useless meetings and "training" in what was already known. Western women's NGOs working in the region on joint projects were criticized for retaining decision-making power over budgets, projects, and salaries even on joint projects, for using women in the region for information to build their own NGOs, for paying much lower salaries to those in the region, even considering differences in the cost of living, for having only token representation of women from the region on their boards when they purported to be joint boards. Such criticisms were even made of U.S. feminist NGOs such as the Network of East-West Women in the early 1990s. Some Western feminists criticized women from the region for not having a conception of gender or described women in the region as not having had a gender identity in state socialism, without ever explaining what that meant.[14] This in turn led to criticism, for example, by some Ukrainian women for false Western claims that women in state socialism did not know that they were women.

Many women in the region criticized and challenged Western writers, including Western women, for characterizing women in the region as victims or "losers in the transformation." It was argued that women were neither simply passive victims, "economic losers," or simply "raped women." Böhm, Nickel, and Dölling all claimed that eastern German women should be recognized for their active persistence in finding paid employment in spite of the difficulties they faced.[15] The numbers of women who remained employed testified to this, as did their participation in job retraining programs.

In the first six years of the twenty-first century the normative discourse continued after gender programs had developed in the region, although fewer women engaged in this form of discourse. This included Elena Gapova (Belarus), Ralitsa Muharska (Bulgaria), Ingrid Miethe and Ute Gerhard (eastern and western Germans respectively), Mihaela Miroiu (Romania), and, in this volume, Ewa Grigar (Poland), Azra Hromadzic (Bosnia-Herzogovina), and Svitlana Taraban (Ukraine), among others. Miroiu critically characterizes the importation of Western feminisms as "room-service feminism," "a superficial substitute for the development of local political feminism."[16] Hromadzic uses excerpts of testimonies by women survivors of rape in the war in Bosnia-Herzegovina to criticize Western accounts of women as passive rape victims without reference to their individual stories, some of which included taking dramatic action against their rapists. She criticizes such accounts for failing to represent these women as agents and accord them the respect and dignity they deserve. Interestingly, Hromadzic reflects the East-West division of labor, characterized by Muharska and Dölling, of providing the facts rather than the theories. Grigar criticizes Western art critics' accounts of women artists in central eastern Europe as imitators of Western art. She argues that those claims are based on ignorance of the gender themes already in those women's art under state socialism and the failure of Western critics to place "Eastern" art in the political context of state formation and dissolution, which led to a need to question their identity, a theme with which they were dealing. Taraban criticizes writers who ignore the agency of women "Internet brides" who actively manipulate multiple gender identities.

Self-reflective normative discourse is also necessary given that one's position, whether from within the region or without, risks misunderstanding and problematic practices of which one is not immediately aware and which hamper cooperation and mutual understanding. In an example of self-reflection, West German feminist Müller herself criticized West German feminists' "benevolent degradation" of GDR women. In another example of self-reflective criticism, Muharska writes: "Perhaps I should also mention here that in writing this text I cannot help realizing that I seem to myself an example in support of my own point. . . . Sometimes I can see the distortion as I am making it."[17] Self-reflective and critical discourse helps to expose the biases of pre-reflective claims, beliefs, presuppositions, and stereotypes, both by oneself and by others, that distort communication and hamper the possibility of fair, constructive democratic cooperation.

In the best cases, active listening and discussion of the moral and cognitive criticisms of the other can lead to honest, if unpleasant, self-reflection. This in turn can lead to cognitive and epistemic change, in both self-understanding and understanding of the other, and to a change in practices and attitudes, thereby easing cooperation. It can also help to promote conditions necessary for more open, deliberative, democratic decision making in joint East and West NGO activities, fairer cooperation, and a mutual sharing of power East and West in organizing joint meetings, deciding on topics, and discussing terminology. It can lead to instituting greater transparency in financial practices on the part of Western feminist NGOS, inviting women from the region onto the board of women's journals, especially in Europe, and including topics of interest to all of Europe, the East as well as the West.

Such normative criticisms and discussion of them can also lead to sensitivity in the differences in meanings and to the recognition of the necessity to explain the specific historical context in which concepts, such as that of gender, arose. It can prevent future false moves and hostilities. Normative discourse is thus an important and necessary corrective in transnational feminism.

Explanatory Discourse

The explanations of the problematic East-West women's discourse and interactions were very diverse, in both explanans and explanandum. Such discourse grew as gender problems in the region developed. Some offered explanations of the discourse and behavior of women in the region; others explained Western women's discourse and behavior toward women from the region. Some provided self-reflective explanations; others offered explanations of "the other." Western women and women in the region in their first meetings offered explanations of why women in the region weren't feminist, weren't interested in gender issues, or were suspicions of feminism or why they rejected political participation. Other women in the region questioned the assumptions behind these explanations.[18] Some explained the difficulties as due to misunderstandings and resentment of Western feminist categories and the failure of Western feminists to explain their concepts, the contexts, and needs out of which they arose.[19] Some explanations emphasized conceptual differences about "gender" that did not have a meaning in the East, or "naturalized" or "essentialized" conceptions of gender in some countries in the region, or different conceptions of gender identity.[20] The list of problematic terms noted in explanations kept on growing and has become familiar: "restaurant," "shopping," "daycare," "feminism," "gender," "gender identity," "woman," "public/private," "studies," "empowerment," "lobbying," "liberalism," "democracy," "state,"[21] *"parteilichkeit"* (partisanship),[22] and "professionalization." Ulrike Helwerth and Gislinde Schwarz, a West and East German respectively, in discussing the East-West German women's conflict gave one of the most multi-factoral explanations of "how we are different," employing twelve different categories. Miethe, an eastern German woman, explained in 2004 that pre-1989 self-defined GDR feminists meant not only what was meant in the West by public/private, but also that "Something is political if one succeeds in making it private."[23]

Others, including Miethe and Gerhard, a prominent western German feminist, in 2004 explained the early 1990s "deficient" West German women's criticisms of eastern German women. They agreed that West Germans criticized East Germans inappropriately, presupposing the West German context as a basis for their evaluation.[24] This mirrors Havelková's earlier claim that Western feminists who came to eastern Europe presumed their feminism was universal, rather than specific to their own political, historical, and social context. Even in 2004 East and West explanations of the East-West women's conflicts in Germany also have different emphases. Gerhard's self-reflective explanation of the conflicts in the early 1990s stressed West and East German feminists' different pre-1989 histories and circumstances as well as West German feminists' frustration at the lack of opportunity to influence the course of the German unification.[25] Miethe stresses the importance of "equally taking into account the common (divided) experiences since 1989"[26] and that each treated the other not as an individual but as representative of the other political system. In one of the best cases of self-critical description and explanation, Gerhard also adds that western German feminists were "characterized by a complete ignorance of the actual needs of East German women which they expressed by a know-it-all attitude" that "until today [2004] are repeatedly remembered." Miethe acknowledges "[the still existing] . . . conflicts and differences between East and West."[27]

Müller explained self-reflectively how West German women researchers criticized East German women researchers' methodology as naively empiricist, which though arguably true, was invoked ideologically, that is, only when GDR women researchers challenged Western assumptions.[28] Müller also noted that West German researchers used empirical methods similar to those they criticized.

What stands out about the explanations is the difference between explanations of tensions as primarily due to conceptual misunderstandings and those explanations for which power differences are primary, resulting from a "a massive inequality of material and intellectual resources."[29] In the German case, Miethe explains West German women's power of definition as due to their position in a "social structural hierarchy" that included greater access to the public discourse and greater economic, social, and cultural capital.[30] Muharska, speaking of other countries in the region, argues that the Western power came from their arriving with ready-made theories and concepts that eastern women did not have.[31] Differences in power also arose from the funding of some women's NGOs in the region by Western or transnational sources, who thereby determined the concepts one had to adopt if one wanted to get funding. Project descriptions had to incorporate the "buzz words" of the moment, such as "gender democracy," "empowerment," "lobbying," "domestic violence," "trafficking in women," or "gender mainstreaming." Western women's NGOs, especially U.S. women's NGOs in the early 1990s, sometimes had a role as intermediaries in this process of grant giving. Many authors also insisted on the importance of understanding "how we are the same" with a shared culture and history, as did Havelková, Helwerth and Schwarz, and Miethe.

The explanatory form of discourse is certainly necessary to correct the problems that hamper cooperation. It also contributes to the development of both gender theory in the region and Western feminist theory. Gender theory in the region develops in part in response to the problems in the region and incorporates the gendered nature of these problems. This has meant in large part attention to the gendered nature of the public rather than the private sphere, including state dissolution, formation, and transformation, war, rape in war and the violence toward women that war increased, corruption, ethnic nationalism, neoliberalism, the church, the welfare state and consequent economic crises, and the relevance in these circumstances of one's identity as woman. In addition, it does include private-sphere issues of the family and abortion in some countries. It often adopts the language of postmodernism. From the early 1990s conceptions of masculinity in the region and their contribution to the changes in the public sphere have been a central topic. Most of these had not been central issues of the beginning of second-wave Western feminisms and certainly were not the issues that many women from the region identified with Western feminism. Today, U.S. feminists also address the horrors of the public sphere, including war and its gendered dimensions, whether in violation of civil and human rights, abuse of prisoners, the sexualization of torture, the justification for war by appeals to saving women, or the resurrection of traditional conceptions of masculinity.

How and Why the Discourse Changed

After the mid-1990s, all forms of discourse about the East-West conflicts and differences diminished, at least as reflected in writings published in English and German, but did not disappear; tensions sometimes remained buried, differing in intensity by country. East and West German women generally have little to do with each other organizationally or individually. Others claimed that by 2000 the East-West dichotomy no longer had significance.

Several factors explain this change of emphasis. First, by the mid to late 1990s some women from the region had greater exposure to Western feminist literature. Although a relatively small group in each country, gender scholars and activists in the region selectively appropriated, translated, and challenged Western feminist writings, making Western feminist ideas theirs, to some extent. Anna Brzozowska, in this volume, writes of the hyper-feminization of Belarusians' concept of their nation, showing that she has adopted a non-naturalized conception of gender. Scholars and activists (and they are often one and the same in the region) produced a growing body of gender literature; they also retrieved the feminist history of their country and collected women's memories of the twentieth century and of the most recent wars. They created archives for doing comparative studies of these accounts. They challenged Western theories; for example, Mihaela Miroiu (Romania) challenged the claim that the welfare state benefits women in postcommunism, arguing that in Romania the greater burden fell on women.[32]

Secondly, fifteen years is long enough for a younger generation of gender scholars and activists to have entered the field, East and West. For some of them feminist theory was no longer exclusively "other." Some claimed that the categories of East and West, categories long contested, were no longer useful.[33] Some of their own professors, once gender studies was institutionalized, taught gender studies courses in the universities. Others, such as Hromadzic, a young Bosnian graduate student in the United States, drew the distinction of who is an East or West gender scholar differently. She identifies feminists in the former Yugoslavia who adopt Western feminist models to discuss the rapes in war as themselves Western feminist authors. The younger generation also reacted to the literature and practices of the first post-1989 generation of gender activists, writers, artists, and academics in their countries and not simply to those in the West. For example, a younger author, Anca Gheaus, examines Mihaela Miroiu's (Romania) claim, raising the question of the conditions under which the welfare state is defensible.[34] In Poland some younger feminists reacted against the early post-1989 activists' model of the NGO, forming less professionalized, more anarchist forms of demonstrations and street theater.[35] In eastern Germany some younger women moved to, or studied in, western Germany, having a blended experience. Others from the region, such as Agnieszka Graff (Poland), Ralitsa Muharska (Bulgaria), and Agnes Hochberg (Hungary), before her untimely death, made the history of Western or U.S. feminism the object of their study as had feminists in the former Yugoslavia even before 1989. Therefore, there was much more for younger women to react to than to the Western women.

The younger women scholars and activists from the region also have little personal knowledge of life in state socialism and did not experience the more volatile interactions of the early 1990s. Miethe claimed that only the next generation of eastern and western German women will be able to explain the East-West German women's conflict.[36] But will they be interested?

Thirdly, "binational" women coming from the region or returning to the region having studied in the West, have a joint insider/outsider status. To some extent they believe they are in a position to avoid some of the errors of either pure "insiders" or "outsiders." Hromadzic claims her research is more committed to the dignity and agency of those she studies than is that of Western authors. To some extent it is true, but it may also lead her and others to believe they don't need to engage in self-reflective discourse. "Binational women" do have to be self-reflective. They risk the danger of "flip-flopping" between

221

cultures and discourses, incorporating the blind spots of both cultures, rather than using concepts consistently. To some extent, as Muharska notes, they remain outsiders because of their experiences and knowledge gained abroad but "insiders" possibly blind to their own presuppositions. Women from the West who are "outsider-insiders" through spending extensive time in a country in the region risk "going native," unreflectively adopting the beliefs, prejudices, and presuppositions of those in the country. Muharska, at once both an "insider" and "outsider," self-reflectively says:

> Needless to say, I am quite aware (now maybe even more than before) of myself also being in the position in question, and the double-ness, dubiousness and maybe even duplicity in the very fact of my undertaking to comment on the ongoing discourses. This I do from the perspective of both an insider: to the reality of Eastern Europe, the women's movement in the region, and gender theory, and an outsider: my own professional area is American Studies.[37]

Thirdly, there were fewer U.S. women coming to many of the countries in the region after the initial contacts. Much U.S. aid to Western and local women's NGOs in the region ended by the late 1990s, contributing to that change. In other countries, as in Bosnia or Croatia, many active women's NGOs are funded primarily by European NGOs, especially Kvinna till Kvinna, a Swedish foundation that does not require partner organizations from Sweden. Kvinna till Kvinna has consistently been regarded by those in the region as among the most sensitive funders in the region. There are thus fewer problematic contacts since the early days, when the region was "flooded" with U.S. women initiating contacts in the region. Thus, there is not the same provocation for dialogue, self-reflection, and reflection about the other.

Fourthly, the expansion of the EU to include eight countries of the former Soviet bloc focused the attention of some women in the region on the gendered nature of that economic and political integration, rather than on the dialogue with women. But the expansion of the EU also opens up the East-West dialogue. Hana Havelková, a Charles University Gender Studies professor, was invited to join the editorial board of the formerly Western feminist journal in Vienna, *L'Homme: Europäische Zeitschrift für Feministische Geschichtswissenschaft*. Shortly thereafter, in 2004 and 2005, they published two issues highlighting East-West feminisms. Ute Gerhard, the well-known West German feminist and editor, wrote that with this issue "a new beginning is made for the East-West dialog."[38] Other journals also continue the dialogue, for example, *Central Europe Review*. Elena Gapova (Belarus and the United States) also continues to write on this topic.[39] In 2004, the important dialogue between Miethe and Gerhard on the East-West German women's conflict was published.

Thus, the descriptive, normative, and explanatory forms of the discourse do continue in 2006, albeit with less frequency.

Conclusion

I have argued that all three forms of the discourse are necessary if there is to be a fair, just, democratic, deliberative transnational feminism. Transnational feminism involving women in east and central Europe and the former Soviet Union and those from Western countries, especially the United States, did not develop without conflict. In my estimation, power inequalities explain much of these conflicts. Self-reflection, including self-expression and reflection about the other, reflection on the critical judgments made by the other, and efforts to explain one's own behavior and that of the other by all parties is crucial if conflicts and misunderstandings are to be negotiated. Only by this means can there be a more just transnational movement. East-West feminism arising out of the fall of the Berlin Wall is one of the latest additions to transnational feminism. It has been among the most self-reflective. At a time when transnational governance and the new forms it can take, including both state and non-state bodies, is under discussion, it is important that transnational feminism be a part of that global governance. This can occur through its local activities, the power of gender norms over state and local governments, the strengthening of UN and EU offices on women, and the cooperation and learning of women cross borders. Transnational feminism can better contribute to a vision of such transnational governance as it works out its problems. It would be a shame if reflection and self-reflection on these matters did not continue as long as necessary.

NOTES

This article could not possible have been written without the contributions, insights, and criticisms of Vanda Božičević, Vesna Kesić, Hana Havelková, and above all Karin Aleksander. For fifteen years, Karin Aleksander has been a wonderful librarian in the Center for Interdisciplinary Women's Studies at Humboldt University in Berlin. She has worked tirelessly, bringing to my attention articles and books relevant to my research. She has done more that I would ever have dared to ask of her. Without her efforts I would know even less than I do now. Her bibliography of all the existing literature on eastern German women will be a tremendous contribution for further researchers. I am also grateful to all the women from the region, both in the United States and in the region, with whom I have ongoing contacts. I also thank Robert Roth and the editor Janet Elise Johnson for helpful suggestions.

1. Vesna Kesić, Vesna Janković, and Biljana Bijelić, eds., *Women Recollecting Memories: The Center for Women War Victims Ten Years Later,* 2nd ed. [in English] (Zagreb: Center for Women War Victims, 2003), 48.

2. I am indebted to Hana Havelková for describing some of these contexts, although she is not responsible for the use I made of them.

3. For women, not only for men, the "other woman" was seen as the representative of the "other" suspect political system. To praise the extensive daycare that GDR women had utilized was to praise the suspect GDR as a political system.

4. Ute Gerhard and Ingrid Miethe, "Debatten und Missverständnisse unter Feministinnen aus Ost- und Westdeutschland in der Nachwendezeit-ein nachholender Dialog" [Debates and Misunderstandings among Feminists from East and West Germany in the Post-Transformation—A Catch-up Dialogue], in *Geschlechterkonstruktionen in Ost und West. Biographische Perspektiven* [*Gender Constructions in East and West. Biographical Perspectives*], ed. Ingrid Miethe, Claudia Kajatin, and Jana Pohl (Münster, Germany: LIT Verlag, 2004), 334.

5. Gerald Gaus, *Justificatory Liberalism: An Essay on Epistemology and Political Theory* (New York: Oxford University Press, 1996), 128.

6. Ibid., 119.

7. Hana Havelková, interview by the author, Prague, Czech Republic, 1996; Hana Havelková and Marie Cervinková, "Uneasy Dialogues: Reinventing Feminism in Post-socialist Europe" (unpublished paper, April 4, 1996), 9.

8. Ralitsa Muharska, "This Started As a Review" (unpublished manuscript, 2005).

9. Muharska, "Silences and Parodies in the East-West Feminist Dialogue," *L'Homme: Zeitschrift für feministische Geschichtswissenschaft* [L'Homme: European Review of Feminist History] 16, no. 1 (2005): 44.

10. Muharska, "Silences and Parodies in the East-West Feminist Dialogue," 38.

11. Muharska, "This Started As a Review."

12. Gerhard and Miethe, 330, 342.

13. This included writings by Ann Snitow, Beth Holmgren, Frances Olsen and Nanette Funk (U.S.), Laura Busheikin (Canada), Susan.J. Koch, Kristina.L. Koch and Zoya Moneva (U.S. and Bulgaria), Kornelia Merdjanska and Tatyana Kotzeva (Bulgaria), Mihaela Miroiu (Romania), Maria Adamic (Hungary), Vesna Kesić, Djurdja Knesević and Slavenka Drakulić (Croatia), Jiřina Šmejkalová-Strickland, Nora Jung (Canada), Hana Havelková, Jiřina Šiklová and Alena Wagnerová (Czech Republic), and Zuszana Kizcková (Slovakia). In Germany the names are too many to mention, and even more was said than was written. The latter was the case in all the countries in the region.

14. Peggy Watson, "Civil Society and the Politics of Difference in Eastern Europe," in *Transitions, Environments, Translations: Feminisms in International Politics*, ed. Joan Wallach Scott, Temma Kaplan, and Debra Keates (London: Routledge, 1997).

15. Tatiana Böhm, "Women's Issues and Democracy," paper presented at conference on Can They Build a State without Us? Women and German Unification, Über sas Schicksal, April 16–18, 1993, in Goethe House, New York; Irene Dölling, "Identitäten von Ost-Frauen im Transformationsprozess: Probleme ostdeutscher Frauenforschung" [Identities of East German Women in the Transformation Process: Problems of East German Women's Research], in *German Monitor: Women and the Wende: Social Effects and Cultural Reflections of the German Unification Process*, ed. Elizabeth Boa and Janet Wharton, proceedings of a conference held by Women in German Studies, September 9–11, 1993, at the University of Nottingham (Amsterdam: Rodopi, 1993); and Hildegard Maria Nickel and Eva Kolinsky, "Vom Umgang mit Differenzen. Statement zur Podiumsdebatte "Auf dem Weg zur normalisierten Wissenschaft? Über das Schicksal subversiver Ansprüche in der Frauen- und Geschlechterforschung" [In Dealing with Differences. Statement for a Plenary Debate: Toward a Normalized Science? On the Fate of Subversive Claims in Women's and Gender Research], in *Reinventing Gender, Women in Eastern Germany Since Unification*, ed. Eva Kolinsky

and Hildegard Maria Nickel (London: Frank Cass, 2003).

16. Mihaela Miroiu, "State Men, Market Women: The Effects of Left Conservatism on Gender Politics in Romanian Transition" (unpublished manuscript, 2003).

17. Muharska, "Silences and Parodies in the East-West Feminist Dialogue," 45.

18. Hana Havelková, "A Few Pre-Feminist Thoughts," in *Gender Politics and Post-Communism: Reflections from Eastern Europe and the Former Soviet Union*, ed. Nanette Funk and Magda Mueller (London: Routledge, 1993), 65.

19. Zuzana Kiczková and Etela Farkašová, Jiřina Šiklová, Jiřina Šmejkalová-Strickland, Hana Havelková, Nora Jung, Peggy Wallace, Beth Holmgren, Nanette Funk.

20. Ulrike Helwerth and Gislinde Schwarz, Hana Havelková, Marie Čermáková, Eva Hauserová, Janet Elise Johnson, Mira Marody, Jirina Šiklová, Peggy Watson.

21. Muharska notes that in some instances in the region "democracy" is understood as "facade democracy," and "state" as "criminalized state" ("This Started As a Review").

22. Gerhard and Miethe, 331.

23. Members of the GDR group "Women for Peace" kept their children out of the public kindergarten as a political act because daycare included exposure to militarism. Gerhard and Miethe, 331; Marina Beyer, a member of this group, referred to the alternative pedagogy this group developed for raising children "in peace"; interview by the author, Berlin, 1999.

24. Gerhard and Miethe, 330, 339. The differences in East and West Germany included differences in gender identity, the role of family, the relations of their respective states to their sense of identity, and post-1989 circumstances. For example, it was part of an East German identity as a woman that she work outside the home to provide for her family, but this was not the case for the West German women.

25. Gerhard and Miethe, 326–29, 340–41.

26. Ibid., 331.

27. Ibid., 330.

28. For example, GDR women researchers reported their findings that GDR woman were satisfied with the GDR model of the unification of work and family, although discontent with the length of the work day. Some East German women sociologists' research was later confirmed by West German researchers. Ursula Müller, " 'Besserwisende Schwestern?' Eine erfahrungsgesättigte Polemik" [Know-It-All Sisters? An Experience Saturated Polemic], in *Weschselnde Blicke: Frauenforschung in internationaler Perspektive* [Changing Viewpoints: Women's Research in International Perspective], ed. Ilse Lenz and Andrea Germer (Opladen, Germany: Leske + Budrich, 1996), 191

29. Gerhard and Miethe, 334.

30. Ibid., 334–35.

31. Muharska, "This Started As a Review."

32. Mihaela Miroiu, "State Men, Market Women."

33. Interview by the author, eastern Germany, 2001.

34. Personal Communication by the author with Anca Gheaus, July 1, 2005.

35. I am speaking only of tendencies because such street actions and non-NGO organized groups existed both before and after 1989 in different ways in different countries.

36. Gerhard and Miethe, 343.

37. Ralitsa Muharska, "This Started As a Review."

38. Ute Gerhard, "Editorial," *L'Homme: Europäische Zeitschrift für Feministische Geschichtswissenschaft* [L'Homme: European Journal of Feminist History] 16, no. 1 (2005): 8.

39. Tiffany Petros, "Mop, Shop and Shut Up. Feminism in the Czech Republic," *Central European Review* 2, no. 43 (2000), http://www.ce-review.org/00/43/petros43 .html (accessed June 2005); Elena Gapova, "Understanding the Other: A Response to Tiffany Petros' article," *Central Europe Review* 3, no. 2 (2001), http://www.ce-review .org/01/2/gapova2.html (accessed June 2005).

WORKS CITED

Abubikirova, N. I., et al. 1998. *Directory of Women's Non-Governmental Organizations in Russia and the NIS.* Moscow: Aslan Publishers.

Achim, Viorel. 1998. *Ţiganii in Istoria României* [Ţigani in the History of Romania]. Bucharest: Editura Enciclopedica.

Acsady, Judie. 1997. "Stehende Gewässer" [Still-standing Waters]. *Weiblick: Informationsblatt von Frauen für Frauen* [Weiblick: Informational Newspaper by Women for Women] 29: 4–7.

Allen, Beverly. 1996. *Rape Warfare: The Hidden Genocide in Bosnia-Herzegovina and Croatia.* Minneapolis: University of Minnesota Press.

Alsop, Rachel, and Jennifer Hockey. 2001. "Women's Reproductive Lives as a Symbolic Resource in Central and Eastern Europe." *European Journal of Women's Studies* 8, no. 4: 454–71.

Amza, Tudor. 1995. *Fenomenul infractional în rindul ţiganilor: Activitaţi specific Poliţiei Române pentru protenjarea etniei si prevenirea faptelor antisociale* [The Infractional Phenomenon amongst the Ţiganii: Specific Activities of the Romanian Police for Protection of the Ethnicity and Prevention of Antisocial Factors]. Bucharest: Academie de Politiei Alexandru Ioan Cuza.

Anderson, Michelle J. 1993. "A License to Abuse: The Impact of Conditional Status on Female Immigrants." *Yale Law Journal* 102, no. 6: 1401–30.

Ashwin, Sarah. 2000. "Gender, State and Society in Soviet and Post-Soviet Russia." In *Gender, State and Society in Soviet and Post-Soviet Russia,* ed. Sarah Ashwin. London: Routledge.

———. 2002. "'A Woman Is Everything': The Reproduction of Soviet Ideals of Womanhood in Post-Communist Russia." In *Work, Employment and Transition: Restructuring Livelihoods in Post-Communism,* ed. Al Rainnie, Adrian Smith, and Adam Swain. London: Routledge.

Ashwin, Sarah, and Elain Bowers. 1997. "Do Russian Women Want to Work?" In *Post-Soviet Women: From the Baltic to Central Asia,* ed. Mary Buckley. Cambridge: Cambridge University Press.

Asociatia pentru Promovarea Femeii din Romania, Centrul de Informare [Association for the Protection of Women in Romania, Information Center]. 2002. *Educaţie si Consiliere Timişoara pentru femeile si feţele victime ale violenţei domestice şi abuzului sexual* [For the Women and Girl Victims of Domestic Violence]. PHARE-ACCESS program. July 5–7.

Attwood, Lynne. 1990. *The New Soviet Man and Woman: Sex Role Socialization in the USSR.* Bloomington: Indiana University Press.

———. 1996. "The Post-Soviet Woman in the Move to the Market: A Return to Domesticity and Dependence?" In *Women in Russia and Ukraine*, ed. Rosalind Marsh. Cambridge: Cambridge University Press.

——. 1997. "'She Was Asking for It': Rape and Domestic Violence against Women." In *Post-Soviet Women: From the Baltic to Central Asia*, ed. Mary Buckley. Cambridge: Cambridge University Press.

Baban, Adriana. 2000. "Women's Sexuality and Reproductive Behavior in Post-Ceausescu Romania: A Psychological Approach." In *Reproducing Gender*, ed. Susan Gal and Gail Kligman. Princeton, N.J.: Princeton University Press.

Balsamo, Anne. 1996. *Technologies of the Gendered Body: Reading Cyborg Women*. Durham: Duke University Press.

Balzer, Harley. 1998. "Russia's Middle Classes." *Post-Soviet Affairs* 14, no. 2: 165–86.

Bărbulescu, Alina. 2003. "Violenţa intrafamilialâ şi neliniştea justiţiei" [Intrafamilial Violence and the Restlessness of Justice]. *Dilema* 530 (30 May–5 June). http://www.algoritma.ro/dilema/530/AlinaBA.htm. Accessed Feb. 7, 2006.

Barkan, Joanne. 2002. "As Old as Rape Itself: Rape in Foca." *Dissent* 49, no. 1: 60–66.

Barnello, Michele A. 1999. "Gender and Roll Call Voting in the New York State Assembly." *Women and Politics* 20, no. 4: 77–93.

Beck, Paul Allen. 1996. *Party Politics in America*. 8th ed. New York: Longman.

Belin, Laura, and Robert W. Orttung. 1997. *The Russian Parliamentary Elections of 1995: The Battle for the Duma*. Armonk, N.Y.: M. E. Sharpe.

Bell, David, ed. 2001. *An Introduction to Cyberculture*. London: Routledge.

Bellér-Hann, Ildiko. "Prostitution and Its Effects in Northeast Turkey." *European Journal of Women's Studies* 2, no. 2 (1995): 219–35.

Belousova, M. P., et al. 2001. *Gender: Obshchedostrupnyi slovar'-spravochnik* [Gender: Popular Dictionary-Directory]. Barnaul, Russia: AKZhOO "Otklik."

Belousova, M. P., L. K. Cintsova, and S. G. Chudova. 2002. *Zhenskie obshchestvennye organizatsii Altaiskogo kraiia* [Women's Social Organizations in the Altai Krai]. Barnaul: Pegas.

Benford, Robert D., and David A. Snow. 2000. "Framing Processes and Social Movements: An Overview and Assessment." *Annual Review of Sociology* 26, no. 1: 611–39.

Berger, Ronald J., Patricia Searles, and Charles E. Cottle. 1991. *Feminism and Pornography*. New York: Praeger.

Berkman, Michael B., and Robert E. O'Connor. 1993. "Do Women Legislators Matter? Female Legislators and State Abortion Policy." *American Politics Quarterly* 21, no. 1: 102–24.

Betterton, Rosemary. 1996. *An Intimate Distance: Women Artists and the Body*. London: Routledge.

Bhabha, Homi K. 1994. *The Location of Culture*. London: Routledge.

Biemann, Ursula. 2001. *Been There and Back to Nowhere: Geschlecht in Transnationalen Orten*. Berlin: B—books.

Björnberg, Ulla, ed. 1992. *European Parents in the 1990s: Contradictions and Comparisons*. New Brunswick, N.J.: Transaction.

Blocker, T. Jean. 1997. "Gender and Environmentalism: Results from the 1993 General Social Survey." *Social Science Quarterly* 78 (December): 841–58.

Bodrova, Valentina. 1993. "Glasnost and 'the Woman Question' in the Mirror of Public Opinion: Attitudes towards Women, Work, and the Family." In *Democratic Reform and the Position of Women in Transitional Economies*, ed. Valentine M. Moghadam. Oxford: Clarendon Press.

Böhm, Tatiana. 1993. "Women's Issues and Democracy." Paper presented at conference on "Can They Build a State without Us? Women and German Unification," April 16–18, at Goethe House, New York.

Boia, Lucian. 2001. *Romania: Borderland of Europe*. London: Reaktion Books.

Bordo, Susan. 1993. *Unbearable Weight: Feminism, Western Culture, and the Body*. Berkeley: University of California Press.

Boric, Rada. 1997. "Against the War: Women Organizing across the National Divide in the Countries of the Former Yugoslavia." In *Gender and Catastrophe*, ed. Ronit Lentin. New York: Zed Books.

Bourdieu, Pierre. 1993. *Language and Symbolic Power*. Cambridge: Polity Press.

Bracewell, Wendy. 2000. "Rape in Kosovo: Masculinity and Serbian Nationalism." *Nations and Nationalism* 6, no. 4: 563–90.

Brah, Avtah. 2000. "The Scent of Memory: Strangers, Our Own and Others." In *Hybridity and Its Discontents: Politics, Science, Culture*, ed. Avtah Brah and Annie E. Coombes. London: Routledge.

Bridger, Sue, ed. 1999. *Women and Political Chance: Perspectives from East-Central Europe*. New York: St. Martin's Press.

Bridger, Sue, Kathryn Pinnick, and Rebecca Kay, eds. 1996. *No More Heroines? Russia, Women and the Market*. London: Routledge.

Brook, Barbara. 1999. *Feminist Perspectives on the Body*. New York: Longman.

Brubaker, Rogers. 1996. *Nationalism Reframed: Nationhood and the National Question in the New Europe*. Cambridge: Cambridge University Press.

Bruthansová, Tereza. 1997. "Worlds Temptingly Marked 'Top Secret.'" In *On the Edge of the Horizon*, exhibition catalog. Prague: Prague City Gallery.

Buckley, Mary. 1997. "Adaptation of the Soviet Women's Committee: Deputies' Voices from 'Women of Russia.'" In *Post-Soviet Women: From the Baltic to Central Asia*, ed. Mary Buckley. Cambridge: Cambridge University Press.

Bucur, Maria. 2002. *Eugenics and Modernization in Interwar Romania*. Pittsburgh: Pittsburgh University Press.

Buica, C., M. Popescu, and O. Tomescu. 1995. "Bucureştiul vazut de Bucureşteni; reprezentari speciale ale spaţiului urban" [Bucharest as Seen by Bucharesteans: Special Representations of Urban Space]. *Revista de Cercetari Sociale* [Journal of Social Research] 13: 111–15.

Bulbeck, Chilla. 2005. "'Women Are Exploited Way Too Often': Feminist Rhetorics at the End of Equality." *Australian Feminist Studies* 20 (March): 65–76.

Burbank, John, and Peter Steiner, eds. 1978. *Structure, Sign, and Function: Selected Essays by Jan Mukařovský*. New Haven, Conn.: Yale University Press.

Busheikin, Laura. 1993. "Is Sisterhood Really Global? Western Feminism in Eastern Europe." In *Bodies of Bread and Butter: Reconfiguring Women's Lives in Post-Communist Czech Republic*, ed. Susana Trnka and Laura Busheikin. Prague: Prague Gender Center.

Butler, Judith. 1990. *Gender Trouble: Feminism and the Subversion of Identity*. London: Routledge.

———. 1997. *Excitable Speech: A Politics of the Performative*. London: Routledge.

Buzan, Barry. 1996. "The Idea of the State and National Security." In *Perspectives on World Politics*, ed. R. Little and M. Smith. London: Routledge.

Caldas-Coulthard, Carmen Rosa. 1995. "Man in the News: The Misrepresentation of Women Speaking in News-as-Narrative-Discourse." In *Language and Gender: Interdisciplinary Perspective*, ed. Sara Mills. London: Longman.

Calling the Ghosts: A Story about Rape, War and Women. 1996. Executive producer: Julia Ormond. Directed by Mandy Jacobson and Karmen Jelincic.

Cameron, Deborah. 1997. "Performing Gender Identity: Young Men's Talk and the Construction of Heterosexual Masculinity." In *Language and Masculinity*, ed. Sally Johnson and Urlike Hanna Meinhof. Oxford: Blackwell.

Caputi, Jane. 1987. *The Age of Sex Crime.* London: Women's Press.

Carroll, Susan J., Debra L. Dodson, and Ruth B. Mandel. 1991. *The Impact of Women in Public Office: An Overview.* New Brunswick, N.J.: Center for the American Women and Politics.

CBOS (Centrum Badania Opinii Społecznej) [Public Opinion Research Center]. 1989–1996. Serwis Informacyjny [Information Service]. 1989–1996. Warsaw.

Centar za istrazivanje i dokumentaciju Saveza logorasa Bosne i Hercegovine. 1999. *Molila sam ih da me ubiju: Zlocin nad zenom Bosne i Hercegovine* [I Begged Them to Kill Me: Crimes against Women of Bosnia and Herzegovina]. Sarajevo: Association of War Prisoners.

Centeno, Miguel Angel, and Tania Rands. 1996. "The World They Have Lost: An Assessment of Change in Eastern Europe." *Social Research* 63, no. 2: 369–402.

Ciumăgeanu Mugur, Daniel. 2003. "Vorbele bune" [Good Words]. *Dilema* 530 (30 May–5 June). http://www.algoritma.ro/dilema/fw.htm?current=arhiva_dilema/search1.htm. Accessed Feb. 7, 2006.

Coates, Jennifer. 1996. "Thank God I Am a Woman." In *Gender and Discourse*, ed. R. Wodak. Oxford: Blackwell.

Cockburn, Cynthia. 1998. *The Space between Us: Negotiating Gender and National Identities in Conflict.* London: Zed Books.

Connell, R. W. 1987. *Gender and Power.* Stanford, Calif.: Stanford University Press.

Connor, Walker. 1994. *Ethnonationalism: The Quest for Understanding.* Princeton, N.J.: Princeton University Press.

Considine, Mark, and Iva Ellen Deutchman. 1996. "Instituting Gender: State Legislators in Australia and the United States." *Women and Politics* 16, no. 4: 1–19.

Cooper, Belinda. 1997. "Building Feminism from the Ground Up." *Civnet's Journal for Civil Society* 1, no. 3. http://www.civnet.org/journal/issue3/cfbeco.htm. Accessed Oct. 2001; URL no longer active.

Council of Europe. 1999. *Gender Mainstreaming: Conceptual Frameworks, Methodology and Presentation of Good Practices; Final Report of the Group of Specialists on Mainstreaming.* Strasbourg.

Cusack, Tricia. 2000. "Janus and Gender: Women and the Nation's Backward Look." *Nations and Nationalism* 6, no. 4: 541–61.

Dahbour, Omar, and Ishay, Micheline, eds. 1995. "Considerations on Representative Government." *The Nationalism Reader.* Atlantic Highlangs, N.J.: Humanities Press.

Das, Veena, et al. 2000. *Violence and Subjectivity.* Berkeley: University of California Press.

Daskalova, Krassimira. 2000. "Women's Problems, Women's Discourses in Bulgaria." In *Reproducing Gender: Politics, Publics, and Everyday Life After Socialism*, ed. Susan Gal and Gail Kligman, 337–69. Princeton, N.J.: Princeton University Press.

DaVanzo, Julie, and Clifford Grammich. 2001. *Dire Demographics: Population Trends in the Russian Federation.* Santa Monica: RAND.

Derrida, Jacques. 1976. *Of Grammatology.* Baltimore, Md.: John Hopkins Press.

Diamond, Irene, and Gloria Feman Orenstein, eds. 1990. *Reweaving the World: The Emergence of Ecofeminism.* San Francisco: Sierra Club Books.

Dietz, Mary. 1998. "Context Is All: Feminism and Theories of Citizenship." In *Feminism and Politics,* ed. Anne Phillips. Oxford: Oxford University Press.

Dodson, Debra L., et al. 1995. *Voices, Views, Votes: The Impact of Women in the 103rd Congress.* New Brunswick, N.J.: Center for the American Women and Politics.

Dölling, Irene. 1993. "Identitäten von Ost-Frauen im Transformationsprozess: Probleme ostdeutscher Frauenforschung" [Identities of East German Women in the Transformation Process: Problems of East German Women's Research]. In *German Monitor: Women and the Wende: Social Effects and Cultural Reflections of the German Unification Process,* ed. Elizabeth Boa and Janet Wharton. Proceedings of a conference held by Women in German Studies, September 9–11 at the University of Nottingham. Amsterdam: Rodopi.

Drakulić, Slavenka. 1993. *How We Survived Communism and Even Laughed.* London: Vantage.

Dubaviec, Sergej. 2000. Strona i Narod v zerkale publitsistiki [The Country and the Nation in the Mirror of the Publicists]. In *Beloruskaya Tragedia, 1986–1999,* ed. Semen Bukchin. Warsaw: n.p.

Eckert, Lynn Mills. 2003. "The Incoherence of the Zoning Approach to Regulating Pornography: The Exclusion of Gender and a Call for Category Refinement in Free Speech Doctrine." *Georgetown Journal of Gender and the Law* 4 (Summer): 863–87.

Efimova, Nadiezhda. 1998. "Sredstva massovoy informatsii i problema natsionalno-kulturalnogo wozrozhdenya Belarusov [Mass Media and the Problem of the National and Cultural Revival of the Belarusian(s)]. In *Belorusia i Rossija: Obschestva i gosudarstva* [Belarus and Russia: Societies and States], ed. D. E. Furman. Moscow: Prava Tscheloveka.

Ehrenreich, Barbara, and Arlie Russell Hochschild. 2003. *Global Woman: Nannies, Maids, and Sex Workers in the New Economy.* New York: Metropolitan Books.

Einhorn, Barbara. 1993. *Cinderella Goes to Market: Citizenship, Gender and Women's Movements in East Central Europe.* New York: Verso.

———. 1995. "Ironies of History: Citizenship Issues in the New Market Economies of East Central Europe." In *Women and Market Societies: Crisis and Opportunity,* ed. Barbara Einhorn and Eileen Janes Yeo. Aldershot, UK: Edward Elgar.

———. 2000. "Gender and Citizenship in the Context of Democratisation and Economic Transformation in East Central Europe." In *International Perspectives on Gender and Democratisation,* ed. Shirin Rai. Basingstoke: Macmillan.

Ellman, Maud. 1993. *The Hunger Artists: Starving, Writing and Imprisonment.* London: Virago.

Elman, R. Amy. 1996. *Sexual Subordination and State Intervention: Comparing Sweden and the United States.* Providence. R.I.: Berghahn Books.

Enloe, Cynthia. 2000. *Maneuvers. The International Politics of Militarizing Women's Lives.* Berkeley: University of California Press.

Equal Chances for Women Foundation. 1998. Survey of Women Victims of Domestic Violence. http://www.proiectns.org/archives/000050.html.

Federation for Women and Family Planning. 2000. *The Anti-Abortion Law in Poland: The Functioning, Social Effects, Attitudes and Behaviors.* http://www.federa.org.pl/english/reports/report00/rep00_2.htm. Accessed Oct. 28, 2003.

Feldman, Allen. 2002. "Strange Fruit: The South African Truth Commission and the Domestic Economies of Violence." *Social Analysis* 46, no. 3: 234–66.

Fell, Alison. 1995. "Language and the Body." *Critical Quarterly* 37, no. 4: 60–65.

Flax, Jane. 1986. "Postmodernism and Gender Relations in Feminist Theory." In *Feminist Theory in Practice and Process*, ed. Micheline R. Malson et al. Chicago: University of Chicago Press.

Foucault, Michel. 1972. *The Archeology of Knowledge and the Discourse on Language.* New York: Pantheon Books.

Fraser, Nancy. 1990. "Struggle over Needs: Outline of a Socialist-Feminist Critical Theory of Late-Capitalist Political Culture." In *Women, the State, and Welfare*, ed. Linda Gordon. Madison: University of Wisconsin Press.

Funk, Nanette. 1993. "Feminism East and West." In *Gender Politics and Post-Communism: Reflections from Eastern Europe and the Former Soviet Union*, ed. Nanette Funk and Magda Mueller. New York: Routledge Press

——. 1994. "Feminism Meets Post-Communism: The Case of the United Germany." In *Feminist Nightmares. Women at Odds: Feminism and the Problem of Sisterhood*, ed. Susan Ostrov Weisser and Jennifer Fleischner. New York: New York University Press.

Funk, Nanette, and Magda Mueller, eds. 1993. *Gender Politics and Post-Communism: Reflections from Eastern Europe and the Former Soviet Union.* London: Routledge.

Fuszara, Malgorzata. 2000. "New Gender Relations in Poland in the 1990s." In *Reproducing Gender: Politics, Publics, and Everyday Life After Socialism*, ed. Susan Gal and Gail Kligman, 259–85. Princeton, N.J.: Princeton University Press.

Gal, Susan, and Gail Kligman. 2000. *The Politics of Gender after Socialism.* Princeton, N.J.: Princeton University Press.

Gal, Susan, and Gail Kligman, eds. 2000. *Reproducing Gender: Politics, Publics, and Everyday Life after Socialism.* Princeton, N.J.: Princeton University Press.

Gallup Organization Romania Survey. 2003. "Violenţei împotriva femeilor" [Violence against Women]. Conducted April 12–23, 2003, Bucharest.

Gapova, Elena. 2001. "Understanding the Other: A Response to Tiffany Petros' Article." *Central Europe Review* 3, no. 2. http://www.zenskestudie.edu.yu/wgsact/e-library/e-lib0007html. Accessed June 2005.

——. 2002. "On Nation, Gender, and Class Formation in Belarus and Elsewhere in the Post-Soviet World." *Nationalities Papers* 30, no. 4: 639–62.

——. 2004. "Conceptualising Gender, Nation, and Class in Post-Soviet Belarus." In *Post-Soviet Women Encountering Transition: Nation Building, Economic Survival, and Civic Activism*, ed. Kathleen Kuehnast and Carol Nechemias. Washington, D.C.: Woodrow Wilson Center Press.

Gaus, Gerald. 1996. *Justificatory Liberalism: An Essay on Epistemology and Political Theory.* New York: Oxford University Press.

Gerhard, Ute. 2005. "Editorial." *L'Homme.Europäische Zeitschrift für Feministische Geschichtswissenschaft* [L'Homme: European Review of Feminist History] 16, no. 1: 7–11.

Gerhard, Ute, and Ingrid Miethe. 2004. "Debatten und Missverständnisse unter Feministinnen aus Ost- und Westdeutschland in der Nachwendezeit—ein nachholender Dialog" [Debates and Misunderstandings among Feminists from East and West Germany in the Post-transformation Period—A Catch-up Dialogue]. In *Geschlechterkonstruktionen in Ost und West: Biographische Perspektiven* [Gender

Constructions in East and West: Biographical perspectives], ed. Ingrid Miethe, Claudia Kajatin, Jana Pohl. Münster, Germany: LIT Verlag.

Gerson, Kathleen. 1985. *Hard Choices: How Women Decide about Work, Career, and Motherhood*. Berkeley: University of California Press.

Gerzová, Jana. 2001. "Art and the Question of Gender in Slovak Art." *N. Paradoxa International Feminist Art Journal* 8 (August): 74–82.

Ghinea, Cristian. 2001. "Între noi fie vorba, rromii tot Țigani sînt" [Just between Us, Rromi Are All Țiganii]. *Dilema* 19, no. 3. http://www.algoritma.ro/dilema/arhiva _dilema/451/Cristian.htm. Accessed Feb. 7, 2006.

Ghodsee, Kristen. "Feminism-by-Design: Emerging Capitalisms, Cultural Feminism, and Women's Nongovernmental Organizations in Postsocialist Eastern Europe." *Signs: Journal of Women in Culture and Society* 29, no. 3 (2004): 727–53.

Gilmore, David. 1990. *Manhood in the Making: Cultural Concepts of Masculinity*. New Haven, Conn.: Yale University Press.

Girard, Françoise, and Wanda Nowicka. 2002. "Clear and Compelling Evidence: The Polish Tribunal on Abortion Rights." *Reproductive Health Matters* 10, no. 19: 22–30.

Goldfarb, Jeffrey C. 1997. "Why Is There No Feminism after Communism?" *Social Research* 64, no. 2: 235–57.

Golosov, Grigorii V. 2001. "Political Parties, Electoral Systems, and Women's Representation in the Regional Legislative Assemblies of Russia, 1995–1998." *Party Politics* 7, no. 1: 45–68.

Goodin, Robert E. 2004. "Representing Diversity." *British Journal of Political Science* 34, no. 3: 453–69.

Gorbachev, Mikhail S. 1987. *Perestroika: New Thinking for Our Country and the World*. New York: Harper and Row.

Goscilo, Helena. 1993. "Domostroika or Perestroika? The Construction of Womanhood in Soviet Culture under Glasnost." In *Late Soviet Culture: From Perestroika to Novostroika*, ed. Thomas Lahusen with Gene Kuperman. Durham, N.C.: Duke University Press.

———. 1994. *Dehexing Sex: Russian Womanhood During and After Glasnost*. Ann Arbor: University of Michigan Press.

Goskomstat. 2002. "Russia in Figures 1999." Moscow.

Goven, Joanna. 2000. "New Parliament, Old Discourse? The Parental Leave Debate in Hungary." In *Reproducing Gender: Politics, Publics, and Everyday Life after Socialism*, ed. Susan Gal and Gail Kligman. Princeton, N.J.: Princeton University Press.

Granik, Lisa. 1997. "The Trials of the Proletarka: Sexual Harassment Claims in the 1920s." In *Reforming Justice in Russia, 1864–1996: Power, Culture, and the Limits of Legal Order*, ed. Peter H. Solomon Jr. Armonk, N.Y.: M. E. Sharpe.

Greene, Diana. 1998. "Mid-nineteenth Century Domestic Ideology in Russia." In *Women and Russian Culture: Projections and Self-Perceptions*, ed. Rosalind Marsh. New York: Berghahn Books.

Grosz, Elisabeth. 1994. *Volatile Bodies: Toward a Corporal Feminism*. Bloomington: Indiana University Press.

———. 2001. *Architecture from the Outside: Essays on Virtual and Real Space*. Cambridge: Massachusetts Institute of Technology Press.

Grunberg, Laura. 1999. "Povestiri din vremea cand am incercat sa fiu o buna Foisoreanca" [Stories from the Time I Tried to Be a Good Neighbor]. *ANAlize: Revista de Studii Feministe* 5, no. 16. http://www.anasaf.ro/romana/index(rom).html. Accessed Feb. 7, 2006.

——. 2000. "Women's NGOs in Romania." In *Reproducing Gender: Politics, Publics, and Everyday Life After Socialism,* ed. Susan Gal and Gail Kligman, 307–36. Princeton, N.J.: Princeton University Press.

Gupte, Manjusha. 2002. "Gender, Feminist Consciousness, and the Environment: Exploring the 'Natural' Connection." *Women and Politics* 24, no. 1: 47–62.

Gutman, Roy. 1993. *A Witness to Genocide.* New York: MacMillan.

Hancock, Ian. 1988. *The Pariah Syndrome: An Account of Gypsy Slavery and Persecution.* Ann Arbor, Mich.: Karoma.

Haraway, Donna. 2001. *Simians, Cyborgs, and Women: The Reinvention of Nature.* London: Routledge.

Harding, Sandra. 1986. *The Science Question in Feminism.* Ithaca, N.Y.: Cornell University Press.

Hartmann, Heidi. 1981. "The Family as the Locus of Gender, Class, and Political Struggle: The Example of Housework." *Signs: Journal of Women in Culture and Society* 6, no. 3: 366–94.

Haukanes, Haldis. 2001. "Anthropological Debates on Gender and the Post-Communist Transformation." *NORA—Nordic Journal of Women's Studies* 9, no. 1: 16–20.

Havelková, Hana. 1993. "A Few Prefeminist Thoughts." In *Gender Politics and Post-Communism: Reflections from Eastern Europe and the former Soviet Union,* ed. Nanette Funk and Magda Mueller. London: Routledge.

——. 1997. "Transitory and Persistent Differences: Feminism East and West." In *Transitions, Environments, Translations: Feminisms in International Politics,* ed. Joan Wallach Scott, Temma Kaplan, and Debra Keates. London: Routledge.

Havelková, Hana, and Marie Cervinková. 1996. "Uneasy Dialogues: Reinventing Feminism in Post-Socialist Europe." Unpublished paper. April 4.

Hayden, Robert M. 2000. "Rape and Rape Avoidance in Ethno-National Conflicts: Sexual Violence in Liminalized States." *American Anthropologist* 102, no. 1: 27–41.

Hearn, Jeff, and Wendy Parkin. 2001. *Gender, Sexuality and Violence in Organizations.* London: Sage.

Hediger, Paul. 2000. "3% Increase in Internet Users in Austria in Last 3 Months." *Europe Media.* http://www.europemedia.net. Accessed June 10, 2002; URL no longer active.

Helwerth, Ulrike, and Gislinde Schwarz. 1995. *Von Muttis und Emanzen. Feministinnen in Ost- und Westdeutschland* [From Mommies and Libbers. Feminists in East and West Germany]. Frankfurt/M, Germany: Fischer Taschenbuch Verlag.

Hemment, Julie. 2004. "Global Civil Society and the Local Costs of Belonging: Defining 'Violence against Women' in Russia." *Signs: Journal of Women in Culture and Society* 29, no. 3: 815–40.

Henderson, Sarah L. 2003. *Building Democracy in Contemporary Russia: Western Support for Grassroots Organizations.* Ithaca, N.Y.: Cornell University Press.

Henn, Matt. 1993. "Polls, Politics and Perestroika: The Emergence of Political Opinion Polling in Central and Eastern Europe." *European Business and Economic Development* 1, no. 5: 11–17.

——. 1997. "Polls and the Political Process: The Use of Opinion Polls by Political Parties and Mass Media Organizations in European Post-communist Societies (1990–1995)." *Journal of Communist Studies and Transition Politics* 13, 3: 127–47.

———. 1998. "Opinion Polling in Central and Eastern Europe under Communism." *Journal of Contemporary History* 33, no. 2: 229–40.

Hirshmann, Nancy. 1992. *Rethinking Obligation: A Feminist Method for Political Theory*. Ithaca, N.Y.: Cornell University Press.

Hochschild, Arlie, with Anne Machung. 1989. *The Second Shift*. New York: Avon Books.

Holmgren, Beth. 1995. "Bug Inspectors and Beauty Queens: The Problems of Translating Feminism into Russian." In *Postcommunism and the Body Politic*, ed. Ellen E. Berry. New York: New York University Press.

Hoptman, Laura J., ed. 1995. *Beyond Belief: Contemporary Art from East Central Europe*. Chicago: Museum of Contemporary Art.

Howard, Marc Morje. 2003. *The Weakness of Civil Society in Post-Communist Europe*. Cambridge: Cambridge University Press.

Hughes, Donna. 2000. "The 'Natasha' Trade: The Transnational Shadow Market of Trafficking in Women." *Journal of International Affairs* 53, no. 2. http://www.uri.edu/artsci/wms/hughes/natasha.html. Accessed Aug. 12, 2003; URL no longer active.

———. 2000. "Prostitution Online." http://www.uri.edu/artsci/wms/hughes/prostitution_online.pdf. Accessed July 20, 2005.

———. 2001. *The Impact of the Use of New Communications and Information Technologies on Trafficking in Human Beings for Sexual Exploitation: The Study of Users*. Strasbourg: Council of Europe. http://www.uri.edu/artsci/wms/hughes/study_of_users.pdf. Accessed Aug. 28, 2005.

———. 2004. "The Role of Marriage Agencies in the Sexual Exploitation and Trafficking of Women from the Former Soviet Union." *International Review of Victimology* 11, no. 1: 49–71. http://www.uri.edu/artsci/wms/hughes/marriage_agencies_fsu.pdf. Accessed Feb. 23, 2006.

Hughes, Donna, and Tatiana Denisova. 2002. "Trafficking in Women from Ukraine." http://www.ncjrs.org/pdffiles1/nij/grants/203275.pdf. Accessed Feb. 23, 2006.

Human Rights Watch. 1995. "Russia: Neither Jobs nor Justice: State Discrimination Against Woman in Russia." *Human Rights Watch* 7, no. 5: 1–31.

———. 1997. "Russia—Too Little, Too Late: State Response to Violence Against Women." *Human Rights Watch* 9, no. 13: 1–51.

———. 2003. "Women's Work: Discrimination against Women in the Ukrainian Labor Force." http://www.hrw.org/reports/2003/ukraine0803. Accessed June 15, 2004.

Human Rights Watch International Gay and Lesbian Human Rights Commission Report. 1998. *Public Scandals: Sexual Orientation and Criminal Law in Romania*. New York: Arta Grafica.

Hunt, Swanee. 1999. "Silovannje" [Rape]. In *Molila sam ih da me ubiju: Zlocin nad zenom Bosne i Hercegovine* [I Begged Them to Kill Me: Crimes against Women of Bosnia-Herzegovina]. Sarajevo: Centar za istrazivanje i dokumentaciju Saveza logorasa Bosne i Hercegovine [Association of the War Prisoners].

International Helsinki Foundation for Human Rights. 2000. *Women 2000: An Investigation into the Status of Women's Rights in Central and South-Eastern Europe and Newly Independent States*. Helsinki: International Helsinki Foundation for Human Rights.

International Organization for Migration. 1999. *Information Campaign against Traf-*

ficking in Women from Ukraine—Research Report. Geneva, Switzerland. http://
www.iom.int/DOCUMENTS/PUBLICATION/EN/ukr_traf_wom_res_
rep.pdf. Accessed June 10, 2003.

Internet World Stats. 2005. Usage and Population Statistics. http://www.internetworld
stats.com/europa2.htm#ua. Accessed June 23, 2005.

Janin, Zuzanna. 2001. Interview by Przemysław Jedroski. "Patrze Na Swiat Jak Patrze"
[I Look at the World as I Look]. Arteon 18, no. 10: 34.

Johnson, Janet Elise. 2001. "Privatizing Pain: The Problem of Woman Battery in
Russia." NWSA Journal 13, no. 3: 153–68.

———. 2001. "State Transformation and Violence against Women in Postcommunist
Russia." Ph.D diss., Indiana University.

———. 2005. "Public-Private Permutations: Domestic Violence Crisis Centers in Barnaul." In Russian Civil Society: A Critical Assessment, ed. Al Evans, Laura Henry,
and Lisa McIntosh Sundstrom. Armonk, N.Y.: M. E. Sharpe.

Jones, Amelia. 1998. Body Art: Performing the Subject. Minneapolis: University of
Minnesota Press.

Jones, Kathleen B. 1990. "Citizenship in a Woman-Friendly Polity." Signs: Journal of
Women in Culture and Society 15, no. 4: 781–812.

Judd, Ellen R. 1994. Gender and Power in Rural North China. Stanford, Calif.: Stanford University Press.

Jung, Nora. 1994. "Eastern European Women with Western Eyes." In Stirring It: Challenges for Feminism, ed. Gabriele Griffin et al. London: Taylor and Francis.

Kanter, Rosabeth M. 1977. "Some Effects of Proportions on Group Life: Skewed Sex
Ratios and Responses to Token Women." American Journal of Sociology 82, no. 5:
965–90.

Karatnycky, Adrian, Alexander Motyl, and Amanda Schnetzer. 2002. Nations in Transit
2001: Civil Society, Democracy, and Market in East Central Europe and the Newly
Independent States. New York: Freedom House. http://www.freedomhouse.org/
research/nitransit/2001/index.htm. Accessed Oct. 2003; URL no longer active.

Katerina Vincourova. 1997. Exhibition catalogue with interview by Marta Smolikova.
Prague: Nova Sin Gallery and Behemot Gallery.

Kay, Rebecca. 1997. "Images of an Ideal Woman: Perceptions of Russian Womanhood
through the Media, Education and Women's Own Eyes." In Post-Soviet Women:
From the Baltic to Central Asia, ed. Mary Buckley. Cambridge: Cambridge University Press.

———. 2000. Russian Women and Their Organizations. New York: St. Martin's Press.

———. 2004. "Meeting the Challenge Together? Russian Grassroots Women's Organizations and the Shortcomings of Western Aid." In Post-Soviet Women Encountering Transition: Nation-Building, Economic Survival, and Civic Activism, ed. Kathleen Kuenhast and Carol Nechemias. Washington, D.C.: Woodrow Wilson
Center Press/Johns Hopkins University Press.

———. 2004. "Working with Single Fathers in Western Siberia: A New Departure in
Russian Social Provision." Europe-Asia Studies 56, no. 7: 941–61.

Keck, Margaret, and Kathryn Sikkink. 1998. Activists beyond Borders: Transnational
Advocacy Networks in International Politics. Ithaca, N.Y.: Cornell University Press.

Keller, Evelyn Fox. 1985. Reflections of Gender and Science. New Haven, Conn.: Yale
University Press.

Kelly, Catriona. 2001. Refining Russia: Advice Literature, Polite Culture, and Gender
from Catherine to Yeltsin. Oxford: Oxford University Press.

Kelly, Petra K. 1994. "Women and Power." *Earth Island Journal* 9, no. 1: 38–40.

Kesić, Vesna. 2002. "Muslim Women, Croatian Women, Serbian Women, Albanian Women . . ." In *Balkan as Metaphor: Between Globalization and Fragmentation*, ed. D. Bjelic and O. Savic. Cambridge: Massachusetts Institute of Technology Press.

Kesić, Vesna, Vesna Janković, and Biljana Bijelić, eds. 2003. *Women Recollecting Memories: The Center for Women War Victims Ten Years Later.* 2nd ed. Zagreb: Center for Women War Victims.

Khasbulatova, Ol'ga A. 2004. "Obzor opyta sovetskoi gosudarstvennoi politiki v otnoshenii zhenshchin" [A Review of the Experience of Soviet State Policies toward Women]. In *Gendernaia rekonstruktsiia politicheskikh sistem* [Gender Reconstruction of Political Systems], ed. N. M. Stepanova and E. V. Kochkina. St. Petersburg: Aleteiia.

Kiblitskaya, Marina. 2000. " 'Once We Were Kings': Male Experiences of Loss of Status." In *Gender, State and Society in Soviet and Post-Soviet Russia*, ed. Sarah Ashwin. London: Routledge.

Kiczková, Zuzana, and Etela Farkašová. 1993. "The Emancipation of Women: A Concept that Failed." In *Gender Politics and Post-Communism: Reflections from Eastern Europe and the Former Soviet Union*, ed. Nanette Funk and Magda Mueller. New York: Routledge.

Kirkup, Gail, et al., eds. 1999. *The Gendered Cyborg: A Reader.* London: Routledge.

Kligman, Gail. 1998. *The Politics of Duplicity: Controlling Reproduction in Ceausescu's Romania.* Berkeley: University of California Press.

Klimenkova, Tat'iana. 1994. "What Does Our New Democracy Offer Society?" In *Women in Russia: A New Era in Russian Feminism*, ed. Anastasia Posadskaya et al. London: Verso.

———. 1996. *Zhenshchina kak fenomen kul'tury: Vzgliad iz Rossii* [Women as a Phenomenon of Culture: View from Russia]. Moscow: Preobrazhenie.

Knesević, Djurdja. 1995. "Women From East and West—How We See and How We Understand Each Other." In *Feminist Theory and Practice—East-West Conference June 9–June 12.* Papers presented at International Conference. St. Petersburg Repino: Petersburg Center for Gender Issues.

Koch, Susan J., Kristina L. Koch, and Zoya Moneva. 1994. "In Their Own Words. An Ethnographic Study of the Quality of Life of Bulgarian Women and Their Children." Paper presented at Transitions and Transcendence: Mutual Perspectives of East and West—Conference on Women's Issues, May, at American University in Blagoevgrad, Bulgaria.

Kochkina, Elena B. 2004. "Politicheskaia sistema preimushchestv dlia grazhdan muzhskogo pola v Rossii (1917–2002)" [Political System of Advantages for Citizens of the Male Sex in Russia (1917–2002)]. In *Gendernaia rekonstruktsiia politicheskikh sistem*, ed. N. M. Stepanova and E. V. Kochkina. St. Petersburg: Aleteiia.

Kogalniceanu, Mihail. 1891. "Dezrobirea Ţiganilor, Ştergerea privilegiilor boiereşti, emanciparea Ţăranilor" [The Unslaving of the Ţigani: The Erasure of Boyar Privileges, and the Emancipation of the Peasants]. Speech given at the Romanian Academy, April 1, 1891. In *Scrieri Literare.* Bucharest: Editura 100+1, undated.

Korac, Maja. 1991. "Prisoners of Their Sex." M.A. thesis, Institute for Sociology, Faculty of Philosophy, University of Belgrade.

———. 1999. "Refugee Women in Serbia: Their Experiences of War, Nationalism, and State Building." In *Women, Citizenship, and Difference*, ed. Nira Yuval-Davis and Pnina Werbner. London: Zed Books.

Kostenko, Maksim. 2003. "Work with Batterers in the Altay Regional Centre for Men." In *NCRB: A Network for Crisis Centres for Women in the Barents Region (Report of the Nordic-Russian Development Project, 1999–2002).* Vol. 5, ed. Aino Saarinen, Olga Liapounova, and Irina Drachova. Arkhangelsk, Russia: Pomor State University.

Kotovskaya, Marija, and Natal'ia Shalygina. 1996. "Love, Sex and Marriage—The Female Mirror: Value Orientation of Young Women in Russia." In *Gender, Generation and Identity in Contemporary Russia*, ed. Hilary Pilkington. London: Routledge.

Kotzeva, Tatyana. 1995. "Women's Experience: Chronicle of a Lost Illusion." *Sociologicheski problemi* 27, no. 4: 64–77. Cited by Kornelia Merdjanska in "Gender in Transition: Does Feminism Speak East-European." Unpublished manuscript.

Kovac, Leonida. 2000. "Whose Body? Whose desire?" N. *Paradoxa International Feminist Art Journal* 6: 22–28.

Koval, Vitalina. 1995. "Women and Work in Russia." In *Women in Contemporary Russia*, ed. Vitalina Koval. Providence, R.I.: Berghahn Books.

Kowalczyk, Izabela. 1999. "Feminist Art in Poland Today." N. *Paradoxa International Feminist Art Journal* 11. http://web.ukonline.co.uk/n.paradoxa/kowa12.html. Accessed Oct. 2001; URL no longer active.

Kuenhast, Kathleen, and Carol Nechemias, eds. 2004. *Post-Soviet Women Encountering Transition: Nation-Building, Economic Survival, and Civic Activism.* Washington, D.C.: Woodrow Wilson Center Press/Johns Hopkins University Press.

Kukhterin, Sergei. 2000. "Fathers and Patriarchs in Communist and Post-communist Russia." In *Gender, State and Society in Soviet and Post-Soviet Russia*, ed. Sarah Ashwin. London: Routledge.

Kuzio, Taras, and Marc Nordberg. 1999. "Nation and State Building, Historical Legacies and National Identities in Belarus and Ukraine: A Comparative Analysis." *Canadian Review of Studies in Nationalism* 26, no. 1–2: 69–90.

Kvinna till Kvinna. 2003. *Report on Testifying about Sexualized Violence in War.* Stockholm.

Lakoff, George. 1995. "Metaphor, Morality, and Politics, or Why Conservatives Have Left Liberals in the Dust." http://www.wwcd.org/issues/Lakoff.html. Accessed April 18, 2005.

Lapidus, Gail Warshofsky. 1978. *Women in Soviet Society: Equality, Development and Social Change.* Berkeley: University of California Press.

———. 1982. *Women, Work, and Family in the Soviet Union.* New York: M. E. Sharpe.

———. 1993. "Gender and Restructuring: The Impact of Perestroika and Its Aftermath on Soviet Women." In *Democratic Reform and the Position of Women in Transitional Economies*, ed. Valentine M. Moghadam. Oxford: Clarendon Press.

Lemon, Alaina. 2000. "Talking Transit and Spectating Transition: The Moscow Metro." In *Altering States: Ethnographies of Transition in Eastern Europe and the Former Soviet Union*, ed. Daphne Berdahl, Matti Bunzl, and Martha Lampland. Ann Arbor: University of Michigan Press.

Lewis, Justin. 1999. "The Opinion Poll as Cultural Form." *International Journal of Cultural Studies* 2, no. 2: 199–221.

Lienau, Sasha, and Barbel Butterweck. 1995. "Theses about the Phenomenon 'Western Women in the East.'" In *Feminist Theory and Practice—East-West. Conference, June 9–12.* Papers presented at International Conference. St. Petersburg Repino: Petersburg Center for Gender Issues.

Liepins, Ruth. 1998. "'Women of Broad Vision': Nature and Gender in the Environmental Activism of Australia's 'Women in Agriculture' Movement." *Environment and Planning* 30, 7: 1179–96.

Light, Jennifer. 1995. "The Digital Landscape: New Space for Women?" *Gender, Place and Culture* 2, 2: 133–43.

Lindsey, Rose. 2002. "From Atrocity to Data: Historiographies of Rape in Former Yugoslavia and the Gendering of Genocide." *Patterns of Prejudice* 36, no. 4: 59–78.

Lipari, Lisbeth. 2000. "Toward a Discourse Approach to Polling." *Discourse Studies* 2, no. 2: 187–216.

Lipovskaya, Olga. 1994. "The Mythology of Womanhood in Contemporary 'Soviet' Culture." In *Women in Russia: A New Era in Russian Feminism*, ed. Anastasia Posadskaya. New York: Verso.

Lissyutkina, Larissa. 1993. "Soviet Women at the Crossroads of Perestroika." In *Gender Politics and Post-Communism: Reflections from Eastern Europe and the Former Soviet Union*, ed. Nanette Funk and Magda Mueller. London: Routledge.

Lister, Ruth. 1997. "Citizenship: Towards a Feminist Synthesis." *Feminist Review* 57: 28–48.

Lockridge, Rebecca Bryant. 1992. "Six Readers Reading Six Photographs." In *Constructing and Reconstructing Gender*, ed. Linda A. M. Perry, Lynn H. Turner, and Helen M. Sterk. New York: State University of New York Press.

Lokshin, Michael, and Barry M. Popkin. 1999. "The Emerging Underclass in the Russian Federation: Income Dynamics, 1992–1996." *Journal of Economic and Cultural Development* 47, no. 4: 803–29.

MacKinnon, Catharine A. 1995. "Crimes of War, Crimes of Peace." In *The Aftermath of Rape: Women's Rights: Women's Rights, War Crimes and Genocide*, ed. Elenor Richter-Lyonette. Ancien College: Coordination of Women's Advocacy.

Magyari-Vincze, Enikő, ed. 2001. *Femei şi Bărbaţi în Clujul Multietnic*, vols. 1–3 [Women and Men in Multiethnic Cluj]. Cluj-Napoca: Editură Fundaţiei Desire.

———. 2002. *Diferenţa care conteaza: Diversitatea social-culturală prin lentila antropologiei feministe* [Differences That Matter: Socio-Cultural Diversity through the Lens of Feminist Anthropology]. Cluj-Napoca: Editură Fundaţiei Desire.

Makhovskaya, Olga. 2003. Interview, "Zamuzh za Ameriku" [To Marry America], Radio Svoboda, April 26. http://www.svoboda.org/programs/rt/2003/rt.042603 .asp. Accessed June 27, 2005.

Malarek, Victor. 2003. *The Natashas: The New Global Sex Trade.* Toronto: Viking.

Maleck-Lewy, Ewa, and Myra Marx Ferree. 2000. "Talking about Women and Wombs: The Discourse of Abortion and Reproductive Rights in the GDR during and after the Wende." In *Reproducing Gender: Politics, Publics and Everyday Life After Socialism*, ed. Susan Gal and Gail Kligman. Princeton, N.J.: Princeton University Press.

Malkki, Liisa H. 1995. "Refugees and Exile: From 'Refugee Studies' to the National Order of Things." *Annual Review of Anthropology* 24, no. 1: 495–523.

Mansbridge, Jane. 1999. "Should Blacks Represent Blacks and Women Represent Women? A Contingent 'Yes.'" *Journal of Politics* 61, no. 3: 628–57.

———. 2003. "Rethinking Representation." *American Political Science Review* 97, no. 4: 515–28.

Marchetti, Gina. 2003. Film review for *Writing Desire* by Ursula Biemann. *Women Make Movies Catalog.* http://www.wmm.com/filmcatalog/pages/c537.shtml. Accessed June 10, 2003.

Marody, Mira. 1993. "Why I Am Not a Feminist: Some Remarks on the Problem of Gender Identity in the United States and Poland." *Social Research* 60, no. 4: 853–65.

Marples, David. 1999. *Belarus: A Denationalised Nation.* Amsterdam: Harwood.

Marsh, Rosalind. 1998. "Women in Contemporary Russia and the Former Soviet Union." In *Women, Ethnicity, and Nationalism: The Politics of Transition,* ed. Rick Wilford and Robert L. Miller. London: Routledge.

Marsh, Rosalind, ed. 1996. *Women in Russia and Ukraine.* New York: Cambridge University Press.

Matynia, Elzbieta. 1994. "Women after Communism: A Bitter Freedom." *Social Research* 61, no. 2: 351–78.

Mayer, Tamar, ed. 2000. *Gender Ironies of Nationalism: Sexing the Nation.* London: Routledge.

McFaul, Michael. 2001. *Russia's Unfinished Revolution: Political Change from Gorbachev to Putin.* Ithaca, N.Y.: Cornell University Press.

Me, Angela, and Marie Sicat. 2004. "Statistics on Women and Men and ICT: The ECE Region." Paper presented at the Regional Symposium on Mainstreaming Gender into Economic Policies, Geneva, Switzerland, January 28–30. http://www.unece.org/oes/gender/documents/ICT%20paper.pdf?OpenAgentandDS=ENERGY/GE.1/2001/1andLang=E. Accessed July 2, 2005.

Mendelson, Sarah E., and John K. Glenn, eds. 2002. *The Power and Limits of NGOs: A Critical Look at Building Democracy in Eastern Europe and Eurasia.* New York: Columbia University Press.

Merdjanska, Kornelia. n.d. "Gender in Transition: Does Feminism Speak Eastern European?" Unpublished manuscript.

Mihalec, Kristina, and Nevenka Sudar. 2004. *Women and Internet: Croatian Perspective.* Zagreb, Croatia: B.a.B.e.

Mikhalisko, Kathleen J. 1997. "Belarus Retreat to Authoritarism." In *Democratic Changes and Authoritarian Reactions in Russia, Ukraine, Belarus and Moldova,* ed. Karen Dawisha and Bruce Parrot. Cambridge: Cambridge University Press.

Mill, John Stuart. "Considerations on Representative Government." In *The Nationalism Reader,* ed. Omar Dahbour and Micheline R. Ishay. Atlantic Highlands, N.J.: Humanities Press, 1995.

Mills, Sara, ed. 1995. *Language and Gender: Interdisciplinary Perspectives.* London: Longman.

Miroiu, Mihaela. 1997. "Experienţele Femeilor" [Experiences of Women]. In *Gen şi Societate* [Gender and Society]. Bucharest: Alternative.

———. 2003. "State Men, Market Women: The Effects of Left Conservatism on Gender Politics in Romanian Transition." Unpublished manuscript.

Molila sam ih da me ubiju: zlocin nad zenom Bosne i Hercegovine. 1999. Sarajevo: Centar za istrazivanje i dokumentaciju Saveza logorasa Bosne i Hercegovine.

Monkiewicz, Dorota. "A Panoramic View: Art by Women, Feminine and Feminist Art in Poland After 1945." In *Architecture of Gender: Contemporary Women's Art in Poland,* ed. Aneta Szyłak. Warsaw: National Museum in Warsaw, 2003.

Moon, Nick. 1999. *Opinion Polls: History, Theory and Practice*. Manchester: Manchester University Press.

Mostov, Julie. 1995. "Our Women, Their Women: Symbolic Boundaries, Territorial Markers, and Violence in the Balkans." *Peace and Change: A Journal of Peace Research* 20, no. 4: 515–29.

———. 2001. "Sexing the Nation/Desexing the Body: Politics of National Identity in the Former Yugoslavia." In *Gender Ironies of Nationalism: Sexing the Nation*, ed. Tamar Mayer. London: Routledge.

Muharska, Ralitsa. 2005. "Silences and Parodies in the East-West Feminist Dialogue." *L'Homme. Zeitschrift für feministische Geschichtswissenschaft* [L'Homme: European Review of Feminist History] 16, no. 1: 36–47.

———. 2005. "This Started as a Review." Unpublished manuscript.

Müller, Ursula. 1996. "'Besserwisende Schwestern?' Eine erfahrungsgesättigte Polemik" [Know-It-All Sisters? An Experience Saturated Polemic]. In *Weschselnde Blicke. Frauenforschung in internationaler Perspektive* [Changing Viewpoints: Women's Research in International Perspective], ed. Ilse Lenz and Andrea Germer. Opladen, Germany: Leske + Budrich.

Narayan, Uma. 1997. *Dislocating Cultures: Identities, Traditions, and Third World Feminism*. London: Routledge.

National Institute of Strategic Studies. 1993. "Emigration of the Ukrainian Population: Socio-Economic Aspects and Potential Consequences." http://www.niss.gov.ua. Accessed August 12, 2003.

Neculaescu, Sorina. 2000. "Corpul Femeii—Trofeu al Dominaţiei Masculine" [The Female Body: Trophy of Masculine Domination]. *ANAlize: Revista de Studii Feministe* (September): 15–16.

Nicholson, Linda. 1986. *Gender and History: The Limits of Social Theory in the Age of the Family*. New York: Columbia University Press.

Nickel, Hildegard Maria, and Eva Kolinsky. 2003. "Vom Umgang mit Differenzen. Statement zur Podiumsdebatte "Auf dem Weg zur normalisierten Wissenschaft? Über das Schicksal subversiver Ansprüche in der Frauen- und Geschlechterforschung" [In Dealing with Differences. Statement for a Plenary Debate: Toward a Normalized Science? On the Fate of Subversive Claims in Women's and Gender Research]. In *Reinventing Gender, Women in Eastern Germany Since Unification*, ed. Eva Kolinsky and Hildegard Maria Nickel. London: Frank Cass.

Nikolic-Ristanovic, Vesna. 2000. *Women, Violence, and War: Wartime Victimization of Refugees in the Balkans*. Budapest: Central European University Press.

Noonan, Norma Corigliano, and Carol Nechemias, eds. 2001. *Encyclopedia of Russian Women's Movements*. Westport, Conn.: Praeger.

Norris, Pippa. 1996. "Women Politicians: Transforming Westminster?" *Parliamentary Affairs* 49, no. 1: 89–102.

Norton, Anne. 1993. *Reflections of Political Identity*. Baltimore, Md.: Johns Hopkins University Press.

Notz, Gisela. 1994. "Frauenemanzipation und Frauenrealität in Ost und West" [Women's Emancipation and Women's Reality in East and West]. In *EigenArtige Ostfrauen. Frauenemanzipation in der DDR und den neuen Bundesländern* [Singular East German Women: Women's Emancipation in the GDR and the New German States], ed. Birgit Bütow and Heidi Stecker. Bielefeld, Germany: Kleine Verlag.

O'Brien, Jodi. 2000. "Changing the Subject." *Women and Performance: A Journal of*

Feminist Theory 9, issue 17, no. 1. http://www.ucm.es/info/rqtr/biblioteca/cibere spacio%20gltb/CHANGING%20THE%20SUBJECT.pdf. Accessed Feb. 22, 2006.

Oleksy, Elżbieta H. 1998. "Plight in Common? Women's Studies in the New Democracies." *Outskirts: Online Journal* 3 (November). http://www.chloe.uwa.edu.au/otskirts/archive/VOL3/commentary1.html. Accessed Oct. 2001; URL no longer active.

Olsen, Frances Elisabeth. 1997. "Feminism in Central and Eastern Europe: Risks and Possibilities of American Engagement." *Yale Law Journal* 106: 2215–57.

Olteanu, Tatiana. 1998. *Studiu de opinie privind violența asupra femeii in familie.* Manuscript published at http://www.pitesti.ro/grado/studui_ro.html. Accessed Aug. 5, 2002.

Olujic, Maria B. 1998. "Embodiment of Terror: Gendered Violence in Peacetime and Wartime in Croatia and Bosnia-Herzegovina." *Medical Anthropology Quarterly* 12, no. 1: 31–50.

Oommen, T. K. 1997. *Citizenship, Nationality and Ethnicity.* Cambridge: Polity Press.

Open Society Institute's European Union Monitoring Program. 2001. *Protecția Minoritatilor în România.* Budapest: Central European University Press.

Osipovich, Tatiana. 2004. "Russian Mail-Order Brides in U.S. Public Discourse: Sex, Crime, and Cultural Stereotypes." In *Sexuality and Gender in Postcommunist Eastern Europe and Russia*, ed. Aleksandar Štulhofer and Theo Sandfort. New York: Haworth Press.

Oushakine, Serguei Alex. 2001. "The Fatal Splitting: Symbolizing Anxiety in Post-Soviet Russia." *Ethnos: Journal of Anthropology* 66, no. 3: 291–319.

———. 2006. "The Politics of Pity: Domesticating Loss in a Russian Province." *American Anthropologist* 108, no. 2: 312–23.

Pachmanova, Martina. 2000. "The Muzzle: Gender and Sexual Politics in Contemporary Czech Art." *ArtMargins* (January 27). http://www.artmargins.com/content/feature/pachmanova2.html.

Pauwels, Anne. 1998. *Women Changing Language.* London: Longman.

Pawluczuk, Włodzimierz. 1998. *Ukraina, Polityka i Mistyka.* Krakow: Nomos.

Perevedentsev, V. 1995. "Women, the Family, and Reproduction." In *Women in Contemporary Russia*, ed. Vitalina Koval. Providence, R.I.: Berghahn Books.

Petricek, Miroslav, Olga Mala, and Karel Srp. 1998. *Contemporary Collection: Czech Art in the '90s.* Exhibition catalogue. Prague: Prague City Gallery.

Petros, Tiffany. 2000. "'Mop, Shop and Shut Up: Feminism in the Czech Republic." *Central European Review* 2, no. 43. http://www.ce-review.org/00/43/petros43.html. Accessed June 2005.

Phillips, Anne. 1995. *Politics of Presence.* Oxford: Clarendon Press.

Pilkington, Hilary. 1996. "'Youth Culture' in Contemporary Russia: Gender, Consumption and Identity." In *Gender, Generation and Identity in Contemporary Russia*, ed. Hilary Pilkington. London: Routledge.

Piotrowski, Piotr. 1995. "The Old Attitude and the New Faith." In *Beyond Belief: Contemporary Art from East Central Europe*, ed. Laura J. Hoptman. Chicago: Museum of Contemporary Art.

———. 2000. "Sztuka Wedlug Polityki." In *Negotiators of Art*, ed. Bożena Czubak. Gdansk: Centre of Contemporary Art Łaznia.

Pisklakova, Marina, and Andrei Sinel'nikov. 2000. "Mezhdu molchaniem i krikom"

[Between Silence and the Scream]. In *Nasilie i sotsial'nye izmeneniia* [Violence and Social Change], ed. Tsentr ANNA. Moscow: Tacis, Caritas.

Pollock, Griselda, ed. 1996. *Generations and Geographies in the Visual Arts: Feminist Readings*. London: Routledge.

Popov, A., and Henry P. David. 1999. "Russian Federation and USSR Successor States." In *From Abortion to Contraception: A Resource to Public Policies and Reproductive Behavior in Central and Eastern Europe from 1917 to the Present*, ed. Henry P. David. Westport, Conn.: Greenwood Press.

Posadskaya, Anastasia. 1996. "The Feminine Dimension of Social Reform." In *Women in Russia and Ukraine*, ed. Rosalind Marsh. Cambridge: Cambridge University Press.

———, ed. 1994. *Women in Russia: A New Era in Russian Feminism*. Trans. Kate Clark. London: Verso.

Post, Dianne. 2002. "Russian Women, American Eyes: The Rebirth of Feminism in Russia." Draft manuscript prepared for the Kennan Workshop on Women in the Former Soviet Union.

Price, Lisa. 2002. "Sexual Violence and Ethnic Cleansing: Attacking the Family." In *Thinking Differently: A Reader in European Women's Studies*, ed. Gabriele Griffin and Rosi Braidotti. London: Zed Press.

Prizel, I. *National Identity and Foreign Policy*. Cambridge: Cambridge University Press, 1998.

Pupavac, Vanessa. 2002. "Pathologizing Populations and Colonizing Minds: International Psychosocial Programs in Kosovo." *Alternatives: Global, Local, Political* 27, no. 4: 489–512.

Racioppi, Linda, and Katherine O'Sullivan See. 1997. *Women's Activism in Contemporary Russia*. Philadelphia, Pa.: Temple University Press.

Reingold, Beth. 1992. "Concepts of Representation among Female and Male State Legislators." *Legislative Studies Quarterly* 17, no. 4: 509–37.

Remennick, Larissa. 1999. " 'Women with a Russian Accent' in Israel: On the Gender Aspects of Immigration." *European Journal of Women's Studies* 6, no. 4: 441–61.

Riach, David. 2000. "Nation Building: Identity Politics in Belarus." *Canadian Review in Nationalism* 27, no. 1–2: 49–63.

Richter, James. 2002. "Evaluating Western Assistance to Russian Women's Organizations." In *The Power and Limits of NGOs: A Critical Look at Building Democracy in Eastern Europe and Eurasia*, ed. Sarah E. Mendelson and John K. Glenn. New York: Columbia University Press.

Richter-Lyonette, Elenor. 1995. *The Aftermath of Rape: Women's Rights, War Crimes and Genocide*. Ancien College: Coordination of Women's Advocacy.

Ries, Nancy. 1997. *Russian Talk: Culture and Conversation during Perestroika*. Ithaca, N.Y.: Cornell University Press.

Rivkin-Fish, Michele. 2004. "Gender and Democracy: Strategies for Engagement and Dialogue on Women's Issues after Socialism in St. Petersburg." In *Post-Soviet Women Encountering Transition: Nation-Building, Economic Survival, and Civic Activism*, ed. Kathleen Kuenhast and Carol Nechemias. Washington, D.C.: Woodrow Wilson Center Press/Johns Hopkins University Press.

———. 2005. *Women's Health in Post-Soviet Russia: The Politics of Intervention*. Bloomington: Indiana University Press.

Roman, Denise. 2003. *Fragmented Identities: Popular Culture, Sex, and Everyday Life in Postcommunist Romania*. New York: Lexington Books.

Roman, Petre. 2000. "Termeni folositi pentru denumirea etniei romilor/tiganilor" [Terminology for the Naming of the Ethnicity of Roma/Ţigani]. Memorandum of the Minister of External Affairs, February 29.

Romani Criss si Argentia de monitizoare a presei [Romani Crisis and the Agency for the Monitoring of the Press]. 2000. *Prezentarea romilor in presa româneasca* [Representation of Romani People in the Romanian Press]. February–August.

Rose, Lindsey. 2000 "From Atrocity to Data: Historiographies of Rape in Former Yugoslavia and the Gendering of Genocide." *Patterns of Prejudice* 36, no. 4: 59–79.

Rubchak, Marian J. 1996. "Christian Virgin or Pagan Goddess: Feminism Versus the Eternally Feminine." In *Women in Russia and Ukraine*, ed. Rosalind Marsh. New York: Cambridge University Press.

Rudd, Elizabeth C. 2000. "Reconceptualizing Gender in Postsocialist Transformation." *Gender and Society* 14, no. 4: 517–39.

Rusnakova, Katarina. 1997. *Between Man and Woman*. Exhibition catalog. Zilina: Povazska.

———. 2000. *The End of the World: Prague*. Exhibition catalog. Prague: National Gallery in Prague.

Rutland, Peter. "How the SU Ended." *EOMRI Analytical Brief*, no. 453 (November 11, 1996).

Saarinen, Aino, Olga Liapounova, and Irina Drachova, eds. 2003. *NCRB: A Network for Crisis Centres for Women in the Barents Region (Report of the Nordic-Russian Development Project, 1999–2002)*. 1–248. Arkhangelsk, Russia: Pomor State University.

Sadovská, Dorota. Interview by Jan Gerzová. "The End of Geography?" *Praesens* 2 (2002). http://www.praesens.net/szamok_en.php?d_id=9. Accessed June 2002.

Saint-Germain, Michelle A. 1989. "Does Their Difference Make a Difference? The Impact of Women on Public Policy in the Arizona Legislature." *Social Science Quarterly* 70, no. 4: 956–98.

Sakwa, Richard. 1993. *Russian Politics and Society*. London: Routledge.

Salecl, Renate. 1994. *The Spoils of Freedom. Psychoanalysis and Feminism after the Fall of Socialism*. London: Routledge.

Sandoval, Chela. 2000. *Methodology of the Oppressed*. Minneapolis: University of Minnesota Press.

Sanford, George. 1996. "Belarus on the Road to Nationhood." *Survival* 38, no. 1: 131–54.

Schaeffer, Eva. 1998. "Postmodern Implikationen im Feminismus—der ost-Deutsche Kontext." [Postmodern Implications in Feminism—the East German Context.] *Feministische Studien* [Feminist Studies] 16, no. 1: 95–105.

Schneider, Elizabeth M. 2002. *Battered Women and Feminist Lawmaking*. New Haven, Conn.: Yale University Press.

Segal, Elizabeth A., and Stephanie Brzuzy. 1995. "Gender and Congressional Voting: A Legislative Analysis." *Journal of Women and Social Work* 10, no. 1: 8–23.

Seifert, Ruth. 1994. "War and Rape: Preliminary Analysis." In *Mass Rape: The War against Women in Bosnia-Herzegovina*, ed. Alexandra Stiglmayer. Lincoln: University of Nebraska Press.

———. 1996. "Der weibliche Koerper als Symbol und Zeichen. Geschlechtsspezifische Gewalt und die kulturelle Konstruktion des Krieges" [The Female Body as a Symbol and a Sign: Gender-Specific Violence and the Cultural Construction of War]. In *Gewalt im Krieg*, ed. Andreas Gestrich. Muenster: Lit Verlag.

——. 2001. "The Use of Women and the Role of Women in the Yugoslav War." In *Gender, Peace and Conflict*, ed. Inger Skjelsbaek and Dan Smith. London: Sage Publications.

Serghiuţă, Stela. 2003. "Violenţa domestică—în lume şi în România" [Domestic Violence—in the World and in Romania]. *Dilema* 530. http://www.algoritma.ro/dilema/fw.htm?current=arhiva_dilema/search1.htm. Accessed Feb. 2006.

Sharpe, Christine. 1999. "Racialized Fantasies on the Internet." *Signs: Journal of Women in Culture and Society* 24, no. 4: 1089–96.

Shelley, Louise. 1987. "Inter-personal Violence in the USSR." *Violence, Aggression and Terrorism* 1, no. 2: 41–67.

Shevchenko, Iulia. 1999. "Explaining Electoral Results: 1993–1996." In *Elections in Russia, 1993–1996: Analyses, Documents, and Data*, ed. Vladimir Gel'man and Grigorii V. Golosov. Berlin: Edition Sigma.

——. 2002. "Who Cares about Women's Problems? Female Legislators in the 1995 and 1999 Russian State Dumas." *Europe-Asia Studies* 54, no. 8: 1201–22.

Shevchenko, Iulia, and Grigorii V. Golosov. 2001. "Legislative Activism of Russian Duma Deputies, 1996–99." *Europe-Asia Studies* 53, no. 2: 239–61.

Shitova, Elena. 2002. "Women's Alliance." *Bradley Herald*. Washington, D.C.: Bureau of Education and Cultural Affairs, U.S. State Dept.

Šiklová, Jiřina. 1993. "Are Women in Central and Eastern Europe Conservative?" In *Gender Politics and Post-Communism: Reflections from Eastern Europe and the Former Soviet Union*, ed. Nanette Funk and Magda Mueller. London: Routledge.

——. 1993. "McDonalds, Terminators, Coca Cola Ads and Feminism?" In *Bodies of Bread and Butter: Reconfiguring Women's Lives in Post-Communist Czech Republic*, ed. Susana Trnka and Laura Busheikin. Prague: Prague Gender Center.

——. 1997. "Feminism and the Roots of Apathy in the Czech Republic." *Social Research* 64, no. 2: 8–80.

Silverman, Kaja. 2001. Interview by Martina Pachmanova. *Vernost v Pochybu* [Loyalty in a Movement]. Prague: One Woman Press.

Simerska, Lenka, and Katerina Fialova. 2004. *Bridging the Gender Digital Divide: A Report on Gender and ICT in Central and Eastern Europe and the Commonwealth of Independent States*. Bratislava, Slovak Republic: UNDP/UNIFEM: 2004. http://web.undp.sk/uploads/Gender%20and%20ICT%20reg_rep_eng.pdf.

Skak, Mette. 1996. *From Empire to Anarchy: Postcommunist Foreign Policy and International Relations*. London: Hurst.

Slapsak, Svetlana. 2001. "The Use of Women and the Role of Women in the Yugoslav War." In *Gender, Peace and Conflict*, ed. Inger Skjelsbaek and Dan Smith. London: Sage.

Slater, Wendy. 1995. "'Women of Russia' and Women's Representation in Russian Politics." In *Russia in Transition*, ed. David Lane. New York: Longman.

Śmejkalová-Strickland, Jiřina. 1994. "Do Czech Women Need Feminism?" *Women's Studies International Forum* 17, no. 2–3: 277–82.

——. 1995. "Revival? Gender Studies in the 'Other' Europa." *Signs: Journal of Women in Culture and Society* 20, no. 4: 1000–1007.

——. 1997. "The Other Monster: 'American Feminism' in the Post-communist World." *ZIF Bulletin* 14: 1–7. Berlin: Zentrum für interdisziplinäre Frauenforschung der Humboldt Universität [Center for Interdisciplinary Women's Studies of Humboldt University].

Snitow, Ann. 1993. "Feminist Futures in the Former East Bloc." *Peace and Democracy News* 7, no. 1: 40–41.

Soble, Alan. 1986. *Pornography: Marxism, Feminism, and the Future of Sexuality.* New Haven, Conn.: Yale University Press.

Spencer, Metta. 1996. "Post-Socialist Patriarchy." In *Women in Post-Communism: Research on Russia and Eastern Europe.* Vol. 2, ed. Barbara Wejnert and Metta Spencer with Slobodan Drakulic. Greenwich, Conn.: Jai Press.

Sperling, Valerie. 1990. "Rape and Domestic Violence in the USSR." *Response to the Victimization of Women and Children: Journal of the Center for Women Policy Studies* 13, no. 3: 16–22.

———. 1998. "Gender Politics and the State during Russia's Transition Period." In *Gender, Politics and the State,* ed. Vicky Randall and Georgina Waylen. London: Routledge.

———. 1999. *Organizing Women in Contemporary Russia: Engendering Transition.* Cambridge: Cambridge University Press.

Spivak, Gayatri. 1999. *A Critique of Postcolonial Reason: Toward a History of the Vanishing Present.* Cambridge, Mass.: Harvard University Press.

Stark, Evan. 1993. "Mandatory Arrest of Batterers: A Reply to Its Critics." *American Behavioral Scientist* 36, no. 5: 651–80.

Stewart, Michael. 1993. "Gypsies, the Work Ethic and Hungarian Socialism." In *Socialism: Ideals, Ideologies and Local Practice,* ed. C. M. Hann. London: Routledge.

Stiglmayer, Alexandra, ed. 1994. *Rape: The War against Women in Bosnia-Herzegovina.* Lincoln: University of Nebraska Press.

Sundstrom, Lisa McIntosh. 2002. "Women's NGOs in Russia: Struggling from the Margins." *Demokratizatsiya* 10, no. 2: 207–29.

———. 2005. "Foreign Assistance, International Norms, and NGO Development: Lessons from the Russian Campaign." *International Organization* 59, no. 3: 419–49.

Swers, Michele L. 1998. "Are Women More Likely to Vote for Women's Issue Bills than Their Male Colleagues?" *Legislative Studies Quarterly* 23, no. 3: 435–48.

Swidler, Ann. 1986. "Culture in Action: Symbols and Strategies." *American Sociological Review* 51 (April): 273–86.

———. 1995. "Cultural Power and Social Movements." In *Social Movements and Culture,* ed. Bert Klandermans and Hank Johnston. Minneapolis: University of Minnesota Press.

Synnott, Anthony. 1993. *The Body Social.* London: Routledge.

Szyłak, Aneta. 2000. "The New Art from the New Reality: Some Remarks on Contemporary Art in Poland." *Art Journal* 59, no. 1: 54–64.

———. 2003. *Architecture of Gender Contemporary Women's Art in Poland.* Warsaw: National Museum in Warsaw.

Tabbi, Matthew. 2000. "Russian Girls." *Playboy,* November, 109, 154–55.

Talbot, Mary M. 1998. *Language and Gender, An Introduction.* Cambridge: Polity Press.

Talpade Mohanty, Chandra. 1995. "Under Western Eyes: Feminist Scholarship and Colonial Discourses." In *The Postcolonial Studies Reader,* ed. Bill Ashcroft, Gareth Griffins, and Helen Tiffin. London: Routledge.

Tanesini, Alessandra. 1999. *An Introduction to Feminist Epistemologies.* Malden, Mass.: Blackwell.

Taras, Ray. 1998. "Nations and Language Building: Old Theories, Contemporary Cases." *Nationalism and Ethnic Politics* 4, 3: 79–101.

Tartakovskaya, Irina. 2000. "The Changing Representation of Gender Roles in the Soviet and Post-Soviet Press." In *Gender, State and Society in Soviet and Post-Soviet Russia*, ed. Sarah Ashwin. London: Routledge.

Taylor, Christopher. 1999. *Sacrifice as Terror: The Rwandan Genocide of 1994*. Oxford: Berg.

Thiesmeyer, Lynn. 1999. "The West's 'Comfort Women' and the Discourse of Seduction." In *Transnational Asia Pacific: Gender, Culture and the Public Sphere*, ed. Shirley Geok-lin Lim, Larry E. Smith, and Wimal Dissanayake. Urbana: University of Illinois Press.

Thomas, Sue. 1994. *How Women Legislate*. New York: Oxford University Press.

Tickner, Ann. 1996. "A Critique of Morgenthau's Principles of Political Realism." In *International Politics*, ed. Robert C. Art and Robert Jervis. New York: Harper Collins College.

Tsygankov, Andrei P. 2000. "Defining State Interests after Empire: National Identity, Domestic Structures and Foreign Trade Policies of Latvia and Belarus." *Review of International Political Economy* 7, no. 1: 101–29.

U.S. Department of State. 2005. *Trafficking in Persons Report*. Washington, D.C. http://www.state.gov/g/tip/rls/tiprpt/2005. Accessed July 20, 2005.

U.S. Immigration and Naturalization Service. 1999. *International Matchmaking Organizations: A Report to the Congress*. Washington, D.C. http://uscis.gov/graphics/aboutus/repsstudies/Mobrept_full.pdf. Accessed Aug. 12, 2003.

United Nations Development Program (UNDP). 2003. "Gender Issues in Ukraine: Challenges and Opportunities." http://www.undp.org.ua/?page=documents. Accessed June 15, 2004.

United Nations Division for the Advancement of Women. "Women and the Information Revolution." *Women 2000*, no. 1 (October 1996). http://www.un.org/womenwatch/daw/public/w2cont.htm. Accessed March 8, 2002.

Văetiși, Lorena. 2004. *Discursuri identitare și intersectoralitate: O analiză privind identitatea de gen și identitatea etnică în cazul femeilor rrome* [Analysis concerning Gendered and Ethnic Identity in the Case of Romani Women]. M.A. thesis, Babeș-Bolyai University, Cluj-Napoca.

Vannoy, Dana, et al. 1999. *Marriages in Russia: Couples during the Economic Transition*. Westport, Conn.: Praeger.

Verdery, Katherine. 1994. "From Parent-State to Family Patriarchs: Gender and Nation in Contemporary Eastern Europe." *East European Politics and Societies* 8, no. 2: 225–55.

———. 1996. *What Was Socialism and What Comes Next?* Princeton, N.J.: Princeton University Press.

Vincourová Kateřina. 1997. Exhibition catalogue with interviews by Marta Smolikova and text by Jiři Švestaka and Tereza Bruthansova. Prague: Soros Centre of Contemporary Art.

Voronina, Olga. 1993. "Soviet Patriarchy: Past and Present." *Hypatia* 8 no. 4: 99–111.

———. 1994. "Virgin Mary or Mary Magdalene? The Construction and Reconstruction of Sex during the Perestroika Period." In *Women in Russia: A New Era in Russian Feminism*, ed. Anastasia Posadskaya. New York: Verso.

Vranic, Seada. 1996. *Breaking the Wall of Silence: The Voices of Raped Bosnia*. Zagreb: Izdanja Antibarbarus.

Works Cited

Vybory deputatov Gosudarstvennoi Dumy 1995: Electoral'naia statistika [The 1995 Elections of the Deputies of the State Duma: Electoral Statistics]. 1996. Moscow: Ves' Mir.

Vybory deputatov Gosudarstvennoi Dumy Federal'nogo sobraniia Rossiiskoi Federatsii 1999: Electoral'naia statistika [The 1999 Elections of the Deputies of the Federal Assembly of the Russian Federation: Electoral Statistics]. 2000. Moscow: Ves' Mir.

Wagner, William G. 2002. "'Orthodox Domesticity': Creating a Social Role for Women in Late Imperial Russia." Paper presented to the conference on Sacred Stories: Religion and Spirituality in Modern Russian Culture. University of Illinois at Urbana-Champaign. February 21–23, 2002.

Wagnerová, Alena. 1993. "Der Sozialismus entlässt die tschechischen Frauen" [Socialism Relieves the Czech Women]. *Beiträge zur feministischen theorie und praxis* [Contributions to Feminist Theory and Practice] 34: 107–12.

Walsh, Martha. 1998. "Mind the Gap: Where Feminist Theory Failed to Meet Development Practice: A Missed Opportunity in Bosnia and Herzegovina." *European Journal of Women's Studies* 5, no. 3–4: 329–43.

Waters, Malcolm. 1995. *Globalization*. London: Routledge.

Watson, Peggy. 1993. "Eastern Europe's Silent Revolution: Gender." *Sociology* 27, no. 3: 471–87.

———. 1997. "Civil Society and the Politics of Difference in Eastern Europe." In *Transitions, Environments, Translations: Feminisms in International Politics*, ed. Joan Wallach Scott, Temma Kaplan, and Debra Keates. London: Routledge.

———. 2000. "Rethinking Transition: Globalism, Gender, and Class." *International Feminist Journal of Politics* 2, no. 2: 185–213.

Weaver, Ole. 1999. "Identity, Communities and Foreign Policy: Discourse Analysis as Foreign Policy Theory." In *Between Nations and Europe: Regionalism, Nationalism and the Politics of Union*, ed. L. Hansen and O. Weaver. London: Routledge.

Webster, Wendy. 1998. *Imagining Home: Gender, "Race" and National Identity, 1945–64*. London: University College of London Press.

Wedel, Janine. 2001. *Collision and Collusion: The Strange Case of Western Aid to Eastern Europe*. New York: St. Martin's Press.

Weldon, S. Laurel. 2002. *Protest, Policy, and the Problem of Violence against Women: A Cross-National Comparison*. Pittsburgh: University of Pittsburgh Press.

West, Candace, and Don H. Zimmerman. 1987. "Doing Gender." *Gender and Society* 1, no. 2: 125–51.

Williams, Simon J., and Gillian Bendelow. 1998. *The Lived Body: Sociological Themes, Embodied Issues*. London: Routledge.

Wodak, Ruth. 1996. *Gender and Discourse*. Oxford: Blackwell.

Women in Transition. 1999. Economies in Transition Studies: Regional Monitoring Report, no. 6. Florence, Italy: UNICEF.

Woodcock, Shannon. 2003. "How to be a Real Romanian: Articulations of Ţigani Others and the Construction of Ethno-National Romanian Selves." Ph.D. diss., Sydney University.

World Health Organization. 2002. "Core Health Indicators by Country." http://www3 .who.int/whosis/country/compare.cfm?country=RUS&indicator=HALE0Male, HALE0Female&language=english. Accessed Feb. 21, 2006.

Yang, Mayfair. *Spaces of Their Own: Women's Public Sphere in Transnational China*. Minneapolis: University of Minnesota Press, 1999.

Young, Iris Marion. 1990. *Justice and the Politics of Difference.* Princeton, N.J.: Princeton University Press.

Yurchak, Alexei. 2002. "Entrepreneurial Governmentality in Postsocialist Russia." In *The New Entrepreneurs of Europe and Asia,* ed. Victoria Bonnell and Thomas Gold. Armonk, N.Y.: M. E. Sharpe.

Yuval-Davis, Nira. 1997. *Gender and Nation.* London: Sage.

———. 1997. "Women, Citizenship and Difference." *Feminist Review* 57 (Autumn): 4–27.

Zabelina, Tat'iana. 1996. "Sexual Violence towards Women." In *Gender, Generation and Identity in Contemporary Russia,* ed. Hilary Pilkington. London: Routledge.

Zabelina, Tat'iana Iu., ed. 2002. *Rossiia: Nasilie v sem'e—nasilie v obshchestve* [Russia: Violence on the Family—Violence in Society]. Moscow: UNIFEM, UNFPA.

Zalewski, Marysia, and Jane Parpart. 1998. *The "Man" Question in International Relations.* Oxford: Westview Press.

Zaprudnik, Jan. 1994. "Development of Belarusian National Identity and Its Influence on Belarus Foreign Policy Orientation." In *National Identity and Ethnicity in Russia and the New States of Eurasia,* ed. R. Szporluk. Armonk, N.Y.: M. E. Sharpe.

Zarkov, Dubravka. 1995. "Gender, Orientalism and the History of Ethnic Hatred in the Former Yugoslavia." In *Crossfires: Nationalism, Racism and Gender in Europe,* ed. Helma Lutz, Ann Phoenix, and Nira Yuval-Davis. London: European Forum for Left Feminists.

Zhurzhenko, Tatiana. 2001. "Free Market Ideology and New Women's Identities in Post-Socialist Ukraine." *The European Journal of Women's Studies* 8, no. 1: 24–49.

———. 2001. "Ukrainian Feminism(s): Between Nationalist Myth and Anti-Nationalist Critique." *IWM Working Paper* No. 2: Vienna. http://www.iwm.at/publ-wp/wp-01–04.pdf. Accessed June 10, 2002.

Zielińska, Eleonora. 2000. "Between Ideology, Politics, and Common Sense: The Discourse of Reproductive Rights in Poland." In *Reproducing Gender: Politics, Publics, and Everyday Life After Socialism,* ed. Susan Gal and Gail Kligman. Princeton, N.J.: Princeton University Press.

Zvinkliene, Alina. 1999. "Neo-Conservatism in Family Ideology in Lithuania: Between the West and the Former USSR." In *Women and Political Change: Perspectives from East-Central Europe,* ed. Sue Bridger. New York: St. Martin's Press.

CONTRIBUTORS

Anna Brzozowska is a Ph.D. candidate in International Relations at the Central European University. She has a Masters in Literature from Adam Mickiewicz University, Poznań (Poland), and a Masters in International Relations (CEU). Since 1992 she has worked for public administration, and she currently deals with the administration of EU programs at the European Training Foundation in Turin. Her research interests involve IR theories, gender and literary studies, democracy, and local governance.

Karen Dawisha is the Walter E. Havighurst Professor in the Department of Political Science and Director of the Havighurst Center for Russian and Post-Soviet Studies at Miami University in Oxford, Ohio. Her publications include *Russia and the New States of Eurasia* (1994), *Eastern Europe, Gorbachev and Reform* (1988), *The Kremlin and the Prague Spring* (1984), and articles in *Foreign Affairs*, *Slavic Review*, and *East European Politics and Societies*.

Nanette Funk is Professor of Philosophy at Brooklyn College, City University of New York. She co-edited *Gender Politics and Postcommunism: Reflections on Eastern Europe and the Former Soviet Union* (1993). Her recent writing has been published in *Signs* (2004), *femina politika* (2006), and *Women and Citizenship in Central and Eastern Europe* (2006). She co-directs the Gender and Transformation Workshop at New York University at the Center for European Studies.

Ewa Grigar is currently a Ph.D. student in Sociology of Culture at the New School for Social Research, New York. She is originally from Poland. Her research focuses on modern and contemporary art in Central Eastern Europe. Most recently Grigar has been teaching at Yeshiva University in New York.

Azra Hromadzic is a Bosnian Muslim woman from the northwest Bosnian town of Bihac. During the war (1992–1995), she lived under siege, with no electricity or regular food supplies. In 1996, after receiving a scholarship, Hromadzic came to the United States. She received her B.A. and M.A. in Cultural Anthropology at the University of Pennsylvania. Hromadzic has published her research on Bosnian war rapes in Germany, and also has presented at a number of conferences. She is currently in Bosnia working on her dissertation, "Emerging Citizens: Youth, Education, and Reconciliation in Post-conflict Bosnia and Herzegovina."

Janet Elise Johnson is Assistant Professor of Political Science at Brooklyn College, City University of New York. Her research, based on fieldwork in Russia and other postcommunist societies, covers gender politics, especially women's organizations and violence against women. Her current project examines the influence of foreign assistance and transnational feminism on the women's crisis center movement in Russia. Johnson's publications have appeared in the NWSA Journal and edited volumes such as Post-Soviet Women Encountering Transition (2004), Ruling Russia (2005), and Russian Civil Society (2005).

Anne-Marie Kramer is a lecturer in the Sociology Department, University of Warwick in the United Kingdom. Her doctoral and postdoctoral research has focused on reproductive politics in Poland. Further interests include gender and nation and feminist theorizing around the body. She has contributed the chapter "Gender, Nation and the Abortion Debate in the Polish Media" to Nation and Gender in Contemporary Europe, edited by Vera Tolz and Stephenie Booth (2006).

Tania Rands Lyon received her Ph.D. in sociology from Princeton University and has focused her academic research on the relationship between family and state in Post-Soviet Russia. She currently works as a consultant in Pittsburgh, Pennsylvania.

Jean C. Robinson is Professor of Political Science and Gender Studies, and affiliated with the Russian and East European Institute and East Asian Languages and Culture at Indiana University, Bloomington. Her research focuses on comparative gender policies; she has done field research in Poland, China, France, and Germany. She contributed to Communist Dialectic: The Political Implications of Economic Reform in Communist Countries (1990); The Reconstruction of Family Policy (1991); Comparative State Feminism (1995); and Abortion Politics, Women's Movements, and the Democratic State (2001). Robinson was co-editor of Women and Social Policy (2001) and has published in numerous journals, including China Quarterly, NWSA Journal, and Signs.

Iulia Shevchenko holds a Ph.D. in political science and is currently a research fellow at the European University at St. Petersburg (Russia), where she specializes in political and institutional development in the postcommunist world, including issues related to women's rights and political participation. She is author of The Central Government of Russia: From Gorbachev to Putin. Shevchenko is a recipient of fellowships from the John W. Kluge Center at the Library of Congress, (U.S.) Social Science Research Council, and the Mac-Arthur Foundation.

Svitlana Taraban was born in Ukraine, where she received her B.A. in Russian and Ukrainian Languages and worked as a high school teacher. Currently she is a Ph.D. candidate in the Faculty of Education at York University, Toronto, where she is writing a dissertation that examines the processes of identity construction among Post-Soviet immigrant youth in Germany.

Shannon Woodcock is an Australian who has lived and worked in Hungary, Romania, and Albania since 1997. She recently received her Ph.D. from Sydney University, focusing on the reliance of Romanian nationalisms on stereotypes of the Țigani Other. Her current research interests extend to stereotypes of Úigani in Nazi policy, ethnic Romani communities, and the Western mainstream fashion scene. More of her work can be accessed at the Genderomania website: www.genderomania.ro.

Index

Index

Index